Nobody's Fool

Nobody's Fool

THE LIFE OF ARCHBISHOP
ROBIN EAMES

ALF McCREARY

Hodder & Stoughton
LONDON SYDNEY AUCKLAND

Copyright © 2004 by Alf McCreary

First published in Great Britain in 2004

The right of Alf McCreary to be identified as the Author of
the Work has been asserted by him in accordance with
the Copyright, Designs and Patents Act 1988.

10 9 8 7 6 5 4 3 2 1

British Library Cataloguing in Publication Data
A record for this book is available from the British Library

ISBN 0 340 86223 8

Typeset in Baskerville by Avon DataSet Ltd,
Bidford-on-Avon, Warwickshire

Printed and bound in Great Britain by
Clays Ltd, St Ives plc

The paper used in this book is a natural recyclable product made from
wood grown in sustainable forests. The hard coverboard is recycled.

Hodder & Stoughton
A Division of Hodder Headline Ltd
338 Euston Road
London NW1 3BH
www.madaboutbooks.com

Where is the wise? where is the scribe? where is the disputer of this world? hath not God made foolish the wisdom of this world? . . . But God hath chosen the foolish things of the world to confound the wise.

St Paul (1 Corinthians 1:20, 27)

Contents

Foreword

This is not the first, and probably will not be the last, biographical study of Robin Eames, but it is certainly the best and most rounded picture we are likely to have for a long time. Archbishop Eames is a many-sided personality, and this book has worked hard to give an impression of the many aspects of his work and the impact he has made on a wide range of people.

For a good many, I suspect that Robin Eames has become a figure who represents something very distinctive about the Anglican Church itself. William Temple, Michael Ramsey and Desmond Tutu, three dramatically different characters, are often seen as telling you things about modern Anglicanism that no amount of textbook discussion could; Robin Eames bids fair to join this company. It is something to do with a temper of mind and soul, a habit of disciplined fairness and patience, a sense of the absolute priority of gospel loyalties over and above anything remotely sectarian, and it is not only a deeply attractive temper but one that achieves things that otherwise would be impossible. When the full history of Northern Ireland's sufferings and triumphs in the twentieth century comes to be written, the significance of Robin's courage and steadiness will undoubtedly emerge in clearer profile than ever; meanwhile, these pages give some sense of just what his witness and imagination have contributed.

And it is this that has given him so demanding a role in the Anglican Church worldwide. The manifest stature of his ministry in Ireland and the strength of his personality have given him a moral authority of a special kind; and he has exercised this, privately and publicly, to powerful effect. In a period when the Anglican Communion has seemed at times to be determined to damage itself beyond repair, his patient service to a larger and more robust vision of what the Communion is and might be has been of immeasurable service.

So it is a delight to read these perceptive and illuminating pages – the portrait of a human being, not a plaster saint, one who has brought enormous delight to his friends and colleagues and been a constant source of joy as well as inspiration. The author, like his subject, has given a real gift to us all, Anglicans and non-Anglicans, Irish and non-Irish. This book deserves every praise and the warmest welcome.

Rowan Cantuar
(Dr Rowan Williams, Archbishop of Canterbury)

Acknowledgments

There are many people whom I wish to thank sincerely for their help, in all kinds of ways. I am grateful to all those who agreed to my requests for interviews and who gave generously of their time. Many did so in the midst of busy careers. I also acknowledge the editors of all the newspapers and of other publications mentioned, and those whose scholarly and literary sources are quoted and duly credited.

I would also like to thank the Church of Ireland Bishop of Down and Dromore, the Rt Reverend Harold Mitchell, the Rector of Knocknagoney, the Reverend David Brown, and members of the Management Committee for making possible the use of the Aslan Centre in Belfast while the book was being written.

I also thank Mrs Roberta Haffey, secretary to the Archbishop of Armagh, for her kindness and considerable expertise, and also my editor Judith Longman and her colleagues at Hodder and Stoughton for all their advice and assistance. I am also most grateful to Roy Lilley, my former editor at the *Belfast Telegraph*, for reading the proofs and for his helpful comments.

I particularly thank Archbishop Robin Eames for his invaluable help in making himself so available for a long series of in-depth interviews during a period of eighteen months, and for his readiness to provide written sources and other material on a wide range of topics to assist in my research. I am also especially grateful to my wife Hilary for her support in every way.

Finally, I thank all those other people, too numerous to mention by name but not forgotten, whose contribution helped to make this publication possible.

Alf McCreary
Belfast
26 September 2004

Prologue:
Crowning Moment

At precisely 3.40 p.m. on a sunny afternoon in late February 2003, a distinguished-looking man in clerical robes stepped forward in the magnificent surroundings of Canterbury Cathedral to play a brief but significant role in the enthronement of Dr Rowan Douglas Williams as the 104th Archbishop of Canterbury.

The honour of pronouncing the Blessing on the Archbishop, following his enthronement to the Chair of St Augustine, had been given to Lord Eames, the Church of Ireland Archbishop of Armagh and Primate of All-Ireland, and the then Senior Primate in the worldwide Anglican Communion.

Praying on behalf of the world's 70 million Anglicans, and speaking slowly in his distinctive Ulster accent, Archbishop Eames said:

> God the Father grant you power to guide and rule the Church with courage and with love.
>
> God the Son, the great Shepherd of the sheep, grant you strength to guard the flock committed to your care.
>
> God the Holy Spirit grant you wisdom and understanding that you may open to all people the riches of the Catholic Faith.
>
> And the blessing of God Almighty rest upon all your work done in his name now and always, Amen.

When Eames finished speaking, the two men exchanged knowing looks. This was no mere symbolic blessing, or simply the performance of an important duty by the then longest-serving Primate in the Anglican Communion. Rather, it was a shared moment between friends who had known each other for more than a decade and who had worked closely together on Anglican projects worldwide. As two Primates representing the Celtic fringe of Ireland and Wales respectively, both men had also played important roles at the very heart of Anglicanism.

Robin Eames had been asked by Rowan Williams to pronounce the Blessing, and the moment was important to both of them. It was witnessed in the cathedral by a packed congregation of some 2,400 people including Prince Charles, the Prime Minister Tony Blair and other senior politicians, church leaders from all parts of the world, as well as representatives from other faiths, and a host of international ambassadors and other distinguished guests.

As the ancient, impressive and moving Service of Enthronement continued with its distinctly Welsh overtones in a truly global setting, Robin Eames moved quietly again into the background. For one brief and important moment he had been given his rightful place as one of the most highly respected Primates in the Church who had given a lifetime of distinguished service to Anglicanism.

For several years he had been a member of one of its key committees, and with great skill he had chaired two important Anglican deliberations, achieving on the potentially divisive subject of women's ordination a remarkable consensus. He had been a trusted senior adviser to successive Archbishops of Canterbury, and at one time he was widely regarded in Anglicanism as a serious contender to succeed Dr Robert Runcie.

As Archbishop of Armagh, he had experienced some of the greatest difficulties facing any senior church figure in the world, as he followed the pilgrimage of an Irish Primate during the years of violent and dramatic change in Ireland. For the greater part of his ministry his native Province of Ulster had suffered from bitterness and continued political deadlock in the midst of one of the most vicious terrorist campaigns in the tortured history of the island.

As a bishop and archbishop he had to preside over territories that included not only divided communities, but also two separate countries. He had to come to terms with a religious and a political role for which no theological training could ever have prepared him adequately. His call to holy orders had transformed his life from a future career as an academic lawyer to that of a minister and pastor at a time when the 'Irish question' began to erupt again in its full fury.

In the years that followed, he found himself thrust into the cauldron of change, of suffering and of revolution, and of the birth of a hesitant new Ireland. In the course of those moment-ous years he became the confidant of prime ministers, poli-ticians and world figures, as well as people of all backgrounds who were seeking to keep alive the candle of hope amid the darkness of Ireland, North and South.

He found himself involved with the paramilitary men and women of violence and also with suffering parishioners and families at the same time as he was being admitted to the corridors of political power and influence.

He had to find a way to balance the inner tension between carrying out his heavy ecclesiastical duties, from his late thirties as the youngest bishop in his church until his mid-sixties as archbishop and Primate, with his role as spokesman for his people in a divided community.

Major political figures became his acquaintances. His con-fidants included Margaret Thatcher, John Major and Tony Blair, and their Irish counterparts Albert Reynolds and Bertie Ahern. The Downing Street Declaration, the Anglo-Irish Agreement and confidential briefings in London, Dublin and elsewhere demanded his attention.

The concept of consent between the communities in Northern Ireland and between all the people of Ireland became his vision. He worked closely with successive Roman Catholic Archbishops of Armagh in extending the hand of friendship to their community throughout Ireland, while also co-operating extensively with other Protestant church leaders.

On a different level, the behind-the-scenes negotiations for a ceasefire called for his previous legal experience. The develop-ment of the peace process became a severe test as people struggled to find a secure and meaningful future in the evolving framework for a political and social stability after more than thirty-five years of upheaval and uncertainty.

Outside Ireland, the work of trying to free the hostages of

Lebanon, including the Irishman Brian Keenan, thrust him into the dark world of Middle East politics. Throughout it all was the constant battle between his mind and heart – what was God's will in a divided and violent world at home and abroad? How was he to try to fulfil his role and his mission in such difficult circumstances?

The journey of Robin Eames is the story of a complex period of history in Ireland, North and South, and within the Anglican Communion through the life of a man whose feelings and sympathy for his own community and the worldwide Church were tested by the stark realities of dramatic and often violent political challenge and change.

The man who briefly took centre stage in Canterbury Cathedral on that memorable day to pronounce a blessing on the new archbishop, and then moved back into the national and international ranks of his senior clerical colleagues, had taken only a few short steps to complete his honoured task, but he had come a very long way indeed since his early days in Northern Ireland.

1

Early Days

Robert Henry Alexander Eames was born on 27 April 1937 in Johnstone Nursing Home on the Malone Road, Belfast, a prosperous residential area of the city. He was the elder child of a Methodist minister, the Reverend William Edward Eames, and his wife Mary. Four years later his only sister Marion was born.

Their parents had a mixed marriage – but not in the usual Northern Ireland sense of a mixed marriage between a Protestant and a Roman Catholic. Their marriage was 'mixed' in that it crossed the political divides in Ireland. His father's family were from Cork and his mother was a Protestant from East Belfast. It proved to be an auspicious start in life for a boy who would one day become the Church of Ireland Archbishop of Armagh and Primate of All-Ireland.

William Eames had been born in Cork and had moved with his family to Dublin during the Irish 'Troubles' of the early twentieth century. His father had owned a car business in Cork, which was then under British rule. Because of the nature of his business he was allowed petrol by the authorities at a time when fuel was rationed during the turbulent days of the Irish Republican struggle for independence. Whether because of this, or the fact that the Eames were Methodists, the family received a threat from local Republicans and decided to flee from the city. The situation was so dangerous that Mr Eames senior and his four sons left Cork by boat, because of the danger of being apprehended at a roadblock. Meanwhile his wife and their daughter were taken out of the city in a car driven by a trusted friend, because the roads were deemed to be safer for women. The family met at a pre-arranged destination north of Cork, and made their way to Dublin. It was here that Robin Eames' paternal grandfather started once again in business. He was given the first franchise in Ireland for Massey Ferguson agricultural vehicles and machinery and established a prosperous network in the Dublin area.

William had been educated at Cork Grammar School and for a period he attended another college in Dublin. He always had a strong vocation for the ministry, and went north to Belfast where he attended Edgehill College to train as a Methodist minister. One of his fellow students was the father of Walton Empey, a future Church of Ireland Archbishop of Dublin – a remarkable coincidence in itself.

His first appointment was as an assistant minister in Limavady, near Londonderry in the north-west of Ulster, and during this period he met Mary Alexander, the only daughter of Robert and Martha Alexander, who were members of a prominent Methodist family from East Belfast. Robert Alexander was a successful businessman and the co-owner of Wilson, Jordan and Alexander, wholesale provision merchants. He was also a well-known Unionist politician who became a Unionist councillor, High Sheriff and Deputy Lord Mayor of Belfast. He was later elected as a Unionist MP for the Victoria constituency at Stormont, the seat of the then Northern Ireland Government.

Mary Alexander, known as Meta, was tall, slim and pretty, and made a big impression on the youthful William Eames. In the Ulster of those days it was an advantage if young people fell in love with people from their own religious background, because marriages between Roman Catholics and Protestants – while by no means unknown – were generally frowned upon.

William Eames courted Meta Alexander as best he could, allowing for the fact that communication in those days was different from today without mobile phones, the Internet or fax machines. It was also a comparatively long distance between Limavady and Belfast at a time when motor cars were owned only by a few well-off people. William, however, kept in touch by mail and he regularly sent Meta a bunch of flowers which were carefully parcelled in a shoebox. She was suitably touched, but wondered how an impecunious assistant minister could afford to buy flowers. Little did she know, until later on, that while William Eames was poor materially he was rich in ideas.

He simply picked the flowers during the course of his ministerial travels and parcelled them off to Belfast. His ingenious and colourful courtship was ultimately successful, and William and Meta were married in Knock Methodist Church, Belfast, where there is still a memorial window to the Alexander family.

William Eames' first church was in Portadown and Lurgan, a relatively prosperous agricultural and manufacturing area in mid-Ulster. Robin Eames was born during this time, while Marion was born during the Second World War when the Reverend William Eames was the Methodist minister in Larne, in wartime a strategically important port north of Belfast on the east coast of Northern Ireland.

Robin, though only a small boy at the time, has a clear recall of those formative years. 'I used to have a biscuit box with a picture of Rupert Bear, and when the air-raid siren went off the first thing I grabbed was my "Rupert Tin". I remember the night of one of the big bombings in Belfast and as we made our way to the air-raid shelters on the Glenarm Road, I could hear the sound of the Luftwaffe planes coming across the Irish Sea as they zoned in on Belfast harbour. I recall creeping up behind the adults at the door of the air-raid shelter and seeing the dark shapes of the bombers etched against the stars on that clear night which helped them find their way to Belfast. It is something which stays clearly in my memory.'

William Eames also took his son to Belfast on the morning after one of the German air raids in the Spring of 1941. Early in April the Luftwaffe bombers destroyed the Harland and Wolff fuselage factory, and a timber yard, and caused extensive damage to the docks. On the night of 15 April – Easter Tuesday – another Luftwaffe raiding party dropped more than 200 metric tons of bombs and around 800 firebomb canisters over a largely unprotected city. They overshot their dockland targets, whether accidentally or on purpose, and dropped bombs on civilian housing in North Belfast. It was estimated that nearly a thousand people had died. The loss of life and devastation was so great that the Irish Prime Minister Eamon de Valera temporarily abandoned his policy of neutrality and responded to calls for help from Belfast by sending fire engines and crews from the Republic into Northern Ireland.

Robin Eames remembers the scene of devastation in Belfast. 'The holes in the hoses of the fire brigade were sprouting little jets of water, like a garden fountain. I remember them particularly because I was a small boy and I had to dodge the jets of water to avoid getting wet. I also remember the smell of the burning that had taken place. I was not frightened, and it was all rather exciting.' It was only many years afterwards that he came to reflect on the degree of violence in which he had lived his life, from that wartime boyhood to the Troubles in Northern Ireland much later on.

His lifetime gift for the detailed observation of people, places and events is well illustrated by his memories of his boyhood in Larne, which at that time was a key marshalling point for American, British and European forces prior to the Allied invasion of Normandy. 'Down the road from the Methodist Manse there was a camp for the "Free" Belgian and French forces. They had painted their guard boxes with their national colours. I also remember a visit to Larne by King George VI and Queen Elizabeth, later the Queen Mother.

'My father had an Austin Seven in those days, and because he was a minister he was issued with petrol to enable him to go on his rounds. Other cars were "jacked up" because they could not get fuel, due to the wartime rationing. My parents organised a tea and soup canteen near the Methodist church, and I remember being there as a child when they worked with the other clergy. The Church of Ireland minister then was the Reverend Alan Buchanan, who later became Archbishop of Dublin.' His sister Marion remembers her mother holding Friday- and Saturday-night receptions in the manse for Allied soldiers. 'They were offered a meal and a bath, because some of them had poor facilities in their billets. My mother believed very much in the ministry of the teapot.'

During his boyhood in Larne, Robin Eames developed a lifelong love for the sea and for railways. 'My father had a feel for the sea and he loved ships and boats. I remember being taken to the hills over the town and watching the British battleships going out of Larne and across the channel to Scotland. It was always a great thrill to travel across Larne Lough in an open motor boat to Islandmagee.'

Robin Eames' years in Larne were his main boyhood experience of rural Ulster, or perhaps more accurately of Northern

Ireland society outside its capital city Belfast. His father spent the rest of his ministry in Belfast churches – in the Crumlin Road where he was chaplain to the prison, then in the impressive church at Donegall Square in the centre of the city (which is now the headquarters of the Ulster Bank), and later at Jennymount, a working-class area of North Belfast.

One of Robin Eames' most searing wartime memories is that of witnessing an ex-prisoner of the Japanese returning home to Belfast to meet his father. 'A taxi drew up to the door and a gaunt figure emerged to be reunited with his father who was a Methodist minister. His son had been working on the Japanese death railroad, and he had been fed on rats. I was only about nine years old but even then I had a deep impression of what war could do to a human being.'

Eames' experience in Belfast marked him indelibly with the atmosphere and character of a tough city which despite its all too obvious troubles has a reputation for kindness and hospitality. He says, 'I think of myself as a Belfast man, as part of a changing city that was my home. I am part of the saga of Belfast in terms of good and bad. I am very proud of its heritage, and while I was totally innocent of what happened in Belfast when I was a child, I am not in any sense ashamed of the city. It was part of my life.'

Significantly, however, he also was familiar with Dublin in his early childhood, an exposure to another culture in the island of Ireland that many of his contemporaries were unable to share. For many Ulster Protestants the relatively new Irish Republic was a 'foreign country', and to some extent looked down upon because it was economically worse off than Northern Ireland which was subsidised by the British Government.

His sister Marion recalls, 'My grandfather owned a big retail petrol garage, as well as the agricultural machinery business, and Robin and I went down to Dublin for a fortnight every summer. Behind the garage there was a huge warehouse where the tractor parts were stored. They were all held in metal cages and carefully catalogued. The men in the store used to allow us to "help" them, and Robin and I would race to see who could find the part first. We had to climb up these huge ladders to find what we wanted, and it was just wonderful. Sometimes we were allowed to take the petrol money in the garage. They also had an ice-cream outlet, and we were allowed to make our own "sliders". It was great fun, and Dublin was always a part of our lives.'

As a boy Robin Eames attended Belfast Royal Academy, a grammar school with a good reputation situated in North Belfast. When his father had yet another change of ministry and moved to South Belfast, Robin went to Methodist College, another outstanding grammar school situated near Queen's University in the then residential suburbs of the city.

A contemporary at Methodist College, Harold Good, who later became a Methodist minister, a President of the Methodist Church in Ireland, and also remained a lifelong friend, remembers Eames in his schooldays: 'He was not gregarious but rather a steady, solid person who was liked and well respected. He was a prefect and I remember him checking that people were arriving at school on time and that they were wearing their school caps. I noticed that he had long outgrown his own school cap, and that he looked more mature than the rest of us.'

Harold Good and Robin Eames had much in common. They shared the same birthday, they were sons of the manse, their parents were friends, and they both struggled with mathematics. A number of their school contemporaries also became ministers. Harold Good recalls: 'Robin would have discovered as I did that there was nothing restrictive or unhappy about being brought up in a manse, and that it was a way of life. It was full of interest, and none of us thought that it was in the least bit odd to be involved in the life of the Church. Robin was a middle-of-the-road son of the manse. There was no rebelliousness, no kicking of the traces. He always looked mature beyond his years. We always got on well together even if I did break my wrist playing "touch" rugby with him in the quadrangle at lunchtime!'

Eames was, however, good at English, history and geography – all of which were to play an important part in his adult career. Of his struggle with mathematics he says, 'I was terrified by maths, but I was a plodder, and I kept at it.' One maths teacher exclaimed to him in exasperation, 'Eames, you will never be out of work as long as snow needs to be cleared from our streets.' This now sounds ironic, given that Archbishop Eames became Chair of the Anglican Communion Finance Committee handling millions of pounds.

Most probably because of his lack of confidence with mathematics, Robin Eames failed the very first 11-plus examination in Northern Ireland. This was a controversial method of selection for young people hoping to progress to grammar school, but he passed the so-called 'Review' a couple of years later. He remembers sitting the 11-plus with two friends – one of whom became a stockbroker and the other a doctor. They both passed, but Eames says, 'I had no sense of failure in not getting the 11-plus. It was all a great adventure, and many other people did not pass either.'

His sister Marion confirms that even then he was a worker. She says, with a smile, 'He had to work hard for his exams and I think it irritated him at times that he had to work so hard and that I seemed to do just enough to get through. He was always being held up to me by our teachers as a model of hard work and diligence. I was reminded of that frequently.'

They were close as brother and sister, while retaining their strongly individual personalities. Marion says: 'My parents used to think that Robin took me to school by bus every day. In fact he used to sprint off to be with his friends, rather than walk with his little sister. This suited me perfectly well at the time. It was only many years later that I told my mother what had happened, and she just laughed.'

The young Robin Eames was good at sport and won his school colours in athletics and rugby, as well as a number of Ulster Grammar School sports awards. Today it is difficult to reconcile the rounded Archbishop with the youth who was a keen sprinter. He retains an abiding love of sport, particularly rugby and sailing.

Robin Eames' early life was predictable. As a son of the manse, he was brought up in a traditional Methodist atmosphere. His mother was a born 'homemaker' with a gift for friendship. There was rarely a week when visitors were not entertained in the manse. She was also a woman of strict religious observance and of prayer. Robin recalls, 'My mother was totally involved in congregational life with my father and identified completely with his ministry. She was a woman of determination, and I rarely saw her undecided, whether publicly or domestically. She may have passed on to me some of that trait. I may take longer than some people to reach a decision, and that's the lawyer in me who takes everything into

consideration. Once I make a decision, however, I am determined to see it through. I can be very stubborn when I want to
be.'

Robin Eames remains deeply aware of the positive influence
of his parents. 'I often count my blessings because of a happy
and fulfilled childhood at home. The balance created by my
mother and father between a secure home life and the demands
of a "public" church life still fills me with admiration. My
parents' lifestyle was more eloquent than any sermon I heard
preached.'

His sister Marion remembers life in the various manses: 'We
had great times together, and some mishaps. I recall the day
when our piano fell through the floor at our house on the
Antrim Road. This was due to dry rot. My father happened to
be holding onto the piano at the time, and he went through the
floor as well. There was nothing for it but to move, and we
ended up in another house off the Antrim Road.

'I also remember my mother listening carefully to our reading
exercises when we were children. She was an elocution teacher
and she used to make us stand at one end of a long room while
she sat at the other end as we read out loud. I always think that
this helped us greatly in later life because both Robin and I
have to speak in public. Robin was good at amateur dramatics
and he played the lead in the school play – *The Rivals*, by
Sheridan. He was also a very good boy soprano and won
trophies at Belfast Music Festival.'

One of Eames' assets in public life has been his clear and
impressive diction, and his keen sense of timing when delivering
a sermon or speech. Clearly those early elocution lessons, as
well as treading the boards with the school amateur dramatic
society, paid off in later life.

Marion later married a Church of Ireland clergyman, the
Reverend Tom Gibson, and when he died from cancer at fifty-
four she was left to bring up their son Paul. She built up a
distinguished career in social work, and she is now a consultant
in stress and trauma. Both she and Robin keep their careers
separate, and although there is a strong family resemblance,
many people are surprised when Dr Marion Gibson, the trauma
expert, turns out to be the sister of Robin Eames, the Primate.

Robin remembers being taught the values of service, as trans-
mitted by both parents. 'I experienced traditional church

involvement as a son of the manse. I attended Sunday School, joined the Boys' Brigade and Scouts, and sang in the choir. But at that stage I never thought beyond the traditional demands which were made of me. I had no desire to become a clergyman. I had an early ambition to become a doctor, but my lack of progress at maths meant that such a course would be unrealistic.'

Marion says, 'Robin inherited my mother's gift of being able to put people at their ease, and there is a lot of my father in him as well. He has my father's quiet determination, a confidence and a faith in what he believes in, and also a sense of humour.'

Robin was particularly close to his father. 'Without realising it during my formative years, he instilled in me what vocation meant. As chaplain to the Crumlin Road prison in Belfast he became involved in the welfare of prisoners' families who frequently called at our home.

'His study was a place where I first discovered books as a child. He was a constant reader, and I recall his weekly change of books at the library. Biography was his favourite form of reading, and I still remember many of the titles. He instilled in me a love for the printed word.

'His sermons frequently influenced my youthful thinking. As I listened to him preaching Sunday after Sunday I learned so much more about his inner dedication. He never once tried to convert me or to ram religion down my throat. He was devout and dedicated, and he passed on to me a very deep sense of what it meant to be of service to people.'

Robin's father paid attention to the tiniest detail. 'He was small of stature but immaculately turned out. He insisted on smoothing down his naturally wavy hair with the then equivalent of Brylcreem, and he always wore well-polished shoes. He once said to me, "If people come to Communion and look down and see the minister with dirty shoes that is not a good advertisement for the church." '

Unfortunately his health was poor, and in mid-life he suffered from heart problems. 'In those days the only cure was rest and more rest. After the early heart attacks he was not allowed to drive, so I acted as his driver as often as I could. We were close and we became even closer as time went on. He shared my love of rugby and sport, and our bond was very deep. He was a friend as well as my father, and I will always recall his life with deep affection. I often wonder whether or not the deep thinking I was to experience as I sought my vocation later on would ever have progressed without his influence.'

Despite his gentle, thoughtful qualities the Reverend William Eames was very much his own man. Although he was born and brought up in the Irish Republic, when he came North he joined the Orange Order and rose to become a County Grand Chaplain. He also held high rank in the Masonic Order. He was partly a man of his time in that a number of senior clergymen, including Church of Ireland bishops and middle-class professional and business people, were members of the Orange Order which had been formed in the late eighteenth century in Co. Armagh to protect and to promote Protestantism in Ireland.

Today there is a very different outlook, with comparatively few middle-class professionals in the Order and even fewer clergymen at all levels – and not a single Church of Ireland bishop. The Order today is much more political and hard-edged than in previous generations, and because of the Troubles in Northern Ireland over the last thirty-five years or so, it has developed even more of a siege mentality partly because it feels that Unionism is fighting for its survival in the face of an apparently implacable Irish Republicanism, as well as British indifference.

As Archbishop, Robin Eames' later career was to be embroiled in the Drumcree stand-off between Orangemen and Republicans which took place in his own Armagh diocese. This became one of the gravest problems facing not only community relations in Northern Ireland but also the Church of Ireland in the North and in the Irish Republic. He says, 'My father's involvement in the Orange Order is something which my critics may latch onto, but I have to say that it meant a great deal to him even though his own father in Dublin disapproved of his connections with the Order. I can only surmise that having come from the South at a time when Protestants had to readjust to a new way of life in the recently formed Irish Republic, he may have swung the other way. He was very fond of the Ulster people and he had a high regard for their attributes and character.

'In my father's day it was part of the life of many middle-class Protestants to join the Orange Order. He loved church life and he was anxious to try to be an influence for good on others, so the Orange Order would have provided extra points of contact with members of his congregation who were also Orangemen. He must also have believed in it, but I don't think he would have been happy with the way in which the Orange Order, which I perceive in my lifetime, has developed.

'To take his Orangeism from him would have been to take a great deal of my father away, but it helped me to understand the attitudes with which I had to deal later as Primate. It also helped me to understand why people south of the border thought and felt the way they did.'

There was another strong Unionist influence on his mother's side of the family. 'I have memories of my maternal grandfather R. B. Alexander as a great "father-figure". I recall being taken as a young child to Stormont, where he was an MP, and of being shown round the building.' Eames also remembers as a boy being taken on the back of a lorry by his grandfather during a Unionist celebration of a tripartite election victory in East Belfast, a Protestant stronghold. 'I remember the parade going along the Newtownards Road, with bands playing, people waving Union Jacks, and cries of "No Surrender" and "Not an Inch". There were also references to King William and the Battle of the Boyne. As a boy, all of this meant nothing to me, but I still remember the noise and the bustle and the feeling of excitement.'

It is a memory which many Protestants of his generation will share. Robin Eames was born into a Northern Ireland which in the late 1930s still looked on itself as an integral part of the United Kingdom with historic and seemingly unbreakable links with the Crown and the British way of life. The partition of Ireland in the early 1920s had not brought peace to Northern Ireland, and the eloquent plea from King George V fell on deaf ears when he opened the new Northern Ireland Parliament in Belfast on 22 June 1921. He said: 'I speak from a full heart when I pray that my coming to Ireland today may prove to be the first step towards an end of strife amongst her people, whatever their race or creed.'

Instead of heeding the King's wise words, both sides in Northern Ireland continued their dispute in the coming decades, and this resulted in intermittent but serious violence between the Unionist and Nationalist communities in Belfast, and elsewhere in the Province. The stalemate persisted, and even after the Second World War when the political map of Europe and the world had changed, the Unionists in Northern Ireland largely failed to see the need for radical change and to develop a shared approach to joint government with the Roman Catholic Nationalist minority. It could be argued, however, that the Nationalist and Republican opposition was feeble, and certainly insufficient to shake the Unionist majority out of its political torpor. The dreariness of Ulster politics, which Winston Churchill had described in a House of Commons speech just after the First World War, could easily have applied to the boyhood years of Robin Eames and his contemporaries on both sides:

> Then came the Great War. Every institution, almost, in the world was strained. Great Empires have been overturned. The whole map of Europe has been changed. The position of countries has been violently altered. The modes of thought of men, the whole outlook on affairs, the grouping of parties, all have encountered violent and tremendous changes in the deluge of the world. But as the deluge subsides and the waters fall short we see the dreary steeples of Fermanagh and Tyrone emerging once again. The integrity of their quarrel is one of the few institutions that has been unaltered in the cataclysm which has swept the world.

Sadly, the 'dreary steeples of Fermanagh and Tyrone' and the bomb-sites of Belfast and elsewhere for the rest of the twentieth century were reminders of the extent to which that quarrel between Unionists and Irish Nationalists remained unaltered. At the start of the twenty-first century the quarrel is still not resolved, though arguably less murderous and vicious than in the recent past, and the final outcome is still imponderable. It has been against this daunting background that Robin Eames has carried out his ministry as a rector, a bishop and an archbishop.

Eames, however, has always retained a sensitive 'feel' for complex issues, including the role of the Orange Order, and he was aware of its existence from his earliest days. Not only was his father an Orangeman, his maternal grandfather R. B. Alexander was a typical Unionist politician of his time. A whole generation of Ulster Protestants, including the middle classes, waved the Union Jack and took refuge in the slogans of the past. Such slogans meant nothing to Eames as a boy, but as a young man he would begin to reflect on the emptiness and inherent danger of such an unenlightened policy. 'I asked myself why such men of faith, including my own kith and kin, did not realise the monster that they were allowing to grow in their midst. When they said their prayers did they not have any indication of the growing storm, with their blind allegiance to a "Protestant Parliament for a Protestant people"?'

There was an air of triumphalism, but one of defensiveness as well. Robin Eames reflects, 'The great "enemy" was the Republic of Ireland, which was known as "Eire". Unionist politics had only one agenda – looking back to the Border issue. For them it was important at all costs that Northern Ireland should remain part of the United Kingdom.

'So much we have lived through could have been avoided if there had been real statesmanship on the Protestant side. Of course I can sound very wise today, but in my grandfather's time those questions simply did not arise. The Unionists did not have to look beyond what they were seeing. There was no challenge, no civil rights movement. It was only later that things would change utterly.'

Things were also to change utterly indeed for the youthful Robin Eames. Having decided against a career in medicine, he applied to Queen's University for a place in its famed Law School and he was successful. He was embarking upon one of the most formative influences of his career, and he was also about to experience important and traumatic family events. These unexpected developments, and the influence of Queen's, would change dramatically the direction of his entire life and future career.

2

Between Two Worlds

The Queen's University that Robin Eames entered in 1955 was a very different seat of learning from that of today. There were around 3,000 undergraduate students, compared to some 14,000 at the beginning of the twenty-first century. In the 1950s, the University was a much more compact, even cosy, place and though a large number of undergraduates – including Eames – lived at home, they mixed in and around the campus in the leafy suburbs of South Belfast.

Queen's was one of the 'redbrick' universities which had received its charter in 1908, but which traced its origins back to 1845 as one of the three 'Queen's Colleges' founded in Ireland during the reign of Queen Victoria. The others were established in Cork and Galway. Thus from the mid-nineteenth century, Queen's College, Belfast had played a vital role in educating the sons and daughters largely of the professional classes who could afford to send their children to such an institution.

Previously the Scottish universities had provided an education for many young Ulster students, mostly Presbyterians, and the Irish Colleges on the Continent catered for Catholics.

Queen's College, Belfast had a good reputation as a seat of learning, particularly in law, medicine and engineering. In earlier times it was noted for classics, and one distinguished classics graduate – Cahal Daly – became a member of the teaching staff, and later the Cardinal Archbishop of Armagh.

During the Second World War many Queen's undergraduates served in the Armed Forces, and those who returned in the post-war years brought to the University a cosmopolitan sophistication that had been missing in earlier times when the institution had primarily a more regional role.

The growing reputation of Queen's was further enhanced in the 1950s with the appointment of Dr Eric Ashby as Vice-Chancellor. Later Lord Ashby of Brandon, he was a tall, urbane figure who was to make a considerable reputation for himself in the world of university education. He left Queen's after nearly a decade to become Master of Clare College, Cambridge.

A later Vice-Chancellor Sir Peter Froggatt wrote, in a tribute in the *Independent* of 28 October 1992: 'Eric Ashby became Vice-Chancellor of Queen's University . . . at an important stage in the development of both. At 45, Ashby's aptitudes and ambitions stretched far beyond the laboratory and lecture room: while Queen's was poised for expansion in its size and horizons after its relative quiescence and continued provincialism between the wars. It was to prove a fruitful partnership.'

Ashby and his University Secretary, a redoubtable Scotsman called George Cowie, ran Queen's with commendable efficiency at a time when government funding was much more available than it is today. Ashby often reflected with a sense of amused wonder at being able to lift the phone and simply ask for more money from the Minister of Education in the Stormont Government.

Ashby was able to attract to Belfast some of the brightest young university staff of their generation. As he said himself later on, 'What I did achieve was appointing a staff who really put Queen's on the world map in a way it hadn't been before. Someone called Queen's "Britain's nursery for good professors". That summed up the position admirably.'[1]

The Law Faculty was prestigious, with such luminaries as Professor J. L. Montrose, a larger-than-life academic lawyer and philosopher of Dickensian appearance and eccentricities, who was Dean for twenty-nine years, and Professor Francis Newark who was appointed to the new Chair of Jurisprudence in 1946, and who succeeded Montrose as Dean. They, and others, imbued generations of law students with the finer points of their chosen discipline and also encouraged them to think outside it.

As an essentially regional institution, Queen's provided the education and training for the overwhelming number of professionals in the Province. As Ashby said, in a BBC broadcast on the Northern Ireland 'Home Service' on 12 January 1951, Queen's touched the lives of almost every Ulsterman:

It was probable that a Queen's doctor presided over his birth. Likely as not, if he had an operation it was performed by a Queen's graduate, and another graduate fitted his false teeth. If his children were working for Senior Certificate, some of their teachers were sure to be Queen's men and Queen's women. Many of the engineers who maintained the roads and railways were Queensmen. And if the Ulsterman was unfortunate enough to find himself in a Court of Law, there might well be a Queen's Graduate at the Bar, or on the Bench.[2]

This was the Queen's University that Robin Eames entered in 1955 as an eighteen-year-old law student. In physical terms he was moving a short distance from a large grammar school just across the road from Queen's to the more rarefied atmosphere of a redbrick university with unique ties to the local community. Intellectually, however, he was embarking on a longer and more challenging journey which would stretch his mind and also awaken him to some of the stern realities of life in Northern Ireland from which he had been relatively sheltered by his middle-class Protestant upbringing.

Entry to the Law School opened up an entirely new and influential chapter in his life. He had always loved reading, but now the challenge to master legal and philosophical concepts, the real meaning of justice and the theories about democracy, allied to the implications of case law and precedent, completely enthralled him. He says, 'The hours spent in the Queen's library poring over books, the tutorials and the visits to courts became food and drink to me. The Law Faculty in the Fifties was a "place apart" from other disciplines, and we all felt a sort of intellectual superiority over medical students and engineers. I was conscious of the efforts of the staff to broaden our attitudes, and lectures by Professor Montrose opened for me the whole field of ethics and philosophy. I recall attending a lecture on philosophy by Dr Cahal Daly, and little did he or I imagine that one day we would occupy the respective Primacies in Armagh.'

The friendships that Robin Eames made at Queen's were a revelation to him in more ways than one. 'I had been brought up in the largely Protestant grammar school atmosphere of Methody, but Queen's presented me with my first significant contacts with Roman Catholics. Many of these friendships remain precious today.'

He talked a great deal with his new Roman Catholic friends. 'Many of their thoughts were new to me. They talked about discrimination against Roman Catholics and of alienation. They painted a picture of a tightly knit community which felt "outside" any privileged life in the Province. Many of them saw a legal career in terms of human or civil rights. After visiting their homes and working alongside them, I became deeply conscious of factors which until then had been largely hidden from my experience. I began to ask serious questions of myself, and those friendships grew.'

There was also a sense of guilt. He asked himself, 'What had Protestants done to Roman Catholics?' He began to read extensively through Irish history, something which he had not been taught at school. He recalls: 'I began to be more aware of the complexities of the Ulster question. I asked myself what Northern Ireland was going to be like in the future.'

However, it was his personal contact and friendships with Roman Catholics at Queen's that taught him most of all. 'Something was born which was to return to me often in my years of church leadership – an admiration for the "community" sense of Roman Catholics compared to the fragmented nature of Protestant areas. Long before my decision to be ordained, I was developing a deep sense of the nature of justice, and an equal sense of what made injustice. My involvement in the University's debating societies opened my mind further. I led several debating teams to the Irish Republic and to England, and I began to appreciate what outsiders felt about Northern Ireland. I came to recognise that my upbringing had been sheltered from so much. I have never forgotten those student impressions.'

Robin Eames was typical of his middle-class Protestant background because the Province's grammar schools from which most of the Queen's undergraduates came were either Catholic or Protestant establishments. As such they mirrored the social and political divisions in Northern Ireland society. The large majority of Protestants were Unionists, and the large majority of Roman Catholics were Irish Nationalists. Judge Patrick Markey QC, now a county court judge in Northern Ireland, and then a young Catholic law student from

21

Andersonstown in Belfast, remembers his friendship with Eames during their undergraduate days in the Law Faculty: 'Robin was a very straightforward, honest fellow, with no "side" and no arrogance. One knew that he was a religious type of person, and not one of the guys who drank in the Club Bar and played billiards.

'He was not a back-slapper nor "Hail fellow, well met!" He was almost reserved, but you could have had what passed then for an intelligent and considered conversation with him. I knew that Protestantism was not necessarily coterminous with Orangeism or Unionism, and that there was more to it than that. Robin was a Unionist with traditional instincts, but he did not give you an impression of triumphalism in any way.

'I learned that not all Protestants had horns, and he probably learned the same about Catholics. It was helpful to realise that people from different backgrounds were capable of being civilised. At that age one did not know enough and I might have had a bias against England, though not a very strong one. This was a misdiagnosis in one sense. One blamed England for the situation in Ireland, and for all that had gone before, but not long afterwards you came to realise that this was not really the situation, or the problem, or the diagnosis.'

Markey began to discover that in Northern Ireland there were two communities, and that each was a prisoner of history. He says, 'Meeting people like Robin helped me to realise that there were other legitimate points of view, that you were capable of having a civilised exchange about such matters, and that there were many things about which your thinking was not all that far apart. We had a genuine friendship and I have always had a warm regard for Robin Eames.'

During his time at Queen's, Robin Eames was elected Chairman of the Law Society. 'In my choice of debates and speakers I included an equal number of Protestant and Roman Catholic personalities and subjects, much to the suspicion of confirmed Unionist students.' He was also Chairman of the Queen's University United Nations Society, and says that he 'flirted' with the politics of the Young Unionists. He recollects, 'I dabbled at a number of things, and the possibility of a political career crossed my mind, though not seriously.'

In fact he would have been a prime contender for a career in politics, given his legal training and his family background –

particularly as Eames' maternal grandfather had been such a prominent Unionist in East Belfast. Indeed, it is not too fanciful to speculate that if Eames had chosen such a path, he might have ended up as a senior Stormont Cabinet Minister. His sensitive antennae for people and situations, and his shrewd political judgment, were to stand him in good stead later on, in a career outside party politics but also in countless situations where his political skills proved to be important – both within the Church and also in dealing with party politicians.

His initial career choice was academic law. 'This was a gradual process. I had had several articles published in learned journals such as the *Criminal Law Review*, the *Cambridge Law Journal*, the *Northern Ireland Legal Quarterly* and others. As far as I know, I am the only Church of Ireland Primate to have had published an article on "Receiving stolen property". To my amazement, on a primatial visit to a police station some years ago I was asked by a young policeman if I was any relation to the author of that article!'

When Eames made it known that he wanted to be an academic lawyer, Professor Montrose suggested that he should enrol for a doctorate, following his primary degree in law. 'Montrose also hinted for the first time that I should go to the United States for further study. Following my graduation I began to study for a Ph.D., and under the influence of the late Professor V. T. H. Delaney I chose as my subject the legal implications of the disestablishment of the Church of Ireland.'

His other supervisor was Dr George Simms, the then Archbishop of Dublin who later became Archbishop of Armagh. It was during his first year of doctorate study that serious consideration was given by the Queen's staff to his possible move to Harvard Law School. Montrose arranged the contacts, and Eames began to adjust himself to the idea.

It seemed that he was set for a career as an academic lawyer, but the sudden death of his father in 1959 changed everything. William Eames had been to a Belfast library to pick up books for a holiday and suffered a massive heart attack on the bus on the way home. He was already dead when the bus conductor came to collect his ticket. At about that time Robin had been sitting in Crumlin Road court listening to a murder case about a police sergeant who had been killed in an IRA booby-trap bomb. He immediately left, and went to identify formally his deceased father. Even though he had been in poor health, his father's death was an immense shock.

Robin was conscious of his responsibilities to his widowed mother, and postponed any move to Harvard. Another important factor in his decision not to go to the United States, and by implication not to continue with a career in academic law, was the growing influence of a call to the ministry – something with which he was to struggle for some time.

Significantly, however, this heart-searching about possible ordination took place as an Anglican and not within the Methodist Church which had nurtured his Christian faith since childhood. This was partly due to the crucial decision taken by his father to join the Church of Ireland ministry after a long career as a Methodist clergyman. The Reverend William Eames had been due to end his term of service at Jennymount in North Belfast, and had been offered a 'light duty' posting at Moy in Co. Tyrone, but this would have meant moving the family out of Belfast, and also out of close proximity to his medical specialist who was based in the city.

He was not alone in facing such a dilemma, and other ministers before and since have wrestled with the demands of fulfilling an itinerant ministry in the Methodist Church which requires a move every few years. William Eames and the church authorities were unable to reach a compromise and he resigned his post, no doubt with much heart-searching.

Such a move would have required courage and strong-mindedness, as well as faith in God for the future. The move also doubtless caused a wrench among his colleagues. The Reverend Dr Harold Good, whose parents were close to William Eames, says, 'He was a much-respected man, and a good minister who had held important posts within the Methodist Church.'

However, Eames senior had long admired the liturgical life of Anglicanism and he prepared himself for ordination in the Church of Ireland. Robin Eames recalls, 'My youthful preoccupations at that stage were concerned with a university career, and my memories of this period are vague, but I do recall the tensions surrounding his decision.'

His sister Marion has a clearer recollection. 'It was a time of great decision-making. My father was always very ecumenical and he had lots of friends across the religious spectrum, particularly in Anglicanism. I believe my father had been thinking about this for some time, so when it happened it wasn't a complete surprise. We had a number of family conversations about the implications of it all, about losing our church house and what it would all mean for our way of life.

'Our parents had decided to make the move but Robin and I were given a choice. My father made it clear that we were not expected to follow him if it was something we did not want to do. Robin and I decided that we would move together as a family, and I clearly remember the day when our family was confirmed into the Church of Ireland. It was a private ceremony conducted by the Bishop of Down and Dromore Dr Mitchell, and it was something that I will never forget.'

The Reverend William Eames became a deacon in Knockbreda Parish in Belfast where the Rector, Canon Louis Crooks, was an older man. Marion Gibson says, 'It was a very wise move by the Bishop to place my father in a parish where he was not just an assistant curate but where he would be able to do things in his own right. However, for the first year he could not administer Holy Communion on his own, so the Bishop asked another young curate – the Reverend Tom Gibson – to assist him. It turned out that Tom was to be my future husband.'

William Eames' decision was fundamental. If he had remained in the Methodist Church would Robin Eames have become a minister and ended up as a Methodist President with tenure of office for only one year? To what extent did his father's change of office open up a path which, after Robin subsequently decided on ordination, would lead him to the Primacy of the Church of Ireland where his influence was to be felt nationally and internationally for nearly two decades? Was this all a coincidence, or was there a Divine purpose working amid what then appeared to be unconnected circumstances? Non-believers may regard this as mere chance, but believers may see a deeper significance in the unfolding of events.

Marion Gibson says, 'As you get older and look back, you see a path, but when you are actually on that path it is hard to see where it is leading. However, I believe that if we have faith there are opportunities and challenges in everything. It is how you accept those challenges which counts.'

Robin Eames reflects, 'Perhaps I was not turned on to church affairs sufficiently enough at the time of the change, but with hindsight I am aware of a significance which I probably did not see then. However, one should not overestimate the fact that I was not ordained within the Methodist Church. At that stage of my life when ordination beckoned I was convinced that Anglicanism was my spiritual home.

'I am not saying that I would never have been a Methodist minister, but it was an Anglican young man who was considering ordination, not a Methodist. When I was a Methodist I was not thinking seriously of the ministry. When I became an Anglican I was absorbed and enthralled by it. Anglicanism has been my adult life, but as I address other Christian traditions, I am convinced that Anglicanism alone meets my particular outlook and inner feelings. It is the breadth of Anglicanism and its corporate witness to the centrality of Scripture, worship and witness that makes most sense to me. I was never blind to the Church's failings in institutional life, but I have always remained a convinced Anglican.'

Many years later – in 2002 – Archbishop Eames signed the Church of Ireland–Methodist Covenant, together with his old school friend Dr Harold Good, the then Methodist President. He says, 'For both of us that was an important moment. Personally I could not help thinking back on history and of how some things come full circle.'

Though Robin Eames eventually was ordained in the Anglican Church his path to the ministry was not, by his own admission, 'a Damascus Road experience. I could not rid myself of the promptings of vocation to the church despite the deep desire to further my academic life in the States. This was a real and a deep conflict for me. At Queen's I became involved by choice with the Church of Ireland Student Centre and I was greatly influenced by the then Chaplain, the Reverend Edgar Turner. I began to feel drawn to the further study of Anglicanism. The language and worship fascinated me, and I became a lay reader in the Church of Ireland.'

Canon Turner remembers Eames as quiet, observant and questioning. He joined some of the Sunday evening meetings, and was also a member of the 'Heretics Club' – a group of students who took part in a residential weekend in camp-like conditions where they shared worship and domestic chores. Turner recalls, 'They became involved in uninhibited discussions and were free to ask outlandish or critical questions, hence the term "Heretics Club". Robin seemed less "heavy" and more boyish at the residential weekends. There was a degree of mild horseplay which you would not have expected of him. It meant that he was learning to relax.'

Eames was religious not in any ostentatious manner, 'but more so in an enquiring way. He asked pertinent and searching questions, but I did not see him as a candidate for the ministry. He appeared quite content in his pursuit of the law. My view was that we needed convinced and practising Christians working in their professions, rather than nudging people into the ministry. I had a reputation for saying to the students, "Keep away from the ministry if you can. If it is the right thing for you, you won't be able to keep away from it." '

Turner clearly felt that Eames would go far. 'He demonstrated a capacity, which came out strongly later, for good chairmanship. Robin had the ability to examine questions thoroughly and not in any partisan way. You knew that he would go somewhere in life, though not necessarily in the church.'

Dr Joan Turner, later Edgar's wife and at that stage a medical undergraduate at Queen's, also knew Robin Eames through the Church of Ireland Student Centre. 'He came to meetings but never sat in the front row. He always took a position where he could observe what was going on. He did not seem to belong to any particular group, and I would have been worried that he was not integrating – not realising then how much of an observer he is. He seemed to be a bit of a loner. I did not know whether he was a natural loner or a former Methodist who felt that he did not belong.'

She remembers Eames as very much an independent observer. 'I tended to try to bring him in more to things and he responded with lower-case "yes". I recognised his interest in law, but I was surprised when he went on to pursue law as a career. He seemed to have a degree of interest in people that most academic lawyers did not have. I knew that he was slightly interested in Unionism and I presumed that he might have been a politician. He was always his own man.'

Edgar Turner says, 'As someone noted about him a little later, if he had stayed in Law he would have been a judge. He was even then showing a capacity for maturity, for leadership and for whatever other qualities he has.' There is no doubt that Turner also impressed Eames greatly. Turner says, 'I cannot remember any long heart-to-heart talks with Robin, but he may have been observing me much more closely than I was aware of at the time. It must have been what I did rather than what I said that caught his attention.'

A turning-point may have been the time when Turner asked Eames to help him in a difficult pastoral case involving a student who was estranged from his parents. 'Initially he was wary of being asked to help because he thought it might involve him being a "sneak" on a student. Once he discovered that it was anything but that, he was impressed by the degree of care needed in order to bring about a reconciliation. If I had intervened directly myself it would not have resolved the situation. I did not take either side – the parents' or the student's – and I think Robin noticed that. He came to me afterwards and told me how much he valued this insight into the exercise of pastoral care.'

Robin Eames' call to the ministry persisted and he sought an interview with the local bishop, Dr Mitchell. He was advised by the Bishop and by Edgar Turner to 'test' his vocation in Trinity College, Dublin. He did so, and was accepted by the Divinity School, where he started his three-year course in 1960.

There was still one problem to be resolved, however. He had to inform his law professor about his decision to become a minister and not an academic lawyer. 'I went to see Professor Montrose in Belfast and, as honestly as I could, I explained my thinking. His attitude was all too clear – while accepting my privilege to make such a decision he must have wondered if I had done the right thing. Later I discovered that he had said to a colleague, "Eames has had some sort of a mental problem." '

Though he enjoyed reading Divinity in Dublin, and also being in that lively city, he had reservations about the intellectual content of the course. At Queen's he had won a number of awards, including the Austin Memorial Jurisprudence Prize in 1958 and 1959, and in 1960 he graduated with a good upper-second-class honours degree. He had been an able student, and he wanted to continue to achieve the highest standards. He recalls, 'As one of the first Queen's graduates to enter the hallowed halls of the Divinity School after taking a degree in Belfast, I was viewed with some curiosity. I was left in no doubt by some lecturers that education in a "redbrick" university was nothing to what I would expect in Trinity College, Dublin.'

However, the course failed to satisfy him intellectually, in many ways. He says, 'After the depth of the intellectual stretching at Queen's I found a great change required in the levels then required in the Divinity School. Part of this was due to the level of my work at Queen's where I had also conducted tutorials and given some lectures. It was well known in the Divinity School at that time that if you reproduced your lecture notes, it would be sufficient for success in the examinations. Years later the bishops revised the whole course when we established our own theological college. The course is now varied and intense, and I have complete confidence in our own training process.'

At that time, however, he questioned whether he was doing the right thing in Dublin, though he greatly enjoyed the city and the vitality of its people. He says, 'We lived in our hostel in Mountjoy Square and walked down to Trinity every morning and back in the evening. That area was full of tenement beggars and my room looked across the roofs to Croke Park Gaelic football ground. I was familiar with much of the cultural background of Dublin, and I well recall being taken there on holidays at the end of the Second World War. The lights of Dublin made a vivid impression after the darkness of Larne.'

He also learned much more about Dublin and its people. 'As a student I became aware of the different attitudes represented by students from Northern Ireland and the Irish Republic. There was a sort of defensiveness on the part of Northern Ireland students, and critical attitudes to Northern life by others, though I felt that these were uninformed.' This was all part of the mutually suspicious cross-border mentality in both parts of Ireland, which knew so little about one another.

Eames says, 'The Orange Order was seen as highly suspicious by Southerners, though any question of links to the Church rarely, if ever, emerged during those days. Southern students who were thinking of curacies in Northern Ireland were viewed by many as "courageous". Few, if any, Northern students sought Southern curacies. There was a feeling that Northern Ireland was a "missionary" area. Nowadays, however, we have an elaborate system where curacy vacancies are matched to those who are completing their training in Dublin. The House of Bishops is involved in this, and the system is very sophisticated.'

Eames won a number of endowment prizes in the Divinity School, which enabled him to meet the cost of books, meals out and visits to the theatre. Apart from clearly enjoying living in Dublin, he became more assured towards the end of his studies there that he had done the right thing. He recalls, 'My real difficulty was to move from the analytical analysis of a lawyer to the appreciation of the concepts of theology. My philosophical studies at Queen's had given me insights which helped in coming to terms with theology, but I found it difficult to grasp the change from that to the "presumption" of theological thought.'

This was a largely intellectual struggle but one he valued more and more. He says, 'It was when I read Dietrich Bonhoeffer that I began to feel something more of the real meaning of the equation between theoretical philosophy and practical theology. My belief in a God of love and justice never wavered. In those days my struggle was whether full-time ministry should be the expression of my vocation rather than a life of lay dedication to the things of God. I did have a gradual consciousness that ordination was beckoning and that I had made the right choice.'

In his prayers, Bible study and personal thoughts, his vocation became firm. He says, 'I still could not explain the "call" but it was clear that I had to respond. I asked myself constantly, "Why me?", as did all my colleagues in their own cases. However, God calls at times without easily understood reasons. One intellectual barrier I had to overcome was the question whether I was going forward simply because people were not surprised, or because they expected me to. I knew that this must not be the real reason, but the conviction was overwhelming. I had found peace of mind. No longer was I "testing" my vocation. I was convinced.'

His sense of being aware of the expectations, or perhaps the intuitions, of other people was not unfounded. His sister Marion says, 'I was aware that Robin was deciding his future. The Law was there but I knew that the church was there too. There was a short period when an incredible amount happened – my parents had their first real home after spending so many years in manses, Robin became more active in the Church and was a lay reader while a student at Queen's, I met my future husband at that time, and my father died.

'It was an enormous crossroads for us all, and I believe it was Divine guidance. There were too many different developments for it all to have been a coincidence. It seemed less significant as it happened and everything appeared as a natural sequence, but looking back there was a pattern.'

Marion always thought that Robin would be something more than a lawyer, or a 'will-writing' solicitor. She says, 'He would always have had something else. I was very aware of his potential. If he had gone into politics the same qualities would have brought him through to wherever. In a wonderful way all his qualities made him who he is.

'He greatly respected my Dad and all that he did. However, I don't think that he went into the church because of what Dad was, but he certainly knew what it was to live the life of a dedicated servant of God because we had been brought up by one. Our religion was never a "Sunday" religion, it was a way of life.'

There is no doubt that William Eames had had a profound effect on his son, and probably more so after his death. Robin says, 'I am convinced that his influence played a vital role in my own vocation. After his sudden death the memories of his life and dedication became even more clear to me. I had no illusions about the life of a clergyman, and I knew that it would be very different from the life of many of my friends in the secular professions.'

As his ordination approached, Robin Eames was no longer between two worlds. His head had been with the law but his heart was in the church. At last he had peace of mind, and as he looked forward, he paid tribute to his past. He was ordained holding the Bible that his father had been given at his own baptism many years previously. The past and the present were to coincide in the life of this new Anglican curate, and in a way that neither he nor anyone else could have even begun to predict.

3

Beatitudes and Barricades –
Man of the People

Robin Eames was ordained as a deacon in June 1963 in St
Clement's Parish Church in Belfast. It was a simple but moving
ceremony attended by the Eames family and friends and by
local parishioners. During the ceremony Robin wore a clerical
stole that had belonged to his father, whose spirit was never far
from his son's ministry.

 Eames approached his ordination with a clear conviction of
the 'rightness' of his 'call'. He attended a pre-ordination
retreat at Murlough House on the County Down coast, under
the shadow of the Mourne Mountains. It was an area of great
physical beauty and there was also an air of tranquillity which
matched his own mood. He recalls: 'The earlier mental turmoil was behind me, and at the laying on of hands I had great
peace of mind. I felt that my father would have understood and would have approved of the important step I was
taking.'

Robin Eames was appointed to the busy parish of St
Comgall's in Bangor, a prosperous seaside town some twelve
miles east of Belfast on the County Down coast. He worked
with a clergy team under the direction of Archdeacon George
Quin, who had been a friend of his father. It was George Quin
who had handed over to Robin his father's stole at his graveside,
before the coffin was interred. He said to the young law student,
'You might need this some day.'

In 1963 Eames was awarded a Doctorate in Philosophy from
Queen's University and became known throughout the parish
as 'the Doc', whereupon the Rector's son Charlie announced,

'He'll always be Robin to me.' Even today Lord Eames the Archbishop is still known to many people simply as 'Robin'.

Robin Eames' days in Bangor as a young deacon and then as a curate were happy and fulfilled. However, this was a very different Northern Ireland compared to the troubled Province of later years which was to provide the background to the greater part of his ministry. In the early 1960s there was an air of hope and of prosperity in Northern Ireland after the austerity and sacrifice of the Second World War and of the slow build-up towards economic regeneration in the 1950s.

In the same year that Eames was ordained, a new and more liberal Northern Ireland Prime Minister emerged from the ruling Unionist oligarchy. Captain Terence O'Neill, with a background of Eton and the Irish Guards, succeeded the patrician Lord Brookeborough who had been in office since 1943. Brookeborough and his colleagues had seen no need to introduce reforms to counter widespread discrimination against Roman Catholics or to move towards any meaningful form of shared government between the two communities.

O'Neill, by contrast, made reconciliation one of his major objectives and he attempted to move away from the siege mentality of his predecessors. In symbolic bridge-building gestures he met the Catholic Cardinal Dr William Conway, and he made a point of visiting Catholic hospitals and schools. Sadly, it would all eventually end in tears, with O'Neill and his supporters underestimating the Unionist recalcitrance that still existed, and by the end of the decade Northern Ireland would be plunged into some of the worst continued civil unrest anywhere in Western Europe since the end of the Second World War.

By the early 1960s, however, when Robin Eames began his ministry there was still a sense of hope that the worst of the past violence was over. There had been a sporadic IRA border campaign in the 1950s but it lacked widespread support. The police on both sides of the Irish border were informed about the IRA's movements, and they were well placed to take strong counter-security measures. The campaign gradually fizzled out and it was finally called off in February 1962. It looked as if violence was gradually being eliminated from the Republican struggle to unite Ireland.

In the 1960s Northern Ireland was also enjoying an economic boom particularly with the manufacture of manmade fibres, and, given relative peace and increasing prosperity, many people (particularly in the Protestant community) hoped that the Province could look forward to a long period of stability and affluence.

It was also felt that greater employment and prosperity would iron out many of the inequalities of the past, and that more and more traditional Irish Nationalists in the Catholic community would gradually accept the status quo of Northern Ireland. Robin Eames and other middle-class Protestants were also aware of Catholic alienation, but no one apart from the most diehard Republicans could have forecast the upheaval which was to come.

Thus the Northern Ireland in which Robin Eames was starting his ministry was enjoying a rich, warm spring before the political ice age returned again. Tourists were flocking to the picturesque Province, and the general atmosphere was forward-looking. Eames recalls, 'These were the days before people went to Spain on package holidays, and every summer Bangor was transformed by the gaiety and spirit of visiting holidaymakers, many of them coming over from Scotland. I also found our parishioners delightful, and the church was the centre for many of their interests. I introduced a men's club which drew good numbers of the committed as well as the uncommitted, and we were greatly encouraged by the overall growth in our membership.'

Young curates were expected to carry out a set number of house visits each week, and Robin Eames was no exception. 'I met a great cross-section of people, who were mostly middle class. Many of them seemed largely untouched by or unaware of Catholic alienation which I had discovered during my time at Queen's. I came to realise that our town had been sheltered from much of what went on in Nationalist areas, and visiting the homes of our people I was struck by the general comforts of middle-class Ulster life.'

He also learned the ingredients of a parish row, and how to deal with it. 'I always tried to be a step ahead before it developed, with varying degrees of success. The blend for a happy parish is when people take each other for what they are, but recognise that they are there for the good of the organisation. I've seen rows split a choir or a bowling club or a badminton club in half. I also learned that there are times

34

when people come to you to mediate, but that the price of mediation is that sometimes they go away blaming you.'

One man who remembers him from those days is Michael Davey, then a young lawyer himself. He later became Eames' assessor and worked closely with him at General Synod and also at the Armagh Diocesan Synod. Davey recalls, 'The congregation had a high regard for Robin, and the feeling was that he would go far, though I don't know if anyone would have thought in terms of Armagh at that stage. He was approachable and courteous, and he had a way with him. He continues to have those qualities. If he wants you to do something he always asks you and he thanks you. This might not seem much, but an awful lot of people take things for granted nowadays. Robin is not like that.'

Eames was highly regarded as a preacher. Davey says, 'I remember feeling that what he had preached was terrific stuff, but I could never quite put my finger on what he was saying. It was eloquent and inspirational, without being specific. However, my reaction would not have been typical. I was a lawyer and there weren't all that many lawyers around the church. Maybe I was more questioning than others, on the few occasions I turned up at the Young Men's Group!

'I still work with Robin regularly and I still recognise some of the very good qualities he had even then. I recall a degree of devotion to him from members of the congregation in those early days of his ministry. I respected him and I liked him, but not blindly so.'

In 1964, Robin Eames was ordained as an Anglican priest in Dromore Cathedral and he was looking forward to several more relatively carefree years as a curate in Bangor and to learning more about the job. In 1966, however, his life changed significantly. In that year he married his childhood sweetheart Christine Daly, and he was also appointed Rector of the Parish of St Dorothea's in largely Protestant East Belfast.

Robin and Christine were married on 25 June 1966 at Knockbreda Parish Church. They had known each other for a number of years, and the family friendship had developed when Robin's father had been one of the chaplains to the Forster Green Hospital. The Matron was Christine's mother Olive, who had been widowed with her only child when her husband Captain Ward Daly had been killed while serving with the

Royal Inniskilling Fusiliers in North Africa during the Second World War. Christine was then only six weeks old.

The family friendships grew, and Christine was in her last year at school and head girl at Ashleigh when she was a bridesmaid for Marion Eames. While Robin was at Trinity College, Dublin, Christine began studying for a law degree at Queen's, which she completed in 1965. She had ambitions to be a doctor and returned to Queen's to study medicine but this was overtaken by marriage and the arrival of a family.

Robin and Christine had been going out together for some time and became engaged in 1965. A year later they were married and on their way to their honeymoon in Switzerland when Robin was informed by telephone of his appointment as Rector of St Dorothea's in Gilnahirk. It was an appropriate appointment for a young couple who were just recently married. St Dorothea's was one of the 'new area' parishes which were a church priority in the 1960s to meet the growing demands of new housing estates.

The church had been built and opened as the focus of a daughter parish of St Columba's, Knock, to serve the housing areas of Braniel and Tullycarnet. There were around six hundred families, many of them young married couples who were either homebuyers or tenants. Many of the parishioners worked in the centre of Belfast and in local factories. Eames reflects, 'It was a very busy time, and I had a feeling of great delight at being given the opportunity so early in my career to run my own parish. Many of my people had come from settled parishes elsewhere. There were so many babies to be baptised and children, it seemed like hundreds of them, to be confirmed.'

There were also enormous challenges. 'Many of the people had no church connection whatever, and during our door-to-door visiting in the housing estates we received a rude awakening. People would ask us, "What is the Church for? Who are you and why are you calling?" I organised teams of lay visitors to cope with the rapid growth of the new housing and to help people to make contact with the Church.'

The social contact seemed almost as important as Sunday worship. 'Many problems were caused by the need for people to readjust to life on a new housing estate. People had moved from older and poorer housing in the Newtownards Road and

Short Strand area of East Belfast, and although the new housing had better facilities including indoor toilets, there was not the same atmosphere.'

People missed being able to lean over the garden wall of the older housing areas and gossip with their neighbours. Eames recalls, 'I faced a real social problem – how could you build up a sense of community in these new estates which people initially looked on as "places apart"? As well as this, a number of the men were drifting down to their old "local" pubs on a Friday night and returning to a dissatisfied family. Marriages were under pressure, and the young people were wandering.'

St Dorothea's had a number of church organisations including the Bowling Club, the Men's Club and the Mothers' Union, but the focal points of the estates were the schools, the health clinic and the shops. Something special was needed to give the Church its own point of social focus. Eames rose to the challenge.

'I got hold of an old Territorial Army hut, and with the help of local people it was refurbished alongside the parish hall as a coffee bar for young people who used it each night of the week. We were swamped by the numbers who came. A "youth community" emerged and they would begin to speak to me openly about their lives. Gradually the barriers came down, and we built up real trust. Many of them started to come to church, and some wonderful memories remain of those times. It was a "sweater and shirt" ministry which knew no barriers of denomination. I still hear from grown-up parents whom I first met as teenagers in our "Coffee Bar".'

Michael Beattie, a freelance television producer from Belfast, frequented the Coffee Bar in his mid-teens, and he was a member of the church's Scout group. He recollects, 'I came to the conclusion fairly quickly that Robin was a "man's man". You felt that there was nothing you needed to hide from him. You would not have been embarrassed if he had seen you hanging out with the lads at a street corner, or if you had your arm around a girl. He was an open, friendly character who seemed much more modern than other clergy you knew. The fact that he was known to all and sundry as "the Doc" demonstrated people's attitude to him.'

Eames also had an element of inner steel. 'One evening a few outsiders aged around seventeen came into the Coffee Bar and started messing around. One of the youth leaders phoned "the Doc" who came down immediately. He was polite to the outsiders and told them they were welcome provided they obeyed the rules. However, they persisted in trying to throw their weight about, and I remember Robin taking off his jacket and clerical collar and confronting them. He said, "I am asking you to leave, now will you go of your own accord or will I have to make you leave?" So they left. Robin had made his point. Behind the charm he had a tough edge, and when something like that happened he was a hero to us.'

He also had the knack of making worship seem attractive. 'He encouraged more openness in church, and the services were much more informal. You were not embarrassed about being there. None of our parents had to force us to go to church while Robin was Rector of Gilnahirk.'

Above all, he was understanding. Michael Beattie recalls his misguided youthful ambition to get drunk on his seventeenth birthday, and succeeding in doing so in a nearby hostelry. 'I vaguely remember making my way back to the Coffee Bar, don't ask me why, and ending up lying on the floor. Someone was bending over me and asking if I was all right. I could make out vaguely the anxious the face of Robin Eames. Obviously he did not approve of what I had done, but he was concerned for me, and I was aware that this was something he would not cast up to me again. I knew that Robin knew about these things. To a youngster like me Robin was a real person, and that was kind of unusual in a minister. He seemed to live in the real world.'

Meanwhile, the 'real world' was changing for the worse in Northern Ireland. The political reforms which the Unionist leader Terence O'Neill had envisaged did not materialise quickly enough to satisfy the justified aspirations of the Roman Catholic minority in Northern Ireland. In the late 1960s a determined, disruptive and successful civil rights campaign put the Stormont Government under enormous pressure, and O'Neill was forced to resign. The civil rights campaign was overtaken by a new and sinister group, the Provisional IRA, which in turn led to severe counter-terrorism measures by the security forces, and also the growth of Loyalist paramilitary organisations.

All of these complex factors led to more than thirty years of sustained and widespread violence, allied to continued political deadlock. The bright new Northern Ireland in which Robin Eames had started his ministry was rapidly disappearing, to be replaced by a nightmare of mayhem and violence. By far the worst year was 1972, when 470 people died and many hundreds of others were wounded and maimed as a result of violence – and all in a Province smaller than Yorkshire.

In 1972 the year began disastrously when thirteen civilians were shot dead on 30 January by the army in Londonderry, in what became known as 'Bloody Sunday'. On 22 February seven people were killed at Aldershot military barracks by a bomb for which the Official IRA claimed responsibility. On 4 March two young women died and many other people were badly injured by a no-warning Provisional IRA bomb in the Abercorn Restaurant in Belfast.

On 24 March the British Government imposed direct rule on Northern Ireland after the Stormont Government, which was losing control of the situation, refused to relinquish its powers over law and order. On 21 July nine people died and many others were badly hurt when twenty-two no-warning bombs were detonated by the Provisional IRA all over Belfast at the height of a busy shopping afternoon. This atrocity came to be known as 'Bloody Friday'. In the same month the Loyalist group the Ulster Defence Association set up 'no-go' areas in Belfast, where Loyalist territories were patrolled by their own paramilitaries.

At the start of the Troubles in 1968, Robin Eames had spent only two short years at St Dorothea's before the Northern Ireland violence started to overshadow all of life in the Province, and like every other parish minister in the land, he had to react as best he could to the spiralling horror and social upheaval.

From his early days at St Dorothea's, Eames had been aware of the alienation between the people in the Protestant estates in his parish and the Unionist politicians. 'People were asking, "What have they done for us?" I became convinced of the need for a new social outreach by the churches, and I shared my ideas with the local clergy. Eventually we formed a local community association to give voice to local social concerns – such as faults in houses, the lack of recreation amenities and other matters.'

The clergy became the spokesmen for local dissatisfactions. 'We built up trust with the people, because they came to realise that the Church was interested in aspects of their lives and not just in filling pews. These totally Protestant estates did not ask about integration with Catholics because these issues simply did not arise. They had enough social issues of their own to worry about.'

As the community tensions in Northern Ireland increased, the mood in the housing estates changed. Eames recalls, 'One night a group of "faceless men" organised a "community meeting" in the local hall, and the clergy were invited. We were told, "You need to be prepared for an attack by the IRA on your estate, and you must be ready to protect yourselves." I asked, "What evidence do you have for this?" They replied, "We come from the Shankill Road (a well-known Protestant area) and we know what we are talking about." '

Despite reassurance from the clergy and their attempts to maintain calm, Loyalist vigilante groups with white armbands were formed to report anything suspicious. Anxiety was spreading across other Protestant estates. 'The vigilantes were more visible. There was another public meeting in the community hall, and more warnings of forthcoming attacks. I recognised that the Loyalist paramilitary group, the so-called Ulster Defence Association, was being born.'

Some Roman Catholic families on the edge of the estate were driven from their homes. The clergy, including Robin Eames, were involved day and night in pastoral work to try to reassure people. 'It was soon obvious that other forces were at work. They said to the people, "Don't listen to the clergy, we know best." Groups of men left the estate at night to join rioters in the Short Strand flashpoint area. Tension in the estates grew.

'One night I confronted a group of men on the Lower Braniel Road who were intent on burning a Catholic home and driving the people away. We had an argument and finally I persuaded them to "think things over". Tragically the next night they succeeded in what they had set out to do. What now, I thought, of the church's social outreach? What can we do?'

The numbers at the youth Coffee Bar began to fall. 'I feared for the young people's safety, and I asked a group of parishioners to join me at the Coffee Bar. I was told by the faceless men, "You must close this place, it is too easy a target for our enemies." I refused, but threats to our young people followed.

Eventually we closed. I was bitterly disappointed, but I felt that I had no option as tensions in the locality continued to grow. The safety of our young people was paramount.'

Eames believes that this was a turning-point for life in the estate. 'Fears spread, and these were encouraged by the UDA. Parish life continued as best we could but now the whole of East Belfast was caught up in street riots. Local churches were asked to send volunteers to the Newtownards Road to help patrol the trouble spots. When crowds gathered we moved among them to try to persuade people to remain peaceful. We had some success but we also had our failures.'

The troubles in the Nationalist West Belfast area also spread. There was heightened tension each night, and the patrols increased. The fears themselves had a cumulative factor. 'Genuine apprehension and fear increased throughout East Belfast, and the Protestant estates became focal points for UDA recruitment, particularly among young people.

'Despite strenuous and genuine efforts by the churches, people were turning to the paramilitaries for help. There were increased appeals to the clergy, particularly from wives and mothers who were worried about the welfare of husbands and sons. For me this was a period of totally exhausting pastoral care. I was learning many lessons which were never taught in any Divinity School.'

It was during this period that Robin Eames was part of a scene of terror that he would remember for the rest of his life. 'One night while working with a church patrol near the Braniel, I was told that a Catholic home was under attack. I went immediately to find out what was going on. There was an angry crowd outside the house carrying lighted torches. Someone said to me that there was a little child alone in the house. I confronted the attackers and pleaded with them to go away. They ignored me, so in desperation I ran round to the back of the house.'

There were no lights on anywhere. Eames asked himself frantically, 'Where on earth is the child? Just before I gave up, I heard someone crying from the coal shed at the rear. Behind a pile of coal I found a little girl trying to hide. She was absolutely terrified. There was no time to think and I simply picked her up in my arms and ran. By now the house was on fire. I had got to her not a moment too soon.'

Eventually he made his way to a nearby Roman Catholic church and handed the child over to the priest while he tried to explain as best he could what had happened. He recalls, 'At last she was in safe hands. I never heard of her again, but for the rest of my life I have wondered about what happened to her and her family. All of this was a far cry from my training in the lecture halls of a university. We were now facing the vastly new challenge of witnessing to a divided and frightened community.'

Eames, like other clergy, had to face up to the challenges and the strong pressures of church life in the new situation. 'What should be the nature of the Church's ministry in these new tensions and circumstances? Did we support our own "local" people and risk being over-identified with their political views, or did we take the easier option and remain aloof, seeking the safety of the pulpit and the sanctuary, but removed from what was actually concerning real people leading lives of uncertainty and fear?'

This dilemma was to dominate his leadership in later years. He says, 'I developed a philosophy which has been called "the theology of the instantaneous". You did not have time to consult books. You reacted to the best of your ability, and the heart-searching came later. Those days in the Protestant estates of East Belfast taught me so much which I would lean on as a church leader many years later.'

He will always remember them with a mixture of sadness, yet of appreciation of the best and worst of human nature. 'Fear was the key word. It took only enough to persuade people that there was truth in a rumour, for totally irrational behaviour to follow. My heart bled for the people of East Belfast, who were largely Protestant. They were being manipulated, and their traditional fears were surfacing in new ways.'

There were also the wider considerations about the role of the Church in a divided society. 'How far would the Protestant churches take any blame for what was happening? Commentators, particularly from the Irish Republic, would say, "They have failed", but the clergy in the North replied, "If you had been here would you have done any better?"'

The personal demands on many clergy, including Robin Eames, were enormous. One of the early casualties of the Troubles was Constable John Haslett, a member of St

Dorothea's congregation who was murdered by the Provisional IRA. He and another policeman were killed when terrorists opened fire on their car on 15 October 1971. The policemen were keeping watch on a savings bank and post office in North Belfast. Both were in plain clothes and were armed.

Robin Eames recalls, 'John had been a helper in the Scout group, and his death was an immense shock to all of us. How well I remember having to conduct that funeral, and of trying to bring comfort to his parents and wider family as well as his friends and our parishioners. It was a terrible time. How was I to know then that I would have to conduct countless funerals of my people as the Troubles spread?'

Michael Beattie also remembers the toll it took on Eames personally. 'I was part of a guard of honour from the Scout group at John's funeral. It was a very emotional occasion, and I was aware that Robin, who conducted the funeral service, was deeply affected by it all.'

Events in the Province were leading to a breakdown in law and order. Eames recalls, 'Sectarianism was nothing new. Manipulation through fear was nothing new, except it had taken on a very sinister form with the creation of paramilitaries. The clergy were preaching a gospel of love and reconciliation but we were being met with the philosophy on the ground of "There is only one way to deal with this situation – we have to meet force with force." '

Sectarianism was not born in those years, because it had already infected Ulster life for generations. Eames says, 'What was new was the fact that paramilitaries had been organised by playing on traditional fears, and they knew how to use that organisation to influence whole communities. Church life in the Sixties was largely unprepared for such a strenuous challenge, and the distinctions between church leadership and the local church became obvious to those of us working on the ground. Those were very tough times, but I learned a great deal about the true nature of ministering to people in the midst of their needs.'

Despite the dark days and the grave challenges, Robin Eames felt that his years at St Dorothea's were among the happiest and the most fulfilling of his ministry. 'Our sons Niall and Michael were born there, and the fellowship of working in a "new" area brought me very close to my people. Pastorally I was admitted to the lives of the young and the old, and some of the friendships made in those times have lasted ever since.'

Christine Eames recalls, 'We were extremely happy in Gilnahirk. Both our sons were born during that period of our lives, and there were lots of other young families in the parish. The people were lovely to work with, and I was never conscious of having "had" to do anything. I became involved with the Mothers' Union and in many parish activities, and the people were most supportive.

'Robin was extremely busy as Rector, but he was always able to carry it all very well. He always had time for me and the boys. Our family life has always been extremely important, and we are very close. We were both fortunate enough to have come from extremely happy homes.'

Because St Dorothea's was a new church, it was possible for Robin Eames to experiment with forms of worship and to relate them directly to people's experience. 'During the summer months, many people went to their caravans on the coast at weekends, so I introduced a late evening Epilogue for their return home on Sunday nights, and these services attracted large numbers. Traditions were not "inherited" at St Dorothea's – instead they were "established".

'I have always believed in the maxim "a home-going parson means a church-going people". I visited their homes regularly, in addition to special calls, and I saw the results in our church-attendance figures. I know that not all the clergy today follow this maxim, and I believe that this is a mistake.'

Though Robin Eames was concentrating on running his first parish, with all its challenges, he was attracting attention from outside. When he was only a few years at St Dorothea's he was invited to consider becoming Dean of Cork, potentially a rapid promotion for a young rector. He consulted his Bishop, George Quin, who was not best pleased at the prospect of losing such a promising young minister. He also talked to the Primate, the saintly but sharp-witted Archbishop George Otto Simms who himself was a former Dean of Cork. Simms advised him, 'Pray to God about it. At the end of the day you must make up your own mind, but the Almighty might help you.'

There was a certain irony in Eames being asked to consider moving to Cork, where his forebears had set down roots, and the elevation to Dean at such an early stage in a clerical career would have been attractive to any young man. However, Eames turned down the offer. He believed that in such difficult circumstances he ought to stay in Belfast. 'I felt that I would have been walking away from people.'

Even today there are veteran Church of Ireland clerics who point out that Eames turned down the job in Cork after it had been announced publicly. Eames admits privately that there may have been some 'feeling' in the South about his change of mind, though nothing was said to him directly. Every young man, however, is entitled to change his mind, and only the most sceptical observer would fail to recognise an element of Divine guidance in the way that Eames' future career developed.

Cork was an attractive city, but it was light years away from the situation in Northern Ireland. If he had gone to Cork he might well have surfaced, sooner or later, in the Church of Ireland hierarchy – perhaps as Archbishop of Dublin, or as Primate through the Southern route. However, by staying in the North Eames was to gain an invaluable, though bruising, experience of the Troubles, which stood him in good stead later on as Archbishop of Armagh.

Eames was content that he had made the right decision to stay in Northern Ireland but in his eighth year at St Dorothea's he was invited to become Rector of St Mark's Dundela in Belfast, known as 'The Lion on the Hill', and also the home parish of the celebrated Christian writer and academic C. S. Lewis. The invitation came unexpectedly, and although Eames knew that he would be moving to a 'High-Church' traditional parish, he felt that he should accept the call.

'I always felt that there is a point where a parish, especially a "new area" parish, needs a change of leadership. I felt that I had done all I could there, and the Diocese wanted me to take on St Mark's. Nevertheless, we were sad to leave Gilnahirk, and I knew that the move would mean many changes of approach and attitude. St Mark's dominated the skyline of East Belfast and had had a long list of distinguished rectors. My predecessor Canon Edmund Parke had been there for many years, and the St Mark's of C. S. Lewis had stood for a traditional church-manship and membership, with regular Eucharists and daily prayers.'

C. S. Lewis had been baptised in the church on 29 January 1899 by his grandfather the Reverend Thomas Hamilton, who was Rector from 1878 to 1900. The Lewis family sat near the front so the young 'Jack' Lewis would have been very close to his grandfather when he was preaching the sermon. In 1935 C. S. Lewis and his brother Warren presented a stained-glass window to St Mark's in memory of their parents. Three saints are depicted – the two gospel writers St Mark and St Luke on either side of St James. Above his head is a picture of St Mark's Church. Lewis's father died in 1929, aged sixty-seven, and his mother had died in 1908, when she was only forty-seven. Her early death greatly affected both boys for the rest of their lives.

At St Mark's, Robin Eames was given a warm welcome, and some sixty-five fellow clergy attended his institution as Rector in 1974. 'I found that some of the practices did not reflect what I had learned of church life in a new area like St Dorothea's, but I had to match my impatience with diplomacy so far as change was concerned. I was grateful for the warmth of my reception, but I also knew that I was being watched carefully.'

He was very aware that St Mark's had been the church of C. S. Lewis. 'It was a good feeling to be able to say, "This is where he worshipped", or, "This is where he was born". Some people in St Mark's were steeped in this sort of thing, but frankly I was just too busy at that stage of my career to think much of that kind of heritage. I read some of his work at the time, and much more since then, and I have taken a lot from him.'

Eames soon felt that he wanted to make changes. 'I introduced the laity to take part in the services, established a side chapel for weekday services and re-established a youth club. Being aware of the length of service of my predecessor, I realised that while some changes had to be made immediately, I had to settle down for the "long haul". We had a large number of elderly parishioners, many of them in old people's homes, and this required a great deal of pastoral care. The musical tradition was excellent, and there was a widespread respect for Anglican worship.

'I enjoyed the worship pattern and I was settling in. I found many families who had drifted away from the church, and I was also putting down roots for the establishment of a separate parish at Knocknagoney. I gave little thought to the long-term future, and I was happy to concentrate on my ministry one day at a time.'

Eames, however, was also making an impression outside his parish. Given his abilities, drive and wide-ranging interests, it was highly unlikely that he would have spent his entire career in a parish ministry. He became involved in central church government in Dublin, particularly in finance and in the role of the church committee, and people soon began to notice him. He reflects, 'This wider involvement greatly helped my understanding of the Church at large, because up to then my experience had been largely parochial. In Dublin I met clergy and laity from all over the island, and my experience and knowledge of Ireland and of her churches developed quickly.

'This wider involvement helped to balance my experience in St Mark's, where I was having the valuable experience of training our two curates, which interested me greatly. In the parish with all its traditions, I also had a strong sense of "community" and of a historic background which had been unknown to me in my experience in the "new area" situation in St Dorothea's.'

Suddenly, however, all this changed. The ageing Bishop of Derry and Raphoe, Cuthbert Peacocke, announced that he intended to resign, and Eames was approached by senior representatives of the diocese at a meeting in Dublin to find out if he wanted to be considered for the forthcoming vacancy.

'I had had only a passing interest in the situation. I had met Bishop Peacocke at Dublin committees, but I would not have claimed any close friendship. However, when I was approached by the Derry and Raphoe people I was surprised and somewhat taken aback. My first reaction was "Thank you – but definitely 'No'." I had had only a short experience in St Mark's, and I had so many plans for what I wanted to do there.'

However, the approaches intensified. 'They asked me if I would at least allow them to consider my name. I consulted my Bishop, to whom I had been appointed Domestic and Examining Chaplain, and also George Simms. Their advice was similar: "In matters of this nature, no priest can refuse to consider the will of the Church." '

Rumours began to circulate about names being considered, and Eames was aware that his was among them. He found this disconcerting, as he was still continuing his ministry at St Mark's. Eventually the Diocese of Derry and Raphoe produced three names, and Eames was their first choice. In those days, there were two stages to such an appointment. First, a vacant diocese would make a selection, and then the Episcopal College would meet.

Eames recalls, 'The days between the two processes seemed like an eternity. On the day when the Electoral College had made its decision, I received a telephone call from Archbishop Simms. He said, "Robin, the Church has decided that you are to be Bishop of Derry and Raphoe. God Bless you." ' It was 9 May 1975, and at the age of thirty-eight Eames would be the youngest bishop in the Church of Ireland. He could hardly take in the news. He recalls, 'At first it was a devastating experience. St Mark's was shocked by the news. Some people must have thought, not unreasonably, "Surely you could have stayed with us a little longer." Besides, I did not know Derry and Raphoe. I knew only a handful of people in that diocese, and I had only visited Londonderry once. I felt that there were many men senior to me who deserved to be appointed. Up to that time bishops had been much older on appointment than me, and I felt genuine feelings of inadequacy.'

Robin Dunbar, a churchwarden at St Mark's, remembers the mixed feelings of delight and disappointment felt by the parishioners. 'We were pleased for Robin when we heard of his appointment, but we were also disappointed. We had already begun to plan our centenary celebrations for 1978 and Robin would have been part of that.'

Dunbar believes that Eames was both pleased and disappointed about moving. 'He felt that he had not been able to spend enough time at St Mark's. He had made a good impression during his short stay there. He was good at chairing meetings of the Select Vestry and we quickly found out that he did not allow any waffle. He was also a good preacher. He could say things in ten minutes which it would have taken others half an hour to do so. We were sorry to lose him but we knew that he was bishop material. Indeed some of the senior people at St Mark's felt that he would go much further, even after Derry and Raphoe.'

The call to Eames from Derry and Raphoe was an offer that he simply could not refuse. 'People whose judgment I trusted said to me, "You have no option, you must go." Warm messages of support poured into my home from Derry and Raphoe. Such a move would mean leaving my home diocese where I had been ordained, as had been my late father. I wondered what a move would mean for my wife and our young family.'

Eames accepted the appointment, and as plans were being made for his consecration as Bishop, he was greatly heartened by the support from his two former parishes. 'St Dorothea's presented me with my episcopal ring, and St Mark's with my pectoral cross – both following subscriptions from parishioners. Even though I had served in St Mark's, my first parish of St Dorothea's still seemed to think of me as "their man, the Doc".'

Robin Eames went on retreat to the theological college in Dublin to prepare himself for the huge challenges that lay ahead. He had risen through the ranks of the priesthood remarkably quickly since his ordination as a deacon only twelve years previously. Now he was ready to move on and to set down his roots in the north-west frontier of Derry and Raphoe. He knew that he was taking a big step into the unknown, but he took it nevertheless. The next stage of the adventure was about to begin.

4

The North-West Frontier

When Robin Eames left his home in Down and Dromore and set off for his new diocese in the north-west, he was conscious that he was starting another long journey, not only across the hilly Glenshane Pass and through beautiful countryside all the way to Londonderry and Donegal, but also across the years of history, prejudice and misunderstanding. Derry had been one of the cockpits of Irish history, particularly in the seventeenth century, and it had played a major role in the civil rights campaign and more recently in the political and social up-heavals since the latest outbreak of the Troubles in 1968.

Situated on the banks of the River Foyle, the great natural beauty surrounding Derry belied its often troublesome history. Even its very name symbolised the divisions in the city, in the Province and on the island. Protestants, the vast majority of whom were Unionists, called it 'Londonderry', the name given to the city after the Ulster Plantation in the seventeenth century. The Roman Catholics, almost exclusively Irish Nationalists or Republicans, referred to it as 'Derry', thus reflecting its Gaelic roots and its foundation by Saint Columba in the sixth century as 'Doire' – the 'place of oaks'.

Despite the very different outlooks of both communities, they shared a loyalty to and a regard for their native city that was not reflected in other areas, and notably in Belfast. Even today, however, the controversy about the name remains, although the City Council officially designated the title as 'Derry'. With typical Ulster humour, some local wits satirise the 'Derry/Londonderry' dilemma by referring to it as 'Stroke City'.

Such nuances might seem trivial to outsiders, but they are taken seriously in a Province where labels are still regarded as important. Nevertheless there are many anomalies, and logic has little impact in the tortuous world of Northern Ireland politics and religion. In the Anglican tradition, the Church of Ireland diocese was always referred to as 'Derry' and not 'Londonderry', though many of the members of the church would regard themselves as British rather than Irish. Any new bishop coming to the city of Derry, including a Belfast man like Robin Eames, would have had to learn quickly how best to walk the tightrope.

For Unionists in Northern Ireland, Londonderry was very much a Protestant icon. It had survived the long siege by the Jacobite forces in 1689, until its liberation by the Williamites. This was the beginning of the military breakthrough to success in Ireland by King William of Orange and his troops, which eventually led to the comprehensive defeat of his Roman Catholic father-in-law King James II, and which helped to secure the Protestant succession to the English throne.

The heroism and sacrifice of those days is mirrored by many of the plaques and artefacts in St Columb's Church of Ireland Cathedral. They include a cannon ball from the Siege, a table made of wood from the city gates, and a copy of the menu available at the height of the Siege – a dog cost 2/6, a cat 4/6, a rat 1/– and a mouse 6p.

Happily, however, there are also more peaceful features of the cathedral, including a memorial window to Mrs Cecil Frances Alexander, illustrating three of her famous hymns – 'There is a Green Hill Far Away', 'Once in Royal David's City', and 'The Golden Gates Are Lifted Up'. Mrs Alexander's husband was a former Bishop of Derry and Primate of All-Ireland.

The city, however, was also an icon to the Roman Catholic community. Its Gaelic and Irish identity, in their eyes, had not been subsumed by the creation of Northern Ireland in the early 1920s, and many felt that its natural links remained with the hinterland of Co. Donegal which was predominantly Roman Catholic and which, they believed, had been excluded deliberately from the new state to ensure a permanent Protestant majority in the new Northern Ireland.

By the late 1960s the social unrest in Derry and the frustration of its Nationalist people at the unwillingness or inability of successive Unionist governments to tackle discrimination against Catholics led to fierce rioting in the city, and the emergence of an armed and unscrupulous Provisional IRA, which was determined to take on the British and Unionist establishment by force. Derry became the centre of protracted and vicious violence from both sides, and of strong and in some cases excessive counter-security measures from the police and the army. The grief, despair and anger at the tragic events of Bloody Sunday, referred to earlier, left a legacy of bitterness and mistrust in Derry that was to last for decades.

It was into this cauldron that Robin Eames entered as Bishop of Derry and Raphoe, with his wife and two young sons. Not only that, he also had to preside over a geographically large diocese that stretched into two different countries, with different political jurisdictions, different aspirations, different problems, different perceptions, even a different coinage, and in some regions a different language. It was no easy task for a young man who had spent most of his life in Belfast, and largely among Protestants and Unionists.

Even before his appointment, there was no shortage of advice. The *Church of Ireland Gazette* quoted the Reverend Maurice Bolton, Presbyterian Minister of Strand Road in Derry, who was clear about the kind of person needed. 'We want a man whose purpose is to lead, not one who will be dictated to by events. He must not see himself as a high dignitary of the church, but as a person within the community. The position of the Church of Ireland Bishop of Derry does not change. However, he must be able to adjust to the changing leadership of the other Protestant denominations within Derry.'

The newly appointed and young Roman Catholic Bishop of Derry Dr Edward Daly was equally forthcoming. He stated a strong preference 'for someone from a pastoral background', someone 'with an easy kind of ability to meet and talk to people at all levels about their problems'. He also said, with the benefit of a somewhat limited experience in his new post, 'A person may not get a breathing-space at the beginning of an episcopate. A bishop, at the present time in the North, is not allowed to make many mistakes. Make one mistake, and you are damned for ever.'

Eames' appointment was welcomed widely. Canon John Barry, whose perceptive and often provocative column under the pseudonym 'Cromlyn' was a highlight of the *Church of Ireland Gazette* for many years, reflected the delight that the church had produced such a young bishop. In the edition of 16 May 1975 he wrote:

So at last we have done it. We have appointed a really young bishop. And how often over the years we have pleaded for just that, asking that a man should be elevated on account of what he might do in the future rather than as a sort of reward for what he had done in the past . . . an era of great promise has opened up for the Diocese of Derry and indeed for the Church of Ireland as a whole.

Eames, who had shown his sensitive political antennae in his previous appointments, began on the right foot. His Enthronement in the Cathedral Church of St Patrick in Armagh was planned for the Feast Day of St Columba, the Patron Saint of Derry, and took place on 9 June 1975. The point was not lost on the people of Derry. The Consecration was performed by Dr George Otto Simms, the Primate, who was assisted by other Church of Ireland bishops. Significantly the ceremony was attended, at Eames' request, by the Roman Catholic Bishop of Derry Dr Edward Daly. Nowadays this would be commonplace, but in the Northern Ireland of the mid-1970s, it was a courageous step by both young bishops just starting their episcopates.

The point was well taken by the *Belfast Telegraph*. It stated in its editorial of 10 June 1975: '. . . in Armagh the new Bishop was consecrated, with his Catholic counterpart in close attendance. Even in Britain, this might raise a few eyebrows and warm a few hearts. Here, it inspires the hope that these two young representatives of Derry's two traditions can help to map out a future for the Maiden City much more harmonious than in the past.'

However, there were also warnings about the challenges that lay ahead. John Cooney, the then Religious Affairs Correspondent of the *Irish Times*, noted in the edition of 10 June 1975:

The presence of Bishop Daly [at the Consecration] was of particular interest in view of the fact that since he came into office in Derry last year, the ecumenical climate over there has become tropical in comparison with other languid areas.

Indeed, the election of Dr Eames is seen as a realisation by the Church of Ireland that it needed in that area a vigorous man to co-operate with Bishop Daly . . . Given the cross-border status of the Diocese, given the youth of the bishop and given the urgency of even greater ecumenical co-operation in Ireland, Dr Eames' performance as bishop will be keenly watched for signs of a fresh interpretation of the Anglican ethos in Inter-Church relations.

In his sermon at the Enthronement, Canon J. S. Brown, Professor of Pastoral Theology at Trinity College Dublin, Warden of the Divinity Hostel and a former teacher of Robin Eames, struck a prophetic note. He said: 'Bishops today are less remote from the common mind than people imagined them once to be. The lifestyle is simpler. Gaiters have gone and palaces are going, but a holy and a humble man of heart may still be found in a palace and an authoritarian can lurk in a cottage.' He urged Eames to be like St Columba, 'one to whom men can turn as a living approachable person, and as a true father in God, that men might say of him, as they did of his Master, "the common people heard him gladly".'

Overall it was a challenging and an inspiring ceremony, held in the presence of a large congregation including official representatives of the British and Irish Governments, thus underlining the new Bishop of Derry's jurisdiction on both sides of the Irish border.

However, the official ceremonies were not all over. On 26 June 1975 Eames was enthroned as the 58th Bishop of Derry in St Columb's Cathedral, and on 11 September he was enthroned as Bishop of Raphoe in St Eunan's Cathedral in Donegal.

On each occasion, Bishop Eames spoke out strongly. At his Enthronement in Derry he totally condemned the sectarian killings in Northern Ireland. 'Such actions cannot be justified by any argument, any philosophy, any political ideal or any human emotion. Those who commit such bestial actions, whether they claim to be Protestant or Roman Catholic, put themselves beyond any human comprehension. One day they will have to give a reason before the God who made them: may He have mercy on them.'

Eames gave a stark warning to his parishioners in the large and sprawling Diocese of Raphoe in Donegal, which seemed to some people to be a far cry from the Troubles in Northern Ireland. The new bishop said, 'The challenge which is being presented to normal life in Northern Ireland is no longer a challenge to any one political ideal or philosophy. It is a challenge to the Christian heritage of this island.'

He also talked about the 'Irish dimension' which was to become an important part of his ministry:

> There is a sense in which members of the Church of Ireland can, and must, speak of an Irish dimension to the future of Ulster – the dimension to the almost unbelievable suffering which is, at this moment, being endured by our fellow Church members and people of all denominations across the border, which is a dimension that is deeply spiritual as well as practical.
>
> We are separated from them by a man-made frontier, but we are united with them in a way which owes nothing to man. We are united by common bonds of humanity, by our common concern for the future of the country we love, and above all else we are united to them when we call on the same God.

It was clear that the new bishop was going to speak his mind. Robin Eames immersed himself in the work of his new diocese, and while he carried out a wide range of ecclesiastical and administrative duties, he had his own agenda. He wanted to be a leader and a pastor to his own flock, he wanted to make meaningful comments on the major political and social issues of the day, he was keen to be a bishop and pastor to his people in the Irish Republic, and he also wanted to reach out directly to the Roman Catholic community.

He was conscious that he was following an older cleric, Bishop Peacocke, who had seen the situation in Derry through the eyes of his generation. Eames says, 'I wanted to be the younger man doing things hands on.' From his earliest days in Derry he was acutely aware of the anxieties of the Protestants who feared a sell-out by the British Government. These fears were compounded by an article in the *Sunday Times*, shortly after his Enthronement, which claimed inter alia that 'an epic change is being accomplished in Britain's relationship with Northern Ireland. British withdrawal is becoming a fact.'

He recalls, 'Clergy spoke to me soon after my Enthronement and I was aware of their apprehensions about a rumoured "British withdrawal". Such fears were having devastating effects on many parishes which had already suffered attacks from the Provisional IRA. When the Northern Ireland Secretary Merlyn

Rees visited me in Derry, I mentioned these points to him and he played them down as "media hype".'

Eames was constantly aware of the need to underline the apprehensions of Protestants. When the newly appointed Roman Catholic Archbishop of Armagh Dr (later Cardinal) Tomas O'Fiaich supported a call from the Irish Premier Jack Lynch for a British declaration of intent to withdraw from Northern Ireland, Eames wrote to him. 'I stated that I could understand his position, but I had to point out that many members of the Church of Ireland were asking, "What is our future, do we have to contemplate a withdrawal of our culture?" '

Eames appealed for greater sensitivity to all cultural disciplines, rather than the use of broad phrases such as a 'British withdrawal'. He recalls, 'We met for a wide-ranging conversation through the good offices of Edward Daly, and the Archbishop acknowledged that the phraseology was misleading.' This was an important meeting, and was the beginning of a warm and fruitful relationship, especially when Eames became Archbishop of Armagh.

Throughout his ministry Eames had always been sensitive to the party political allegiance of members of his church. 'I quickly realised that few conversations in Northern Ireland fail to involve political discussion. As a curate I entered the church at a time when all that mattered for political Protestants was "the border question". For generations people had been nurtured on a fear of what would happen if a United Ireland became a reality. In my days as a rector the "not an inch" philosophy dominated Unionism. Most members of my church would have been Unionists.'

The leadership of the Church of Ireland in the North was seen as basically Unionist in sympathy. Eames recalls, 'At parish level, members of the Orange Order stood firm on their "Britishness", and any sermon or remark which appeared to be slightly favourable to the Irish Republic or to life in the South could produce opposition from the pews.

'From an early stage at Queen's University I had been convinced that this preoccupation with the border issue was overriding many social and community needs. I had seen those needs at St Dorothea's in East Belfast. Colleagues in North and West Belfast had seen them even more clearly. I also saw the needs in and around Derry. Housing, jobs and education cried out for attention, but the dominance of Ulster Unionism failed to give social needs the attention they deserved. It was left to local councils to address such needs as best they could.'

He felt that those clergy who had failed to win the confidence of their people to allow them to preach freely in effect encouraged a hard line in the pews. 'I felt that the real secret of trust was knowing the people in their homes, at their work or play, and allowing them to know me. Thus I never felt constrained by preaching at the parochial level. I could understand my people's emotions, having been born and educated in Northern Ireland. I always felt that leadership had to be Bible-based, but also practised with the utmost sensitivity to local conditions.'

That was precisely what he was trying to achieve in Derry, and he was particularly conscious of the fears of Protestants there. 'They felt that they were a besieged people because they did not know what the future held for them. A lot of people told me that they felt they had no future on the "city" side which was mainly Roman Catholic, and a great many moved across the River Foyle to the Waterside on the east bank. They just did not feel safe elsewhere.'

At one stage there was a lengthy debate as to whether or not Foyle College, a Protestant grammar school in Derry, should be moved from the city side to another area. Eames was the Chairman of the Governors. 'We had a tremendous intellectual struggle in trying to decide whether or not there would be a future for the school if it remained where it was. In the end we decided to stay put, but it was not an easy decision.'

Eames adapted the title of Charles Dickens' novel *A Tale of Two Cities* to the situation, and warned of the dangers of a city divided along sectarian lines. Speaking at the ordination of a curate for a Waterside parish he said, 'The future of Londonderry depends so much on the recognition that there are two communities which have an immense amount to give to each other . . . Polarisation in these two communities by a river will bring "a tale of two cities" much closer.

'Throughout the Troubles in the city we have found so much evidence of goodwill from so many responsible, thinking and practical Christians in each community. Both sections will be the losers if we reach a point of talking about a totally Protestant bank and a totally Roman Catholic bank of the Foyle.'

His comments drew a supportive response from the Mayor of Derry Hugh Doherty, who said that Bishop Eames had touched on one of the most serious problems facing the city. He said, 'It is disturbing to realise just how many people have crossed from one side of the River Foyle to the other in the past few years. If the trend continues we could become a totally divided community, and no responsible person wants that.' He said, however, that local people had told their elected represent-atives that they wanted to work and live together in peace and added, 'I am confident that all of us will join with the Bishop and work to encourage all of our people to live together in peace.'

While Robin Eames kept the dangers of polarisation clearly in focus, both publicly and privately, he was also aware of the need to address other issues not only in his large diocese but also in Northern Ireland as a whole. In May 1977, an industrial strike by the Loyalist Ulster Workers' Council attempted to mobilise Protestant support for an all-out stoppage to protest against the Government's perceived lack of resolve in dealing with the threat of militant Irish Republicanism. A similar strike three years previously had led to the overthrow of the inter-community Northern Ireland Executive. Eames recalls, 'This second stoppage was strongly opposed by the majority of the Unionist community. The Reverend Ian Paisley attacked my opposition to the strike on the grounds that I was an "ecumenical friend of the South". The electricity power station at Culmore was in my constituency, and I visited the men who remained on duty. They were frightened and feared for their families because of intimidation. Though there was not the degree of support that there had been in 1974, the strike again demonstrated the power which extremism could exert within the Protestant working class. I counselled calm, and with local clergy I visited the homes of those who had been intimidated. The Secretary of State Roy Mason thanked us for our stance.'

The sheer range of duties and situations which Eames, like other churchmen in Northern Ireland, had to face was very different from most other parts of the Anglican communion. Eames had to bring comfort to the families of those found guilty of paramilitary crime, without condoning their behav-iour. In June 1977, nine members of the Loyalist paramilitary Ulster Volunteer Force in Coleraine were jailed for a total of

108 years for terrorist activities. 'Some of them claimed Church of Ireland links. I met with our clergy to discuss our attitudes, and I stressed the need for pastoral support for people, without pre-judging political views or in any way supporting terrorism. This highlighted the real nature of pastoral care, and the dilemma facing clergy – how to avoid the perception that pastoral care for families was tacit support for the actions of those in prison. I visited the prisoners, but emphasised my opposition to their violence.'

As always, he had to be even-handed. When Derry Guildhall, the town hall, was badly damaged by a Provisional IRA bomb, Eames called for a cessation of violence 'against all the people of Derry'. When members of the Provisional IRA became active in prison protests, Eames visited several Roman Catholic families whose relatives were involved.

He was quick to point out perceived Republican provocation. When tension escalated in Derry after a march by Sinn Fein near a Protestant area, Eames said that the authorities were wrong to have allowed it in the first place. He received praise from an unexpected quarter. The Reverend Ian Paisley's Democratic Unionists noted that 'perhaps Eames is now learning the real facts of Londonderry'.

He was also learning in the grimmest possible circumstances about the trauma of ministering to families in the aftermath of vicious killings, and particularly to families of murdered members of the security forces. He had already encountered this in his previous diocese, but now in Derry and later on in the Dioceses of Down and Dromore and Armagh, where he was successively Bishop and Archbishop, the numbers steadily grew.

He not only had to bring words of comfort to the families and relatives, but also to condemn the killers and on occasions to chide the politicians and many others. Early on in the Derry Diocese, for example, he spoke at the funeral of Constable Robert McPherson, who was shot in Dungiven. He said, 'When the politician allows policing to become a perpetual political football, he places the ordinary constable on the beat in a situation which becomes intolerable.' These funerals, and their aftermath, took a considerable personal toll of Robin Eames, as a bishop and also as a human being, and it was a burden carried by many clergy of all denominations during those traumatic times.[1]

59

5

Walking the Tightrope

Given such a background of death and destruction in his Northern Ireland Diocese of Derry, Bishop Eames also had to reach out to his people in the Diocese of Raphoe who were living in, technically, another country – the Irish Republic. They had different loyalties, and a different political outlook, and were chiefly bound to their co-religionists in Derry by their loyalty to and membership of the Church of Ireland. It was not easy for any bishop to minister comprehensively to both parts of such a disparate joint diocese, but Eames – like those before and after him – managed to do so. He recalls, 'The ethos changed when I went across to Donegal. Those parishes along the border were Derry-oriented, but the further into Donegal I went, the further I found that the Protestants had assimilated totally with the local community. I also discovered that they did not want to be associated with what was going on across the border.'

The Donegal people had direct church ties with their Anglican counterparts across the border, but they did not feel part of the Northern Ireland state. Their direct loyalty was to the Irish Republic and to its ethos, and they regarded themselves as Irish. This was very different from the situation in Northern Ireland, which was part of the United Kingdom and where the vast majority of Northern Ireland Protestants thought of themselves as British.

One of the things that Eames instantly recognised about Donegal was the feeling of isolation of some of its people, and he tried to rectify that. He recalls, 'I instituted a practice which later became commonplace. I would go to a local parish and spend two or three days there, and during that time I would visit the old people, the sick and the schools in the company of the local rector. I felt it was important the people realised that the church was caring for them and was identifying with their needs. That was also why I held a special synod in Raphoe itself, the first for very many years. I really enjoyed being with the Donegal people. They helped to give me a new dimension and I learned a great deal from them.'

They also had a self-effacing sense of humour which appealed to their new bishop. Eames tells the story of setting off one Sunday morning with his wife Christine and their two boys for a morning service in a remote Donegal church where he was to be the guest preacher. He thought he knew how to get there, but took a circuitous route which meant that he and his family arrived late. However, he was quickly reassured by one of the parishioners who said, 'Sure don't worry yerself – nothing starts on time in Donegal anyway!'

He was well received throughout the Diocese of Raphoe. Archdeacon Scott Harte, the Rector of Dunfanaghy in Donegal and earlier a much younger rector in Ardara, remembers Robin Eames as Bishop. He says, 'He had a wonderful gift of making people feel special, even when he was asking them to do something! He was close to the clergy, and on visits to parishes he was also concerned about their material well-being, even in matters such as the water supply to the rectory. When he went back to Derry he followed it up. He was pragmatic.'

He also showed strong leadership qualities. 'He was clearly a big person who was deeply involved in community and inter-church issues. He had a positive influence, and he was an eloquent voice for the Church of Ireland. People in remote parishes can become discouraged, and Robin was an encourager. He could draw out the best in people, and they responded to him well. He was also keen to ensure that those from more remote or less populated areas were given a voice in central decision-making.'

Whitby McClay, who has been Lay Secretary to the Diocese of Raphoe for a quarter of a century, says, 'Bishop Eames was a good administrator and a man of the people. Even now when I meet him he instantly knows my name and my face. He is that kind of a person.

'We always felt safe about him representing us when it was an awkward time to be Bishop of Derry. The Troubles affected everyone, including the Church of Ireland, but we knew that he would make statements that were firm but tactful. People thought highly of him, and over all the years I have not met anyone who said otherwise.'

Significantly, Eames took the opportunity as the bishop of a cross-border diocese to challenge people on both sides on the validity of their concept of Irish unity, and in doing so he instituted an important debate. In October 1977 he told the Derry and Raphoe synod that the real question in Ireland was the nature of the relationship between the two communities which would allow them both to inherit the island in peace and prosperity. He said, 'The quality of life that both Protestants and Roman Catholics will enjoy or be denied in the years to come will depend entirely on how this question is answered both in Northern Ireland and the Irish Republic . . . There are two minorities in Ireland and taking the island as a whole surely we can now see very clearly that the last few years have shown that there are equal rights and obligations on the part of a minority as well as on the part of a majority.'

A few months later, Eames returned to the same theme. On 11 March 1978 he addressed a historic synod of Raphoe, the first to be held in that small Irish town for many years. He used the occasion to make an important speech. He said:

> The years of trouble and suffering in the North and a feeling by many Northerners that Southern politicians are, somehow, insensitive to their position, are matched by a genuine fear by the majority in Northern Ireland that political unity involves a 'sell-out' and domination of their political, cultural and religious life.
>
> No longer can we in Ireland afford the luxury of talking about unity in vague terms or generalisations. What are the practical implications of what we call Irish unity? How far are civil, religious and personal rights and freedoms important when we talk about unity? How far are we prepared to embrace change or reform to accommodate and recognise the justifiable rights of a majority and a minority of Irish people when we argue about unity?

Emphasising that the time had long passed when there was any point in talking in abstracts about Irish unity, Eames said:

We must recognise and remember constantly that, for those who have endured years of suffering brought about in many instances by organisations claiming to desire a united Ireland, it is very hard to distinguish between peaceful and violent aspirations of unity. It is vital, therefore, that the Church and the politicians adopt a sense of honesty and realism when thinking about the future of this island.

His remarks drew a lively response from people all over Ireland. The *Irish Times* stated in an editorial:

There is more to unity, said the Bishop, than is intended in the party political sense. Of course; and he mentioned the cultural, social, religious and economic dimension. There is more to unity, too, than in blending what are known as the two traditions. This is a useful enough phrase for someone in a hurry, but it implies divisive possibilities.

The newspaper's editorial concluded, rather haughtily, 'Let Bishop Eames and his flock forget the two traditions and concentrate on the larger river of Irish heritage.'

The *Derry Journal*, a Nationalist weekly newspaper, regarded Eames' speech as being 'critical of the advocacy of the case for a United Ireland and an apologia for the attitude of its opponents in this area'. It noted that Eames had said it was difficult for those people who had endured years of suffering from organisations desiring a United Ireland to distinguish between peaceful and violent aspirations of unity. The newspaper added:

It is certainly not for want of repeated and explicit condemnations by the minority's spiritual leaders and political representatives of the violence that is no less abhorrent to them than to Protestants that the latter should have any reason for failing to distinguish between the peaceful and the violent aspirations.

We find it hard to believe that they can be under any misconception on the point. But this we must say: that the Unionist intransigence that has baulked every effort to achieve a solution of the Six County question by conciliation is the greatest handicap there is to the minority's representatives' peaceful aspirations in their opposition to the violent.

The *Derry Sentinel*, on the Unionist side, contributed to the debate, and gave short shrift to any idea of 'interference' from the South. It stated, somewhat testily: 'When the people of the North commence interfering in the affairs of the South, that will be the time for the Southern Government to become embroiled in Northern affairs.'

Eames, on the whole, received a favourable reaction from Nationalist politicians. The Mayor of Derry Hugh Doherty said, 'I congratulate him on the deeply sincere and, may I say, courageous speech he made in Raphoe. Bishop Eames opened a door to the future of Ireland. The significance of this speech is probably not realised yet, but it will be in time. Bishop Eames asked certain questions, and I hope that people with courage to match his will give the answers.'

The Irish Foreign Minister Michael O'Kennedy also praised Eames' speech, at an Easter Sunday commemoration ceremony on the centenary of the birth of Thomas MacDonough, one of the leaders of the 1916 Easter Rising. Referring to the fears of the Northern Protestants of a 'sell-out', he said, 'Those of us here today honouring the true Republican tradition know that these fears are groundless. But we must also accept that our saying so is not sufficient. In seeking the accommodation which all of us desire, we must go beyond mere. words and show evidence of our good faith.'

O'Kennedy wrote to Eames privately later on and said that he was encouraged that the debate was continuing 'not just in public but also through private contacts and conversations. The debate cannot but have a positive long-term benefit for all of us in Ireland, and your own generous contribution has certainly created a favourable climate for further discussion.' The Irish Foreign Minister also suggested an informal, private conversation with Eames during his next visit to the North.

Whatever the merits of the debate, the important point was that a speech made by the Bishop of Derry and Raphoe in a corner of Donegal was being discussed by politicians, leader-writers and other opinion-makers throughout Ireland, from Dublin to Derry and beyond. Though Eames was at that point stationed on the north-west frontier, he was making a much wider impact elsewhere. He was also showing that the Church could still have an important voice in local and national politics.

While emphasising the importance of cross-border issues, another significant part of Eames' agenda was to forge direct links with the Roman Catholics of Derry city and of the surrounding area. In setting out to achieve this objective, he was fortunate in that his counterpart was Bishop Edward Daly, who had earlier gained local, national and international prominence as the priest who had waved a white handkerchief as he came round a corner in Derry with a group carrying a badly wounded man who had been shot on Bloody Sunday.

It was not for this reason, of course, that he had been appointed a bishop shortly afterwards, but rather for his qualities as a pastor and a gifted communicator in succession to his elderly predecessor Bishop Neil Farren, a conservative figure. In fact one of the reasons why some Church of Ireland members welcomed Robin Eames' elevation to Derry was because they felt he could match the communication skills of Edward Daly.

Both men had much in common. They were young and energetic, they were able, they were good communicators, they were ecumenically minded, and they got on well together. They regularly travelled together by car, they dined together and they could share informally their concerns. While holding to their own religious and political views, they had an important understanding.

Bishop Daly recalled, 'We hit it off together, and we had a healthy respect for one another. We were from the younger generation and we had the freedom to try to do things differently. We discussed religious and social issues, and we reached a local agreement about mixed marriages between Catholics and Protestants, about which we were both quite liberal. If there was a difficulty we would do our best to sort it out.'[1]

However, they had their differences. 'We hadn't any problems from a religious point of view, but there was a bit of reservation about how political one was. Robin was quite Unionist in his thinking, and I was Nationalist, as opposed to Republican. I think we skirted around the politics a few times, but I don't think we ever got around to talking about it in depth.'

They made a point of working together. 'It came naturally to both of us to be seen together in public. I remember when a shared carol service in the Guildhall was interrupted by a huge bomb, with glass flying everywhere. After a period, however, we continued with the service. We could not allow things like that to stop what was going on.'

In 1976, shortly after Robin Eames arrived in Derry, both bishops joined other clergy in a walk across the city, after a series of 'tit-for-tat' killings. Daly recalled, 'We decided to hold a silent procession of all clergy and almost every clergyman took part. (Those were the days when there were few, if any, women clergy.) It was a very impressive turn-out, and the series of killings stopped, and never re-occurred. Whether or not that was a coincidence I don't know, but the walk by the clergy from nearly every church was a powerful statement against violence.'

Both bishops were working in a situation of almost continual crisis. 'We were having to issue statements at every turn. We were so busy addressing what had happened two hours ago, that it was very difficult to take a long-term view on things.'

At times, there were differences of emphasis or presentation. Daly says, 'On occasions Robin would be inclined to see a thing one way, and then say, "On the other hand . . ." He would have two views, rather than coming down on one side or the other. Perhaps that was a wise and diplomatic thing to do, looking at something in broad context. It could have been indecision or good judgment, and I am not going to judge, but I am making the observation that this happened a number of times.

'I think he tended to fudge some issues, but again that might be described as good judgment, and certainly he was more diplomatic than perhaps I would have been. What came through often in what Robin said was his background in law. He had very much a legal outlook on things. I am not making that point in any way critically, but as an observation.'

The two men undoubtedly got on well together. 'A bishop can be quite isolated because of the nature of his office and he might need to talk to someone. It was reassuring to know that there was a man down the road who would understand, and Robin and I could confide in one another completely. We could speak a similar language, we were also able to respect our differences, and we had a great deal in common. We were young bishops at the same time in the same place, both learning our pastoral skills and both facing much the same problems.'

It was no surprise that Eames asked Daly's advice about visiting Catholics in the Bogside area of the city. 'I said to Edward, "Is there anything against my going there? Would you be annoyed if I wandered about the place?", and he said, "I'd be delighted." All I asked him was that he would not make formal arrangements, I wanted to be free to walk about on my own. I decided, however, that I would not go in there as a "mate" dressed informally in an open-neck shirt. I came to them as the Church of Ireland bishop who wanted to get to know them.'

The visits were well received. 'As a Protestant bishop I said to them, "I want you to see that I haven't got horns. I have come to Derry and I have inherited a situation where I want to do something, because I represent a new generation. I want to know what makes your worries as real as they are, and I want to confirm to you the worries I am getting from my own people, because I don't think you have been able to hear anything beyond the rhetoric of the politicians." '

The Catholics were also keen to put their points to the new Protestant bishop. 'They would ask me questions like, "Do all Protestants think like Ian Paisley? Why can we talk to you at our fireside about things like unemployment and outside loos, yet the Unionist politicians do not want to listen about those things?" I am sure that some of the people I met had sympathy for the Provisional IRA. They did not say, "Johnny was out on a job last night," but they did say that the Provisionals were the only people who were doing anything for them. They also spoke with great respect for Edward Daly who was expressing some of their inner worries.'

These direct contacts with the Catholic community in Derry also led to a secret meeting with a Republican paramilitary and the beginning of many years working behind the scenes with both sides. It was an important part of Eames' work, which he did not speak about publicly, partly to retain the credibility and trust with his contacts, and partly because he knew that such meetings could easily bring condemnation and misunderstanding from the Protestant community at large.

Eames had made it known during his meetings in the Bogside that he would be prepared to meet anyone. One night he received a late phone call asking if he would be prepared to talk to a certain individual. 'What about?' he asked. The reply came, 'It's in relation to your conversation in the Bogside.' Eames knew that more likely than not it was a 'feeler' from the Provisional IRA, and he agreed to a meeting in the Protestant Bishop's House.

Eames describes what happened. 'A car was driven up to the house, and a youngish man got out. I invited him into the house, and the car sped away. The stranger and I talked for about two hours. He never told me who he was, but he was obviously a member of the IRA. He certainly knew a lot about what was going on.'

The stranger wanted to talk in particular about a problem in South Derry, which was part of Eames' diocese. 'He said that Catholic families had received threats that they would be put out of their homes, and asked me if I could do anything to prevent it. He asked me if I could get the message through to Loyalists in that area that the Catholic families did not pose a threat, but that if the intimidation continued his organisation was going to have to retaliate.'

Eames replied that he would do what he could, but that he could not guarantee miracles. He recalls, 'This was the first time that I had met a man from such a background, and I asked him, "Are you on the run?" He replied, "Yes." I asked him, "Are you not afraid of being caught? You have no guarantee that I did not tip off the security forces." He said, "I'm trusting you." '

Eames could not work out why he felt so safe. Then the stranger said something which has stayed with Eames ever since. 'He said, "I know when it is safe to visit a house." I asked him, "Do you actually know when you are not likely to be accosted?" He nodded. "Yes." I asked myself, "Does he know the timings of the security patrols on the road outside my house? Does this mean that there are talks going on somewhere and that there is a safe passage for some of these people?" In that two-hour conversation was I seeing a tip of the iceberg of collusion with the authorities, in that this fellow was sitting in the Bishop's House feeling safe, although he was on the wanted list? I still don't know the answer, but it has always struck me as very odd.'

People might ask why Eames did not turn this man over to the law. He says, 'I felt that it was not my job to do that. I didn't know what he had been accused of, or what he had done. I didn't even know his name. If I had turned him in or made it possible for him to be arrested, it would have totally undermined my independence as a church man. I felt that the criminal aspect was a matter for the police. This man had not come to me to confess to a murder or anything like that. He had come to talk about a serious problem in the community, and I was trying to reach out and to make a practical contribution.'

Nevertheless if Eames were to tell his parishioners that he had met a Provisional IRA activist and had a two-hour conversation with him, or if the news had leaked out, it would have caused an uproar. Eames says, 'I did not talk about what I had done, apart from telling Edward Daly afterwards. He was not a party to what had happened, but he was able to confirm that it had been a genuine approach. Over the years there have been many things which I have tried to do, things which would have been totally obliterated if they had been talked about, so I have tended to play my cards close to my chest.'

Following the meeting in Derry, Eames visited his clergy in the southern part of the diocese. 'First I had the facts clarified and I said to them, "We have to get some assurance going here, otherwise we are going to have a big problem." Those clergy did things on the ground, and I never heard from the IRA man again. The rectors would have known the activists in the Loyalist areas and they made it known that things would be much better if the hassle stopped. And it stopped.'

This was the first tangible result of Eames' meeting with a Republican paramilitary. 'It was the first time in my life that I had met such a shadowy figure, and it was a world I did not know. However, it was the beginning of something else, and to the present day this has been a part of my life, talking to people on both sides.'

Some three years before Eames went to Derry, an incident had occurred in the diocese which later led to suspicions about possible collusion between the Government and the Roman Catholic Church. In July 1972 a Provisional IRA bomb in Claudy killed nine people, including three children, and injured more than thirty others. In late December 2002, a police review of the massacre indicated that an unnamed priest – identified elsewhere as a Father James Chesney, who has since died – was actively involved in terrorism at that time.

A report in the *Belfast Telegraph* of 20 December 2002 claimed:

Rediscovered documents show that Father Chesney's apparent involvement in IRA terrorism was discussed at the highest levels of the Government and the Catholic Church, but the priest was never questioned by police.

Instead he was moved from a Co. Londonderry parish to Donegal after the case was discussed privately by the then Secretary of State William Whitelaw and the Catholic Primate Cardinal William Conway.

Following these claims, the Catholic Primate Dr Sean Brady, in a statement carried by the *Irish Times* of 21 December 2002, expressed his horror at 'the possibility of any such allegation being true' and said, 'every effort must be made to find answers to the yet outstanding questions. The Catholic Church will obviously co-operate in that search.'

As Bishop of Derry and Raphoe, Robin Eames visited Claudy in 1975. 'The memories of the families who had lost loved ones were vivid, and the hurt ran deep. A number of people claimed that a Roman Catholic priest had been involved, or they claimed to know a good deal about it. I treated such rumours at arm's length, but they persisted. I gather that it was general knowledge, but that no one could prove it. At the time I felt it was the sort of rumour which could easily be spread but without foundation. When it was confirmed late in 2002 I was horrified to think back on what I had heard all those years ago. "Was such a thing possible?" I had asked myself. The rumours were rife at the time, but nothing could alleviate the depth of the feeling of sadness in that little village.'

During his time in Derry and Raphoe, Eames constantly tried to build bridges. 'It was walking a tightrope, a tightrope I have walked ever since. I saw many injustices in Derry, and I saw the consequences of discrimination. Some of those Catholic people talked to me about their children who, once they had finished school, had to leave Derry to get a job, and would never return. Today the Protestants in Derry are saying that their children are going to England or Wales or wherever, and will not come back. It's amazing how the story has turned round.

'When I was in Derry I don't think that some of my people understood the hurts of the Catholics because they had only been enunciated in the "them and us" syndrome. I found it possible to be involved because I saw it in a non-party sense. I saw it in terms of injustice, and in the sense of ordinary people facing ordinary problems. That's what I had encountered in St Dorothea's.'

The problems in Derry, however, were different from the rest of Northern Ireland in important respects. 'One of the keys to understanding Derry was to recognise a mutual feeling of disenchantment with the Government. There was an anti-Belfast feeling because they believed that the only power base was in Belfast, and that the politicians there did not speak the language of Derry. In Derry there was more reconciliation with a small "r" than would have been possible in Belfast.

'Hence when the Apprentice Boys from other parts came to Derry, they thought that the Derry Protestants were thinking the same as them, but they did not realise that they were bringing with them a culture that was foreign to many Protestants in Derry, and that remains true today. Derry people are softer, but they can also rise to the bait, and some terrible things happened in Derry – yet there wasn't the same viciousness that I had encountered in Belfast.'

Eames greatly admired the work of John Hume who was making his name as a civil rights leader and Nationalist politician during part of the time the Bishop was serving in Derry. Eames recalls, 'I used to say to him, "John, you have great vision and wonderful views for this city but try to remember that it may not be acceptable in a place like Belfast." I used to call it the "Glenshane complex". It was amazing the difference in attitudes once you had driven south of the Glenshane Pass.'

All too soon the Glenshane Pass was beckoning again. After five years in Derry and Raphoe, Robin Eames was invited to become Bishop of Down and Dromore, his home diocese. Again it was an offer he could not refuse, and for a young man thought by many to be on his way to Armagh, it was an obvious appointment.

Eames says, 'I experienced the usual mental torment. I was very happy in Derry and Raphoe, and I felt that there was still much to do. However, there is a level in the Church of Ireland at which bishops are being appointed and you realise, "This is what is going to happen."'

At the end of his five years of office in Derry and Raphoe, there was a general feeling that Eames had done a good job. Bishop James Mehaffey succeeded Eames, whom he had known as a parish minister and with whom he had shared a very long friendship. Now retired, he talked about his predecessor as Bishop. 'He achieved more in five years than others would have done in ten or fifteen. He came to the diocese as a young man with enthusiasm and fresh ideas.'

One of his achievements was to raise the profile of the Church of Ireland. Bishop Mehaffey said, 'Until he came, the church simply got on with its role, but it did not have the same impact on the community. Robin Eames raised the profile, and even though the Church of Ireland was a minority church, it showed that it had a contribution to make to society at large. I did my best to build on that during my time as Bishop over the next twenty-one and a half years.'

Eames also helped to bring about important changes within the diocese. 'He inherited a fixed regime with a tradition of conservatism and he began to open it up. Life was easier for me because of some of the changes he had initiated. The diocese was no longer dominated by a number of senior clergy and laity, and more women were elected to office. There was more openness, and I was also able to build on that. Robin made a significant contribution as Bishop, he had a big impact on the diocese, as well as the city and the wider community, and he was liked and respected.'

As the Eames family left the north-west for the last time, they thought fondly of their time in Derry and Raphoe. Christine Eames reflects, 'We lived in a beautiful house and we had a lovely home. Despite the bad times in terms of the Troubles, it was a great place to live. The diocese took in a great diversity of situations, and the people of Derry and Raphoe were fantastic.

'Although I was the Bishop's wife, I was first and foremost Robin's wife wherever he happened to be, and I was happy to be involved in whatever came my way. Clergy wives have great privileges. They have instant entrances to people's lives in an often vulnerable way. People take you into their lives in a way that it might take other people years to be accepted. That is a huge privilege. You can be with people at that level and not be untouched by what happens to them. It is not just a job.'

Robin says, 'I had been impressed by the basic decency of ordinary people in both communities, and I felt so privileged to have made such personal contacts. I was aware that I was leaving many friends, but in the spiritual life you do what you feel you are called to do. Who was I to say it was the wrong or the right time to move? I think I was being guided. Having gone through the trauma at Queen's of changing my career from academe to the ministry, my life has been one of constant change and I have an urgency about the things I want to do which is probably a consequence of that experience.

'When I have the idea to do something I try to do it, because I fear that the time to do it will pass. I was surprised by how much I grew to love Derry, which I had not known beforehand, and its people. When I left I felt that I was an honorary Derryman, but when I drove down through the Glenshane Pass on the way back to Belfast I also felt that in another sense I was returning to my home city. Sadly, however, it proved to be very different from the place I had left some five years previously. I had left a Belfast of riots, and I came back to a Belfast of atrocities. In the interim, things had changed very much for the worse.'

6

More Trouble and Strife

On Saturday 14 June 1980 Robin Eames was enthroned as Bishop of Down and Dromore in Down Cathedral, Downpatrick – a small town some twenty miles south-east of Belfast and within sight of the Mountains of Mourne. It was not far from the Murlough House retreat centre where Eames had spent a few days prior to his ordination as a young deacon in June 1963.

The Enthronement Service was attended by a wide range of the laity, including local community leaders, and by a broad spectrum of Church of Ireland and other clergy. Significantly, it was the first time that the Roman Catholic Bishop of Connor, the Most Reverend Dr William Philbin, had attended a service in the Protestant cathedral.

The service itself was impressive, and the ever-observant 'Cromlyn', the columnist in the *Church of Ireland Gazette*, gave it his seal of approval. He wrote: 'It had movement, colour and form, but a commendable absence of gush. It did it without over-doing it. So much depends on knowing where to stop.'

Earlier in the article Cromlyn had poked fun at some other Enthronement ceremonies:

> Think of the way we require ... the new man to biff a stick on the closed door of the Cathedral, someone inside to shout 'Who's there?', and the Bishop to shout back 'It's me' (as if the fellow inside didn't know that either!) and then for the door to be opened and have him allowed in. Surely to goodness it would not be hard to make a funny bit about this sort of thing if the mood was on you. Could anything be closer to goonery?

There was no 'goonery' about the new bishop's sermon which was typically challenging and well delivered. Eames chose as his text the words from 1 Timothy 6:20: 'Keep safe that which has been entrusted to you.' It was a theme which was relevant for the occasion, and which reflected his sense of the steward-ship of his new diocese. It was also a text which could be applied as the guiding principle of his entire ministry.

One of the most striking aspects of his Enthronement sermon was his emphasis on the work of the bridge-builders in a divided Northern Ireland which was under great stress. 'So often the work of the peacemaker, the agent of reconciliation, the bridge-builder, never hits the headlines, but let us always remember that when the smoke of hatred and division clears, it will be this work which will endure.'

He paid particular tribute to the work of clergy from all denominations. 'Clergy are not immune to feelings of ordinary people. It has not been a time when it was always easy to put forward a message of hope and joy. The strain on clergy has been immense. Yet without their pastoral caring and leadership many a situation would have taken on dimensions of suffering and hardship much in excess of what we have seen.'

The theme of courage, resilience and hope remained central to his public and private philosophy even in the darkest days of the Troubles. Having come from Derry and Raphoe he was conscious that he was returning to the capital city of Belfast that had been battered and bruised by more than a decade of civil strife and paramilitary bombardment and to a divided community where what he called 'the knife-edge sectarianism' was much worse than anything he had experienced in the north-west.

During his installation in St Anne's Cathedral, Belfast on 5 October 1980, he paid tribute to his native city and its people, and he also managed to sound a note of hope. He said, 'Visitors come to us expecting to find a community beaten into the ground and constantly at war with itself. They are amazed when they find the level of normality so many people can maintain in their lives.'

In a central passage of his address he outlined one of the major underlying priorities of his episcopate and of his ministry: 'We the Church must constantly remind Belfast that individuals matter. That life and its values matter. That in the new Belfast emerging around us what will really matter at the end of the day is the value we place on the quality of life of its people. Every other consideration must stem from this.'

He also paid tribute to the then Dean of Belfast, the Very Reverend Samuel Crooks, who had pioneered a novel way of showing to the population at large that the institutional Church was indeed demonstrating its concern for ordinary people. The Dean had instituted an annual Christmas sit-out on the pavement outside St Anne's Cathedral to collect money for local and overseas charities, including Christian Aid, and the public responded with great generosity. Dubbed the 'Black Santa' he became one of the best-known clerics in Northern Ireland, and the tradition he began continues to this day – to the great financial benefit of a large number of charities.

Eames always had a genuine recognition of the work being doing by his hard-pressed clergy. He once told a journalist, 'The clergy have been neglected in many instances. They spend time giving to their people, and who gives to them if it is not me? In a sense, I am a rector of rectors. The person-to-person ministry is the most important thing I do.'

Despite his outward demeanour of calm and confidence, he approached his new role as Bishop of Down and Dromore with trepidation. 'This was my home diocese, and I knew that I would be working with men who were my seniors. I asked myself, "Will I have difficulty in giving leadership to these colleagues? Will I be able to get the work done?" Events proved that I need not have worried. The "office of Bishop" carried the day, and I was grateful that my colleagues gave such allegiance to the office I held.'

The diocese had long prided itself in the elaborate support it had given to junior clergy before and after ordination, but Eames recognised the need to bring in a wider range of professional outsiders to help in the training sessions. Another challenge was the recruitment of clergy. As Bishop, Eames was attempting to offer a broad spectrum of what the training of a Church of Ireland minister should be.

A good insight into his views on the priesthood is contained in a sermon he preached at St Columba's, Knock during the ordination service for six young clergymen on 24 June 1980, only ten days after his Enthronement as Bishop. He said that a cleric is first a priest and secondly a pastor. He said, 'He will be concerned about and involved with people. In the end it is people who matter. It is for all sorts and conditions of men that he will live, for it was for people that Christ died.'

He emphasised that for the cleric the key was to know the people. 'To be associated with the joys and sorrows of his people, to share their confidences, to be with them in their homes, to be at the bedside of suffering, to be involved in every facet of their lives, and if necessary to suffer with them – this is truly to know his people.'

A few months later, in an article for the church magazine in his old parish St Dorothea's, he developed his thoughts on the role of a bishop. In doing so he gave a number of clues about the inner man, something that he has tended to keep closely to himself, partly because of the special nature of his public and private role.

The life of a bishop, he stated, could be regarded as lonely insofar as there is so much of his work which must involve utter confidentiality and decisions which will not always make him the most popular person in the diocese. There could be loneliness in that he could share so little of his problems and decisions with anyone else.

> A bishop requires strength which is much more than physical ability. He will find that he must lean very heavily on his faith. His prayer life and his reading, thinking and preparation will be priorities. He will also find that there is an even greater urgency to plan for time with his family and to guard more jealously than ever his times of relaxation. In return he will find a warmth and friendliness from his people, for which I know no substitute in the world.

Sadly, the world had become more cynical since he left his parish in Belfast just some five years previously. During this period over nine hundred people in Northern Ireland had died violently in the Troubles, thousands had been injured, and millions of pounds of damage had been caused by terrorist explosions.

Robin Eames found that some things had changed in his old parish, while others had not. He recalls, 'Some of the Protestant housing estates had become entrenched islands on their own, and they were very much under the influence of the paramilitaries. The people seemed to be no happier than they had been many years previously when they had lived in their old homes down on the Newtownards Road.'

He also noticed a widening gulf between the Church and the politicians. 'The politicians liked it when the Church said, "We are supporting you", but they did not like some of the other things which the churches were saying. I was conscious that the Church had to make serious decisions as to how it expressed community opinion. It was not that people were beginning to doubt the relevance of the Church, but they were beginning to question to a much greater extent the role of authority and leadership, and I attributed that to the trauma of the Troubles.'

It seemed to him to be a moral duty, as it had been in Derry, to reach out to the Roman Catholic population. He says, 'I visited Roman Catholic clergy, I worked with the local Roman Catholic bishops, and I tried to encourage as many cross-community efforts as possible.'

He was also conscious of the power of the media and of the importance of getting across the Church's point of view, at home and abroad. 'I had always been conscious of the need to present the Church's message, and I had long been interested in communication and the mass media. In the old days there had been a feeling that it was better to try to keep stories about the Church out of the newspapers.'

That was not Eames' view. He believed that the Church's communications outreach should take the best possible advantage of the important developments in communications and media technology, and the Church of Ireland built up an efficient communications office through the work of Charles Freer, Alan Johnston, Elizabeth Gibson-Harries, the Reverend Brian Parker and a number of others.

A significant, and at that time a somewhat controversial, initiative was taken by the Church of Ireland in sending a delegation led by Bishop Eames to the United States early in 1981 for talks with American church leaders, politicians and journalists. Eames recalls, 'The idea was to give the Americans the view of moderates in Northern Ireland. Militant Republicanism had been there before us talking in terms of the drama of the injustices in Northern Ireland, but that was before others had been able to indicate that there were two sides to the story, and that the "Green" version was not the only one.'

The Church of Ireland delegation included David Bird, a layman from Cork, Canon William Arlow, a former Secretary of the Irish Council of Churches whose work brought him into contact with paramilitary groups including the Provisional IRA – some of whose leaders he had met secretly at Feakle in Co. Clare in 1974 with other senior Protestant churchmen which the churches claimed had been on an individual rather than an official capacity – and the Reverend Houston McKelvey, an experienced communicator who edited the *Church of Ireland Gazette.*[1]

The composition of the delegation was criticised in some quarters. Mr Robert Overend, at that time a well-known figure in conservative Ulster Unionism, said that while not disagreeing with the American visit, he believed that Canon Arlow, Mr McKelvey and Mr Bird could in no way project the 'true situation' in Northern Ireland. Mr McKelvey gave a typically spirited reply concerning his own stance on moderation. He said, 'I leave it to God and to those who know me better to judge, rather than to Mr Overend.'

The Churches Correspondent in the *Belfast Telegraph* wondered why there could not have been a joint delegation from the Church of Ireland, the Presbyterians and the Roman Catholics. He wrote, 'To put it bluntly, the visitors would have carried more weight as representing the broad spread of the community here rather than a segment of it.'

However, there were more encouraging messages for the delegation. The *Irish Times*, in an editorial of 5 March 1981, noted that 'these missionaries of today should have much to tell their audiences, and much that is good and heartening and true. They should not be spokesmen for any party or Establishment view.'

Looking back, it seems extraordinary that such a step by a four-man delegation of Anglicans to the United States could lead to such widespread comment. Nowadays such delegations attract little or no attention within the community, but the Anglican visit to America in 1981 was particularly significant because it attempted to present a moderate and Protestant point of view to try to counter the Republican propaganda which had been giving only one interpretation of the complex events that were taking place in Northern Ireland.

Robin Eames says, 'Following us, other groups began to visit the United States, but I was glad the Church was one of the first. I believe that it was a worthwhile exercise. We also did some industrial lobbying on behalf of Northern Ireland employers in a bid to attract jobs and inward investment and I was told that our efforts were helpful.'

Eames was asked to address the Foreign Affairs Committee of the US Congress in Washington. When he was about to speak, however, the dramatic news came through that President Reagan had been shot and wounded in an assassination attempt nearby. The Chairman of the Committee turned to Eames and asked, 'Bishop, would you say a prayer for our President and our city at this time?' Eames recalls, 'I did so gladly. The next day one of the Washington daily newspapers wrote, "Is this some sort of indication that things are changing in Northern Ireland when a Protestant Bishop can stand in the Congress of the United States and be asked to pray for the President of the United States?" That has always stayed in my memory.'

When Robin Eames was Bishop of Down and Dromore, there were two major developments that had a profound influence on politics and society in Northern Ireland, and that presented considerable challenges to the Church and its members. One was the Republican prisoners' hunger strikes, and the other was the signing of the Anglo-Irish Agreement in November 1985.

The details of the hunger strikes were infinitely complex but essentially it was a battle of wills between the Republican movement and the British Government. The argument centred on the concept of 'political status' – whether a member of a paramilitary organisation convicted of a serious crime could enjoy a special category status in prison or should be treated as an ordinary criminal.

On 27 October 1980, seven Republican prisoners began a hunger strike in support of political status. The Government refused their demands. This phase of the hunger strikes ended in some confusion in December over an offer from the Government of new and improved prison conditions.

However on 25 January 1981, Bobby Sands, the 26-year-old leader of the Provisional IRA inmates in the Maze Prison, claimed that moves towards co-operation between the Government and the prisoners had broken down. On 1 March the struggle entered its most dramatic phase when Sands began a hunger strike and thereby started a campaign which ended in the deaths of ten hunger strikers: seven from the Provisional IRA and three from another militant Republican organisation, the Irish National Liberation Army.

Sands himself was the first to die, on 5 May, after sixty-six days without food. His funeral from the Twinbrook area of West Belfast to Milltown cemetery was attended by an estimated 70,000 people. The hunger-strike campaign greatly polarised public opinion in Northern Ireland, drove an even greater wedge between the Protestant and Roman Catholic communities, caused immense political difficulties between London, Dublin and Belfast and caused widespread and critical interest from around the world.

The British Prime Minister Margaret Thatcher firmly set her face against considering any concessions while the hunger strikes continued. As the condition of Bobby Sands and the others visibly worsened, the Roman Catholic Church was involved at many different levels to try to find a way out. Monsignor John Magee, an Ulsterman who was Secretary to Pope John Paul II, talked to Sands at the Pope's request, but failed to persuade him to abandon his hunger strike. The Roman Catholic Cardinal Dr Tomas O'Fiaich and the Bishop of Derry Dr Edward Daly had several meetings with Government ministers. Father Denis Faul, a prison chaplain, was also involved, and organised meetings with the relatives of those on hunger strike.

By 20 August the tenth Republican prisoner had fasted to death, but in mid-September the campaign began to lose impetus, particularly after the relatives of four men still on strike had intervened to ensure that they would be fed under proper medical supervision. By late September six other prisoners on hunger strike were aware that their relatives would do the same, and on 3 October they agreed to take food.

Shortly afterwards the Government announced that prisoners would be allowed to wear their own clothing, and that they would have 50 per cent of lost remission restored. The campaign slowly petered out, amid protests from Unionists at the concessions made, while Republicans took consolation from having obtained immense worldwide publicity during the hunger-strikes campaign.

Eames spoke out strongly on the issue, conscious of giving a Protestant point of view but also of trying to be just at the same time. During the Church of Ireland Synod in Dublin in May 1981, at the height of the crisis, he said that society would suffer to an even greater extent than before if 'expediency, compromise or surrender to pressure' were to be seen as the only reasons for meeting the H-block prisoners' demands.

He said, 'Society has a responsibility for the conditions under which any prisoner is kept. But society also has a moral duty to safeguard the innocent and those who live within the law. The question should be asked again – who are the real sufferers in this situation? Those who have a choice, or those who are denied it?' The hunger strike was a 'deliberate sacrificing of life'.

The plan, he said, was 'well laid and is conducted with the maximum publicity. It arouses many emotions, not least in the areas outside the prison from which the prisoners come. It has led to violence. It has further divided people, and increased polarisation in the community. The reaction to this calculated form of protest has told us much about the make-up of our society.'

It was not possible, he said, to indulge in this form of protest, and to expect to have no reaction on the streets. 'There is a degree of hypocrisy in any call for calm while still persisting in the hunger strike.'

The hunger strikes had placed immense pressure on the community. Following the death of Bobby Sands, there was widespread rioting in Belfast, and Eames feared for the safety of people in his diocese in East Belfast, particularly in the Roman Catholic Short Strand area, where he visited both Church of Ireland and Roman Catholic families.

The crisis created immense moral issues. Eames says, 'The attitude of the Roman Catholic Church that hunger strikers were not committing suicide compelled deep thinking in the other churches. In public statements and at clergy conferences I urged people to take seriously the moral implications of the situation – the whole question of dying for a cause – but I also reminded them that the hunger strike historically had immense importance for Republicanism as a means of drawing support for their cause. I urged people to think about the moral responsibility of God's gift of life. I also realised that politically the hunger strikes were representing a turning point in the Troubles in drawing widespread international attention to the Republicans' campaign, and I feared that Protestants did not recognise the significance of this.'

The other political turning point in Northern Ireland during Eames' time in Down and Dromore was the Anglo-Irish Agreement. This was signed at Hillsborough by Prime Minister Margaret Thatcher and the Irish Prime Minister (Taoiseach) Garret FitzGerald on 15 November 1985. It was the most radical political development since the partition of Ireland in the 1920s, which had led to the creation of Northern Ireland.

The British and Irish Governments committed themselves formally to work much more closely on Northern Ireland matters, and they set up a joint ministerial conference of British and Irish ministers at Maryfield on the outskirts of Belfast to keep a close watch on issues of concern to the Nationalist minority.

The Anglo-Irish Agreement did not formalise a joint authority of the two Governments in Northern Ireland, but it signalled a major shift in attitude by the British in their willingness to give the Irish Republic much more influence in Northern Irish affairs.

The Agreement was meant to promote peace and stability but it was greeted with fury by the Unionist majority in Northern Ireland – particularly as they had not been consulted beforehand about its contents. The Agreement led to a pro-longed 'Ulster says No' campaign by the Unionists, who felt that it was a 'sell-out' to Irish Republicanism and Nationalism. Even moderate Protestants felt that the Agreement gave the Provisional IRA the political gains that they had failed to achieve through their campaign of violence. However, the Agreement was welcomed by Irish Nationalists both north and south of the border, because they felt that it gave greater recognition to the position, aspirations and protection of Roman Catholics in Northern Ireland.

Eames believed that the Agreement had been a landmark in Anglo-Irish relations. He says, 'It was also the first real attempt by the British and Irish Governments to reach some sort of viable agreement on Northern Ireland and its problems. It marked the end of long years of disenchantment between the two Governments.'

The Church of Ireland's cross-border structure gave it, not for the first or last time in Irish history, a unique perspective which also placed it in a difficult position. Eames recalls, 'On the one hand it could interpret the feelings of those members north of the border to those in the Irish Republic, and vice versa. However, most Church of Ireland members in Northern Ireland were more concerned with feelings in the Province.' Eames found central church meetings in Dublin enlightening. 'Southerners generally welcomed the Agreement and found it hard to understand the apprehensions of those in the North.'

None of his southern colleagues doubted that the Irish Republic now had a defined role in the affairs of the North, and they could not understand why northern dioceses did not feel that a massive step forward had taken place. Eames says, 'I found that the overwhelming view in the South was "At least it will help to bring peace to Northern Ireland." '

Northerners, however, saw it as evidence of a new agenda of the British and Irish Governments. Eames recalls, 'As one widow wrote to me, "Did my husband die in vain now that Britain has sold us out?" Such sentiments were common in my postbag. It is too easy to dismiss these attitudes as traditional Unionist fears of the threat of a united Ireland. I saw how closely such attitudes were linked to their experiences of a community which had been subjected to years of terrorism.'

In simplistic terms, both the IRA terrorism and Irish Republican politics were seen as having the same aim. 'Our people believed that where terrorism had failed, Republican politics had succeeded. The anti-British attitude now visible helped to fragment Unionism. Anti-ecumenists again took the opportunity to attack any overt co-operation with Roman Catholics. While the British Government maintained that the Agreement had "copper-fastened" the position of Northern Ireland within the United Kingdom, many of our parishioners saw it as a step towards the rule of Northern Ireland by the joint authority of Britain and the Irish Republic.'

The Agreement placed particular strains on an all-Ireland church. Eames says, 'The Church of Ireland was subject to this pressure, more than any other denomination. In conversations with Roman Catholic Church leaders, I found a degree of sympathy with our dilemma, although they fully supported the Agreement.'

Eames' own reaction as a bishop was to try to engage people in the view that anything which supported greater understanding between North and South had to be given a chance. He says, 'Rectors continued to tell me of the pressure they were under. Unionist politicians had not been consulted properly by the Government before the Agreement was reached, and this added to the sense of dismay among our people.'

During this period, Eames met the Irish Prime Minister Dr Garret FitzGerald who stressed the need for direct dialogue between North and South. Eames says, 'Not for the first time I was aware of the fundamental difference between the southern perception of life in Northern Ireland, and the reality. I felt the need to explain the human element of people's reactions to events over which they felt they had little or no control.'

The controversy over the Agreement raised basic questions for church leaders. Eames says, 'Church life is lived out in the community, and it must always be seen to be concerned with and to touch the lives of ordinary people. If the Church remains aloof, it will lose credibility and relevance. Church leadership has a clear moral duty to use any avenue available to influence political life, not in any party sense but in a balanced way to promote understanding, justice and reconciliation.'

When presented with such avenues of approach, Eames felt morally bound to use them. He says, 'The late Lord Soper preached a philosophy of Christian social involvement. Archbishop Desmond Tutu also demonstrated a similar involvement. I have found such opportunities throughout my ministry, and I have responded as best I can. Never have I promoted any party political agenda, but I have constantly sought ways to influence justice and reconciliation. This, I believe, is my response to the gospel of Christ who moved among people and who fought for justice and understanding.'

During those years of upheaval and controversy, Eames – like other bishops – also had to look after a busy diocese. Somehow he found time to visit churches, to carry out confirmations, and to be a confidant and pastor to his clergy and their families.

Archdeacon William Macourt, a retired cleric and widely respected throughout the Church of Ireland, worked closely with Eames in the Down and Dromore Diocese. He recalled, 'His gifts of leadership and encouragement were very evident. He was friendly and approachable, and the clergy and laity felt that there was a person at the head of affairs in the diocese to whom they could turn with their problems.'

Mrs Betty McLaughlin, who was Eames' secretary during his six years as Bishop of Down and Dromore, got to know him well. She says, 'As with any church leader who has to make decisions that often prove to be unpopular, he had to take criticism. It may not have been until years later, when the whole story became known, that people would understand the decision he had taken.'

She was also acutely aware of the pressure on Eames because of the Troubles. 'Many people criticised him for mixing the Church with politics, but having experienced so many atrocities, I think he felt it his duty as a servant of God to become mixed in politics with a small "p". Too often he had to visit the families of those bereaved during the Troubles and to prepare funeral addresses.

'He had the ability to put into words what many people felt at such times, whether it was words of comfort or of the condemnation of terrorism which was reported by the media. I personally felt that he was greatly affected by what he saw and heard, and I know that he kept in touch with bereaved families for years. I believe that many people will never really know Robin Eames' contribution to our community as he acted as negotiator and reconciler to try to bring peace and stability to Northern Ireland.'

The burden and the worth of such work was well recognised by Gerald Priestland, the highly regarded Religious Affairs Correspondent of the BBC who had commissioned a series of talks for 'Thought for the Day', including one from Robin Eames.

Priestland stated later, 'I came away from Ireland with many emotions exercised that I may not much use in England: a sense of humility in realising that things are far more complex than it's convenient to admit – and that ordinary people in the North have qualities of solidarity and endurance we might envy for ourselves.'

He paid tribute to the courage and kindness of so many ordinary people who were trying to build bridges with their neighbours, often in the face of difficulties. He concluded: 'Each act, each gesture represents the conscious commitment of some very good people, and it's an affront both to them and their Father in Heaven to brush their commitment aside as valueless. Please, if you think of Northern Ireland, think on these people and not just of the loudmouths and gunmen.'[2]

This was the world in which Robin Eames and other bridge-builders lived, during the long decades of the Troubles in Northern Ireland. At the end of nearly six turbulent years in Down and Dromore during some of the worst of the violence and political deadlock, and earlier in Derry and Raphoe, Robin Eames must have felt that he had had enough experiences of conflict, and of responsibility and challenge.

Still only in his late forties, he had much to do in his Belfast-based diocese but, as before, another call was beckoning and it would prove to be the biggest challenge of his life. Robin Eames was asked by his church to follow in the footsteps of St Patrick as Archbishop of Armagh and Primate of All-Ireland. It was a duty he could not deny and an offer he could not refuse.

7

The Road to Armagh

When Archbishop John Ward Armstrong made his anticipated announcement that he intended to retire on 1 February 1986 as the Church of Ireland Primate, the speculation about his possible successor began almost immediately. Archbishop Armstrong had spent six years as Primate, and on the announcement of his retirement the then Roman Catholic Archbishop of Armagh Cardinal Tomas O'Fiaich paid him a handsome tribute. Both men had worked well together.

However, Dr Armstrong had been in failing health, and when he announced his impending retirement he was aged seventy. Clearly the Church of Ireland needed a younger incumbent in Armagh to undertake one of the most demanding and challenging senior posts in the entire Anglican Communion.

The Churches Correspondent of the *Belfast Telegraph* believed that the field of selection for the new Primate – traditionally from the existing bench of bishops – was unusually restricted, particularly if the preference was likely to be for a younger man. He pointed out that if Robin Eames at the age of forty-eight were elected, the new Primate would be in the leadership for possibly twenty years. He also underlined the importance of a candidate who had a good working knowledge of the North.

The media speculated that Eames was the firm favourite, with Bishop Mehaffey of Derry and Raphoe considered as a close second. Another name mentioned in the general speculation was that of Bishop Samuel Poyntz of Cork, Cloyne and Ross. The *Church of Ireland Gazette* sensibly emphasised that the Church did not need a 'caretaker Primate', and urged the bench of bishops to choose 'the best that is available at the moment'.

The election of the new Primate by the eleven-man House of Bishops took place in Dublin in February 1986 under the presidency of Archbishop Caird. Robin Eames and others left the room and their names were considered in their absence. It is believed that the others with Eames were Bishop Mehaffey and Bishop Ponytz, but Eames to this day declines to mention names.

After due consideration Eames was called back into the meeting of bishops, and Archbishop Caird said in a form of colloquial Latin, 'Habeamus Papa' – we have a Father! There was a mood of joy in the room and Eames was deeply moved. It was a considerable honour and challenge for a man still only in his late forties with – given good health – a likely tenure of some twenty years as Primate. The then Church of Ireland Press Officer Elizabeth Gibson-Harries recalls, 'I have never seen him so taken aback. There had been talk that he was one of the candidates, but once the result of the election was made known I think that he was overwhelmed. The realisation of the sheer magnitude of the job suddenly hit him.'

It was also, literally, a considerable act of faith by the House of Bishops, some of whom might have been tempted to have gone for a slightly older man, thus giving Eames a few more years in Down and Dromore before taking on the Primacy. It was a tradition in the Church of Ireland that a Primate was chosen for a limited period. In the event the bishops made their choice, and Robert Henry Alexander Eames, with almost all his ministry having been spent in Northern Ireland, became Primate of the all-island Church of Ireland.

His election was warmly welcomed by people of all backgrounds. The Auxiliary Roman Catholic Bishop of Armagh Dr James Lennon, deputising for Cardinal O'Fiaich who was away, welcomed him to Armagh, and the Presbyterian Moderator Dr Tom Simpson offered the prayers and good wishes of the Presbyterian community as the new Archbishop 'takes up his duties in one of the most critical periods in our history'.

The Methodist President the Reverend Hamilton Skillen described Eames' election as 'one of the most exciting appointments which the Church of Ireland has made'. No doubt his colleagues throughout Ireland were deeply aware that Robin Eames had started his spiritual journey as a Methodist.

The *Irish Independent* in Dublin gave Archbishop Eames a

warm welcome. It stated in an editorial: 'He is a frank, outspoken man who will obviously articulate the wishes of his flock both North and South. The voice of every churchman of peace and reconciliation needs to be heard, and there is little doubt that he will be in the vanguard.'

The *Irish Press* gave a strong Nationalist slant to its welcome, and issued a veiled warning to Eames, though it stated that there was no doubt that the new head of Irish Anglicanism was an able ecclesiastic.

> While wishing him well in his new and onerous role, it must also be said that it is important not only for him and for the Church of Ireland, but for all of us on this island that his perspective must no longer be an exclusively Northern one. He is now Primate of an All-Ireland Church, and his evaluation of issues must henceforth reflect this. In the end we will all be in his debt if he lives up to his promise to do precisely this.

Eames was sensitive to the widespread implications of his appointment and quickly laid down some of the ground rules for his Primacy. He told a press conference in Dublin:

> I have not been elected to voice any one particular opinion on economic solutions, political solutions or social solutions. It is not the role of any Church in Ireland to give its imprimatur to any one particular party view. Within the Church of Ireland we have every conceivable shade of political, cultural and social outlook. It would be an abject failure on my part were that not to be remembered.

To underline the active role he intended to take in the public life of Northern Ireland, he confirmed that he would be leading a delegation of Church of Ireland bishops to meet the Prime Minister Margaret Thatcher in London to discuss the Anglo-Irish Agreement. The bishops had already met the Irish Taoiseach (Prime Minister) Dr Garret FitzGerald and the Northern Ireland Secretary Tom King to discuss this controversial issue.

The Churches Correspondent of the *Belfast Telegraph* focused quickly on the political dimension to Eames' appointment.

Dr Eames has warned Mrs Thatcher that the work of reconciliation within Northern Ireland will be ten times more
difficult because of the situation that has arisen following
the Hillsborough Treaty.

That amounts to a straight contradiction of the assessment
her own advisers made before the deal was set up – and one
she must personally have accepted. The signs are that the
Primate will find non-domestic concerns bulking largely on
the agendas of the Bishops' regular meetings in the months
ahead.

How prophetic those words would prove, but it is significant to
note the level of public comment on Eames' new role even
before his Enthronement took place.

He had made clear his stance already, during the press
conference immediately after his election. He told reporters, 'It
would be my wish today that while I fully appreciate the job you
have to do, that you would understand that the most important
thing to me . . . is that I believe in my heart I am a spiritual
leader, and that I will resist at this stage drawing either myself
or my Church into party political controversy.'[1]

It was a good start, and illustrated yet again the new
Archbishop's ability to deal confidently with the media and to
communicate a clear message to his many public audiences.
Privately, however, he had much to think about before his
Enthronement as Archbishop on 21 April.

'I realised that if I stayed until the mandatory age of
retirement at seventy-five I would be Primate for some twenty-
six years, and given the obvious pressures, this was a daunting
possibility. Even if I were to retire at sixty-five, it would mean a
long appointment. I asked myself, "Could I do that personally,
and would it be good for the church?" '

Prior to his election as Primate there had been much
speculation in the Republic about the appointment of a
Northerner. His experience of the Church of Ireland in the
Republic had been restricted to Raphoe, and for obvious
reasons the Troubles had identified him with Northern Ireland.

He says, 'The Church of Ireland ethos as an all-Ireland church,
with so much of its structure south of the border, would have to
adjust to a Northerner at the top. I was greatly encouraged,
however, by the many messages from the South congratulating

me, and Southern bishops assured me that "the time has come for a change".'

As with his appointment in Derry and Raphoe, he knew little or nothing of the Armagh diocese or its clergy. However, he received many messages of welcome from them, and he felt that his pastoral experiences in Derry and Raphoe and Down would stand to help him in a largely rural and cross-border diocese.

He recalls, 'Much of my thinking and preparation naturally turned to the Primacy itself. What would the priorities be and how would I as a person see them? As one deeply affected by pastoral ministry I visualised the needs of the clergy in relation to all that I had experienced up to then. But I felt that County Armagh had probably endured and suffered more from the Troubles than any other county in Ireland. When I arrived in Armagh, I saw clearly that my previous thoughts had been correct. The feelings of hurt and resentment ran very deep.'

Eames also felt that while he should give a lead, he had to focus also on delegation and leadership sharing. 'I was determined to make the House of Bishops much more a team effort than had been the practice and to utilise at a central level the greater gifts that they possessed individually. I explained this to my colleagues at some length before my Enthronement, and this intention was welcomed. Hence since my appointment I have always sought a consensus in policy, and on more than one occasion when consensus was not possible, nothing was said.' He continually encouraged a collective voice, collective reaction and collective responsibility. He says, 'This sharing and delegation became a significant part of my Primacy.'

That said, however, Eames became more and more identified as a major church voice on the island of Ireland, partly because he had always been good with the media who in turn welcome a public spokesperson who has a neat turn of phrase and a lawyer's ability to strike to the heart of the matter. Eames, however, while willing to speak out publicly and to give leadership, was constantly conscious of moving too far ahead of his church members across the whole spectrum, from the people in the pews to the House of Bishops. 'Responding to the demands of the media has at times compelled me to speak out, but at all times I have distinguished between my own opinion and that of the Church of Ireland. I also recognised that my pulpit as Primate would be more and more the media.'

Typically, Robin Eames had his broad priorities in mind even before his Enthronement. He intended to give individual leadership when necessary, to speak out when a committee structure would have otherwise made this a slow procedure, to interpret the North of Ireland to the South, and through greater knowledge of the South to try to interpret it better to the North. He also wanted to personalise the role of the Primate to the broader community outside the ecclesiastical structures, and to represent the Church of Ireland ethos to the world Church, and particularly to the Anglican Communion.

It was an ambitious programme, but as the *Church of Ireland Gazette* noted at the time of his Enthronement:

> We do not expect to be disappointed in our belief that in Dr Eames the Church of Ireland has the right man in the right place at the right time. In an organisation not noted for such happy conjunctions, that is a great thing. It is our hope that he will not be left isolated by distant admiration, but will be gladdened by thoughtful support, and strengthened by active re-forcement.

The *Gazette* also stated:

> We are totally confident that Church people in the Republic will come to respect and admire Dr Eames and will point to him with quiet pride as a person of stature, not only in Ireland, but further afield in those consultations within the Anglican Communion to which he has already made an acknowledged contribution.

It continued:

> The occupier of the See of Armagh will see things in an historic perspective, and will understand better that times and people have not materially changed all that much. He may even have time to be thankful that he has not to exercise his Primacy in times infinitely more lawless than ours, and within a Church community far less cohesive and supportive than now.

The new Archbishop took up his duties immediately after his election. Among his first engagements was a meeting with Mrs

Thatcher as head of a delegation of the Irish bishops. She replied to him on 18 April following his letter to her some ten days previously which referred to their recent conversations. Addressing him as 'Dear Archbishop', she stated, 'I entirely agree with you that, in the present difficult situation in Northern Ireland, dialogue rather than confrontation must be our aim ... I am most grateful for your offer of assistance, coming as it does from someone who is uniquely placed with contacts both North and South of the border.'

Despite Eames' willingness to become part of the political process in a non-party way, no politicians from Ireland North or South were invited to the Enthronement Service. This was a break with tradition, but Eames made it known shortly after his election that he wanted the ceremony to be a purely religious occasion. There had been speculation that the Irish Premier Dr FitzGerald and others from the Republic would be attending, and this had led to threats of a hostile reception in Armagh from hardline Loyalists.

Six years previously there had been protests when the then Irish Premier Charles Haughey, a figure hugely unpopular with Loyalists, attended the Enthronement Service in Armagh for Dr John Armstrong. In 1986 feelings were running high in the wake of the Anglo-Irish Agreement, and there was a real possibility of trouble if Southern politicians came to Armagh. The Church Press Officer Liz Gibson-Harries told the *Belfast Telegraph*, 'This is a Church celebration. If we lived in a perfect world, everybody would be invited, but we do not. We do not want unpleasantness. We do not want anybody hurt or injured during our celebration.' That statement in itself said much about the difficult situation in which the new Archbishop found himself.

The Enthronement Service itself was inclusive in a church sense. It was attended by Cardinal Tomas O'Fiaich, by Terry Waite, the Adviser on International Affairs to the Archbishop of Canterbury Dr Robert Runcie, and by other church leaders in Ireland, Scotland and Wales. And in another break with tradition, the service was attended by the recently appointed Archbishop of Dublin Dr Donald Caird.

The service was rich in symbolism. The new Archbishop took his oath while holding a 1913 edition of the ninth-century *Book of Armagh*, and the Secretary-General of the Anglican Consultative Council, Canon S. Van Culin, presented him with the Compasrose, the symbol of the worldwide Anglican Communion. Such symbolism underlined Robin Eames' direct connection with the site of St Patrick's premier church in Ireland and also his membership of and contribution to the worldwide Church.

In his sermon, the new Archbishop spoke out strongly. He stated:

> Violence and hatred have scarred too many lives. Anger rather than reason has dictated too many attitudes. Christianity is not just about belief and worship. Christianity is about how we live and behave. Sometimes as the world watches and listens to what is going on in our land, many have wondered not just about Ireland, but about Christianity itself.
>
> What is the Christian voice to say to our society today? Is it to give bland assurances, to answer questions no one is asking, to utter eternal truths in ways which have no apparent relevance to the here and now? Is it to be a voice which always echoes what society says – or is it to say something, sometimes, about another way – another purpose – another experience?

The Archbishop said that each section of the community had its grievances, its aspirations, hopes and fears. 'Each has its right to be heard. Each has its place in this land. Somehow, some day each has to learn a new respect for the other.'

The Church, he said, must understand these feelings:

> But while we must identify the feelings of people, while we must understand those emotions, while we must at times articulate those feelings, we must never lose sight of our God-given responsibility. We must point the way ahead for the community, we must ask the questions which are prompted by our faith, and be unafraid to face the consequences. I cannot help feeling that the churches in Ireland have been too ready to say to society, 'We will go with you,' without taking time to ask the question, 'Where are we going?'

It was a classic Eames speech. It emphasised the need for partnership and spiritual conviction to try to bring about change, and to prepare people to face the difficult challenges ahead. It was also written in relatively simple language and delivered with the powerful certainty with which a preacher with the gifts of Robin Eames could turn quite ordinary words into an extraordinary message of inspiration and challenge at a time of uncertainty and foreboding in Ireland.

The address was well received by its many different audiences, both inside and outside the cathedral. The Belfast-based nationalist daily the *Irish News* hailed the sermon, in an editorial published the next day. It stated: 'Dr Robin Eames hoisted a new beacon of light yesterday in Armagh. It was a beacon of light directed searchingly into the Church itself and beamed in hope and reassurance to society at large.'

It continued:

> Church leaders should not expect to be listened to as of right. Credibility must be earned. There was an admirable absence of predictability in the new Archbishop's sermon. If one were to choose from his courageous address a section that summed up the whole, it would be those simple words: 'Christianity is not just about belief and worship. Christianity is about how we live and behave. Too many seem to have forgotten that fact.'

The address was also well received by the Unionist morning daily the *News Letter* which praised Eames' comments and also took the opportunity to rebuke the British administration over its Direct Rule policy in Northern Ireland. It noted that the new Archbishop was enthroned 'in a ceremony that was both simple and inspiring', and observed: 'Dr Eames takes over the Archbishopric at a time of great tension and man-made divisions within the community. A man of independent thought and manifest courage and compassion, it was noticeable that the key word in his address yesterday was "partnership".'

The *News Letter* emphasised:

> [Eames' message] must be heeded not just by the ordinary, confused, frustrated people of Northern Ireland but, more importantly by those charged with responsibility for the government of the Province.

It might be tempting for the Northern Ireland Office to

assume that Dr Eames meant that the role of the Church is to act as a blotting-paper for all the mistakes, deliberate and otherwise which a weak, out-of-touch administration has inflicted on the people.

That is far from being the case. The greater the authority, the greater is the responsibility, and the Northern Ireland Office has failed lamentably to give the sort of lead necessary to bring Ulster out of its present strait-jacket.

The faithful Cromlyn in the *Church of Ireland Gazette* understandably reflected the Church's pride in the Enthronement Service and particularly in their new man.

The Primate possesses, of course, the indefinable quality that nowadays is called charisma. It seemed to the onlooker that on this day he was at his best, relaxed and assured, almost casual at times, entering upon his high office with the ease and confidence of one who had not the smallest doubt of the rightness of his being there. It was a confidence that was infectious and can give strength and hope to us all.

The *Belfast Telegraph* also welcomed Eames' message, but in an editorial it stated pointedly:

Dr Eames has shown himself to be concerned about the Province and candid in his expressions. It will be interesting to see how his brand of Unionism works with his Roman Catholic counterpart in Armagh, Cardinal O'Fiaich, who is an equally outspoken Nationalist. Can they set an example of agreement to differ whilst sharing the bond of Christianity?

It was made obvious that while most people had recognised the contribution of Robin Eames on his way to Armagh, he would still be judged not so much on what he said as Primate but on what he did. It was a daunting challenge and nowhere more so than in the field of ecumenism, where his actions would be scrutinised even more than his words.

For far too long in the tortured development of Irish history the two great Christian denominations had worshipped the same God, but on their own terms. Both communities knew the many obstacles which divided them, but there was an urgent need for their church leaders and others to help them to discover what they had in common. That process had begun some years before Robin Eames became Primate, but one of his most important and urgent priorities was to develop even more a meaningful dialogue and practical co-operation across the religious divide.

However, there were other priorities. It was crucial for Eames to get to know his own people in the Diocese of Armagh. He was conscious not only of the national profile of the Primacy but also of his role as a diocesan bishop. From the start, he set out to meet his own clergy and people in Armagh where, as a result of the Troubles, there was great suffering and hurt. Even though he was now Primate of All-Ireland, his pastoral role as a diocesan bishop would prove to be of great importance.

8

The Footsteps of St Patrick

When Robin Eames was elected Archbishop of Armagh, and Primate of All-Ireland, his first reaction was one of shock – even though he knew that he was regarded as a contender for the post. He said later, 'You get to the stage where you know that there is a strong chance they might ask you to do it, but even so when I was told the outcome of the election I was taken aback.

'There was the withering thought that I would now be asked to carry the responsibility that I had watched others shouldering over the years. It was awesome. At that stage there was no question of turning back. You were a part of it, and if your fellow bishops asked you to take on the job that was it. You did it.'

He remembers asking his colleagues for two things, before he went out from the room to meet the media. 'I asked that I be allowed to phone my wife and tell her about my election. I also asked all the bishops to pray for me, that I would carry out not only what they were asking me to do, but that I would be given the wisdom and strength to do it.'

Eames was given little or no time to acclimatise himself to his new role. 'The media wanted my opinions right, left and centre on a whole range of things – on the deaths and murders, on the political attempts to stop the violence, on the international pressure on Northern Ireland. I had very little warning, but I did my best to give my opinions in all sorts of situations.'

This required time and effort but he hoped that gradually, after all the furious activity of Down and Dromore, he would be able to step back a little and to concentrate on the sheer heritage of Armagh. He says, 'I was expected to be Primate of All-Ireland but I also wanted to soak up the atmosphere of

Armagh – with its cathedral and nearby buildings including the public library which was founded by one of my predecessors, Archbishop Richard Robinson in the middle of the eighteenth century.'

Robinson, later Lord Rokeby, was a remarkable churchman who was consecrated as Archbishop of Armagh in 1765. He devoted much of his considerable personal wealth to employ some of the best architects and craftsmen of his day to make Armagh a city of exceptional architectural merit. In the ecclesiastical capital of Ireland he created a city of Georgian splendour to rival Dublin, the secular capital of Ireland, and in doing so he spent between £30,000 and £40,000 – which was a fortune in those days.

In doing so he created much-needed employment for the local population, and he gave the community a pride in their new city. He also created a legacy of architectural beauty for future generations, including Archbishop Robin Eames and his family. Though Armagh had its own dangers and difficulties, it was a significant change of surroundings for the family after their years in Derry and Belfast.

In Armagh, Robin Eames was impressed by the quiet atmosphere around the cathedral. 'Despite the awful things that were happening in other parts of Armagh and Northern Ireland I discovered that St Patrick's Cathedral and its precincts had an air of tranquillity. That helped me to come to terms with all the challenges and responsibilities that were crowding in upon me.'

The Church of Ireland cathedral is situated on the hill in Armagh where it has long been believed that St Patrick established his main church. As if to underline the historical importance of the site in general, a large stone in the wall of the north transept records the burial place of the great Irish King Brian Boru, who was killed at the Battle of Clontarf in 1014.

The Protestant cathedral has a noticeboard showing the names of all the Abbots, Bishops and Archbishops of Armagh in unbroken succession from Patrick's time to the start of Archbishop Eames' Primacy. It is important to note, however, that the list of names up to the Reformation is shared by the Catholic tradition. The foundation stone of a new Roman Catholic cathedral was laid in 1840, but the building was not completed until early in the twentieth century.

The Church of Ireland cathedral is strikingly neat and attractive, but without the soaring splendour of its Catholic counterpart. W. M. Thackeray noted in his book *The Irish Sketch-Book* (published in 1843):

> The Cathedral is quite too complete. It is of the twelfth century, but not the least venerable.
>
>   It is neat and trim like a lady's drawing-room. It wants a hundred years at least to cool the raw colour of the stones, and to dull the brightness of the gilding; all which benefits, no doubt, time will bring to pass, and future Cocknies setting-off from London after breakfast in an aerial machine may come to hear the morning service here, and not remark the faults which have struck a too susceptible tourist of the nineteenth century.

Time has mellowed the colour of the stones of the cathedral and also the sting of Thackeray's comments which, apart from any architectural merit or otherwise, showed a remarkable vision about the future of air travel.

The main point about the cathedral is not its discreet charm, but its location which has a direct connection to St Patrick. From the start of his Primacy, Robin Eames was aware of the significance of the Patrician heritage. 'I said to myself, "If I am going to have any validity in this job I have to try to understand what the heritage of Patrick really means." So I read even more widely about the past in Armagh, as I tried to chart a way forward for the future. Patrick had given Armagh a particular focus on learning, teaching and witness, and I was anxious to build on that.'

The names of Armagh and of St Patrick are synonymous. It was in this city that Patrick founded his main church in AD 445. This led to the establishment of Armagh as the ecclesiastical capital of Ireland.

Despite the numerous legends surrounding Patrick, and the fanciful creations of many writers who attributed to him miraculous powers, he remains a comparatively little-known historical figure. The best and most reliable account of Patrick is his self-portrait in his *Confessio*.

This was written in rudimentary Latin in his old age, and his opening sentence illustrates his deep sense of unworthiness: 'I

101

am Patrick, a sinner, most unlearned, the least of all the faithful, and utterly despised by many.' Referring to his mission in Ireland, he wrote: '. . . it was most necessary to spread our nets so that a great multitude and throng might be caught for God, and that there be clerics everywhere to baptise and to exhort a people in need and want . . .'

In his *Confessio* he tells the remarkable story of his kidnap, his servitude in Ireland, his dramatic escape, and – following a vision – his return to the island to convert the inhabitants. In doing so he laid the foundation for a later flowering of Irish Christianity, which helped from the sixth to the eighth centuries to keep alive the faith on the European continent – from Lindisfarne to Liege, and from Whitby to Wurzburg.

He had to endure considerable hardship and dangers in his mission to the Irish. He wrote:

> I know perfectly well, though not by my own judgement, that poverty and misfortune becomes me better than riches and pleasures. For Christ the Lord, too, was poor for our sakes: and I, unhappy wretch that I am, have no wealth even if I wished for it. Daily I expect murder, fraud or captivity, or whatever it may be: but I fear none of these things because of the promises of heaven. I have cast myself into the hands of God Almighty, who rules everywhere, as the prophet says: Cast thy thought upon God and He shall sustain thee.

Though he was also street-wise, courageous and tough when he had to be, the real St Patrick was a humble and deeply religious man, and with an all-embracing concern for the welfare of his fellow human beings. Anyone walking in the footsteps of St Patrick, as successive Archbishops of Armagh in the Roman Catholic and Protestant traditions had to do, could not but be humbled and inspired by the life and work of this extraordinary Christian from ancient Britain who became the national saint of the Irish.

Robin Eames, according to the Official Guide to St Patrick's Church of Ireland Cathedral, was 103rd in the long succession of Abbots, Bishops and Archbishops of Armagh since the time of St Patrick. However, Eames was not taken in by the sentimentality surrounding the Patrician tradition which sometimes portrays Patrick as little more than a kind of secular folk-hero, and an acceptable icon for a fun-loving rumbustious Irishness of popular concept that has no connection with the austere and lonely Christian pilgrimage of the man himself.

Eames pointed out, later on, the thoughts about Patrick that had occurred to him from the early days of his own ministry:

> One could argue that all of us have let him down. The light of St Patrick has always been there, but it has burned the wick low in many instances. This is simply because we have not taken his message as seriously as we should have done. It shines brightest whenever people have the courage to witness the faith of Patrick and the courage also to say 'I want to help remove the bondage of violence and division from Ireland.' But at times the response to Patrick's message is very dim.

Eames continued:

> Patrick did not see himself as a great prophet, or as a man who would manipulate or change history. He saw himself as 'a servant of servants' who was placed at a particular time in history when all the message he needed to give was the message of the basic gospel. I believe that in the times in which we are living St Patrick, if he were alive, would stress the importance of understanding the nature of forgiveness and of reconciliation, and that this begins on a one-to-one basis, from person to person, before it becomes institutionalised.[1]

This was a central part of Robin Eames' credo, not only in building bridges across the religious divisions but also in getting to know and understand his own people. As a newly elected Archbishop of Armagh he was ready to listen to the stories of hurt and suffering throughout his diocese. He said later: 'Before I knew that I was coming to Armagh, I thought that the area had borne the brunt of the Troubles, and my experience proved that I was right. I had witnessed suffering and despair in Derry, and also in Down and Dromore, but nothing quite like that of the depth of feeling in Armagh.

'The Church of Ireland people talked to me about having good Roman Catholic neighbours, and they meant this sincerely. Yet memories played an important part in the Armagh scene, and the sense of hurt over the attacks by the Provisional IRA on Protestants, often in isolated border areas, ran very deep.'

Robin Eames' judgment about the suffering in Armagh was borne out by the statistics of violence that occurred in the area. At the height of the Troubles, Armagh had a fearsome reputation. It became known, with part of neighbouring Tyrone, as the 'Murder Triangle'. Of the 2,037 civilians killed between 1966 and 1999, 228 were from County Armagh. Only in West and North Belfast, with 436 and 396 civilian deaths in the same period, were the figures worse.

Around half the total civilian deaths for this entire period occurred in Belfast, though per head of population Armagh was the most dangerous county. Of the total of 3,636 deaths associated with the Troubles, within the British Isles and Europe, 1,647 occurred in Belfast. The second highest total was for County Armagh, with 510.[2]

The injuries and deaths affected all communities. The local Unionist politician John Taylor (now Lord Kilclooney) survived an Official IRA assassination attempt in 1972. In 1981, Sir Norman Stronge, aged eighty-six, a prominent Unionist and former Speaker of the Northern Ireland Parliament, was murdered together with his son James when armed intruders forced their way into their stately home at Tynan and shot them both. The terrorists then started a fire which destroyed the building.

In 1983 Charles Armstrong, Chairman of Armagh Council and an officer in the part-time Ulster Defence Regiment, was murdered by the Provisional IRA in the car park near the Council headquarters which used to be the Primatial Palace for the Archbishops of Armagh.

These and many other murders had taken place before Robin Eames went to Armagh, but during his Primacy the grisly litany of deaths and injuries continued – including those along the twisting border with the Irish Republic where Protestants in isolated areas were particularly vulnerable.

Canon William Neely, the veteran Rector of the Parish of Keady near the Irish border, described the trauma of the families of those who were murdered. He said, 'In my ministry I have always tried to teach the essence of Christianity and about forgiveness, love and understanding. I remember one young man who came up to me after I had preached a sermon on forgiveness. He told me, "I heard what you said, but I find myself unable to forgive." His bachelor uncle had been literally hacked to death on the border near Keady by those who wanted him out of the way in the hope that his farm would pass from Protestant ownership.'

Throughout the years of Eames' Primacy the murders and maimings continued. In 1994 two Catholic students were shot dead when a Loyalist paramilitary gunman opened fire, and in 1998 Philip Allen, a Protestant, and his best friend Damien Trainor, a Catholic, were murdered by Loyalist gunmen who burst into a bar at Poyntzpass and opened fire.

Eames reflected, 'I was aware that people had been subjected to a great deal of terror. Not only were they traumatised and hurt, they also needed a voice. Some of the statements I issued in public were more directly linked to events in Armagh than even my previous statements following my experiences in Derry and Down and Dromore, where some of my people had also suffered grievously.'

The Archbishop personally visited homes in the Armagh diocese. He recalls, 'I spent a lot of time in the parishes, I went to the isolated farms and talked to the people, I found out why they felt the way they did, while trying to bring some sort of leadership and help. As the years passed I spent longer in Armagh than in the other dioceses, and what happened in Armagh more and more affected what I said and did as Archbishop.'

As well as the feelings of deep hurt, Eames also detected a sense of isolation in Armagh. 'It was not an anti-Belfast feeling as such. It was simply that people felt that they were far removed from the corridors of power. The degree of despondency and despair in the Armagh diocese was something new to me.'

Eames found that as a result of the violence and general air of fear and uncertainty, clerical vacancies in the country parishes of Armagh were difficult to fill. The area had a reputation for isolation, and younger clergy were not prepared to move, partly for family reasons. Eames also discovered that the divisions ran deep in the towns as well.

'In Portadown, for example, I found that the town was very sharply divided by sectarianism, though I also encountered many good and decent church people in that area. I had never before come across such bitterness, which was plain at almost all levels of that society. The widespread trouble and distress that resulted from the stand-off at nearby Drumcree between the members of the Orange Order and the residents of the Garvaghy Road Nationalists was only one manifestation of this.[3]

'I discovered that Portadown suffered from an absence of local amenities, and that Roman Catholics were afraid to walk in certain areas. I made repeated pleas for a community forum, but with limited success.' David Armstrong, the long-term editor of the *Portadown News*, worked closely with Eames from time to time on certain issues. He says, 'I have a high regard for him. Throughout the crises over Drumcree, Robin Eames showed great courage at a considerable personal cost.[3]

'He came in for great criticism every year from certain quarters, but he continued to work hard behind the scenes – much more so than many people will ever know. Despite the problems he did not throw in the towel. I believe that he is held in high regard by most people in Portadown as someone who genuinely tried to help the town during a time of great difficulty.'

Eames says, 'Throughout my ministry and indeed my Primacy I have been at pains to emphasise the importance of bridge-building, and what I said was not just some well-meaning thoughts that might be expected from a church leader. My private and public statements were based on human suffering, and nowhere more so than in the Diocese of Armagh.'

As well as carrying out his Primatial duties, Eames had to run his diocese. This required a great deal of juggling with dates and diaries and also an ability to delegate. Eames said, 'This has been difficult on occasions, and the pressure on time has been intense. Often I have to drop one or the other to deal with emergencies in either, but I have tried not to neglect the diocese even when the pressure of all-Ireland business has been great.'

He used rural deans and the archdeacon extensively as a back-up by delegating many tasks to them. He reflects, 'I suppose that we should try to copy the Roman Catholic situation where an auxiliary bishop assists the Archbishop of Armagh, but the Church of Ireland has not recognised the role of an assistant bishop anywhere. Good health has enabled me to fulfil both jobs, but I do not know how an older man could be expected to cope.'

Throughout his Primacy Eames has had to depend on a

small support staff. He has not used an official chauffeur, and has spent many hours driving himself all over Ireland, including frequent return journeys from Armagh to Dublin on central church business. It seems a remarkable set-up, compared to other archbishops and bishops in the Anglican Communion who are not quite so hands-on. Eames, however, is the kind of leader who operates quickly and well on his own, and he enjoys long solitary drives which give him space to think.

Of necessity Eames works long hours. When in Armagh he arrives at his desk in the Diocesan House around 8 a.m., and often works late into the evening on his public engagements or on diocesan business. After a half-hour of private devotions each morning in his office, he sets about the business of the day. He deals with paperwork, committees, numerous phone calls, including those from the media, and all the many administrative tasks that fall to someone in his position. He delegates where possible, and relies heavily on his immediate staff and particularly his excellent secretary Mrs Roberta Haffey.

She says, 'No matter who comes to the door of Church House with problems, each one is treated in the same courteous and gracious way. The Archbishop has the great gift of being able to "switch off" from one difficult situation and go straight into seeing someone else, and to concentrate totally on what that person is saying to him. At the height of the Troubles I have often witnessed him prayerfully and calmly helping to keep the lid on the situation, either by a statement or media interview during which he helped to defuse very tense political situations with words of wisdom. He drives himself hard, and doesn't like to refuse any invitation that will provide an opportunity for the Church to be involved in. He is a man of great intellect, ability and spirituality.'

The former Press Officer Elizabeth Gibson-Harries also pays tribute to Robin Eames' capacity for hard work and for remaining calm and considered whatever the circumstances. She recalls, 'I remember that he used to have a picture in his office of a duck gliding serenely across the surface of the water, while paddling furiously underneath. That sums him up very well.'

The Archbishop receives visits from many people in positions of power and influence, including ambassadors, senior politicians, trade union leaders and many others. On those occasions when it is not possible to receive such visitors in Armagh, he goes out of his office to meet them. In private conversation he will mention, almost as a mere matter of fact, that he has just had a meeting with the current Northern Ireland Secretary of State, or that he is scheduled to have dinner with the Irish Prime Minister. This is all part of the job, and he is willing to put much time and effort into maintaining contacts and counsel at this level.

He observes, 'Because of the connection with St Patrick, Armagh is the natural location for the Archbishop's head-quarters, but at the height of the Troubles the centre of power in Northern Ireland was in Belfast. If there had not been a motorway to Belfast, the job would have been that much more difficult.'

The geographical location of Armagh reminded him of the time he was in Derry, well beyond the Glenshane Pass. 'There was a perception of being "out there". During my Primacy in Armagh there has been a sense of important things happening in Belfast, and if I was to remain fully informed, I had to maintain a direct link with the Church of Ireland bishops in Belfast. Otherwise I might have become out of touch. I instilled in my colleagues the need to keep me in the picture and this has worked well.'

Eames, a much sought-after speaker as well as an outstand-ing preacher, accepts many engagements to address major dinners, school prize days and other public and semi-public functions. This, he feels, is part of his mission to bring the Church into the everyday world and to help prevent the gap between the two widening further. In his speaking and other engagements he is ably supported by Lady Eames, an extremely good speaker in her own right. Working together on these and other occasions they are invariably charming and have formed an impressive professional, as well as a devoted personal, partnership.

Despite Eames' public role as Primate and Archbishop, he frequently remarks that one of the most fulfilling aspects of his daily work has been his role as a pastor. 'I never wanted to be desk-bound, and I love to get out among the people. I usually have two or three diocesan services on a Sunday, including confirmations, dedications and anniversaries. Each of these are special occasions for the parish, and the preparation of addresses takes up time. It is still one of my greatest joys to be among the people of the diocese.'

Eames feels that the ordination of deacons and priests is particularly important, as they are for any bishop. He says, 'I have given a lot of attention to the first few years of a cleric's life to training in pastoral matters, including preaching, but as a Primate I have also had the great privilege of consecrating bishops. Nothing can quite compare with the moment when you present a new bishop with his staff, ring and pectoral cross.'

However, as a bishop or archbishop, his first priority is his clergy and their families. He says, 'I often tell my people that I'm only a phone call away if I am needed, and I have cancelled engagements if a rectory family is in trouble. In Primates' meetings abroad I have never been able to understand fully how my fellow Primates in, for example, the USA and Canada can do their job without a diocese of their own. I firmly believe that the role and duties of a diocesan bishop keep you directly in touch with your people.'

Eames also lays great importance on letter-writing, and many people have paid tribute to his thoughtfulness in writing to them in times of sickness or need. He says, 'I have often been reminded of the importance of correspondence in my work. In fact I tell junior clergy that there is a "ministry of letter-writing".

'Once something is written it cannot be taken back. It can be explained – or even withdrawn – but nevertheless, it has been written. It is part of the record, and there are many occasions when a letter can become part of a general pastoral opportunity.'

Though some of the older clergy might grumble at times because Eames is, of necessity, away so much there is a realisation of the work he carries out for the church nationally and internationally. Canon Neely of Keady was a neighbouring rector when Eames was in St Dorothea's. He has known him for some forty-five years and they get on well together. He says, 'Robin works too hard, but his energy amazes me. The job is just too big for one person and essentially there will have to be changes in the future. Robin copes by working every hour God gives him.' However, no one doubts his qualities as a pastor. Neely says, 'I have heard no complaints at all about Robin in that respect. When my mother died he was very sympathetic and helpful. It would be very difficult to find a clergyman who would say that Robin had let him down when he needed help. And that's the great test. He is, as much as his situation allows him, a very good pastor.'

One of Eames' other outstanding qualities, according to Canon Neely, is his people-management. 'He is absolutely brilliant at this. One of the great things he has done is to use the rural deans as his contacts. We meet with him four or five times a year. A lot of bishops make no use of the rural deans network, but Robin has welcomed it as a means of helping to deal with the problem of not being able to give as much time as he would wish to certain matters. His work through the rural deans has been enlightened and very progressive.'

Neely believes that Eames knows how to get the best from people. 'I have seen that so many times. Robin knows what he wants, and he works to achieve it. He knows when to take a strong line, though he doesn't do it very often, and he sometimes retreats. I think he is very wise. I have always said, "Never fight a battle you can't win." Robin is very much of that mentality. He is a caring person with sound common sense who knows his church inside out. He reacts instinctively like an ordinary member of the Church of Ireland.'

As Archbishop of Armagh, Robin Eames has also been conscious of the civic nature of his role, and he has been supportive of the many efforts by the local Armagh City and District Council to promote the city. Desmond Mitchell, the former Chief Executive of the Council who was responsible for initiating many of the more imaginative development schemes for Armagh, said, 'During my tenure of office Archbishop Eames brought a civic dimension to his work.'

He invited many internationally distinguished members of the Anglican Communion to Armagh, including successive Archbishops of Canterbury Dr Runcie and Dr Carey, as well as Archbishop Desmond Tutu, and each one of them paid a visit to the Council offices. Mitchell says, 'Robin Eames did not see the Church as being separate from the civic function of the city, and he continually made the cross-over in a relaxed way. He has a commitment which goes beyond his official role as Archbishop. He has worked hard to develop Armagh, and during his time it has regained its city status, as well as the development of the Queen's University at Armagh and other important assets. Eames has helped to put Armagh on the map, and to consolidate its position as the ecclesiastical capital of Ireland, and to broadcast this locally, nationally and internationally.'

The Archbishop of Armagh is Chairman of the Board of Governors of the Royal School, Armagh, which was founded in 1608. The Primate also has a close connection with Armagh Observatory, which was founded by Archbishop Robinson in 1789 as a School of Sciences for a proposed University at Armagh. The city, however, had to wait until 1995 when the Armagh campus of the Queen's University of Belfast was opened to the first group of students.

As Primate, Archbishop Eames automatically became Chairman of the Governors and Management Committee of the Observatory, with its associated Planetarium founded in 1968. Eames says, 'I never claimed to have scientific qualifications, so it was a sharp learning curve, but I have found the work fascinating. The motto of the Observatory contains the words "The Heavens Declare the Glory of God", and I have found great respect from visitors, many from overseas, for the uniqueness of the institution.' The Governors comprise the canons of the cathedral and elected laity. Eames has consistently encouraged the appointment of people of different denominations to the Management Committee.

This has been symbolic of another important aspect to Eames' work in Armagh. His Primacy, and his ministry, are noted for his efforts at bridge-building between the two traditions, and in Armagh he has worked closely with successive Roman Catholic Archbishops.

The importance of this joint work, and the input of those involved, was neatly summarised by Desmond Mitchell. He said, 'In recent years many people of influence and of power visited Armagh. They included Her Majesty the Queen, the Presidents of Ireland and British and Irish Prime Ministers, as well as President Bill Clinton and the European Union President Jacques Delors.

'These people came to Armagh not just because it is the ecclesiastical capital of Ireland. They also came because Armagh had remarkable Archbishops from both traditions whose words were important concerning life and death issues during a prolonged period when violence, political upheaval and change were taking place all the time. Eames, in particular, was in office so long that he gave a sense of stability and continuity in terms of moving to try to resolve crisis after crisis.

'When we were trying to move the Council and Armagh forward in terms of getting things done, Archbishop Eames and his Roman Catholic counterparts gave a great example to all of us by working closely together to promote the best of St Patrick's tradition in St Patrick's city and much further afield.'

In the best sense, both sides – and their church leaders – were following in the footsteps of St Patrick, but much still needed to be done to help bring peace and healing to a tortured land.

9

Across the Divide

When Robin Eames was elected to the Primacy, one of the first messages he received was from Cardinal Tomas O'Fiaich, the Roman Catholic Archbishop of Armagh. Eames says, 'I remember his letter well. He welcomed me to "St Patrick's Hill", and he added, "May God guide you in shouldering the burden that has been passed on to you." He backed up his letter of welcome with a phone call. I was impressed by the warmth of his welcome to me, a stranger.'

Tomas O'Fiaich, a distinguished scholar and an expert on Irish language and literature, had previously been Professor of History and later President of Maynooth Catholic Seminary near Dublin. He was a native of Crossmaglen in South Armagh. He became Archbishop of Armagh in 1977, following the death of Cardinal Conway, and was appointed a cardinal in 1979. Eames recalls, 'Partly because of his background in Crossmaglen, he would have been viewed by most Protestants as an Irish Republican, so I wondered how he would react to me as someone who was perceived to have come from a different tradition. In fact we got on very well.'

The Cardinal attended Eames' Consecration as Archbishop in the Church of Ireland St Patrick's Cathedral. This was an act of significant symbolism, in that the heads of the two Christian traditions in Ireland were being seen together on such an important public occasion, and at a time of particular tension in Northern Ireland.

The Cardinal's presence at the Consecration Service continued the tradition that had characterised Robin Eames' entire episcopal career – his Consecration as Bishop of Derry and Raphoe, and later of Down and Dromore, had been attended by his Roman Catholic counterparts Bishop Edward Daly and Bishop William Philbin, respectively.

Such visible symbols of bridge-building are common today but at that time they were regarded as ground-breaking, after centuries of coolness between the two traditions. Indeed the architecture of Armagh itself long underlined the divisions in Christendom, with two impressive Cathedrals of St Patrick facing each other from two hills in the city. However, in an ecumenical gesture long before the term became well known, the Roman Catholic cathedral included a picture of the Protestant cathedral in one of its beautiful stained-glass windows.

Since the Reformation, both communities continued to worship in their traditional ways, but apart. In 1923 the main denominations within Protestantism formed the Belfast-based Irish Council of Churches, but the Roman Catholic Church was not, at this stage, involved in ecumenism. This initiative began in earnest after the Second Vatican Council, which opened in October 1962.

It took another ten years for some tangible results to emerge. In 1973 the first inter-church talks between Protestant and Roman Catholic leaders were held at Ballymascanlon, near Dundalk, just across the border in the Irish Republic. The so-called 'Ballymascanlon Talks' built on earlier work by the Joint Group on Social Problems, which included Protestant and Roman Catholic representatives.

The Ballymascanlon Talks took place from time to time, and later became more formalised as the Irish Inter-Church Meeting. This developed good relations at leadership level, and useful work was done in creating better co-operation on the vexed question of mixed marriages between Protestants and Roman Catholics, and other matters. It could be argued, however, that such progress was limited and that the prospects of shared communion – for those who desired to share the Eucharist – remained only an aspiration.[1]

Against this general background, Archbishops Eames and O'Fiaich quickly developed a good personal and working relationship. Shortly after Eames arrived in Armagh he met O'Fiaich at the Cardinal's house for two hours of talks. These ranged widely over ecumenism and the situation in Ireland. They each recognised the other's standpoint on politics, but agreed to work closely on building understanding between their churches. Eames recalls, 'Tomas O'Fiaich had been clearly well briefed by Bishop Daly on my days in Derry, and spoke with appreciation of my previous efforts to reach out to Roman Catholics. This was to be the first of many meetings in our homes.'

Eames found him to be a most friendly, outgoing character who was prepared to listen, and who enjoyed good conversation. 'He was extremely well read, a gifted historian and a man of great personal warmth and charm. I enjoyed my contacts with him greatly, and I learned of his immense love for County Armagh.'

Cardinal O'Fiaich made no secret of his firm Republican views. Eames says, 'He often referred to his early days in Crossmaglen, and his public persona did not appeal to Unionists. I often felt that if more of them had met him personally, they would have appreciated him more. I was determined to introduce him to as many Protestants as possible, and I did so by inviting him to a wide range of gatherings and dinners.

'It was often rumoured that he had dialogue with the Provisional IRA. At the beginning I had no evidence of this, but later on he confided in me that he had his contacts. He condemned totally the IRA's violence, but he spoke of his dream of a united Ireland at some future date.'

O'Fiaich could be very emotional. Eames says, 'This sometimes emerged at the meetings of the Four Church Leaders where he showed immense sympathy for the suffering of Protestants. On one occasion the then Presbyterian Moderator was very critical of something which O'Fiaich had said, and I went with him later on to meet the Cardinal in private. It was clear that O'Fiaich had felt the Moderator's criticism very deeply, and he became quite emotional about it.'

O'Fiaich loved a party, and he hosted an annual ecumenical evening in the Primate's house in Armagh during Church Unity Week. Eames recalls, 'These were highly enjoyable social gatherings. He had a great knowledge of history and often when I referred to an article or a book from the Reformed tradition he would say, "I've read it!" His library was immense, and he could read rapidly and absorb facts easily. He travelled widely and spoke several languages fluently. He had a very good mind, but he was often ruled by his heart.'

115

Eames and O'Fiaich maintained a close relationship. Eames says, 'If either of us didn't like what the other said in public, our friendship was such that we could talk it over in private. The Cardinal was very concerned by the rise of the Loyalist paramilitaries. We often talked about this. He appreciated the Protestant churches' condemnation of attacks on Roman Catholics. He had a less than easy relationship with British Government ministers, though he had no problem with Dublin. He was respectful to British ministers, but I know he often wondered if they had another agenda.'

Eames recalls that during a visit by the Four Church Leaders to Wexford in 1990, Cardinal O'Fiaich appeared to be very tired. 'At supper I asked him if he felt all right. He replied, "I am tired but I am going on a diocesan pilgrimage to Lourdes next week and that always refreshes me." I never saw him again, for he died during that visit.'

Robin Eames attended the Cardinal's funeral in an official capacity, but he felt that he was saying farewell to a good friend with whom he had shared much. 'He died before his wish for an end to suffering in Ireland became a reality. I remember him fondly as a warm-hearted sincere man who was one of the best listeners I ever met. Unknown to many people, his outgoing personality hid a shy man. I will always remember his personal kindness to me.'

O'Fiaich's successor Dr Cahal Daly was also a respected academic who had taught scholastic philosophy at Queen's University and became Bishop of Ardagh and Clonmacnois in the Irish Republic. He was later appointed Bishop of Down and Connor, and was based in Belfast. Whereas O'Fiaich was ebullient, open-hearted and emotional, Daly had a much more measured public personality.

To those who knew him he was also warm-hearted and charming, with a good sense of humour, but he was much more tightly reined within himself, and gave the impression of never speaking in public – or private – without giving each sentence the most careful consideration. He was rightly regarded as an ecclesiastical and political heavyweight, who was credited with drafting a significant part of the keynote speech by Pope John Paul II at Drogheda, during his historic visit to Ireland. Daly was also a fierce critic of the Provisional IRA and with his considerable intellect took on publicly all apologists for violence, including the Sinn Fein leaders.

It was widely acknowledged that Daly and Eames formed a politically adept and formidable clerical partnership in Ireland at a time of great difficulty and danger. This partnership was likened, not surprisingly, to that of Bishop David Sheppard and Bishop Derek Warlock in Liverpool, but the English clerics did not have to work within the same constraints as their Irish counterparts in a society where ill-chosen words could literally cost lives. Daly and Eames worked well together but they were not so closely identified with one another as personally as the Liverpool bishops.

Eames recalls, 'Cardinal O'Fiaich's successor was no surprise to any of us. I had first met Cahal as a student at Queen's University, when I attended some of his lectures. As Bishop of Down and Connor he had long been regarded as the front man for the Roman Catholic Church on public and political issues. We both smiled when he was appointed to Armagh – did either of us imagine when we were at Queen's that we would end up on opposite hills in Armagh as Primates?'

Eames found Daly a considerable contrast to O'Fiaich. 'Cahal was an academic philosopher who weighed up all his words in public and in private most carefully. He had a strong sense of justice. He was fully supportive of ecumenism and anxious to find out as much as he could about Protestant and Unionist feelings.'

Eames felt that Daly was not as openly an Irish Nationalist as O'Fiaich, but he was a Nationalist nevertheless. 'He was a staunch defender of Roman Catholic rights. He was very disciplined, and thoughtful at all times. He was a constant reader, and analysed everything that was said to him most carefully. His formality, however, hid a warm and genuine Christian lifestyle. Soon we had an excellent working arrangement.'

As sectarianism continued to drive wedges between the communities, Daly agreed to Eames' suggestion that he co-sponsor a private one-day conference of Protestant and Roman Catholic clergy at St John's Malone, in Belfast. This in itself was a significant event. Eames says, 'More than a hundred clergy attended from Belfast and other dioceses. It was the first time that such a conference had taken place, and it was widely regarded a success.'

Daly resigned in 1996, when he had reached the retirement age for members of the College of Cardinals. Robin Eames says, 'We remained good friends throughout our time together, and I respected his undoubted integrity and willingness to listen to both sides of the Northern Ireland argument.'

Eames felt that Cahal Daly always went out of his way to try to interpret the reaction of Unionists and Protestants by learning as much about them as he could. Eames recalls, 'We talked about this often, and he was anxious to put himself, as far as he could, in their shoes. I also felt, however, that his intense loyalty to and discipline in Roman Catholic thinking made it impossible for him at times to step totally into those shoes. Having said that, however, no Roman Catholic leader I worked with took greater care to understand the Protestant point of view.

'My memory of his Primacy will always be that of a man of complete honesty, courage and intellectual prowess whose philosophical approach was not always the language of the ordinary man or woman in the street, but who was respected by Protestants for the fairness of his approach to their fears.'

Cardinal Daly also has warm memories of working together with Robin Eames. He met Eames at the Lambeth Conference when Eames was Bishop of Derry and Raphoe, and he was impressed by his commitment to Northern Ireland and his distress – which he shared – at the suffering of people on all sides. Daly says, 'I found Robin to be bright, well informed and deeply spiritual. I formed the impression that he would not end his days in the one diocese.'

Like Eames, he was acutely aware of the difficulties of the situation in Northern Ireland. 'If we were going to say anything that would be conducive to peace, we had to be sensitive to both communities. The risk for Robin and for me as Archbishops was that one or other of us might be seen as mouthpieces for the dominant political view of our own community.

'That would have been fatal, because it would have contributed to the problem rather than to a solution. Of course, that was bound to disappoint many people who thought it was our duty to speak to our own community. That was the role for the politicians, but the churches had a different role – they were not there to deny the differences but to try to transcend them and to speak to both communities with equal respect and love.'

Their respective Primacies were characterised by shared concerns. Daly recalls, 'Our common aim was to try to understand the position from each other's point of view and not just that of oneself. My efforts to understand the Protestant and Unionist community were greatly helped by my contacts with Robin, even though by no means did I see him as a "Unionist" per se.

'He was a "Unionist" in the sense that I was a "Nationalist" but our parallel offices obliged us to take a much wider view than that. I would not have seen myself as a "Nationalist" Archbishop. I came from that background but it was no part of my mission or mandate as Archbishop to propagate a Nationalist point of view, and Robin, I am sure, felt the same about Unionism.'

Both met regularly, though not on a fixed basis, and formed a close working relationship. Daly says, 'If we had not been able to do that, it would have made things much more difficult, because this would have been noticed by the wider community. If we had been at loggerheads, that would have been most damaging. Even out of a sense of duty we would have had to pretend that this was not the case. We did get on, and we were in the business for the long haul. As Archbishops it was a kind of life sentence, and certainly for as long as we held our respective offices.'

They were not close pals or clerical 'blood brothers'. 'We knew each other well, and we grew to know what each other was likely to say or do. We had a very good understanding of one another, we appreciated each other's problems and difficulties, and we shared each other's emotional reactions. We were always conscious that we had similar tasks in relation to our own people and to the wider community, and we trusted one another at all times.'

One of the tangible examples of the common goals and pragmatic co-operation of both Archbishops was their important contribution to the year-long Armagh Together celebration which began on St Patrick's Day in 1994 to mark the 1550th anniversary of the Patron Saint of Ireland in Armagh. Over 250 events were held during the ensuing year, and they included conferences on a wide range of subjects including religion and conflict, science and the environment, and also Georgian architecture.

119

Cardinal Daly said at the time, 'St Patrick is very relevant to our times. It is sad that there are the wounds of pain and division between the Christian churches, but it is also an inspiration. We both feel proud of the heritage of St Patrick. We've become more conscious over the years, and particularly since the Second Vatican Council, of how much more there is that unites us. In the past, we have concentrated on the things that have divided us. In those days it was a different outlook, a different world. It was not that we were always in conflict with each other, but that we understood so little about how we respectively worshipped and what we respectively believed.'[2]

Eames said, 'To set the present mood of co-operation in perspective, it is unthinkable that such progress would have been possible a generation ago. We are doing things today that would not even have been dreamt of then. There were times when the Church of Ireland Archbishop and the Roman Catholic Archbishop were barely on speaking terms.'

When Eames and Daly travelled together to the United States on a joint church delegation, there was surprise in some quarters in America, especially among those who wrongly believed that the Irish conflict was mainly due to religion. Daly reflected, 'It is seen now as a much more complex situation. There was surprise and amazement that we were together, and that we were largely singing from the same hymn-sheet, without anyone being drastically out of tune.'

Despite the greater understanding between both sides, fundamental differences in outlook remained – a point well made by Eames. 'Cardinal Daly . . . would find it very difficult, I am sure, to accept my theology of the Church, just as I could not share his adherence to the Papacy, and to its power and influence. We can have very deep discussions – not arguments – about those things that divide us, as well as those which we share in common.'[3]

The success of the Armagh Together celebration was due to many factors, but the wholehearted support of both Archbishops gave it an important momentum. Desmond Mitchell, the then Chief Executive of the Armagh City and District Council, says, 'It was critical that the project was seen to be cross-community and both Archbishops had no problem with that.'

Their support was also crucial for the restoration of city status to Armagh in 1995, and both Eames and Daly were present when the Queen visited Armagh to hand over the new Charter. At a reception afterwards the Cardinal met Her Majesty, and the symbolism of the head of the Roman Catholic Church shaking hands with the British monarch was not lost on those who were aware of the violent and tragic interrelated history of both islands. As Desmond Mitchell noted, 'It was a most historic handshake.'

It was also a gesture which Robin Eames thoroughly understood and of which he fully approved. Though much remained to be done with regard to ending the violence and to building bridges in the community, the first visible signs of the healing of old wounds were becoming apparent.

However, on the wider canvas of relationships beyond Armagh there were some hiccups along the way. When Cardinal Desmond Connell, the Roman Catholic Archbishop of Dublin, who was not noted for his skill with the media, claimed to a journalist allegedly 'off the record' that his Anglican counterpart Archbishop Walton Empey was not one of the Church's theological 'high-flyers', his words inevitably appeared in a Dublin newspaper. There was understandable irritation within the Church of Ireland, though Archbishop Empey himself made a dignified response.

Robin Eames chose to remain silent in public but privately he was annoyed at the slight to his colleague, whether intentional or not. He said later, 'I felt that Cardinal Connell's comments were out of order, and totally at variance with the ecumenical tone of the times we were in. It was not just ecumenism in the strict sense, but in the understanding that was being built up between the various traditions.'

Another important development in which both the Northern Archbishops took part regularly was the work of the group known as the Four Church Leaders. The origins of this are rooted in an initiative taken during the episcopacy of Cardinal Conway and the then leaders of the Reformed Churches. From the time he became Primate, Robin Eames took part in these 'ad hoc' but regular meetings and with the passage of time he became the longest-serving church leader in the group.

He recalls, 'Over the years the work of the Four Church Leaders has become synonymous with joint action, joint statements and joint witness to a divided community. It is important to note that we in Northern Ireland and the Irish Republic are far ahead of any other part of the British Isles or Europe in this regard.'

The initiative began as a response to the sectarian divisions in Northern Ireland. 'Church leaders had asked themselves and each other, "How can the main churches not only do things, but be seen to be doing them together?" ' Over the decades the relationship has been formalised, and the two Archbishops are joined each year by the incoming Presbyterian Moderator and Methodist President. Eames says, 'I believe that there is a genuine support for the work of the group and also genuine opposition. Those who criticise us are usually anti-ecumenical Protestants. Some Moderators have come from that constituency, but they have always joined the group. Some have had reservations about praying together with the Roman Catholic Primate, but with sensitivity we have overcome this difficulty.'

One of the practical problems, however, is that because Moderators and Methodist Presidents are elected for only one year, there is a lack of personal continuity in the group – although this is provided on a permanent basis by a secretariat comprising the Clerk of the General Assembly and the Secretary of the Methodist Church. Eames says, 'Because the others are with us only for a year, it is impossible to plan ahead, and it means that just as we are getting to know each other, a change has to be made. However, I believe that the very fact we are seen to be working together has an influence on Christian witness in Northern Ireland.'

The group has made regular visits to No. 10 Downing Street. Eames says, 'These meetings have ranged from a virtual lecture to the four of us on Northern Ireland by a forthright Margaret Thatcher, to useful dialogue with John Major and Tony Blair.'

Eames had a mixed personal reaction to working with high-ranking civil servants at this level. 'By and large English civil servants have found it hard to come to terms with the influence of church life in Northern Ireland. Coming from a largely secular background, they are accustomed to estimating the influence of the Church by the actions of individuals, rather than as an institution. So they identify with high-profile figures who happen to be church members, rather than with the Church as a whole.'

Eames found that on occasions the advice of some civil servants to Direct Rule ministers in Northern Ireland had been based on their knowledge of the English church, rather than shaped by the realities of Northern Ireland. He says, 'One Secretary of State told me this personally. In fact he had disregarded the advice of the London civil servants once he came to know the Northern Ireland scene.'

One of the dangers, however, is for the church leaders to assume that they can always deliver what they promise, or what is asked of them. 'Presbyterian Moderators have often asked us to be cautious because of the divisions they have encountered at their General Assemblies. I am also aware of this within the Church of Ireland in the North. Synod debates can and do expose divided opinions of the Northern Ireland members where politics are concerned.'

Another inherent problem was the danger of the media portraying Eames, inadvertently, as the spokesman for all Protestants. A former Moderator, the Very Reverend John Dunlop, and himself a skilled spokesman and media commentator, made the point during a reflective conversation about Robin Eames. He said, 'When I went to my first press conference as Moderator, I was greeted by a battery of television cameras and tape recorders. There is something scary when you find yourself being on the record as a church leader and not as a private individual. So I have every sympathy and regard for Robin who has had to fill this demanding role for many years.

'There are Presbyterians who have long felt, however, that our practice of electing a Moderator for one year has disadvantages regarding a public profile. People do not get to know a Moderator or a Methodist President until half-way through the term of office. That practice is not likely to change.

'The flip side of this is that it appeared sometimes that Robin Eames was speaking on behalf of the Protestant community and not just the Church of Ireland. That was not Robin's fault, it was simply the way the system worked. The wider public, especially in Britain, came to know and recognise Archbishop Eames and Cardinal Daly but not the others. So Robin was sometimes portrayed as the Protestant spokesman, which is not what he was or ever claimed to be.'

Eames was sensitive to the situation. He says, 'There were several factors involved. As a church leader I was there the longest, I knew the media personally, I felt at ease in front of a camera or microphone, and the media tended to seek me out when I would have preferred one of the others to speak.'

He was always conscious that he might be interpreted as the 'Protestant' spokesman. He says, however, 'When I did speak I was basing my comments on what I took to be the views of my own people in the Church of Ireland. There was also the problem that international journalists and those from the Irish Republic tended to seek the views of the two Armagh Primates. However, I was always sensitive to the feelings of my colleagues from the Reformed traditions.'

The Reverend Dr Edmund Mawhinney, a former Methodist President and Joint Secretary of the Four Church Leaders group, makes the point that Eames was always open to new ideas from successive Presbyterian Moderators or Methodist Presidents, 'even though he had been the Anglican Primate for a long time and had faced some of the issues previously. Robin provided steadiness, wisdom and useful insights. The tenure of his office, his experience and his personal qualities meant that his point of view had to be respected.'

The tensions between the churches were not always evident on the surface, but at times they simmered underneath. Eames himself reflected on some of the misunderstandings and tensions at grass-roots level in Armagh. 'On the whole there were always excellent relations between the Church of Ireland and Roman Catholic clergy. In some cases, however, Presbyterian clergy did not welcome contact with their Church of Ireland neighbours. This was partly because some Presbyterians distrusted ecumenism, and partly because there was some feeling that Armagh was referred to as "the ecclesiastical capital of Ireland" – meaning only the Church of Ireland and the Roman Catholics.'

There was no such feeling at leadership level, but over the years the role of the Four Church Leaders group changed, because of the developing political situation – a point made by the Very Reverend Samuel Hutchinson, a former Moderator and Clerk of the General Assembly. One of his ex-officio roles as Clerk was to act as Joint Secretary to the Four Church Leaders. He recalls, 'Particularly in the Eighties when there was a political vacuum in Northern Ireland, the churches had an extra role, and became a kind of subsidiary parliament. At one stage after the Anglo-Irish Agreement, the Unionists were not speaking to the Government, and the Presbyterian Church became virtually a postbox where messages were sent back and forward between them.'

During the political vacuum the Four Church Leaders had a special role. 'Though Cardinal Daly did not take a high profile, he was a key player, as was Robin Eames. Because of the structure of the churches, Cahal had great authority, and when he spoke, he spoke for the entire Roman Catholic Church in Ireland. Others like myself from the Reformed tradition might have had to consult or to inform one or other of our leading church committees.

'Robin Eames was a man of outstanding ability who later on became the number one Protestant church leader in Ireland and, within the Anglican Communion, he became probably second only to the Archbishop of Canterbury. During the period of the political vacuum in Northern Ireland, Robin's profile was high in his own right but it was enhanced to some degree by the presence of Cahal Daly as one of the Four Church Leaders. The authorities were always anxious to have Cahal on board. Northern Ireland politics is like an onion – once you unpeel a layer, there is another one and another one. People who deal with Northern Ireland have to be aware of that.'

Eames, he feels, made a positive contribution to inter-church relations. 'Ecumenism can be an odd activity. The "fanatical" ecumenists do not always make the most progress, because they tend to get some people's backs up. Real progress is often achieved by the person who moves quietly and with sensitivity, and Robin was like that. Without meaning to diminish the role of any of the church leaders with whom I have worked, I believe that Robin Eames and Cahal Daly were two exceptional Primates in the right place at the right time. If they had been in office together thirty years earlier, things might have been very different for Northern Ireland.'

Since the 1998 Good Friday Agreement the political situation has altered significantly. Despite the lack of political trust on all sides, the violence has lessened significantly. Hutchinson says, 'With the diminished level of violence and an imperfect political settlement the Churches have had to adapt to a changing role. They have not been given the same degree of attention compared to the years of the political vacuum. They are now more free to try to be "the Church" but this has its own considerable challenges.'

The changing political order and the new challenge facing the churches is noted by Cardinal Daly's successor Archbishop Sean Brady, who spent his earlier career as a schoolmaster in County Cavan, just across the Irish border, and later in the Irish College in Rome before returning briefly to Cavan as a parish priest. He is a thoughtful and modest man who keeps a low profile compared to his predecessors – though it could be argued that the changing political circumstances have given all church leaders a lower profile.

The two Archbishops have been maintaining the close working relationships in Armagh, as in the past, but they are keenly aware that the challenges are different. Archbishop Brady says, 'When I was appointed as Coadjutor Archbishop in 1995, one of the first people to welcome me was Archbishop Eames. I particularly valued his friendship as I knew that our paths would cross many times over the years. Since then we have come to know each other well and we have become good friends.'

Archbishop Brady says, 'Some of the main challenges today include healing the hurts and helping to "bed down" the peace process. All of us are in a new post-Troubles dimension. We all face the challenge of preaching the good news in a society that is daily becoming more secularised and which is relegating Christ to the margins.'

Reconciliation remains one of the major priorities. Archbishop Brady says, 'A recent consultation on the churches' contribution to improving relations in Northern Ireland agreed that reconciliation of this divided society is the single greatest priority for our ministry at this time. Archbishop Eames and I are both aware that we have an important role to play in our churches in contributing to this. Relations between the two traditions really do matter, and attention must be given to them.'

Robin Eames, for his part, found Sean Brady 'a quiet, sincere and humble man who appeared deeply conscious of his new responsibilities and of the need to become accustomed to Northern Ireland. In conversation he made no secret of his initial lack of knowledge of the Province, but he listened intently as we talked over the problems. My time with him on the opposite hill has been a period of trust, mutual respect and warmth when I have presumed to feel that I could assist him as he came to terms with his new appointment.'

One of the major problems for Archbishop Brady and the Roman Catholic Church in Ireland, as elsewhere, was the growing number of cases involving the sexual abuse of children by priests. Eames says, 'My prayers were with him as he dealt with circumstances of these cases, and the resultant media coverage and public speculation. None of us in our generation within the church was trained or prepared to encounter this. It must have caused Sean Brady great pain and distress. I will long recall his dignity "under fire". On top of all such episodes came the speculation that a priest had been involved with the Claudy bombing – and again Sean had to go public. He did so with growing confidence and with great dignity.'

Eames shared Brady's views about the challenges of the secular society. He says, 'During the worst of the Troubles the churches in Northern Ireland were a kind of social ambulance service – burying the dead, comforting the relatives, appealing for peace and saying instinctively what we knew had to be said.'

Now the situation is much more difficult. 'During the worst of the violence we learned to apply "the theology of the instantaneous" but I believe that the churches will find it much more difficult to work within the peace process. Now there are grey areas, and vast moral issues, within the peace process, and the churches are trying to grapple with them. It may take a new generation of church leaders who have not developed their work through the worst of the violence to address the new situation properly. They will be able to start with a clean sheet and with a new set of ethics and principles.'

Eames did not support the calls from many different groups inside and outside Northern Ireland for a South African style Truth and Reconciliation Commission. He says, 'While sympathising with the objectives of many of those who called for such a Commission, I believed that it would have opened up more wounds than it would have healed.'

Overall, it is difficult to assess precisely what Robin Eames and his senior colleagues in all the churches have achieved with regard to ecumenism. In Northern Ireland there are still considerable obstacles to be overcome and many people, particularly conservative Protestants, remain hostile or indifferent to the vision of better inter-church relations.

Others believe that while the ecumenists cannot point to an outstanding success in a difficult area of outreach, the situation would have been much worse without them. Many members of different churches are now meeting regularly, whereas this would simply not have happened over a generation ago.

Eames, while remaining a committed and pragmatic ecumenist throughout his ministry, retains a hardheaded attitude to the achievements so far. Speaking at the Galway Summer School in July 2002 he said, 'Those who firmly believe in the structures of ecumenism need to be aware that they are regarded by many within the Reformed tradition in Ireland as being out of step, or as being unrelated to reality. We have come a long way from the first Ballymascanlon inter-church talks, but we have yet to convince a majority that realistic and visionary ecumenism has a real contribution to make to healing the wounds in Northern Ireland.'

10

The Valley of Death

Throughout Robin Eames' long ministry the shadow of death loomed large. Like all clergy he had to deal with bereavement in his parish, but as a bishop and an archbishop his ministry to the bereaved was both private and public.

He was called upon to conduct scores of funerals for the victims of violence, and particularly for the police and the army and their reserves. He had to try to provide comfort and hope for those in their very public and private grief and despair, and he also had to find words of condemnation and yet of strength at the funerals to help heal the wounds of the entire community.

These messages were preached invariably in the full glare of the media, and on highly emotional occasions. It was no easy task, and it taxed Robin Eames heavily. Each time he found the right words, but he never lost his public demeanour or compassion, dignity and authority. Years later, however, when he talked privately about these harrowing times, he shed tears. He recalled, 'During the worst years of the violence, my parochial clergy were on the front line. They were subject to the attitudes of their people, while at the same time recognising the Christian call to ministry to people who were frightened, uncertain and angry. I had great sympathy for their position, and kept in constant touch with them to offer support and understanding.'

They all had to face deep theological questions – including the meaning of suffering and concepts of justice, and their identity with other human beings. He says, 'It was not always easy to preach forgiveness or reconciliation when feelings ran so deep. I constantly urged pastoral contact between the clergy and their people.'

He often phoned rectors to ask how they were. 'Several of

my clergy reached despair after atrocities or assassinations. I arranged for some to get away for a while in England, for a break. Some even needed medical aid for their lives as they battled with the tensions.'

Eames also urged his clergy to keep in contact with their Roman Catholic counterparts, particularly where community tensions were high. He recalls, 'When Roman Catholics were murdered it was important for Church of Ireland clergy to make contact with their priests and to tell them, "We know what you are going through." In some cases the paramilitary trappings at the Roman Catholic funerals of IRA "volunteers" caused deep hurt and misunderstanding among Protestants. People asked me, "Does this mean that the Catholic Church supports the Provisional IRA?" '

He felt that Protestants had to try to understand some of the pressures that the local Roman Catholic clergy were under. He says, 'I paid tribute time and again to those Roman Catholic clergy who attended the funerals of the Protestant victims of violence. At a time of heightened emotion their presence could have been misrepresented or misunderstood, and it took courage to be there.'

The newspaper files are full of references to Robin Eames at the funerals of the victims of violence. In the Belfast *News Letter* of 4 March 1985, there is a typical picture of Eames, then Bishop of Down and Dromore, walking grim-faced in front of the cortège of murdered RUC Sergeant John Thomas Dowd. His coffin was draped with the Union flag and his policeman's hat was resting on the top.

Sergeant Dowd was one of nine police officers who died when a Provisional IRA 40lb mortar bomb ripped through a mobile RUC canteen in Newry. The blast injured thirty-seven other people, including twenty-five civilians. It was the biggest loss of police lives during the Troubles, and the attack was widely condemned. The Prime Minister Margaret Thatcher sent a message of condolence to the RUC. The then Chief Constable Sir John Hermon later underlined the traumatic impact in human terms of the RUC loss by recalling how the deaths had had a lasting effect on him. He was so moved that he had kept open in his office desk a police magazine with pictures of the nine dead officers, which he brought back to his study at home when he retired.

Archbishop Eames conducted the funerals of several of the dead, including Sergeant Dowd and Woman Constable Rosemary McGookin. He said later, 'Those were among the toughest of them all. Like a lot of the funerals, the atmosphere was grim and determined, but marvellously composed. You would have had a heart of stone if you had not been affected.'

At the funeral of Sergeant Dowd in the presence of a large congregation of family, former colleagues and friends and community representatives, Robin Eames said:

> We are burying our dead once more when our community is at a crossroads. The crossroads poses a simple question – which way do you want to go? Is it to be the way of violence, destruction, intimidation and the path of fear, or is it to take our own faith and align ourselves with men like John Dowd, who stand in the thin line between us and anarchy?

At the funeral of Policewoman Rosemary McGookin, Robin Eames described her as a 'heroine'. He said, 'Rosemary McGookin would have been horrified if she had ever thought that we would think of her in these terms. She would have said she was an ordinary girl, doing an ordinary job ... with ordinary hopes and fears.'

Referring to the wider implications of the terrorists' attack on the police station, he said:

> Let the world note that what is happening here is far removed from the results the terrorists seek to achieve. The resilience, the courage, the well of human compassion, the determination to lead normal lives, far from being destroyed by terrorism, are strengthened. The determination not to be forced into solutions to our problems at the point of a gun or in a bomb blitz is stronger than ever.

This was the public face of Robin Eames, who, as so many times before and afterwards, was paying tribute to the dead, bringing comfort to the bereaved and giving a lead to the community. Behind the scenes, however, there was a personal cost that the public did not see.

Reflecting on those dark days he says, 'Over the years I came to apply what I termed "the one-hour test". When the news of a killing came over the airwaves, I knew that the "test" had started. If I did not get a phone call within an hour, the chances were that the dead person was not one of my flock. If it was, I nearly always heard within the hour, and I had my clergy geared up for this.'

The reaction was the same in every case. He recalls, 'It was a case of "drop everything and go".' Sometimes he went direct to meet the local clergy, and he would be taken to the victim's house. On one occasion, when he was in Derry, he had to break the news to the widow of a young police reservist who had been blown up by a bomb exploding under his security vehicle.

Robin Eames will never forget it. He says, 'I remember going to the gate of the house and praying, "Please God tell me what to say." There was nobody about, but I could see a child's plastic bike in the garden. I walked up the path with a heavy heart and paused before knocking on the door. I could hear the rustle of a young woman coming into the hall.'

As she opened the door, Robin Eames recognised her, because he had seen her at parish functions. 'She looked me straight in the eye and said, "It's bad news, isn't it?" I said, "Can I come in?" and she ushered me into her home. It was a situation where you didn't know what you were going to say, or how to find the right words. I always said to my clergy, "When you are with grieving relatives, they may forget what you said, but they will remember that you were there."

'I learned that in this situation, because the young policeman's widow was able to say to me years later, "I remember, you were the one who told me." I could not remember exactly what I had said, but the important point was the fact that I was there. If the Church is to have a relevance in this new post-Christian era, the pastoral role is more important than the big public statement.'

Some of the funerals were particularly harrowing. 'I remember one occasion when we were burying a policeman and I was standing by the graveside as they lowered his coffin. Suddenly I felt a tugging on my stole. I looked down and I saw the face of the policeman's 4-year-old daughter. She looked up at me and asked, "What are they doing with my Daddy?" That question from an innocent child has haunted me ever since.'

The sheer number of such funerals took its toll over the years. 'It became easier to the extent that you knew what you were going to face in terms of the funeral service and the arrangements you made with the rector and with the police and the army themselves. It became easier in that the more funerals you had to conduct, the more you could do it. But it became harder each time because it burdened you that bit more. I often thought of the lines from John Donne, "No man is an *Island*, entire of itself ... any man's death diminishes *me*, because I am involved in *Mankind*; And therefore never send to know for whom the *bell* tolls; It tolls for *thee*." '[1]

Each time, Robin Eames had to prepare himself for the funeral service. 'Sometimes I would go to the church the day before on my own, just to absorb the atmosphere. I would see in my mind's eye what would happen the next day – the long snake of the funeral procession coming up the country road towards the church, the solemn music of the police band, the medals gleaming in the sunshine, the crunch of the boots on the gravel, the rows of grieving faces of the relatives and friends, the rows of staring faces of the locals in the church, the political and community representatives, often the same people as last time, but every funeral was different.'

Each time in his address there would be several paragraphs for the media, but he never read out a sermon in full. He says, 'That was not my style. I spoke from notes, and I tried to speak from the heart. The role of the pastor was terribly important, whatever the circumstances and whatever the background.'

There was never an easy way of breaking the bad news. On one occasion the Archbishop went to the house of a Northern Ireland policeman after the news came in of an RAF Chinook helicopter crash on the Mull of Kintyre on 2 June 1994 with heavy loss of life. All twenty-nine passengers and crew were killed, including ten senior RUC Special Branch officers, six MI5 officers and nine Army intelligence officers. Apart from the tragic loss of human life, it was a disastrous loss for the security forces.

Robin Eames was in the home of a missing senior police officer with his wife and colleagues, and they were waiting to hear if there were any survivors. Eventually there was a phone call, and one of the senior policemen looked at him and said, 'Perhaps you should take it.' Eames understood why he had been asked to do so, and he nodded in agreement. He says, 'I left the room and took the phone call. To my horror I was told that there were no survivors. I had to go back into that room and to tell them all, including the policeman's widow who was a lovely woman.

'How do you prepare people for that? I knew the widow and had known her late husband well, so I realised that I did not have to be evasive with the truth. It was stark, but how do you come to terms with handling people in a situation where the news is as bad as it can be? How do you do it?'

Eames' advice to other people in such daunting circumstances is, 'Tell them the truth, because the way you tell them is so important. From a pastoral point of view you should never take a person down a line that you are going to have to contradict totally, but you can take them down a line and let the truth dawn on them.'

If he has bad news to impart, he will think about how to approach it for as long as he can. He says, 'Over the years, one gets an appreciation of how the other person is reacting. There comes a point when the truth has to be conveyed, for the other person is going to have to live with it long after you have gone out of his or her life. What you want them to remember is how they have heard it.'

When Robin Eames' father died he had a sixth sense at what might have happened, because he knew that he had heart trouble. He says, 'I knew also that the police would not have come to bring me out of a courtroom unless something terrible had happened. The doctor took me to the morgue to identify my dead father, and that kept coming back to me in later life. When you have had to do that, you know what it is going to be like for others. I see everything in terms of pastoral theology. That is the key to my ministry.'

He believes it is important that the clergy's contribution to people's lives is different from that of other professions. 'When you go to your GP you expect to get advice and medical help. If you consult your solicitor you expect legal advice. When you talk to your cleric you expect him or her not to be worldly in the sense of saying what your doctor or solicitor or dentist will say.' Nevertheless, people expect their minister to be in touch with the realities, to know the facts of life. Eames says, 'They also expect, without being shocked or surprised, to hear him or her talking about the Almighty and the deeper side of emotion and experience of life.

'I share this with curates, but I will not give them a sheet of paper with a few bullet points. No two situations are the same, but I will try to advise younger clergy on the frame of mind to adopt when talking to people in this kind of situation, and also to learn to recognise the cut-off point. Otherwise, if you are not careful, you will end up acting as a pillar for people, and you may end up protecting them from something which they have to face themselves.'

One of the great temptations of clergy life, Eames believes, is the danger of gossiping. 'I have become really angry when I have caught clergy making little of serious things they have been told in confidence. That should never happen. They have been trusted by someone, and that trust is sacred.'

People may confide in their clergy, who in turn must demonstrate a transparent integrity. 'The further up the line you go, the more serious are the things you are told, and the more dangerous are the implications of breaking that trust, because more people might be affected by your breach of confidence.

'A politician may say to me, "This is what I think I should say and do, though I am not sure about it – would you hear me out?" If I say, "Yes," and I listen to him or her, but nothing is done in the end, he or she knows that I know what might have been done or said.'

Sometimes a particular confession or something told in confidence is not easy to listen to. Eames recalls, 'Years ago a well-known man in Northern Ireland, who has since passed on, said to me that he had to unburden himself to someone before he died. I found it hard to listen to his story which was really dreadful. He said, "I don't know how long I have to live, but I cannot go to my grave without confessing what I have done. And it has to be someone like you who, I would assume, lives by a certain rule of life."

'He told me the story and then he asked, "What is the Christian teaching on forgiveness?" I was plunged into a whole discussion on this very deep subject, and I did my best to explain forgiveness to him. I hope that I was able to bring him some insight and comfort, but I never talked about it to anyone else and I believe that he took that conversation to his grave with him. As a minister you are often surrounded by people, but there are things which you cannot and must not divulge. In this context I think of the inscription on the

135

tomb of the Unknown Soldier – "Known Only Unto God".'

One major challenge Robin Eames faced relatively early on as Archbishop of Armagh was to deal with the aftermath of the horrific Remembrance Day bombing at the War Memorial in Enniskillen on 8 November 1987. A Provisional IRA bomb hidden in a disused building had been intended to kill and maim the security forces, but it exploded without warning and murdered eleven innocent people around the Cenotaph who were waiting for the Remembrance Day Service to begin.

The explosion wounded scores of other civilians, some of them seriously. It was one of the worst atrocities of the Troubles, and Robin Eames was caught up in it almost from the start. He was in Enniskillen that day to preach at the Remembrance Day Service in the Church of Ireland cathedral, but he made his way to the local Erne Hospital to try to bring comfort to the distressed families and relatives of the dead and wounded. He told a newspaper journalist later that evening, 'The grief I witnessed was so private that I do not even want to talk about it. I pray never to see things like that again. Words fail to describe it.'

The Remembrance Day explosion at the Enniskillen Cenotaph will be etched in the public consciousness of the people of Northern Ireland for many years to come, in the way that the memories of earlier atrocities in Anglo-Irish history live on from generation to generation. There was something particularly heinous about an IRA bomb exploding beside civilians waiting to take part in a service to remember the dead of two World Wars and other conflicts. It was literally an intrusion upon sacred ground.

Condemnation of the atrocity was swift and widespread. In a statement, the Queen said, 'I was deeply shocked to hear of the atrocity which took place in Enniskillen today and of the innocent victims who were sharing in the nation's remembrance. My heartfelt sympathy goes out to the bereaved and the injured in their distress.'

The Prime Minister Margaret Thatcher described the explosion as 'barbaric'. She said, 'Every civilised nation honours and respects its dead. To take advantage of people assembled in that way was really a desecration.' The Irish Prime Minister Charles Haughey spoke of his deep horror at the bombing. The United States President Ronald Reagan expressed the 'revulsion' of the American people. Pope John Paul II professed 'profound shock'.

Amid the carnage, suffering and death there were many acts of heroism and selflessness. Ambulance drivers, hospital staff at all levels, the security forces and members of the public did all they could to help the injured and the families of the bereaved. Civilians and others tore frantically with their hands at the rubble of the bombed building which had trapped the innocent bystanders at the Cenotaph. It was a scene of utter devastation.

There were many heroes, but one man who later attracted worldwide attention was a local draper called Gordon Wilson. He and his daughter Marie were caught up in the explosion and were buried in the rubble. Afterwards Gordon spoke movingly about how he held Marie's hand beneath the rubble and how he tried to reassure her, although he was injured himself. Several times he asked her if she was all right. She assured him that she was. Then her voice changed. Gordon said later, 'She sounded different. She held my hand tightly and gripped me as hard as she could. She said, "Daddy, I love you very much." Those were her exact words to me, and those were the last words I ever heard her say.'[2]

Some time later Marie Wilson died in the Erne Hospital's Intensive Care Unit while her mother Joan, brother Peter and sister Julie Anne looked on. Afterwards Joan had the terrible task of breaking the news to Gordon who was downstairs in the Casualty Department with a dislocated shoulder. Shortly afterwards the Wilson family made their way home with breaking hearts.

Later that night Gordon Wilson was asked for a comment by a BBC journalist, and he spoke spontaneously. His words became one of the most moving broadcasts on record. He said:

> I bear no ill-will. I bear no grudge. Dirty sort of talk is not going to bring her back to life. Don't ask me please, for a purpose. I don't have a purpose. I don't have an answer. But I know there has to be a plan . . . It's part of a greater plan, and God is good. And we shall meet again.[3]

The events of that terrible day had pitchforked Robin into scenes of unbelievable suffering and carnage. The then Bishop of Clogher the Right Reverend Brian Hannon had invited him to preach in the cathedral, and the Archbishop left Armagh early to avoid traffic congestion in the town. Everything appeared normal as he drove towards the cathedral. Some people had gathered already at the War Memorial, and at the cathedral itself he met some of the early arrivals for the service. He talked to a 'Greenfinch' (a female member of the part-time Ulster Defence Regiment) and she told him that her husband was on duty at the War Memorial.

Eames recalls, 'A little later we all heard an explosion in the distance. A brown, grey cloud rose above the rooftops. No one knew immediately what had happened, but the first news came through when a member of the Ulster Defence Regiment ran towards the cathedral out of breath, with his uniform covered in dust. He told us, "There's been a bomb. God knows how many people have been killed." '

There was a shocked silence, and then frantic activity. People were running off to find out more. It quickly became obvious that there would be no Remembrance Day parade coming up the hill to the cathedral, and that there would be no service. A little later on Robin Eames had to tell the Greenfinch soldier to whom he had been talking that he believed her husband was among the dead.

When the cathedral service was cancelled Eames and Hannon made their way to the Erne Hospital. Eames recalls, 'I saw ambulances and private cars ferrying the injured to the Accident and Emergency Department. As the news spread, nurses and doctors were coming in from church services and local golf courses. Suddenly a small local hospital became the focus of world attention as the media arrived.'

The corridors were packed with people, and hospital trolleys with patients were being lined up for attention. Doctors were examining casualties and making decisions about surgery and other medical procedures. Eames says, 'Chaos was the order of the day, but my admiration for the staff of the hospital and their loyalty had no bounds. Hospital chaplains appeared, and I also did what I could to help. Names were being scribbled frantically on paper as people searched desperately for their loved ones.'

Robin Eames met Gordon Wilson, who was lying on a hospital trolley. 'I vaguely knew Gordon from the past. He grasped my hand and asked me, "Do you know anything about Marie?" I replied, "No, but I'll try to find out." No one appeared to know anything about her. Gordon murmured, "She was

holding my hand, but I don't know what happened then."
Gordon's wife Joan appeared, and we talked together.'

All the time people were calling out names, and staff, clergy
and the police were attempting to put together lists of names.
Relatives were arriving by the moment, each anxiously trying to
find out what had happened to loved ones. There were cups of
tea and words of sympathy. On more than one occasion Eames
was asked, 'Archbishop, would you say a prayer with me?' I
always said, 'Of course I will.'

For most of the day he stayed at the hospital. 'I offered what
comfort I could, and I prayed with people in distress. As the
hours passed, the routine of the hospital took over, and
complete lists of names were made. The staff worked long
hours, and their spirit was marvellous. The clergy from all
denominations worked together, and a person's religion was of
no importance – only that they were human beings in need.
Not for the first or last time my admiration for the ability of
the Ulster people to cope was uppermost in my mind.'

Looking back years later Robin Eames says that his overall
impression was one of the horror of what happened on a
peaceful Sunday in a beautiful part of Northern Ireland. 'I
recall also the magnificent way in which ordinary people faced
up to the horror and the shock – and I remember the faces of
dust, blood and pain. Throughout the Troubles I have a clear
and very personal regard for the way in which people with no
previous claim to courage or attention rose to meet the
demands of the moment. All divisions of religion or politics
are forgotten, and human relationships emerge where the need
demands. This is what happened in Enniskillen and, sadly, the
same would happen in other places later on.'

The Remembrance Day Service which was abruptly cancelled
on the day of the explosion was rearranged for Sunday 22
November. It was attended by the Prime Minister Margaret
Thatcher, who earlier, in driving rain, had laid a wreath at the
Enniskillen Cenotaph.

The Girls' and Boys' Brigades, Guides and Scouts braved
biting winds and heavy rain to parade to the Cenotaph with
members of the Royal British Legion, the Royal Irish Rangers
and the 4th (Co. Fermanagh) Battalion of the Ulster Defence
Regiment. Most of the same people had been assembling on
8 November to make the same journey to the Cenotaph.

Ballyreagh Silver Band, some of whose members were injured in the explosion, led the marchers.

St McCartin's Cathedral was packed with community and political leaders as the Remembrance Day parade made its way to the church. Hundreds of members of the Royal British Legion associations throughout the United Kingdom were present, and many other people had travelled especially from Britain and the Irish Republic to be there. Significantly, members of the families of the bereaved and injured, and some of the survivors of the Enniskillen bomb, were present, including Gordon Wilson and his wife Joan and the family. The service was televised live throughout the United Kingdom on both the BBC and ITV, and it was also relayed to churches and church halls throughout Enniskillen.

Robin Eames, who preached the sermon, faced a formidable task at such a time and in such an atmosphere. Once again he had to find the right words to condemn the violence, and also to offer comfort and hope. He took as his text the words from Matthew 5:9: 'Blessed are the peacemakers: for they shall be called the children of God.'

He referred to the dead of the two World Wars and the sacrifice of so many in Flanders, the Somme, Normandy, North Africa and the Pacific. He also referred to the suffering in the notorious Changi Prison in Singapore, which he had visited only a few months previously.

He said that the bullet and the bomb in Northern Ireland had produced sadness and loss of life which must be a constant reminder to society that human nature still contains those ingredients for destruction some would want to forget. He continued:

> Recent events in this town remind us that when we become so immune to violence that we fail to react we shall have lost the battle for civilised values. It is only when the voices of those calling for the rejection of violence, calling for greater human understanding and reconciliation, for a better world, become louder than those advocating the bullet and the bomb, only then will the world really come to understand the evil nature of terrorism.

He said that the world had seen in the past few weeks how strong had been the voices of compassion and humanity.

140

Few will ever forget the words of those who suffered so much here a fortnight ago. Out of the darkness of tragedy the world heard the voices of courage. Out of the potential for bitterness came so much that spoke of Christian love. Out of the rubble came a sign of hope.

The Archbishop said that out of the destruction of a world at war, history had recorded so many examples of good out of evil.

Out of our remembrance, out of our memories must shine brighter than ever the Christian hope and certainty that good comes out of evil, that decency overcomes hatred and that life and love are far stronger than death and division. How well I remember the words of a victim of the Enniskillen bombing on a trolley: 'God is here also.'

Robin Eames said that there had been many moments in Northern Ireland when people talked about 'turning points', yet the problems continued.

Over the past few weeks we have asked, 'Is Enniskillen the turning point? Has it really changed the course of events and the way people think?' Time alone will tell. Churchmen, governments, politicians, community leaders, ordinary people, young and old cannot live on as though Enniskillen did not happen. Enniskillen must be an important part in the process of peace. Let none of us forget under God it is the task of the peacemaker to pick up the lessons of the past and go on. It is the task of the Christian to be in the forefront of the search for peace.

His sermon was well received by his listeners, including the Prime Minister. It is said that Eames made such an impact on Mrs Thatcher that she would remember his name for future reference.

Eames said later that he was unaware until the last moment that Mrs Thatcher would be present. 'She sat through the service with a set expression, but afterwards she spoke to me with great feeling about the atrocity. She said, "It should never have happened. It must never be allowed to happen again." She was introduced to relatives of those killed and injured in the bombing, and also the police and the Ulster Defence Regiment.

I saw in their faces such dignity and quiet determination which I often found in ordinary, decent Ulster people. I also paid tribute to the local Roman Catholic clergy in Enniskillen who expressed sympathy to the community.'

The Church of Ireland columnist Cromlyn wrote: 'The sermon of the Archbishop was unforgettably impressive, both in content and delivery. How fortunate we have been to have found a leadership so matched to the hour.'

In the vast audience that shared in the service and watched the broadcast all over the British Isles there was one woman for whom the day had a special poignancy. Mrs Joan Wilson, the mother of the 20-year-old nurse Marie who had died as a result of the explosion found the service and Robin Eames' sermon greatly uplifting. She recalled afterwards how much she had dreaded going to the service, with her husband Gordon, daughter Julie Anne and son Peter and his wife Ingrid.

'I was nervous, sad and apprehensive, and the events of 8 November were going through my mind. The beautiful music including pieces by Telemann, J. S. Bach, Elgar, Vaughan Williams and Benjamin Britten were played by a very talented local organist W. J. McBride, and they began to soothe me. I had been listening to Elgar's "Nimrod" in our church on 8 November when the bomb went off.

'The first hymn, "Praise My Soul the King of Heaven", was written by Henry Francis Lyte who had been educated at Portora Royal School in Enniskillen. I found it uplifting, but I fought back tears during the Last Post, and during the two minutes silence my head was whirring with memories. The words "We will remember them" were spoken firmly, and inwardly I said to myself, "Can we ever forget them?" ' The Reveille sounded a note of triumph, but Joan Wilson remembers crying quietly through the prayers.

She was grateful that Archbishop Eames was preaching the sermon. 'Gordon had greatly valued his words to him in the Erne Hospital on that awful day. No one was better qualified to preach to us because Archbishop Eames had witnessed the whole scene. He had visited the hospital and shared the distress.'

She remembers being deeply impressed when he told the story of Changi Prison in Singapore. She says, 'I snapped out of my own grief and pity and drank in the story which he told with great meaning and depth of feeling. It made me aware of pain and cruelty worldwide and helped to put my grief in perspective. I rose and left the service with a steadier step, a resolve to strive in God's strength, to look for a brighter future, and one day win the crown of life. I had the great assurance that God comforts the mourning.'

She was impressed by the Archbishop's words, and also by the fact that he had never forgotten the events of 8 November 1987. She says, 'After Gordon died on 27 June 1995, Robin Eames sent me a beautiful letter of sympathy. I have kept it and I often read it to help me on my way.'

The former Church of Ireland Bishop of Limerick, the Right Reverend Edward Darling and a close colleague and friend of Robin Eames, talks privately of meeting Gordon Wilson in the city some years earlier. He said, 'Gordon said to me, "On the first Christmas Eve after Marie died our phone rang at 9 p.m. and it was Robin Eames on the line telling me that he knew it was going to be a very difficult Christmas for our family and that Joan and I were in his thoughts and prayers. I will never forget your Primate for that. It meant so much to me." '

The point of this poignant story is not only the phone call from a busy archbishop to the grieving Wilson family on Christmas Eve, but also the fact that Eames himself never mentioned it to anyone else. Such stories of quiet compassion are all the more impressive when they are related by others, and not by the person who shows such Christian concern for those in need.

During all the years of the Troubles, when Robin Eames played a major role in the public eye, there is no doubt that at heart he was essentially a pastor. He says himself, 'I was always happiest in pastoral situations. Listening to, talking with, praying with, helping to make decisions was and is for me the greatest privilege of my ministry. Behind the headlines of leadership this remains true of me. Often in situations where I least expected it a well-known public figure would say, "Please pray with me", and I always considered it a privilege to do so. 'You drink tea with people, you suffer with them, you cry with them, and I know no other way in which to make the gospel relevant. That's far more important to me than a pulpit or sanctuary, or the robes of Canterbury. Being a pastor, that's what matters most.'

11

Cross-Border Politics

Given the harrowing circumstances of the many bereavements in which Robin Eames shared as a pastor and church leader, it is not surprising that one of his constant concerns was to use every means possible to try to break the political deadlock in Northern Ireland which was claiming so many lives and which was plunging so many families into despair. It has been said rightly that there is hardly a family in Northern Ireland that has not been touched directly or indirectly by the suffering during the decades of the Troubles.

From early on in his career, Robin Eames was involved in many situations that had a close connection with politics. His training as an academic lawyer gave him a sharp intellectual insight into complex matters, and his natural fascination with politics, added to his consummate ability in handling people, would have equipped him for a significant political career in Northern Ireland, and perhaps even at Westminster, if he had chosen to follow that path.

As Rector of St Dorothea's in Belfast he had experienced the sharp end of sectarian bigotry as he dealt with the self-appointed vigilantes who took it on themselves to 'protect' the Protestant community. When he became Bishop of Derry and Raphoe his speeches concerning the future of Ireland North and South drew comments from leading politicians, newspapers and other commentators across the island.

As Bishop of Down and Dromore, based in Belfast, he continued to make political statements which drew widespread attention. For example, in his synod address in June 1983 he warmly endorsed the remarks of his Roman Catholic counterpart Bishop Cahal Daly over the latter's recent critical remarks about Sinn Fein.

Eames said that when Daly confronted evil 'with the gospel' he deserved the prayerful support of all Christian communities. He added, 'Whether they realise it or not, the Protestant community throughout the Province has as much to lose as their Roman Catholic neighbours if paramilitary organisations or their paramilitary fellow-travellers win the battle for the hearts and minds of West Belfast.' West Belfast was one of the heartlands of the Provisional IRA and Sinn Fein, its political wing. The distinction between both was blurred in later years by Unionist politicians who simply described them as 'Provisional Sinn Fein/IRA'.

Eames referred to the 'corrosive' nature of militant Irish Republicanism, symbolised by the Provisional IRA and by the smaller, but if anything more extreme, Irish Nationalist Liberation Army (INLA). 'The double-thinking, so often apparent in their statements, their efforts to excuse or to justify murder by mistake, intimidation and not least the poisoning effects of their influence on young people – all these factors are part of their web of self-destruction which can affect the community from which they come and which they claim to represent even more than the community they seek to attack.'

Though Eames' language was invariably more diplomatic and measured than that of a number of the politicians, it cannot be said that he shirked commenting on the major issues of his time. Perhaps the fact that he did not set out to be controversial blurred to some extent the cutting edge of what he had to say, in a period where extreme statements attracted more headlines than those couched in more moderate, though perceptive, language. However, the authority of Eames' approach, his intellectual integrity and his spiritual mission gained him respect and a hearing from those who might not otherwise have listened to a senior representative of the Protestant community.

When he became Archbishop of Armagh he continued his bridge-building work not only in public but also behind the scenes. One of his priorities was to foster better North–South relations in an island where Belfast and Dublin were politically light years and not just miles apart. There were individual exceptions, of course, but the stereotypes prevailed. Many Northern Unionists continued to look down on the Republic as a theocracy – a more popular expression was 'priest-ridden'

– while many in the Republic looked on the North as a bastion of bigoted Unionism where Catholics remained downtrodden until the first stirrings of the civil rights movement in the early 1960s.

Eames reflects, 'As Primate, I found that many doors in Government and politics were opened to me. I had long been convinced that such opportunities should be seized on behalf of the Church, but only in attempts to build peace and understanding as a contribution to a more stable future as a whole.' He was acutely aware that the normal political processes both in the North and the South had been curtailed by the constitutional issue of Northern Ireland remaining part of the United Kingdom, and by the widespread ignorance among Southern politicians about life in the North.

'The lack of sensitivity towards Northern Protestants' fears on the part of Southern Governments amazed me, and the Orange–Green mentality on both sides was a genuine obstacle to building the sort of peaceful, genuine and reconciled co-existence which would benefit both parts of Ireland. After one speech by Charles Haughey, then Taioseach (Prime Minister) of the Irish Republic, in which he castigated Northern Unionists, he asked me, "Why do the Unionists not talk to me?" I replied, "Are you surprised when they hear some of the things you say?" '

Charles Haughey also faced the genuine difficulty that Northern Unionists regarded him with suspicion and hostility. When the Northern Ireland Troubles erupted in earnest in the late 1960s, both the London and Dublin Governments were unprepared for the resultant upheaval. In the Republic the then Taioseach Jack Lynch wisely decided against intervention in the North following the outbreak of sustained violence in 1969, but decided to establish field hospitals and refugee camps south of the border to help Catholics driven from their homes in the North.

Haughey, then Irish Finance Minister, and others were at the centre of gun-running allegations in 1970. In May of that year Lynch dismissed Haughey who was later charged with conspiracy to import arms and ammunition illegally. However, he and three others were acquitted, and Haughey returned to the Irish Government several years later as Health Minister. To complete a remarkable political comeback he succeeded Lynch as Taioseach and Fianna Fail leader in 1979, albeit with a deeply divided parliamentary party.

On taking office Haughey emphasised his opposition to the Provisional IRA, underlined his commitment to continue with strict security measures, and declared that his main political priority was the reunification of Ireland by peaceful means. He was Taioseach on three occasions: from December 1979 to June 1981; from March to December 1982; and from March 1987 to February 1992. Throughout all these years, however, there was no diminution of the Northern Unionists' dislike of Dublin Governments in general and of Charles Haughey in particular.

Nevertheless, Robin Eames believed that when Haughey sent out feelers to him to attend a private meeting, he ought to use his position as Primate to accept every opportunity to influence the thinking of key Southern figures. The initial meeting took place in Haughey's room in Government buildings in Dublin, and it lasted longer than both men had anticipated – so much so that a meeting of the Irish Cabinet began late as a result.

Eames recalls, 'I found Haughey willing to listen to me, but he was clearly conscious of what he had been told by Irish Nationalist sources in the North. He believed that the British Government and the Northern Ireland administration at Stormont had done nothing to address Nationalist and Catholic grievances. He was surprisingly critical of a perceived failure of both the Roman Catholic and Protestant church leaders to address the issue of human rights. He admitted that I was the first Protestant church leader to talk to him so plainly about Protestant grievances. Not for the first time, I was conscious of the failure of church leadership to paint a non-party political picture of life in Northern Ireland.'

'Like most others who met Haughey as Taioseach, I found him affable and easy to talk to. To some extent his private persona, compared to his public image, impressed me. He was quiet-spoken and cultured, and when it came to the arts he knew what he was talking about. However, of all the Taoisigh I met, he was the hardest to predict. I never really felt totally at ease with him, and I still don't quite know why.

'With hindsight, when I consider what he did for the country in some social and artistic areas, it would be wrong to write him off as a total political failure. He did achieve a great deal, but because of other things that emerged later, people tended to lose sight of his achievements.'

Eames was anxious to probe behind the public image of Haughey to find out if there was something on which he could help to build better cross-border understanding. 'There was no doubt that Haughey was confident he could deliver whatever he decided to do. He never gave me the impression that he would not be able to sell his ideas in the Dail. Again with hindsight, perhaps it was not quite as it seemed. Where I was getting the impression that he felt "I'll carry them with me", what he really meant was "I know enough people who will make this work".'

However, Eames formed the overall impression that Haughey was a man who was looking for an opportunity to do business with Northern Ireland. 'He was the first of the leaders in the Irish Republic I got to know and who said, "I will have to examine my past in perspective, and I will have to face the fact that I have baggage." By that I presumed he meant the arms trial and everything else. It was not an admission of involvement or anything like that, but rather an admission that there would be things in his past that Unionists would find it hard to accept.'

Following that first meeting, Dr Martin Mansergh, an English member of the Church of Ireland and a key adviser on policy-making on the North during various government administrations, made it his business to stay in touch with Eames. This led to regular contacts and conversations between the two men.

Eames had a second meeting with Haughey a few months later. 'I found a great change in his attitude. He was anxious to pursue new contacts with Northern opinion, and I saw on his desk a full copy of my recent address to the Church of Ireland General Synod in which I had emphasised the need for a new awareness of the genuine apprehensions both North and South.'

Eames told Haughey about the devastating effects of the Provisional IRA campaign on Church of Ireland families in the North, many of them along the border, and emphasised to him that nothing short of an end to this campaign and the opening of a political avenue for Irish Republicanism would ever move things forward.

'Haughey still talked about reunification as a long-term possibility, but I tried to tell him why the terrorism was pushing such political hopes further and further away. He seemed to find it hard to distinguish between attacks on the Northern security forces and the perception among Northern Protestants that this was an attack on them as a community and on their whole way of life.'

Eames made it clear to Haughey that having buried so many victims of this terrorist campaign in Church of Ireland parishes, he had no doubt about the extent to which attitudes were hardening in the North. Eames recalls, 'His attitude to all this was a reluctance to recognise that there were genuine problems within Unionist areas as well as in Nationalist communities. Once more I felt that the non-party political picture of Northern Ireland had not been put forward in the Republic to those who mattered.'

Meanwhile, Eames had been building up relationships with Northern Unionists and other political figures, and he told them that it would be to their benefit to clarify their position directly with the Southern leadership. However, the Unionists found it difficult to move beyond the constitutional issue of maintaining the link between Great Britain and Northern Ireland, and they were understandably antagonistic towards many things Irish because of the continuing Provisional IRA campaign.

Nevertheless, Eames believed fundamentally that a new platform was needed for greater understanding on both sides of the border. There was no suggestion that he was the only such conduit, and others were also engaged on equally import-ant and parallel initiatives, but Eames believed that in the absence of a solid political basis for such overtures, the Church was well placed to encourage these contacts. He says, 'With great care I encouraged private contacts between church leadership North of the border and the church, political and other opinion-formers in the South. Several sensitive meetings took place as a result, and I was assured afterwards – sometimes years later – that the contacts had been very valuable on both sides.'

Eames believed that a political vacuum in any society placed a non-political agency like the churches in a position to assist greater communication and understanding. 'I have found this to be true across the world, and my contacts with Desmond Tutu among others has reinforced my opinion, as far as the churches are concerned.

'I am totally satisfied that in my position as Primate, it was and continues to be not just an opportunity to help build bridges, but also a Christian obligation to do so. Consequently, while Charles Haughey was in office, the foundations were laid for what was to follow in later years, and I look back to the significant openings that were created in those days. Apart from changes in the political leadership of the Republic, those early contacts established important degrees of trust with the civil servants in Dublin.'

In Eames' conversations with Haughey, he became aware of a significant issue which was to determine much of his future efforts at bridge-building. 'In the South there seemed to be a total absence of any appreciation of the importance of the element of "consent" to the Irish problem. Haughey acknowledged the need for degrees of understanding between the two parts of the island, but he did not seem able to grasp that progress and confidence had first of all to be established in order to address the question of consent in Northern Ireland.'

Among Northern Protestants, Dublin was perceived to be informed solely by Northern Nationalist and Republican input, and the Southern Government did not disguise its long-term objective of Irish unification. Eames felt that Haughey was slow to recognise that the North could not be forced into a united Ireland by world opinion.

Eames says, 'He appeared to believe that Britain would grow tired of Northern Ireland and seek to find a means of getting rid of the problem. I went to great lengths to try to tell him that the more those facts became clearer, the harder would become Northern resistance. He seemed to be greatly impressed by the Ian Paisley line and he had the impression that this was the opinion of all Protestants.'

Eames saw the concept of consent also as a core issue in building Northern confidence in itself. 'There had to be consent to any constitutional change in Northern Ireland, but there also had to be a new recognition that a consent to be governed was needed from a population of Protestants who were being subjected to a terrorist campaign. There was a genuine feeling among Northern Protestants that events were being dictated at a point beyond their power to exert any influence on the process. And that was leading to deep, deep frustration.'

Many Protestants felt that their aspirations to remain in the United Kingdom were being eroded because their voice was not being properly heard in London or Dublin. 'I saw this frustration as highly dangerous, for many reasons, but I needed to make it a priority in Dublin. Looking back now, I am surprised that the concept of consent had not been grasped earlier as an important ingredient to make way for better North–South relations. In those days I saw it as very important that I used every opportunity to put forward the value of consent to anyone who would listen. Future events satisfied me that I was correct.'

Haughey, he believed, was very conscious at all times that his real constituency was the Irish Republic. 'Many of the things he said in public were geared to take that constituency with him. He was shrewd enough to know that there might come a point where he might lose that all-Ireland constituency if he moved too far, too soon.'

Eames still questions himself about Haughey's agenda. Was he saying that he wanted the Unionists to understand where he was coming from, and also to try to understand them, or was it a step further along the road of his own agenda to convince Unionists of the viability of a united Ireland? Eames comments, 'In all these kinds of situations my big dilemma has been to balance the need for reconciliation between the differing political cultures and communities, and the possibility of other people using these talks to drive their own agendas.'

Eames feels, however, that Haughey was not trying to 'use' him in that sense. 'At one point he asked me to do something and I replied to him point blank, "I cannot do that." I said to Haughey and other leaders in the Republic, "I cannot and will not be 'used' by anyone. I will give you my opinions and you can make your own judgments from what I say, but I will not be anyone's message boy."'

Haughey had his own domestic political problems and for some time their private contacts lessened. His final talks with Eames were concentrated on representations regarding Church of Ireland education in the Irish Republic. However, reflecting on their earlier conversations, Eames says, 'I learned much from Haughey, and I hope that he learned something from me. I believe that our talks helped to pave the way to a degree of greater all-round understanding between North and South later on.'

Robin Eames also developed a rapport with Dr Garret FitzGerald, leader of the Fine Gael Party during the decade from 1977. FitzGerald also served twice as Taioseach, from June 1981 to March 1982 and from December 1982 until February 1987. It was in this latter period that Eames, as Archbishop of Armagh from 1986, had particularly significant meetings with FitzGerald, who was altogether better regarded by Unionists than Haughey.

FitzGerald visited the North frequently, and his mother came from Ulster Presbyterian stock. As a former Foreign Minister in the Fine Gael Government of Liam Cosgrave from 1973 to 1977 he had been involved in talks with British ministers on political and security aspects of Northern Ireland affairs. Unlike Haughey, he quickly grasped the need for the consent of Ulster Unionists to a solution of the Irish problem, and he went out of his way to try to reassure them.

He was originally a university lecturer in political economy, and many of his statements had an over-wordy donnish dimension. However, he was regarded widely as a political heavyweight who had an important role to play with regard to the North, which he understood much better than many of his Southern colleagues.

Eames felt that FitzGerald brought a new intellectual approach to North–South relations. 'He always impressed me by his thoughtful approach, and his ability to carry out research. He was an excellent listener, and he seemed eager to make personal contacts with Northern opinion-formers. My memory of FitzGerald was that of his highly intellectual approach, even to the extent of seeming more at home in an academic atmosphere than in the office of Taioseach.

'He had a sense of history, and viewed the North with a refreshing honesty. However, as with Haughey, I was never convinced that he did not believe – given time – that the Northern Protestants' objections to becoming part of an Irish Republic would subside because of a declining British interest to retain the link with Northern Ireland.'

Eames believed that FitzGerald viewed the British Prime Minister Margaret Thatcher as someone who deserved grudging respect, but he suspected the real depth of her allegiance to Unionism. Eames also felt that FitzGerald genuinely wanted good relations between North and South, but was frustrated and exasperated by the continuing violence.

Eames tried to outline to him the root causes of Loyalist violence in the North. 'I did not excuse it in any way, but I tried to explain it in terms of the excuses offered to it because of the Provisional IRA terrorist campaign. FitzGerald certainly had good contacts in the North. He knew Cardinal O'Fiaich personally, and he did appear to be conscious of the non-political facts of life in the Province.'

Nevertheless, Eames was never sure about how much FitzGerald viewed the Anglo-Irish Agreement of 1985 as a personal triumph, although he had been one of its chief architects. 'He could be very subtle, and his words were often veiled in what he termed "logic". Like Haughey, he listened to Nationalist opinions in the North, but I felt that he was also sensitive to fluctuations of opinion at Westminster.' Overall, Eames found in FitzGerald a refreshing appreciation of the deep-rooted nature of the Northern problems, and he was aware that FitzGerald had several private meetings with significant Unionist politicians.

While Eames helped to nurture the cross-border dialogue, he remained closely in touch with the details of Northern politics. As noted earlier, he led a Church of Ireland delegation to meet Prime Minister Margaret Thatcher at No. 10 Downing Street shortly after his election as Primate, and even before his consecration as Archbishop of Armagh.

One of the topics discussed was the need for heads of Government to clarify certain parts of the 1985 Anglo-Irish Agreement that continued to cause controversy in Northern Ireland. A large number of Unionists there felt alienated from a cross-border political process which, they felt, was being implemented without their consent.

The degree of Protestant opposition was reflected in Eames' postbag. One member of the Church of Ireland wrote to him stating:

> There is absolutely no doubt in my mind that you have in the past supported a Government which continually lies to the people in order to surrender to thuggery and to abdicate responsibility to law-abiding people. For this reason my whole family will be resigning from the Church you lead and which you claim to speak for. My only regret is that we did not take this action sooner.

Even when Eames was Bishop of Down and Dromore, shortly before he was elected Primate, he was acutely aware of those feelings of betrayal among his own people. 'The "Ulster Says No!" campaign became a watchword in many areas. In the days before my Primacy, riots throughout the North underlined the sense of widespread ill-feeling that prevailed.'

In May 1987 Robin Eames made a keynote speech during his presidential address to the Church of Ireland Synod, its ruling body, in Dublin. He said that there was a vacuum in Northern politics and that to end this there was a need for the constitutional parties to begin negotiations on a new accord which would supersede the Anglo-Irish Agreement.

He said that if both communities in the North could be reassured by such a new agreement, it would have some chance of success. However, it required two further pre-conditions: 'The Unionist people must be prepared to show a new willingness to listen to and to appreciate the genuine feelings of their Nationalist neighbours, and the Nationalists' people must show a new willingness to make the structures of the community work for all the people of the Province.'

Eames emphasised that the Church of Ireland could not allow itself to be drawn into the party political arena. 'What we must maintain as a priority in both jurisdictions is the independence to speak the truth in love as we see it under God.'

Significantly, two senior bishops from the Irish Republic appeared less than enthusiastic about Eames' proposals. Bishop Samuel Poyntz of Cork told an *Irish Times* reporter that any second agreement could not get rid of the original, which was an international treaty signed by two sovereign states and lodged with the United Nations. He stated, 'Whether we need a second agreement is a moot point.'

Bishop Walton Empey of Meath and Kildare also told the *Irish Times*, 'If something could be done by broadening the existing agreement, or moving on to a second agreement, something could be said for it. However, I wouldn't want to derogate from the present agreement. We don't want to go back to the beginning and to start all over again.' Such comments underlined the sense of unease among Church of Ireland members in the Republic. While they tried to understand mainline Unionist apprehensions, they also feared that the Anglo-Irish Agreement might be tampered with by the

British, in order to accommodate the more intransigent shades of Unionist opinion.

However, Eames' speech was given a generally good welcome by the press and, perhaps more importantly, by Northern politicians. The liberal Unionist newspaper the *Belfast Telegraph* praised Eames' 'realism', and complimented him on identifying the flaw in the existing accord. It echoed his words: 'You cannot impose reconciliation. You cannot impose understanding.' The more conservative Belfast *News Letter* noted: 'Few who really know and care about Ulster and all its people will disagree with the Primate's sentiments.' In Dublin the *Irish Times* stated: 'The Archbishop speaks for so many Unionist people who feel helpless and who are frightened by their apparent inability to break out of the position in which they find themselves.'

One of the most important endorsements came from James Molyneaux, leader of the Official Unionists, and the Reverend Ian Paisley, leader of the Democratic Unionists. They welcomed Eames' suggestions and declared that he had put his finger on the crux of the problem. Eames, no doubt, was conscious of the likelihood of such an endorsement before he made his statement. Politically he was too astute to edge out on a branch that would have been swiftly chopped by the political leaders of Unionism if they had not already given tacit recognition to such an initiative.

Accordingly it was anticipated that Eames' comments were in line with the expected findings of a Unionist task force report on an alternative to the Anglo-Irish Agreement. This was compiled by the then 'Young Turks', including Peter Robinson, deputy leader of the DUP, Frank Millar, the secretary of the Official Unionists, and Harold McCusker, a Unionist MP at Westminster with leanings to the right of the party. He was also a likeable character, despite his often trenchant political views. The reaction of both main parties to the task force report was disappointing, however, and it was thought that as a result Millar resigned as Unionist secretary.

Eames says, 'Frank Millar and Peter Robinson came to me to explain their thinking. While I felt that there was some merit in their approach, I believed that a majority of Northern Ireland Protestants were in no mood to see anything but an outright rejection of the Anglo-Irish Agreement.

'With hindsight, however, I am not sure that my judgment was right. The Millar-Robinson initiative had the backing of a younger generation of Unionists and they had worked hard on the report. Was I wrong not to give them public encouragement? Looking back I feel perhaps that an opportunity to introduce new thinking had been lost. I was told afterwards that they were disappointed by my reaction.'

During this period, Eames worked closely with Tom King, who was Northern Ireland Secretary from September 1985 to July 1989, when he went on to become Defence Secretary at Westminster. King was firm and plain-spoken, and he had to withstand the widespread and determined Unionist dissatisfaction with the Anglo-Irish Agreement, of which they strongly disapproved, partly because it had been imposed on them without consultation.

In fact just after the Agreement was signed, King was jostled by aggrieved and frustrated Loyalist supporters outside the City Hall in Belfast. Despite the considerable difficulties, he worked steadily to try to regain some measure of Unionist confidence while also dealing with pressure from the Dublin Government to address the grievances of Northern Nationalists.

In short, he found himself in the same difficulties as nearly every other Northern Ireland Secretary in trying to meet the very different needs and aspirations of all shades of political opinion. He nevertheless stuck to the task with not a little common sense and stoical good humour.

Eames says, 'Tom King impressed me greatly during this period. We talked together frequently, and he indicated that he had an acute awareness of the depth of Protestant feelings.' King, on his part, also formed a high opinion of Eames. As Secretary of State he needed to hear from opinion-formers who were not directly part of the political process, particularly at a time when Unionist politicians were boycotting Government ministers in protest, though there were still some discreet links at Westminster.

Part of the challenge facing the Secretary of State was to try to help people to develop a better understanding of the Agreement, and also to establish dialogue with Unionists in order to find ways to address their concerns. Among other challenges King faced was the need to keep the Northern Ireland economy going, and to contend at all times with the considerable security threats from terrorist groups on both sides.

The job had challenges and dangers, but King also found it inspiring. He says, 'People who had experienced the Troubles showed great courage in the midst of difficulties, and they had the determination to get on with it, and to make the best of their lives.'

Tom King regarded the role of the Church as particularly important, and he felt that Robin Eames was a good sounding-board as well as a respected adviser. He was, according to King, 'a breath of fresh air', and a leader who was prepared to speak honestly and frankly.

'He knew how to warn and to advise without giving offence. He always struck me as a rather muscular Christian and as an archbishop who was not in an ivory tower, or locked inside his own cathedral. He was someone who got out and became involved. I respected him as someone who was committed to Northern Ireland and who had courage, strength and considerable ability.'

The Secretary of State recognised that Eames was seriously worried about the security situation. There were many casualties, and Tom King knew that Eames was experiencing these tragedies at first hand, and that this was a very tough part of his role. King says, 'He saw the families of the bereaved, he conducted the funeral services, and he was very much involved. It was a time when a less responsible and courageous leadership could have led to real problems. We went through very difficult times, and Robin Eames gave real leadership.'[1]

That leadership would continue to be tested as Northern Ireland withstood as best it could the battering of the terrorists, while the long search for an elusive peace continued.

12

The Road to Downing Street

On 24 July 1989 Peter Brooke became the new Secretary of State for Northern Ireland when Tom King was promoted to Defence Minister in London. Brooke was the son of the former Home Secretary Henry Brooke and he had longstanding family connections in the cross-border areas of Northern Ireland and the Irish Republic.

His period of office in Northern Ireland for nearly three years was associated with a still grim security situation and the hard slog of 'talks about talks' to try to resolve the political deadlock. Though regarded by some as having a less forceful public profile than Tom King, his patient diplomacy and determination of purpose in difficult circumstances helped to pave the way for a significant shift in emphasis in British policy on Northern Ireland. This marked the beginning of a long road towards the Downing Street Declaration of December 1993 and the Good Friday Agreement of April 1998.

Robin Eames developed a high regard for Brooke, with whom he worked closely. He found him to be likeable and cultured, with a genuine appreciation of Irish history. Eames says, 'He was a devout man and he also had a genuine appreciation of the churches in Ireland. His family roots in Ireland made him conscious of the past history of the Troubles. He was not as blunt as Tom King, and at times he could appear as "the gentleman in the Castle" at Hillsborough, but he was a shrewd and able Northern Ireland Secretary.'

One of Eames' important meetings with Brooke, which also involved Cardinal Tomas O'Fiaich, took place not long after the new Secretary of State arrived in Northern Ireland. Late one night the Cardinal phoned Eames to ask if they could

meet. He said that he had received an approach from the
Provisional IRA which he was convinced was genuine. 'In effect,
it was apparently an offer for serious peace talks with the British
Government prior to a possible ceasefire. O'Fiaich and I had a
good relationship and I felt able to question him closely. While
he carefully protected his sources, I could see that he was
impressed by what he had been told.'

The Cardinal asked Eames if he could arrange a meeting
with Peter Brooke as soon as possible. He agreed to do so, and
they went together to Stormont the next day. Brooke was in
London, but a private meeting was held by means of a video
link, with only one other person – a senior civil servant –
present.

Eames says, 'Peter listened to the Cardinal carefully, and with
great patience. O'Fiaich explained that the Provisional IRA
had asked us to approach the British Government to take their
offer seriously. I said that I was convinced from what I had
heard that the request was genuine. Brooke thanked us and
promised to have the request fully examined.'

Neither Eames nor O'Fiaich were subsequently informed of
any follow-up. Eames recalls, 'I sensed that the Cardinal was
disappointed by the outcome, but I also felt that Brooke had
not been too surprised by our approach. I wondered if talks
were already underway. I suggested to O'Fiaich that he should
inform his sources in Dublin and he agreed to do so.'

Eames remains convinced that this was a genuine approach
from the Provisional IRA. 'I believe that our meeting with
Brooke was more significant than even we thought at the time.
It is important to remember that the feed-in to that meeting
was not just what the Cardinal had been told but what we were
both hearing from prisoners in the Maze.'

After he had left office Brooke indicated that secret government talks with Provisional Sinn Fein representatives had begun
in 1990, which would have been shortly after or parallel to the
Provisional IRA's approach through O'Fiaich and Eames.

Referring specifically to the meeting with Eames and
O'Fiaich, he recalls, 'From as early as 1986 there was a debate
inside the terrorist community, particularly on the Republican
side, as to how it would all end. The approach to me by the
Cardinal and the Archbishop reinforced the view that such a
debate was going on. I was encouraged that the prisoners were

sounding as if they could be a force for the resolution of the problem, rather than the opposite.'[1]

In November 1990 Brooke made an important speech to his constituency party in London in which he stated that Britain had no selfish economic or strategic interest in Northern Ireland and that its purpose was not to 'occupy, oppress or exploit'. This statement was to become deeply controversial, but it was also a cornerstone of future British policy. Brooke was underlining in public what the British had been saying in private. The future of Northern Ireland would depend on the wishes of its people, and the British did not have a 'selfish' interest that was separate from the interests of the people of Northern Ireland.

Meanwhile Brooke, with one of his junior ministers – the Ulsterman Brian Mawhinney – had involved themselves closely with attempts to persuade the politicians to agree about talks on three distinct sets of relationships: those within Northern Ireland (strand one); those between North and South (strand two); and those between the United Kingdom and the Irish Republic (strand three).

A crucial feature was that the three strands were interlocked. Nothing would be agreed until everything was agreed. This assuaged Nationalist fears that the Unionists would win agreement on a new assembly and then fail to deliver counterbalancing concessions on a closer North–South relationship. The three-stranded formula, though complex and at times frustrating, helped to chart the way to the Downing Street Declaration and ultimately the Good Friday Agreement.

Some useful progress was made early on in the Brooke talks but, not surprisingly, given the previous history of Ireland they developed into a long-winded process. Brooke presided over the plenary sessions in June and early July 1991, but the Unionists felt that they could not continue because of a planned Anglo-Irish inter-governmental conference. The talks were halted by Brooke on 3 July 1991, and two days later Robin Eames issued a statement as Primate expressing his disappointment that this initial process had come to an end. His words also reflected the sense of despair that many people felt at the apparent breakdown of the first promising talks for years, and the deep desire of many that they should not fail. He said:

> A prolonged vacuum caused by an absence of such political
> dialogue is a most dangerous and tragic threat to this
> community... In the context of the experience of this
> Province we must never allow frustration or disappointment
> to overcome our efforts to bring greater understanding,
> peace and stability for all our people. We have no option
> under God but to try and try again.

It required the intervention of the Prime Minister John Major
to produce a formal restart to the talks in March 1992, with an
important agreement that the process would continue after the
forthcoming British General Election in April of that year.
However, one significant outcome of this was a new Cabinet in
which Brooke was replaced, much to his disappointment, as
Secretary of State for Northern Ireland by Sir Patrick Mayhew
who had made it known for some time that he was attracted to
the post.

Earlier, in January of the same year, Brooke had offered to
resign following an unfortunate incident during which he had
been persuaded, against his better judgment, to sing his party
piece 'Clementine' during his scheduled appearance on the
'live' and widely viewed RTE programme *The Late, Late Show* in
Dublin. Unfortunately for Brooke, this occurred only hours
after news came in from Northern Ireland that eight Protestant
workmen had been massacred by a Provisional IRA bomb in
Co. Tyrone on the same evening.

Brooke, an honourable and a sensitive man, was aghast at
this lapse of judgment, which was a basic human error in the
circumstances, and he subsequently made it his business to
apologise personally to the families of those who had been
murdered. He felt that in no way could he ever 'square the
circle', but he was grateful that the relatives had agreed to see
him. The Prime Minister John Major did not accept his
resignation, but the incident did not improve Brooke's relationship with the Unionists. Brooke managed to stay on in the job,
helped by strong support in the Commons, but the incident
had put him under a handicap.

Robin Eames says, 'This incident was completely out of
character and I know that Peter Brooke deeply regretted what
happened. I blame RTE and the Northern Ireland Office for
creating such an insensitive situation. It was completely in

character for Peter Brooke to offer his resignation.' Brooke, he believes, was a good man who achieved a great deal. He says, 'Like Garret FitzGerald, he had a great sensitivity about Irish history, and those who believed that he was not aware of the political nuances of Northern Ireland could not have been more wrong. He possessed an acute judgment of people and events, and he was totally focused on the job in hand. I do not feel that he was given the credit for what he achieved.'

Peter Brooke, for his part, had a high regard for Eames. He recalls a luncheon in Hillsborough in the aftermath of the RTE incident when Eames made a public speech and mentioned him specifically. He recalls, 'Robin spoke about me in an extra-ordinarily supportive way. I found it a remarkable pastoral contribution, and I appreciated it greatly. I also learned afterwards, though I did not know it at the time, that Robin had talked to John Major privately and had spoken warmly about me. I was a member of the Church of England, and the pastoral support I received from him was a major resource during my time as Secretary of State.'[2]

Brooke was replaced as Northern Ireland Secretary in April 1992 basically because the Prime Minister felt that it was time for him to move on. John Major confirms that the RTE 'gaffe' had nothing to do with it. He recalls, 'The real problem was that all Northern Ireland Secretaries have a certain lifespan before they begin to lose the confidence of the community, and time was running out for Peter. It should be remembered, however, that the three-stranded talks approach was Peter Brooke's, and that remains his tremendous legacy to the peace process.'[3]

Sir Patrick (later Lord) Mayhew, Brooke's successor, remained in post from 1992 until 1997, and became the longest-serving Northern Ireland Secretary up to that time. As the former Attorney General he had experience of legal issues affecting Northern Ireland, which had given him a good understanding of the Province, and he also had Southern Irish roots. Given his expressed desire to come to Northern Ireland, unlike some previous Northern Ireland Secretaries, he seemed a good choice to build on the work of Peter Brooke and his colleagues.

Robin Eames came to know Mayhew well, and found him accessible and willing to listen and to discuss all concerns. Eames says, 'He had a definite sense of justice, and of right and wrong, and he never allowed the complexities of Northern Ireland to overcome his sense of duty to both communities. During his time the process of finding political consensus which had been started by Peter Brooke maintained a definite momentum.'

Mayhew was a tall figure with an almost military bearing. 'He was correct in style, but behind a somewhat formal exterior I found him to be an extremely friendly and warm-hearted man. His legal background was obvious, and his attention to detail was profound. I quickly formed a high opinion of his sincerity and ability.'

One of his first calls was to Armagh where he met the two Primates. He was accompanied by his wife Jean who later played an active role in community affairs in the Province, and this was much appreciated. Eames recalls, 'Sir Patrick was sensitive to the background to his new responsibilities, and he was acutely aware of the need to strike a balance. He had a deep appreciation of church affairs, and the clergy were quick to respond to his willingness to see the churches as active players in the Northern Ireland situation.'

Mayhew also had a high regard for Eames. He recalls the visit with his wife to Armagh shortly after he took up his post in order to meet the Archbishop and the Cardinal. He says, 'As a practising churchman I invited them to pray, which was something I was much in need of. I think that the Cardinal was more surprised than Robin!'[4]

Mayhew recognised the demanding role of the church leaders. Referring to Eames in particular he says, 'Robin had a difficult balancing act to perform, which he did, not just with great dexterity but also with great attachment to principle. If I wanted a non-partisan but informed and accurate impression of what the Unionists were thinking, or would think, I knew that I could do no better than go to Robin.'

The Secretary of State was impressed by Eames' spiritual qualities but also by his political skills. He says, 'He had very considerable political gifts which anyone in that position needed, not only on that side of the water but also in dealing with the Anglican Church worldwide. His detractors might say that he was more of a politician than a churchman. I didn't agree with that, though I could see why they might have thought that.'

Shortly before Mayhew took over as Northern Ireland Secretary there was an important political development in the Irish Republic. Early in 1992 Albert Reynolds became Taioseach, and this gave an added impetus to the drive to try to break the political deadlock in the North. Previously he had held a number of Cabinet posts, including that of Finance Minister, and it was in this key role that he worked closely with John Major, then British Chancellor of the Exchequer. The two developed a good working and personal relationship.

Major, as soon as he had become Prime Minister in 1990, had decided to put Northern Ireland on 'the front burner'. He recalls, 'I felt it was absurd that in the twentieth century an ancient feud like this was continuing to hold back the development of Northern Ireland and creating chaos in the streets.'

Major, however, had no illusions about the difficulties involved. He says, 'There wasn't much support in Cabinet for what I was doing. There was support, of course, from Peter Brooke and Paddy Mayhew and a handful of others, but there were a number of very senior members of the Cabinet who, while not opposed to what I was doing, felt that it would come to nothing and would end in political tears. They really thought that I ought not to be doing it.'

The details of the many political machinations leading to the Downing Street Declaration were extraordinarily complex. The challenge was to keep all sides involved without moving too fast and without losing the confidence and trust of the main players. Major had to keep the Unionists on side with regard to an Irish dimension, which was no easy task, while reassuring the Irish Nationalists in the North that their aspirations were being taken into account.

He and Reynolds had to keep the lines clear, as far as possible, between Dublin and London, and both had to make sure that Provisional Sinn Fein were kept informed. This meant that the Provisional IRA were, de facto, being kept in the picture as well.

Reynolds had excellent Northern contacts within Irish Nationalism and Republicanism, and he worked hard to try to get into the mind of Unionism. In particular he developed a good relationship with Robin Eames, who was widely regarded in London and Dublin as the authentic voice of moderate Protestantism in the North, though not in any party political sense.

Eames was one of a number of influential figures who were consulted during this period, and he was fully aware that others were part of that complex process. However, he was particularly well placed not only as a Northern unionist, with a small 'u', but also as a leader of an all-Ireland Church. As such he was a particularly good contact for Reynolds, though he remained in close touch with John Major whom he greatly respected.

Given the relationship between the two Prime Ministers, there was an obvious symmetry in their approach to the Primate, though Eames kept his own channels clear with each of them as individuals. He had a shrewd idea, however, as to where these channels were likely to lead. Eames recalls, 'Albert Reynolds was the Taioseach with whom I had the most dealings. He talked in Irish colloquialisms and was known as a political "wheeler-dealer".' Shortly after taking up office, Reynolds made the first approach to Eames who recalls, 'We had not met before that, but contrary to much media speculation I found him to be very clear in his mind that dialogue, understanding and an appreciation of what concerned Northern Protestants had to be taken into account.

'Albert and I got on like a house on fire, and I did not know that this would be the case until I met him. Sometimes we talked in his office in Dublin, and sometimes in his home. I also got to know his wife well. I had a real regard for Reynolds. He was an entrepreneur, but also a consummate politician.'

He was very different from Dr Garret FitzGerald. 'Garret had a great knowledge of Irish history and he would often bring an economic dimension into our discussions. Albert Reynolds would say, "Could you sell this idea for me", or, "Could you buy that?", whereas FitzGerald would say, "Let's look at the pros and cons of this." It was essentially the difference between an academic pragmatist and a political wheeler-dealer.'

Eames believed that Reynolds had a firm grip on things and that he knew instinctively what would or would not work in terms of relationships. 'I knew that he had at heart the best interests of Ireland as a whole but perhaps not exclusively of Northern Ireland, at least at the start. I did not know to whom else he was talking in the North, but when I offered him an opinion in answer to a question, he sometimes gave me the impression that he had heard something similar from somebody else.'

Reynolds could be extremely determined if he felt a cause was right. 'Albert gave me the strong impression that he was prepared to take great risks for peace. I also felt that, unlike any other Taioseach I had dealt with, he was confident that he could take his party with him. Early in our conversations he showed a sensitivity towards the apprehensions of Northern Protestants, and he openly admitted the failure in the South to listen to the people in Northern Ireland.'

Eames quickly sensed Reynolds' rapport with the British Prime Minister. 'He said to me early on, "I can do business with John Major, and I want to push the peace process forward. Can I count on your help?" ' Eames believes that part of the chemistry between Major and Reynolds was that they got on well and that they had no significant doubts about one another.

This is also confirmed by Major. During the difficult run-up to the final Downing Street Agreement, when the outcome was on a knife-edge, both men needed to re-establish trust. Before one meeting with their advisers in Dublin, they had a private session which led to a huge row. Major later recalled, amid laughter, 'It was a spectacular row. It takes a long time for me to get so angry that I lose my temper, but Dublin had pushed me so much with "leaks" that I was spoiling for a fight when I got to Dublin. So was Albert, because he probably thought that I was operating behind his back, and I felt the same. So it was an explosion waiting to happen. We cleared everyone out of the room and we had an hour on our own. It is extremely fortunate that posterity does not record what was said!'

Albert Reynolds recalls, 'John and I had plenty of disagreements. Sometimes we would spend an hour, or maybe two, arguing over one point in a draft. The British are classic at this, but I had very good guys with me too. Prior to that Dublin summit I said to Major, "Don't bother coming over, tear it up. What's the point of producing something that isn't going to run?" '[5]

Reynolds confirmed that privately they had had a fierce row in Dublin, but that they had cleared the air. He said, 'When we came out to talk to the media after the subsequent meeting with our officials, I looked at Major and he looked at me. We started speaking together and it was word for word, without any rehearsal. The media could not believe it. We were of one mind.'

The basis of their good relationship had been laid previously when they were both finance ministers in Brussels. Reynolds says, 'On John's first day in Brussels he sat down beside me and said, "You are one of the longer-serving people here, and maybe you will mark my card." I replied, "It's very simple – every issue here is 11–1 against, as far as Great Britain is concerned." At that time Margaret Thatcher was opposing everything. Later on, however, when it was not against Ireland's interests I sometimes made that balance 10–2, which might have made John think that this was not just the usual "Bash the British" campaign!'

When it came to the long haul on the Downing Street Declaration John Major had a slim majority in the House of Commons, and he needed the support of the Ulster Unionists to keep him in power. Reynolds notes, 'At the same time, John Major was not afraid to come on the journey with us to the Downing Street Declaration. John was an underestimated guy, and was certainly not the "grey man" as portrayed by the media. I had a lot of time for him.'

Despite the difficulties, the early contacts between the two when they became Premier of their respective countries boded well for the future. Reynolds recalls that during his first meeting with Major in Downing Street, the British Prime Minister told an aide, 'Albert is going to take us through the Irish scene as he sees it, so you can put away your pen and paper. This is not going to be recorded.' Later on, a senior aide, who had been at the meeting and who had worked for several Irish Premiers, told Reynolds that he had never heard a British Prime Minister open up as Major had done. The official said to Reynolds, 'I have a feeling that you are going to do good business with him.'

Back in Ireland, Eames knew that soundings were being made early on to begin the drafts of what was to become the Downing Street Declaration of December 1993. He recalls, 'I was aware that contacts in North and South were already under way, and I knew that Major had made progress in gaining some sympathy from Unionist leaders. One of my own key contacts among Northern Protestants had also met Reynolds and shared my view that Albert was indeed someone who would look for help in trying to understand Northern Ireland's problems.'

For his part, Reynolds was anxious to hear as wide a spectrum of views as possible from Northern Ireland. He had many contacts on the Catholic side, including Cardinal Daly who had earlier been a bishop in the Irish Republic, but he needed to hear the authentic views of Northern Protestants.

He said later, 'I did not need the ear of Archbishop Eames to get to Major, but I knew that he was an important part of the loop. He was friendly with James Molyneaux, who was talking to Major who was also talking to Eames. However, in his own right Robin Eames was very important because he was an authentic and clear voice of Protestantism. I wanted to know the score in every part of the community in Northern Ireland. There was no point in someone pretending to me. I wanted it straight, and Eames was always straight with me. There was also the fact that Eames had continuity. The other Protestant church leaders were also impressive but after a year they were replaced by someone else.'

There was also the fact that Robin, while a churchman first and foremost, was also a good politician. Reynolds says, 'He could read a situation politically and he understood why certain people would be saying certain things from time to time. It was also helpful that we got on well personally. My wife is a good judge of character and she liked Robin, and his wife Christine. We had a friendship not just because of what we were doing. We were delighted to see him, wherever we met. He was also a highly respected figure throughout the Republic. I never heard anyone say a bad word about him.'

During Eames' second meeting with Reynolds, the Taioseach talked about his vision of an Agreement where there would be a definite acknowledgment of the need to take the concerns of both communities on board. Eames said, 'What impressed me was his wish to learn what were the non-party political worries of people in Northern Ireland.'

He learned later that Major and Reynolds had discussed involving him and others in a period of consultation in the run-up to the Declaration. He says, 'I had misgivings that I could not live up to these expectations, but I was left in no doubt that they wanted to hear what I was able to relay. I also knew from other channels that Northern Ireland political leaders were being sounded out on what was possible.'

Eames wrote a paper for Reynolds outlining his concerns and those of Northern Protestants. Eames says, 'This was well received in Dublin, and I understand that Reynolds shared it with Major. James Molyneaux, the leader of the Official Unionists, was also aware of my involvement, and we talked at length.'

The main thrust of Eames' paper was fourfold. He underlined that Northern Ireland Protestants' fears had not only to be recognised but to be *seen* to be recognised; he indicated, from his contacts, how far he thought that the Ulster Loyalists would move; he gave a brief analysis as to why Northern Protestants were suspicious of Southern intentions; and he included a personal analysis of what could follow a complete ceasefire by Republicans and Loyalists.

Eames was invited to Dublin to enlarge on his paper. Reynolds showed him a working draft of the Declaration, and he took time to read it. He recalls, 'I was horrified and indeed angered to find that in the draft there was little recognition of the genuine fears of Protestants in Northern Ireland, and that there was little enforcement of the idea of "consent". I expressed my doubts openly to Reynolds. He replied, "Would you draft some words for me to think about, and I promise you that we will give them real consideration." '

Reynolds confirmed later that he also felt that the early draft was unsatisfactory. 'It was unbalanced from start to finish. There was no expression of the Protestant views at all. If I thought that it was unbalanced, what on earth would Robin Eames think?'

Eames agreed to accept the offer, having gone so far in the process already. 'I had two aims in my draft – to encourage the importance of an "agreed" Ireland, as opposed to any imposition by one or other nation of a solution that would deny human rights. I also wanted to encourage both Governments to accept the concept of consent as a long-term objective.'

Eames was also in contact with Major separately, and he kept his own bishops informed about the broad thrust of what he was doing, though not the details. He says, 'I received their full support and also took on board their suggestions. I also did all I could to keep the leaders of Protestant political opinion informed.' During that long inter-governmental process, the British sought the advice of Eames, Molyneaux and others when writing their own drafts to try to find middle ground with the Irish, whose early drafts were regarded as 'too green' for Unionist approval.

Major recalls that the early draft from Dublin was 'strictly for the birds'. He says, 'It was so green it was out of sight. None of that survived. The Hume-Adams drafts were not useful because anything that came from that source was never going to be acceptable to the Unionists. So things had to be rewritten.'

In Eames' meetings with Major, the Prime Minister spoke candidly and openly about his hopes for a Declaration. Eames says, 'He found working with Reynolds satisfying, and they obviously had a good rapport. Like Reynolds, Major asked me constantly about non-party political feelings in Northern Ireland, and I took care to keep myself fully informed about the attitudes among the leaders of the local community.'

Eames got on well with Major and found him very different from his predecessor. 'John Major to my mind has not been given enough credit for what he achieved. He was a real pioneer in Northern Ireland and I believe that he laid the foundations for peace which Tony Blair and others inherited. To some extent Major was overshadowed by the Thatcher years and by her dynamism and sheer power.'

Eames did not have the same contact with Thatcher that he had with John Major and later with Tony Blair. He says, 'My judgment of Margaret Thatcher was from a greater distance, though I did meet her on several occasions.' They first met when Eames, then a bishop, was one of an ecumenical group of Northern Ireland clergy who were asked to meet the Prime Minister in Downing Street. He met her again soon after he became Primate, and later on after the Memorial Service for the victims and families of those who died or were injured in the Enniskillen bomb. He was also invited to a reception in Downing Street.

When Eames met her as part of the group of ecumenical clergy, he remembered her jotting down comments in a Marks and Spencer notebook, and also the fact that she seemed to be lecturing them about their responsibilities. He says, 'That did not go down too well. While I respected her as Prime Minister and as a strong woman, I did not agree with much of "Thatcherism". I was also critical of some of her attitudes to Northern Ireland.

'She did not appear to have a great deal of sensitivity, and I really did not warm to her. I think she saw Northern Ireland in terms of breaking the Provisional IRA. She seemed to believe that if that could be achieved, Northern Ireland could find its own level. Her philosophy appeared to be "Don't give in to the hunger strikers or to intimidation, don't show any weakness in Northern Ireland".'

Eames felt that Thatcher was 'too militarily orientated' in Northern Ireland. 'Of course many people in the Province admired her because they felt that she was standing up to the Provisional IRA. I wondered if she was as clear-sighted as she liked to think she was. I asked myself if there was any room in her philosophy where she was willing to address the causes of the alienation in society which was helping to create the terrorists of tomorrow.'

Major was a complete contrast. 'He genuinely wanted to try to solve the Northern Ireland situation and he was the first British Prime Minister to recognise the need for the consent of the Ulster Unionists to any proposals, and also the importance of developing an all-Ireland dimension. He also realised that the British Government would have to deal with the Provisional IRA and he was willing to involve the Dublin Government in trying to find a solution. I don't think that Margaret Thatcher would have done that.'

Eames found Major to be straight with him at all times. 'He was not only one of the most reliable but also one of the best informed Prime Ministers on Northern Ireland affairs. The cartoonists' image of "the grey man" was most unfair. I knew from my dealings with him that he was neither weak nor dilatory.'

Eames, on the contrary, found him definitive and decisive. 'On one occasion I met him in Downing Street, together with Sir Patrick Mayhew and his own private secretary. We sat on chairs in a semi-circle in the Cabinet room, and I was impressed by how quickly he put aside the subjects they had been discussing in Cabinet, and focused on Northern Ireland.'

Major was not at his best on television, but he was much more impressive in groups and above all in one-to-one situations. 'He would come straight into a group and start talking, without hanging back. He had a presence and he was a professional. I often wondered about his "anger" during the crossfire of Prime Minister's Question Time, and how deep that went. He was perfectly capable of a professional "performance".'

However, on one occasion when they were together Eames found Major seething with anger following a Provisional IRA outrage. 'I said to him, "That might help you to understand the emotions and the degree of hurt of the people I am dealing with every day." He replied, "It does, and I do." '

Major was always conscious of Eames' position. 'He worried about the repercussions for me if it became known that I was working so closely with the process. I said to him, "If the thing is worth doing, it is worth taking risks." When we met in Downing Street I sometimes used the back entrance, and when he came to Hillsborough he would say, "I feel more comfortable for you on your own territory." We also communicated by phone, often early in the morning, and I know that on one occasion the phone call was made when he was shaving. We talked a great deal and I said to him once, "Prime Minister, do you have an open line?" He replied, "Don't worry, my line is secure." '

Major was also extremely appreciative of Eames. He says, 'What I needed was someone who would vouch for the fact that what the British Government was doing was genuine. That person could not be an elected politician, because in Northern Ireland politics were too divisive. I either had to do it myself, or find a community figure who commanded respect. Robin was perfect for that.'

Major showed Eames parts of relevant and highly confidential documents. He says, 'It's been a long time in the affairs of Church and State since a churchman would have seen such intimate documents as Robin saw. Albert Reynolds and I squabbled over every dot and comma, but when I had got as far as I could, I needed an independent view that the deal would be accepted by Unionists. Robin understood the nuances which an outsider like me, or the Civil Service, might not have known.'

He found in Eames what he wanted – a 'worldly cleric'. He says, 'I don't mean by that to question his religious credentials, but Robin did not carry with him an air of sanctimony. He was a man whose religion was out in the community, and not stuck behind the walls of his church. That is true among the best clerics.'

Their meetings, though dealing with serious matters, were not 'grey and grisly', according to Major. 'Robin had a wry sense of humour and we had many chuckles. Our meetings were enjoyable as well as very serious.'

Family man: Dr. Robin Eames with his wife Christine and
sons Niall and Michael, pictured in the mid-eighties when he
was elected Archbishop of Armagh and Primate of All Ireland.

Archbishop Eames at a meeting with the late Archbishop of
Canterbury, Dr. Robert Runcie.

Pictured with Cardinal Cahal Daly, the then
Roman Catholic Primate of All Ireland, at Armagh in 1991.

Archbishop Eames with President Arafat in Gaza.

With Archbishop Desmond Tutu at the ACC meeting
in Nigeria in 1984.

Greeting the Duke of York with Bishop Samuel Poyntz in
St. Anne's Cathedral, Belfast.

In Jerusalem with President Ariel Sharon and Archbishop George Carey, during a visit to the Middle East.

Archbishop Eames with Archbishop Tutu, President Nelson Mandela and Archbishop George Carey.

Archbishop Eames with the Archbishop of Canterbury
Dr. Rowan Williams, a colleague and also a friend.

In conversation with President Bill Clinton on one of his visits to Northern Ireland.

The time-conscious Archbishop with yet another deadline to meet.

The Portadown Orange parade, with Drumcree Parish Church in the background, passed off peacefully on 4th July 2004, but the long standoff in recent years involved Archbishop Eames in protracted peacemaking efforts. He described Drumcree as 'My Calvary'.

Major trusted Eames totally. He points out that Margaret Thatcher once said that she could make up her mind in two minutes about whether or not she liked and could trust a person. 'She did say, "Sometimes I was wrong," and indeed she was. I did not make up my mind on people quite so quickly as that, but I did make up my mind pretty quickly as to the people I could trust, and Robin was one of them.'

Major says that never once after a meeting with Robin did he worry that anything he had said might be retold inaccurately elsewhere, or if it was a private conversation that it would be retold at all. 'If you are a senior politician, almost everything you say becomes good dinner-table gossip, often embellished. I discovered very quickly with Robin that what I said wasn't going to become "tittle-tattle" and that it would not be embellished. Without that I don't think we could have done what we did.'

John Major felt that Eames was fully prepared to become a player in the search for a settlement. 'I saw him as an effective bridge-builder between the policy I wished to carry out and also the Unionist politicians, and more important, the Unionist population. I felt that if I could frame policies that Robin Eames could accept, it was going a long way to producing a policy that would be accepted by the Unionist population generally.'

Eames was aware that Major knew about the drafts he was writing for Reynolds. 'I am sure that they talked about it and that Major had read the drafts, but he never asked me to change a word. Albert might say to me occasionally, "There are difficulties", but I also realised the momentum that had been built up, particularly by both sets of civil servants as well as the two Prime Ministers.'

He also assumed that both Prime Ministers were fully aware that he was closely in touch with the Unionist leader James Molyneaux. Major confirms this. He says, 'We all knew that we were talking to each other. It was a game we all played because we had to play it that way, but it was also serious politics. Jim Molyneaux was a wise old bird who was slow to rush to conclusions, but when he reached a judgment, it was secure. For ever he had to watch the Unionists at his back.'

Eames also had a high regard for Lord Molyneaux. He says, 'I never wanted to overstep the mark in our relationship, and I always emphasised that any support or information that I conveyed to him had to be left to his judgment. He was a master of Westminster procedure, and often operated through contacts with British politicians. He never betrayed a confidence I shared with him, and it was mutual.'

Molyneaux has reciprocal views. He says, 'It was not a matter of wheeling and dealing, or negotiating. I knew that the lines were open. Robin was sounding me out and he was also keeping another line to Major and Reynolds. I trusted him completely.'[6]

Eames became more and more convinced that the Declaration was absolutely crucial if it could address honestly the British and Irish intentions for the future of Northern Ireland. 'My clergy continued to tell me of their anger and the frustrations of their people over the continued violence, as well as their doubts about the future of the Province. John Hume, the SDLP leader, and Gerry Adams, the President of Sinn Fein, had already gone a long way in their joint dialogue to try to break the political deadlock, but among Church of Ireland people in Northern Ireland there was only a grudging acceptance of their importance.'

Eames continued to be impressed by Reynolds' anxiety to accommodate the fears of the Northern Protestants. 'I told him so, and his response was quite candid. He said, "For too long down here we have not taken them on board." '

Eames continued with his drafting. 'I tried to take on board the wording which would bring the Protestant community into the process, rather than do anything to push them further into alienation from a process that was becoming more and more inevitable. I sensed a growing frustration in London that "nothing will satisfy Northern Ireland Protestants", and I found this highly dangerous. It encouraged me to try even harder to ensure that they would be part of the growing peace process.'

In his conversations in London and Dublin, Eames sensed that the real debate would turn on how serious the Republican movement was about peace. He recalls, 'On 11 September 1993, Sir Patrick Mayhew addressed the British-Irish Association at Cambridge. He emphasised the need to renew the talks process, but not the need to involve the men and women of violence in the political process. In the event, the Downing Street Declaration did the opposite.'

Eames' first draft was well received by Reynolds. 'There were further drafts, of course, but these retained the essence of what I had suggested. I believe that what I drafted was to become eventually a substantive part of paragraphs 6–8 of the Downing Street Declaration, and I recognised some of my words and phrases in the finished product.'

This was summarised by Reynolds in his statement on the Joint Declaration on Peace (i.e. the Downing Street Agreement) on 15 December 1993:

Paragraphs 6–8 reflect my desire to respond to Unionist fears. They include a willingness to accept and examine representations by them across the negotiating table with regard to the aspects of life in the South which they believe to be discriminatory or which threaten their way of life.

In the declaration I also ask them to look on the people of the Republic as friends, who share their grief and shame over all the suffering in the last quarter of a century, and who want to develop the best possible relationship with them, in which trust and new understanding can flourish and grow.

In it I also pledge to consider how the hopes and identities of all in relation to constitutional matters can be expressed in more balanced ways, which no longer cause division. I have stated that the Irish Government will, as part of a balanced constitutional accommodation, put forward and support proposals for change in the Irish Constitution, which would fully reflect the principle of consent in Northern Ireland.

Reynolds confirmed that Eames' draft of the crucial paragraphs had been virtually unchanged. He also revealed that paragraph 5 of the Declaration had been drafted with the help of Loyalist sources in Belfast. He said, 'It was important that their voices were being heard and that when the Declaration was made public they would identify with it.'

Eames, for his part, was giving the broad Protestant view. Reynolds said, 'The Archbishop's contribution was significant, because I could rely on him and I could say so with complete confidence, to John Major or anyone else. Through Robin I felt that I had the true feelings of the Protestant community. It gave the final document real credibility on all sides.'

After the Downing Street Declaration was announced on 15 December it was well received by both the British and Irish Parliaments and by the world's media, though the British continued to try to soothe the fears of the Ulster Unionists who reacted to it rather more cautiously.

The importance of the Downing Street Declaration was seminal. It was a powerful symbol which guaranteed that Unionists would not have a United Ireland imposed on them, while Nationalists were assured that their traditions and aspirations would be respected. Equally the paramilitaries were assured that they could enter political life if they accepted the rules of law and democracy, and abandoned violence. The Declaration was not designed as a blueprint for a settlement, but it helped to pave the way.

Robin Eames shares that view. 'The Downing Street Declaration was a historic document whose time had come and it was seen as part of a greater and a developing understanding between the two sovereign Governments. I had lived through the years of megaphone diplomacy across the Irish Sea and I had witnessed at a high level the events which were bringing the two Governments together. Without the Downing Street Declaration there could have been no Good Friday Agreement.'

Frequently on his journeys home from Dublin or London he asked himself, 'Are we turning British-Irish history on its head, are we seeing the beginning of the end of the desperate difficulties between two neighbouring nations? At times I had to pinch myself to make sure that it was all happening.'

It was a most unusual situation for an archbishop to be in, but Eames says that he would do the same again if the situation arose. 'I felt that my role as Primate was much more than being head of the Church of Ireland, which was very important in itself. It was my duty under God to do everything I could to try to bring an end to the death and destruction among my people and their neighbours.

'We were living in highly unusual and dangerous times, when lives were being lost, and if I was asked to be part of the process of trying to bring this to an end, I felt that there was no way in which I could stand aside.'

John Major summarises the crucial role which Eames played in the entire process. He says, 'There are a handful of people who, because of what they were, and because they were *where* they were, enabled the others to bring the threads together. Robin is high on that list. His name did not appear on any key documents, he made no public speeches, but he had a very significant role. He was part of the engine that made the motor go. I think that people will only realise, when he is no longer there, what a significant contribution Robin Eames made. When he goes, he will leave a big hole in the church, and a big hole in the community.'

13

Paramilitaries,
Politicians and Paisleyism

The road from the Downing Street Declaration to the Good
Friday Agreement some fifty-two months later was long and
arduous. While the initial reaction was encouraging from
Parliamentarians in London and Dublin, the Declaration was
given a muted welcome by the Ulster Unionists – though
considering the significant cross-border dimensions involved, a
muted welcome by Unionists was an achievement in itself.

The hardline Democratic Unionists under the Reverend
Ian Paisley were predictably hostile, but the reaction of the
Republican movement would prove crucial. Although Gerry
Adams and his senior colleagues were aware of the origin,
evolution and significance of the Downing Street Declaration
they had to sell it to their grass roots in an attempt to continue
the long march from violence towards political engagement
with the British – and, by implication, with the Ulster Unionists,
though Republicans had given little enough thought to the
wishes and aspirations of Northern Protestants.

Another crucial factor was the likely reaction of the Loyalist
paramilitaries who had to be convinced that there was no sell-
out to Irish Republicanism. Equally important, many people
believed that if Republicans could be edged towards a ceasefire
and ultimate disarmament, it would be easier to nudge the
Loyalists along the same path.

Despite a surge of violence from the Provisional IRA in early
1994, a momentum had been growing behind the scenes for a
possible ceasefire. To outsiders this might have appeared
contradictory, but there was an increasing awareness among

178

Republican strategists and also the British establishment that neither side could win the war outright. The British had the resources and the firepower to do so, but a military victory would have required repressive measures against Republicanism and the Catholic minority in Northern Ireland, which would not have been acceptable to the British public at large.

The focus at this stage was how to move forward without making it appear that the Republicans were losing the war or that the British were giving in to terrorism. This dangerous and often deadly minuet continued, but on 31 August 1994 the Provisional IRA leadership made a historic announcement. It stated: 'Recognising the potential of the current situation, and in order to enhance the democratic peace process and under-line our definite commitment to its success, the leadership of the IRA have decided that as of midnight Wednesday 31 August, there will be a complete cessation of military operations.'

Though the British Government and the Unionists remained sceptical, there were celebrations in Irish Nationalist areas. Despite numerous breaches of the ceasefire, the overall level of violence decreased, and on 13 October the Combined Loyalist Military Command also announced a cessation of all Loyalist violence.

As subsequent events demonstrated, the ceasefire on both sides was far from complete, and violence as well as extortion and drug-dealing were all part of the shady paramilitary undergrowth. However, one constant factor was the slow re-education of violent Republicanism and its painful move towards a realisation of the gains to be made through politics – though many of its Unionist critics would still claim that there was more shadow than substance to such a development.

The significant point remained, however, that the Northern Ireland situation was changing markedly from almost total war and the political deadlock of previous years. A delicate plant of understanding was surviving in a hostile climate, and the bridge-builders like Archbishop Eames were finding themselves drawn in to new, and often surprising, avenues of approach.

Eames already had experience of dealing with shadowy figures within Loyalism, from his early days at St Dorothea's in Belfast, and he also had had some direct, though limited, experience of Republicanism when he was Bishop of Derry and Raphoe.

However, like many other church and community leaders, he wrestled with his conscience on the whole issue of making peace. He asked himself many questions – how far could he go in his contact with combatants without sacrificing his own or the Church's integrity? Where was the line between seeking to listen to views and being perceived to accept them? What was the precise role of the Church when people were obsessed with political issues? He asked, 'How do you define church influence if you are only prepared to speak out from the pulpit or the sanctuary; should the church or its leaders even contemplate going outside to engage with politicians and paramilitaries; and how do you define "real" peace anyway?'

Eames never lost his conviction that his role as a church leader also lay outside the traditional structures. 'It would have been a lot easier and more comfortable if I had devoted all my time to the "institutional" church, but my conscience would not let me do that. The pastoral ministry has been my priority and you cannot isolate yourself by speaking only to those people whom you like and with whom you agree.'

Another consideration was that much if not all of Eames' leadership was exercised in a period of political vacuum and also in a prolonged period of violence. 'Time and again people had appealed for their fears to be addressed. I could not ignore them. Secondly, the Christian faith is about real people in real life situations. One argument always has been "Say your prayers, read your Bible – and forget society". How could I do that and not follow through on the ground?'

He has always believed in dialogue, and he could see no other answer to confrontation or violence. 'I have always felt that no situation is hopeless, and that through God's grace anything, no matter how unbelievable, can occur. I have experienced this on endless occasions. You cannot just give up and walk away. When you risk getting your hands dirty, you are paying the price for outreach and human reaction.'

Eames, of course, was not the only public or private figure who was taking risks for peace. He says, 'Over the years I was helped in this work by many whose courage, vision and hard work were at times beyond belief. Many must remain anonymous, even now.'

Eames made the point repeatedly that he was making contacts as a church leader and that he never gave his support to any one political or paramilitary position. 'I have always sought to analyse their point of view, but also to explain what I feel is the Christian standpoint, and to suggest the possibility of solutions based on that principle. If I felt that I had been clear as to the Christian view of what I had to do, I was prepared to take the risk, whatever the criticism.'

However, he was always mindful that he was not a politician, but a church leader and a pastor. 'I remember a letter I received from a woman in Newtownards whose two sons served in the Ulster Defence Regiment, at a period when it was known that I had helped to play a part, with others, in bringing about the Loyalist ceasefire. She wrote, "Thank God you are there and doing what others have not had the courage to do. You have deepened my faith that God is in this situation with us. Please for all of us, keep it up." '

The announcement of the Loyalist ceasefire in October 1994 was the public culmination of a long evolution that involved Robin Eames and many others, though this was to prove an imperfect process. Nevertheless, it was clear that the Loyalist paramilitaries had also been developing their thinking in the twenty-six years since Eames first encountered them in the Belfast working-class estate where he was then a young rector. He recalls, 'Loyalism is a term that has emerged during my years in church leadership. In my early days the vast majority of the Church of Ireland membership in Northern Ireland would have been classified as Unionist, whereas Loyalism emerged with the birth of Protestant paramilitarism. I always felt that it was a flag of convenience for the Protestant working-class areas which wanted their own sense of identity in the face of the growing strength of Republicanism.'

Eames was never convinced that Loyalism was being thought through properly, and that it was applied to communities who knew what they were not. 'They were not Catholics and certainly not Nationalists. Loyalism became a tribal identity, and during the Troubles it was used as a cover name by various groups who committed the most terrible violence against Catholics.'

One of the problems in trying to curb the spread of violence was the fact that traditional Unionism did not appeal to working-class areas. 'As far back as the 1970s I was telling Unionist leaders that unless they addressed properly the needs of these working-class Protestants, they would come to regret it.

I take no pleasure from the fact that I have been proved right. Traditional Unionism embraced the "union" with Great Britain, and Loyalism became the symbol of anti-Catholic self-seeking. The drug trade and other anti-social behaviour became the criminal activity of many involved.'

Significantly, however, there was also a sense of bewilderment in many of the Protestant working-class areas. 'People could not really understand why or how traditional Unionism had become separated from them, but as the peace process developed I became aware of a change. There is now more genuine political thinking going on in those areas than ever before. A new breed of strategists began to emerge after the first Loyalist ceasefire was announced.'

Eames talked at length with the Reverend Roy Magee, a veteran Presbyterian minister who had his finger on the pulse of Loyalism. 'I respected his judgment, and as we talked I became convinced that the future for Loyalism lay in encouraging them to take part in political dialogue. The question was, "Would they have enough vision and incentive to do so?" '

In 1994 there was a move within Loyalist circles to try to pre-empt an anticipated Provisional IRA ceasefire. The Loyalists, however, wanted to make sure that their proposal would be known at the highest levels in Dublin and London. They felt that Robin Eames was the best-placed person to convey that message to Downing Street, and to Dublin – though they had other contacts within the Republic. With the help of the Reverend Roy Magee, a meeting was arranged with Eames at his office in Armagh.

Magee arrived with two senior military figures from the Combined Loyalist Military Command, though Eames did not know how senior they were, or the positions they held. He trusted Magee, and he was trying to help broker a Loyalist ceasefire. He pointed out that he was not going to be 'used' by them, nor could they take advantage of the Church or his position in any way. He listened intently, and the paramilitary leaders felt that they had made their point.

This was followed, however, by an outbreak of vicious tit-for-tat violence which ended with the murder of a number of Catholics when Loyalist gunmen burst into a bar at Loughinisland where a group of men were watching a football match on television. Eames was not only horrified, he also felt utterly betrayed. He thought that the Loyalist paramilitary leaders had tried to use him, and he determined to sever all links with them.

However, the Reverend Roy Magee prevailed on Eames to think it over. Magee, while he knew that he did not have the political clout of Eames, was very close to the Loyalist paramilitary leaders' thinking, and he told the Archbishop that they had not sanctioned the Loughinisland outrage. Eames, after much heart-searching, decided not to sever his contacts with the group, but there were no more approaches from the Loyalists until after the announcement of the Provisional IRA ceasefire some time later, when he played a key role in helping to bring about a Loyalist paramilitary ceasefire.

Roy Magee, as a respected Presbyterian minister, was taking risks associating himself by meeting with such people – even in the name of peace. He pays tribute to Eames for his willingness to help: 'He really was taking a huge ecclesiastical risk by putting himself forward in this way. He was the head of the Church of Ireland, a senior figure in the Anglican Communion, and highly regarded by all sides of the community. If it had got out that he was secretly talking to senior paramilitary figures in this way, I don't think people would have been understanding about it, and it might have backfired on him. He showed great courage in what he was doing for the sake of long-term peace.'

The Provisional IRA ceasefire brought matters to a head. Eames felt that the world was welcoming this development because a major step had been taken on the path to peace, but he was also deeply worried. 'People were concentrating on the IRA, but no one was asking about the Loyalists.'

Eames was phoned by Roy Magee who had been talking at length with Loyalist leaders. He was deeply concerned and told Eames that the Loyalists were worried that the British had done a deal with the Provisional IRA. Eames said that he would do anything in his power to help bring about a Loyalist ceasefire, but that he had certain conditions to put forward. 'I wanted to make it plain that they could not "use" the Church, that they genuinely wanted peace, and that they would abide by any undertaking they received.'

A week later Magee phoned Eames again to ask if he would be prepared to meet the Loyalist leaders face to face. Eames took time to consider the offer, and after days of turning it over in his mind he became convinced that he could not avoid taking any chance to bring about peace. He agreed to meet the Loyalists and they came to his office in Armagh. 'They were respectful to me and I was assured that those present represented all the major players within the combined "Loyalist Command". I stressed that if there was any attempt to "use" the Church I would walk away. I told them that the murder of Catholics for whatever reason was totally repugnant to me, and that I could not and would not condone it. I urged them to try to lead their communities to peace, and warned them that I would "go public" if I felt that they were trying to bluff me.'

A lengthy discussion took place. The Loyalists expressed their worries but they also stressed that they wanted 'to end it all'. They said that they would declare a ceasefire if Eames could assure them that no British–IRA deal had been done. He asked them if they would accept his word for that, and they agreed.

The meeting was adjourned. Eames talked again to Roy Magee who urged him to take the chance to seize peace. Eames decided to do so and quickly arranged a meeting with Prime Minister John Major at No. 10 Downing Street. This had been arranged with the help of the Archbishop of Canterbury Dr George Carey, who was on good terms with Major. Eames did not want to work directly through Major's official staff, given the highly secretive nature of the task.

Eames recalls, 'In his private room I asked John Major, "Have you done a secret deal with the Provisional IRA to gain their ceasefire?" He looked me straight in the eye and said, "Robin, you are Anglican Primate of All-Ireland and I am the British Prime Minister. If I lie to you, history will judge us both. I can assure you that I have *not* made any secret deal with the Provisional IRA." '

Eames asked him another question, 'Have you made any agreement of any sort with them? Just tell me, and I will walk away from this.' John Major said, 'I have not lied to you.' Eames says, 'I always had straight dealings with John, and I trusted his word. I went back to Northern Ireland and met the Loyalist leaders. I told them of the meeting at No. 10 and they said, "We trust you. If you can stand over that assurance we will declare a ceasefire."

'I replied, "There's one thing more. If you are genuine in

your intentions, you must link your ceasefire with a declaration of regret for all the misery you have caused." To my surprise, they agreed to do so. A few days later a press conference was called by Gusty Spence, a senior figure in Loyalism. At that meeting the Combined Loyalist Military Command announced a ceasefire, and expressed regret for the misery they had caused. I prayed that it had all been genuine, but at least a first step had been taken.'

Following the ceasefire, and despite its many breaches, Eames kept in touch with Loyalism. A new generation of leaders had emerged, and new problems had arisen. He came to know the sons and successors of those leaders he first met, but he felt that a degree of trust had remained.

In later years an umbrella group – the Loyalist Commission – was formed. Without hesitation, Eames urged the Church of Ireland clergy to take part. 'Despite the years of paramilitary activity involving individual violence and criminal activity in drugs, prostitution and protection rackets, I still felt that the Church had a role to play in influencing them towards political rather than military action.'

Eames met the Loyalist Commission in East Belfast, together with Presbyterian and Methodist Church leaders. 'They felt that no one was listening to their needs. They believed that their areas had been ignored in terms of education, recreation and the elderly, and that the peace process was way above their heads. In short they felt that they were irrelevant, and that all the attention was being given to the Republicans.'

In the summer of 2003 the Loyalists expressed a wish to meet the Irish Premier Bertie Ahern to express their views to him directly. Eames, who had a good relationship with the Taioseach, made the arrangements, and both sides met in Dublin for what was described as a 'frank exchange of views'. Eames said, 'It was a useful meeting. The Loyalists told Ahern what they felt and he in turn gave them a feeling that they were being genuinely listened to. I feel that if traditional Unionism had done the same all those years ago, much would have been achieved.'

Despite the developments within Loyalism, Eames has remained a realist. He says, 'Much of Loyalism is a cover for criminality, but it still represents those large areas of working-class Protestants who feel alienated from the "high-wire act" of the peace process. When I visit those places, I still see the consequences of the generations of traditional Unionist neglect of those areas.'

For years he felt that the Church had lost much of the 'working-class' Protestants, and because it had not identified with their needs, it faced a mammoth task in relating to them. 'My worry is that apart from party-political alignments, vast working-class areas are becoming alienated from the political process in general. This, I believe, is a very dangerous situation.

'These people are basically Protestant, and tribal. Their suspicion of traditional Unionism says a great deal about them, and about Unionism. However, I believe that the Church *has* influenced them, and if we can continue to do so with integrity, this will remain a powerful opening to help continue the move away from violence towards politics.'

In the search for a political solution in Northern Ireland, one of the more intransigent factors on the Unionist side during Robin Eames' church career has been the phenomenon of 'Paisleyism', which he describes as 'the raw face of imprisoned and uncertain Unionism'.

The Reverend Ian Paisley has been a remarkable figure in Northern Ireland political life, and, as a Westminster MP, a former Northern Ireland MEP and an orator and self-publicist of considerable ability, he has the distinction of founding not only his own church – the Free Presbyterian Church – but also his own party, the Democratic Unionists, which mounted a considerable electoral challenge to the traditional Ulster Unionist Party. This culminated in a triumph in the 2003 Assembly elections, when the DUP for the first time became the biggest Unionist group in the Northern Ireland Assembly.

Even in his advanced years Ian Paisley showed no lack of appetite for a political battle. He was quoted in *The Times* on 25 October 2003 as saying, 'I can work any man in this Province politically off his feet, and I would go to bed refreshed and he would go to bed knackered.'

Robin Eames, who like many other church leaders has observed Paisley closely, points to two different dimensions. 'On the one hand there is the image of the Reverend Ian Paisley, the man in the light raincoat, the tall, physically imposing figure who proclaims "Ulster Says No!" This is the figurehead of the apprehensive and reactionary right wing of

Unionism, but what has been more significant for me has been "Paisleyism" as a thought process.'

Eames believes that, in religious terms, the main Protestant denominations have always viewed the religious-political face of Paisleyism as a threat. 'Disaffected parishioners, for any reason, have viewed Paisley's fundamentalism as a home for their disaffection, but in my experience many of them eventually returned to their parish. Paisleyism in my time has become the catchword for an attitude of mind among many who would not be necessarily members of his political party or denomination.'

In that sense Paisleyism has been a focus for anti-ecumenism, and for opposition to the Roman Catholic Church. Eames says, 'Paisley's protests against any ecumenical stance or development are predictable, and I remember attending the first Ballymascanlon Inter-Church Conference and running the gauntlet of his protests. However, Roman Catholics speak of him highly as a fair-minded MP, and he has been an excellent constituency representative.'

Historically Northern Ireland has always had strong advocates of religious fundamentalism. 'Paisleyism has stemmed from a bedrock of protest, and has remained so ever since. Fundamentalism in various guises is a living reality in Northern Ireland for all denominations. The Church of Ireland in the Province has its own dimension of this, and often the advocates of "biblical truth" are only a short step away from fundamentalism.'

Ian Paisley has criticised Eames in public on a number of occasions. 'When I was Bishop of Down and Dromore he attacked my advocacy of greater understanding between Northern Ireland and the Irish Republic and he has referred to me as "that ecumenical Eames". However, when he attended funeral services of the victims of violence at which I preached, he caused no problems and on one occasion he congratulated me on "preaching the gospel in such circumstances".'

Though a formidable opponent in public, there is another side to Paisley. 'My contacts with him in private have also given me the opportunity to appreciate a warm, generous and thoughtful man. On occasions we have exchanged books. He is greatly interested in religious history, and he appreciated a book I gave him on Archbishop Agar. In return he sent me a book on the Reformation. He is one of the most widely read people I have met, and if he had confined his activities to religion, I believe that he would have made a profound contribution to evangelical thought.'

This 'private' Paisley is transformed, however, when given a platform and an audience. 'The rhetoric is pure Bible-belt, and the anti-ecumenism abounds. His anti-Rome stance lies at the foundation of the enigma. Among Roman Catholic clergy I have found genuine curiosity about Dr Paisley rather than outright opposition, but among Roman Catholic laity I have encountered fear and suspicion. It is interesting that of all the Roman Catholic leaders I have known, Cardinal Cahal Daly has understood Paisleyism best.'

Despite all that has been written and said about Paisley, he remains an enigma – irrevocably opposed to Rome, often a firebrand in public, consistently opposed to ecumenism and Irish Republicanism, and yet reputedly warm and friendly in private, and gifted with a sense of humour. Eames says, 'Ian Paisley has been and is part of the Ulster story because he has seen how to use the innermost, basic fears of Unionists.'

When Unionism comes under enough pressure it fragments. Eames says, 'It also produces the political phenomenon called Paisleyism which was born out of the fragmentation within Presbyterianism, and it had its greatest hour when fundamental Unionism came under attack.' Given the new political dispensation, it remains to be seen if Paisleyism can be more constructive and imaginative in the search for a working relationship with Republicans, and other Unionists, in the interests of a long-term peace.

Although Eames kept in touch throughout his career with Unionism and with Loyalism at all levels, his early association with Irish Republicanism had been confined to the consequences of Provisional IRA terrorism. 'The majority of those killed in my flock had been murdered by PIRA which was regarded by Protestants as the anonymous terrorist face of Republicanism. The heartache and sadness of numerous families of mine was mixed with anger and total opposition to the IRA.'

He believes that for years Protestantism did not allow itself to look ahead to any purely political involvement by Republicanism. Loyalist terrorism was only of spasmodic and definitely secondary importance. On numerous occasions, at the funerals of the police and members of the Ulster Defence Regiment, he condemned the IRA in the most forthright terms. 'In that respect, Protestantism thought in terms of "victory" – nothing encouraged them to think beyond that.'

While Eames was able to understand fully and enunciate clearly the Protestant viewpoint, he was aware that he was largely ignorant of the history of Irish Republicanism. 'I read widely to help me to understand where they were coming from. I began to think, "What will happen when all this trouble and suffering comes to an end?" '

The emergence of the thinking within the British political and military establishment that there could be no obvious victory over the Provisional IRA was not well received by Protestants, but Eames began to think that some day Northern Ireland society would have to face a new situation. His awareness of the changes within South Africa and his close contact with people like Archbishop Desmond Tutu convinced him that eventually a form of dialogue would replace violence.

Despite the widening of his own thinking, Eames was not ready to meet Gerry Adams when an initial contact was made for a meeting with the Archbishop after the Republican ceasefire in August 1994. He gave long and prayerful thought to Adams' request, but decided that the time was not yet ripe to accept it privately or publicly. At that point there was in-sufficient evidence of a desire within Republicanism to move away from violence, and he felt that his involvement with many of the families of the victims of the IRA would make any such meeting counter-productive.

A year later, however, Eames felt that there would be some point to a meeting with Sinn Fein strategists, though he did not meet Adams at that stage. 'Our conversation was frank, and it concentrated on an examination of the feelings in our respective communities. I underlined the depth of Protestant anger and resentment, and explained from my pastoral contacts the reasons which contributed to the Protestant condemnation of all things Republican.'

The Republicans listened intently and asked searching questions. Eames concluded from what they said that, at that time, Sinn Fein did not understand the non-party political reaction of Protestants, and they saw their 'enemy' as Britain, and not the Ulster Protestants. 'I pointed out that their slogan

"Brits Out" compelled the Protestants in Northern Ireland to ask "Does that mean us as well?" '

Eames felt that Irish Republicanism had not taken enough cognisance of Protestant feelings. 'They saw the "British war machine" as the real enemy. We spent a long time at that meeting, and at subsequent meetings, on that point. I became aware of deep divisions within Republicanism over an end to terrorism, and a desire to find out the possible Protestant reaction to any Republican moves toward peace.'

The process of talking continued and at later meetings Eames met a number of senior figures in Sinn Fein. He was advised from different sources that these contacts had no active involvement with the terrorist campaign. 'I cannot tell how important these talks were for Sinn Fein, although I was well aware that contacts were being made with other Protestant church leaders, particularly in the Presbyterian and Methodist traditions.'

While Eames did not compare notes, he was aware that the other Protestant contacts were telling the same story. It was clear to him that the Republicans were reaching a crucial stage in their thinking. If an end to the suffering could be brought about, any small and seemingly insignificant contribution that he could make should not be lost.

Talking was gradually replacing violence, but memories ran deep in the Protestant community. 'I urged Sinn Fein to take what was for them a risk, namely to make renewed efforts to politicise their activities rather than resort to violence. While my arguments were listened to carefully but in silence, I had no way of knowing how effective my argument was.'

Eames received word that Gerry Adams would still like to meet him, and despite some lingering personal reservations, he agreed to do so. They met several times, either alone or with other people. 'I found Gerry Adams courteous, well informed and prepared to listen. Undoubtedly, he was committed to the Republican socialist agenda, but when I challenged him he seemed anxious to assure me that there would be no return to IRA violence if the political process was successful. However, he always resisted any suggestion that the Provisional IRA should announce an end to all violence. For him that was a step too far.'

Eames was surprised to discover the depth of Adams'

thinking on the advantages but also the dangers of a peace process. 'Clearly he wanted to emphasise political points but I was chiefly concerned to talk to him on a personal level, and to relate to him the feelings of ordinary people in my church and my community. He indicated that he now recognised something of the feelings of the Ulster Protestant population and spoke frankly about his own personal feelings. Man to man we were honest, as far as I could judge, with each other.'

Eames did not want to give the impression that he could speak for the whole Protestant community, many of whom might not share his views. This was accepted by Gerry Adams, and he was assured that Adams could not claim to speak for all Roman Catholics. 'However, I found the interplay on his part between "Nationalism" and "Republicanism" most interesting.'

Eames' contacts with British and Irish government ministers encouraged him to believe that the risks he was taking in talking to Sinn Fein were worthwhile. 'Time will tell how much weight they put on my approach. I was aware also that several Unionist politicians hinted at my contacts with Sinn Fein and I was encouraged that they found these to be useful. Sometimes they asked me, "How do you read what you are hearing from the Republican community?" In return I urged the Unionists to think even more in depth about how they read the mood within Irish Nationalism.'

Eames was convinced from his contacts with Sinn Fein of the similarities among Protestant and Catholic working-class areas. 'The thought occurred to me that if you changed the political labels, the unemployment, the lack of amenities, the education facilities and other basic facts were common to both. I asked myself, "Is it just possible that years ahead we might see a socialist alliance between the two sides?" '

Robin Eames felt that Adams was anxious to remove the perception that Republicans saw the Ulster Protestants as enemies. 'This constantly emerged in our dialogue, but Sinn Fein had not recognised sufficiently the depth of the Pro-testants' allegiance to all things British.' Eames formed a firm impression of a party that was prepared to continue carrying out painstaking research, to carry out in-depth planning and to work to an agenda. He knew that he was only part of a widespread consultation by Sinn Fein with figures from the Protestant community. 'I believe that all of these contacts and discussions have contributed undoubtedly to the gradual move away from violence and towards dialogue.'

The Republicans' movement towards politics, despite the reluctance by the Provisional IRA to admit publicly that the 'war is over', was due to many complex factors. The significance of this shift was underlined on the Roman Catholic side by Cardinal Cahal Daly who had been a fierce public critic of the Provisionals' so-called 'armed struggle' which he described as 'armed anarchy'. Speaking after his retirement he observed, 'The Republican leadership has successfully managed their difficult constituency in bringing them from a total commitment to violence and a suspicion of politics to a position where they are seriously committed to the political process, where they have shown considerable skill.'

Daly felt that they were eventually doing and saying many of the things that Pope John Paul II said in Drogheda, and that many church leaders have been trying to say over the years. 'I am not saying this in any triumphalist way, nor would I expect or want them to say that "Daly was right after all", but I would want them to realise the truth that violence is no way to promote justice.

'The magnitude of the task they faced needs to be appreciated and the skill with which they have done it needs to be commended. I am not saying that the Church directly influenced them – maybe it helped – but the prophetic voice of the Church converged with what they eventually came to realise.'[1]

The task facing all church leaders was to continue to pronounce the prophetic message of the Church, without allowing themselves or their respective denominations to become compromised. Robin Eames, like the others, had his moments of doubt during very difficult times.

The doubts were usually caused by such things as the failure of some people to fulfil the promises they had made, or the breakdown of agreements reached after much heart-searching, or unfounded media comment, which derailed good intentions achieved after hours or days of hard work. 'The doubts also surfaced when I did not know whether or not to believe what I had been told, when laboriously agreed plans might encourage the concept that the Church was becoming too political, or when carefully built-up trust evaporated because of external pressures.'

He has had to live with many dilemmas. 'There will always be dilemmas where the gospel imperative meets the actualities of the world as we know it today. There are no easy answers to a host of ethical questions, but above all else I want to emphasise that all I tried to do stemmed from my deep personal belief that no scenario was entirely hopeless, and that God was in every human situation.'

Eames firmly believes that human nature under pressure can reach the heights of courage and nobility, and it can also sink to the lowest depths. 'I have seen both many times. I have often been asked in media interviews whether or not I lost hope when things were at their worst. I had many disappointments and I felt extremely frustrated at times, but my faith in the ultimate triumph of good over evil and in the basic decency of human beings never wavered.'

In talking to the Loyalist paramilitaries and Sinn Fein Eames undoubtedly took risks, at a time when 'respectable' church people would not have seen the point in doing so or would have argued that the Church should remain far above making such questionable contacts.

Brian Rowan, the authoritative BBC Security Correspondent in Northern Ireland, believes that the easier option for Eames would have been to say 'No' to such approaches, but that he decided that there would be no hiding place for him. 'First he talked to the Loyalists, and then to the Republicans. Given his vast range of contacts he realised that there was no security answer, and that there had to be a different approach.'

The easier option for Eames would have been to say 'Let someone else look after that'. However, Rowan believes, he chose the tough option. 'In doing so he took a huge risk. Had it been known what he was doing, it would have been less understood then than it might be now.' Eames was leading from the front. 'He took a course of action that was ahead of the political approach. He was not part of the "posse", he was ahead of it. That took courage, and he constantly had to measure the personal risks he was taking against the greater good. Those who look back at it from a neutral point of view cannot but admire what he did.'

14

Unfinished Business

The Downing Street Declaration of December 1993 paved the way for the Belfast Agreement, which was signed on 10 April 1998 and became popularly known as the Good Friday Agreement. It emerged after a long period of negotiation during which the American politician Senator George Mitchell played a key role as an 'honest broker' who was trusted and respected by the major parties involved. In Northern Ireland this was a rare accolade for any politician.

The final stages of the negotiations in a suite of offices in the Stormont estate were characterised by political brinkmanship and by doubts inside and outside the building that an agreement could or would be reached. It was a revolutionary process in which, for the first time, the political representatives of Republicanism were engaged in major political negotiations with Ulster Unionists, though the hardline Democratic Unionists refused to take part.

The Prime Minister Tony Blair took a leading role in the negotiations, and the US President Bill Clinton also spent a sleepless night in Washington waiting by the phone for calls from Northern Ireland politicians who needed reassurance during the final stages.

The SDLP, whose leader John Hume had previously taken considerable political risks by engaging in talks with the Sinn Fein leader Gerry Adams, also played a key part in the negotiations. It was ironic that having helped to bring political Republicanism in from the cold, the SDLP for the first time was overtaken by votes for Sinn Fein in the Northern Ireland Assembly elections in Northern Ireland over five years later, in November 2003. At the Stormont negotiations in 1998 the smaller cross-community groups including the Alliance Party and the Women's Coalition were also supportive of the agreement.

Late in the afternoon of Good Friday, the parties finally announced that an agreement had been reached, amid general scenes of rejoicing. It was felt by many people that a real political breakthrough had been achieved, though others had reservations about the lack of detail which left a number of significant issues still unresolved. This included the decommissioning of weapons, and it was the failure of the Provisional IRA to do so, to the satisfaction of the Unionists, that bedevilled the peace process and led to continued bitterness and lack of trust between the two sides.

However, the optimistic mood in the immediate aftermath of the Good Friday Agreement was underlined by Archbishop Eames. He said that for the first time in twenty-five years the message of Easter would be heard by people in all communities in Northern Ireland in an atmosphere of peace. The victory of good over evil, and the banishment of fear, would have a special meaning for people of all traditions.

He said in his Easter message:

> For many years we found that our experiences reflected the suffering of Good Friday. This year we find a new identity with the victory and peace of Easter morning. Our prayer must be that the time of violence has gone for ever, that the time of peace has dawned and that it will mature beyond its present fragile state into permanence.

The Archbishop's optimism and support for the Agreement was reflected in the overwhelming endorsement of the people afterwards, in a referendum in Northern Ireland and the Irish Republic on 22 May. Elections were quickly held, and the Northern Ireland Assembly had its first meeting on 1 July. People were aware that there would be inevitable arguments and possible deadlock on the way to the appointment of a Northern Ireland Executive with devolved powers from Westminster, but many were agreeably surprised (and not a few downright astonished) that such apparent political progress had been made.

With the passage of time, however, uncertainty and disillusion began to creep in. Many Unionists found it hard to accept that prisoners including Republican paramilitaries would be released before they had served their full sentences. They were infuriated by what they regarded as the Provisional IRA's prevarication over the decommissioning of weapons, while the Republican movement at large seemed to be intent on wresting as many further concessions as it could from the British Government.

On the other side, hardline Republicans felt that Sinn Fein had betrayed their fundamental principles by agreeing to serve with Unionists and others in a Stormont Assembly that they regarded as a British establishment. This led to a split within Republicanism and the formation of small but dangerous and ruthless paramilitary off-shoots under various names, including the 'Real' and 'Continuity' IRA. It began to look as if the long-awaited and much-lauded Good Friday Agreement was perhaps too good to be true after all.

Robin Eames and other clergy at all levels were quickly aware of the uncertainty about the future, and the price to be paid for a lasting peace. Opinions were sharply divided within the Protestant community, and this was reflected in the Church of Ireland. Eames was criticised by some of his own people for declaring that, despite his reservations, the Agreement was the 'only show in town'.

He says, 'The consent element required in accepting the Good Friday Agreement was lost for many who found that the early euphoria had prevented them from reading the small print. Both communities had to give as well as to receive, but this was not an easy message to proclaim. Protestantism was split, and when Sinn Fein members took ministerial office in the new Northern Ireland Executive the raw nerves became even more jangled.'

The Archbishop received a delegation of parishioners from the border areas whose relatives in the police and army had been killed or maimed by the IRA. He recalls, 'I could see their pain and anger at the release of people they regarded as murderers. It would have been a futile task to ask people in the midst of such raw and understandable emotion to think their way through the political complexities of the Agreement.'

At parochial level the clergy had to deal with the divisions, and they quickly witnessed the emergence of 'pro' and 'anti' camps within Unionism. These divisions increased considerably among the grass roots as the Agreement itself appeared to take hold at governmental level. Many Unionists were asking, 'Why do we have to give up so much and get so little in return?' Eames recalls, 'Memory is a precious element and it often makes us what we are. Within Northern Ireland this is important, and Protestants so often listen to their memories – many of which are negative. People worried about moving into the unknown, or about a drift back to the dark days. Courage and trust were needed, but both were in short supply.'

The apprehension and mistrust within the wider community were greatly increased by the outrage in the country town of Omagh, west of the River Bann, where twenty-eight people were killed and more than three hundred injured on 15 August 1998 when a large car bomb exploded on a busy Saturday afternoon in the main street. Not long afterwards, a twenty-ninth victim died.

It was by far the worst incident of the Troubles, and the harrowing scenes of human distress and utter carnage were broadcast on television to millions by means of video footage taken of the chaos near the centre of the blast, and through the interviews with the bereaved and the suffering. Tragically, the security forces had received a garbled telephone warning shortly before the blast, with the result that people were being moved towards the area of the explosion rather than away from it. The outcome was horrendous.

The bomb was part of a concerted campaign by Republican paramilitaries who opposed the Agreement. Earlier in the month the town of Banbridge had also been devastated by a large bomb – though fortunately there had been no loss of life. Three days after the Omagh bomb, the so-called 'Real IRA' claimed responsibility, and soon afterwards declared that it was suspending all operations, following widespread condemnation and also a warning from the mainstream Republican movement that it should disband. Nevertheless, another splinter Republican group, the 'Continuity IRA', resisted all pressures for a ceasefire.

The Omagh bomb was widely condemned on all sides. In view of the hopes for peace which had been engendered only a few months previously by the Good Friday Agreement, this

197

unprovoked attack on innocent people in a small rural town seemed all the more barbaric and reprehensible.

On the afternoon of the explosion, Robin Eames was taking a rare opportunity to relax at home. A phone call from Ken Magennis (now Lord Magennis), then Westminster MP for the Omagh area, alerted him to the bombing. Eames decided immediately to drive to Omagh, some twenty miles away. He recalls, 'I travelled to the town with the overriding thought, "Not again, please God, not again." Memories came flooding back of the Enniskillen atrocity of 1987, and I had seen wounds there that might never heal. The hospital in Omagh, like that in Enniskillen all those years ago, provided scenes of utter carnage and suffering. That was awful, but the following day was very bad as well.'

The local recreation centre became the focal point for the relatives of the dead and missing. 'It was the silence I will never forget. Once more I marvelled at the dignity and courage of the Ulster people in the face of terrorism. Together with other church leaders I moved among the people, offering them what comfort or prayers I could.'

As more information became available, family members were called into a side room. 'Not far away a temporary morgue had been prepared. It was an unforgettable sight, with personal belongings laid out with the remains of those who had died. I spoke to ambulance workers, soldiers and the police, who were coping as best they could. I was full of admiration for their quiet efficiency, but most of all for their dignity as they went about their desperately sad work.'

Eames, like everyone else, was deeply disturbed by what had happened, but deep down he was also very angry – though he did not show it. He says, 'Despite all the atrocities I had seen, Omagh stood out for several reasons, not only because of the sheer scale of the suffering but also for the blatant disregard of those who planted a bomb on a Saturday afternoon in the heart of a busy town. I was nauseated by some of the excuses offered for the Omagh bombing and by the fact that after all we had endured, violence seemed the only way in which terrorists could make their point.'

The anger of so many people, including the Archbishop, was well expressed by the *Church of Ireland Gazette*. In its editorial the next week it referred to the dreadful, cold anger at those men and women from the so-called 'Real IRA' who had the arrogance to believe that they knew better than anyone, that the future for this island lay through violence . . .

There is utter revulsion on all sides and in all parts of this island, indeed in these islands and world-wide, at their totally cynical and crude attempt to apologise, as if mass murder could somehow be shrugged off as a mistake. The 'Real IRA' and their political fellow-travellers deserve no sympathy, no pity, no quarter.

The then Church of Ireland Press Officer Elizabeth Gibson-Harries, who was also in Omagh to assist with press enquiries in the aftermath of the bomb, remembers watching Eames pace up and down on his own, deep in thought. She says, 'The media, as always, were looking for a quote, but I knew when to approach Robin and when to leave him alone. You sensed when he needed the time and space to talk to and to listen to his God, and when he had done that, somehow he was ready to make a statement, and to come up with the right words. People tend to forget how often he had to do that throughout the Troubles, and what it took out of him.'

In one sense, the Archbishop was never off duty, and he was always aware of the challenges and opportunities of his public role to offer words of comfort and reassurance or of challenge and criticism. However, in the years after the Downing Street Agreement and in the run-up to the Good Friday Agreement, part of his background role in Northern Ireland changed subtly but significantly.

Earlier he had been drawn in almost to the point of policy-making in trying to build political bridges between North and South and to foster and develop greater understanding between the communities in the North. However, after the Downing Street Agreement it was clear that the only long-term settlement would be one that contained significant constitutional change by Britain and the Irish Republic, with the consent of the people North and South.

Whereas in the past there had been limited and painful attempts in developing dialogue, the politicians were now talking more openly, even if it appeared in the North that it was 'at' rather than 'to' one another. Accordingly, Eames found himself involved in another kind of dialogue in his secret and politically highly sensitive encounters with Loyalist paramilitaries, and also with Sinn Fein representatives – as outlined in a previous chapter.

Notwithstanding this subtle but important change of direction in his background meetings, he continued to maintain the closest possible ties with leading politicians, including the Prime Ministers of Britain and Ireland and with successive Northern Ireland Secretaries.

Eames formed a good working relationship with Tony Blair, though not as close as that with his predecessor John Major, with whom he had been involved in the build-up to the Downing Street Declaration and the first Loyalist ceasefire. The Archbishop found Blair a good listener, with a sound knowledge of local attitudes, but the Prime Minister started on the wrong foot when he first met the church leaders at Stormont. Eames recalls, 'He asked us, "What can you do for me?" in helping the peace process, and seemed disappointed when we did not produce any clear-cut response. Life was not quite as simple as that, even though the Church had been involved for decades in the peace process. Tony Blair was known to have had a poor regard for our leadership at that point, but he was a quick learner, and later on the relationships improved greatly.' Blair invited the church leaders to Downing Street for breakfast on at least two occasions, and the atmosphere was cordial. One of the results was a new joint initiative on sectarianism in Northern Ireland which the churches spearheaded.

During the meetings with Blair, Eames noted that the Prime Minister, a regular churchgoer, asked for prayers at the start, which seemed an appropriate request in such a gathering. Eames says, 'Some people outside our circle might have regarded that as a cynical attempt by Tony Blair to win us over, but I never thought that. I felt that he was sincere.'

Eames paid tribute to the immense amount of time that Blair devoted to Ulster. 'Protestants treat him with varying degrees of suspicion over what many regard as broken promises, but no one can fault him over the energy he has exerted in addressing the Northern Ireland problem, trying to bring about a solution. Unfortunately all his efforts to date – and those of many other people, it must be said – have failed to produce a lasting solution.'

Robin Eames found the Irish Premier Bertie Ahern very approachable, though he did not have the same degree of contact that he had had with Albert Reynolds. As noted earlier, Ahern readily agreed, at Eames' request, to meet representatives of the Loyalist Commission umbrella group in 2003. Eames says, 'I liked Bertie Ahern. He was well versed in Northern Ireland matters, and in dealing with him in the Irish Republic he was most sympathetic to the Church of Ireland.'

Within Northern Ireland, Eames dealt with various Secretaries of State during both Tory and latterly the Labour administrations. Though each one had considerable power and influence, each one varied greatly in ability, style and temperament. Eames, in his characteristic way, dealt with each one on an individual basis.

He regarded Mo Mowlam, an exuberant and larger-than-life Secretary of State, to be a good listener who appreciated a carefully argued case. Eames, however, was furious when one of Mowlam's aides leaked his name as a senior public figure who would give his full support to a Stormont cross-community initiative before it had even been announced. Eames protested strongly to the Northern Ireland Office, and Mowlam rang him back urgently to express her 'deep regret', and to thank him for not calling for the sacking of her official who had leaked the material.

Eames recoils at the memory of such spin. He says, 'I had agreed to support the initiative because I felt that it would help the general situation, and not just because it had come from Stormont. However, I was angry that my name had been leaked in that way. I do not believe that the people of Northern Ireland ever realised how much power the civil servants in the Northern Ireland Office had. The story of that "leak" showed the kind of planning that went on behind the scenes.'

Peter Mandelson, a very different character from Mowlam, also made a highly individualistic impression during his short tenure as Northern Ireland Secretary. Eames found him warm, friendly and determined – but much influenced by the prevailing line from London. The Archbishop had a good relationship with Mandelson and appreciated, among other things, his sense of humour. 'Peter discovered a chess set designed for tourists, and it had an effigy of me. He had much glee in presenting me with the piece.'

Eames found Mandelson's successor John Reid a no-nonsense politician who was not easily bruised by the hurly-burly of politics in general or by Northern Ireland in particular. Reid was followed by Paul Murphy, who had previous experience in Ulster as a junior minister before his promotion to Welsh Secretary and later Northern Ireland Secretary. Eames was impressed by Murphy who had an acute political sense, allied to a strong Christian faith, and a Welsh background which enabled him to understand much of the local reaction in Northern Ireland. Eames says, 'He was one of the most dedicated Secretaries of State we have had.'

Although Eames had been used to moving easily among the corridors of power and influence for many years, he was faced with a personal dilemma when he was offered a life peerage in 1995. On the one hand he knew that it would give him a voice in the Lords, particularly on Northern Ireland, and he was drawn to the tradition and history of the House which, he also recognised, would still be open to him long after he left clerical office.

He also felt that Anglicans in the North would perceive this as a recognition of the constructive role played by the Church of Ireland and other churches during the Troubles. On the other hand he was well aware of the likely reaction of some of his flock in the Republic who might feel that by accepting a peerage he would align himself too closely with the British Establishment.

By custom, senior Church of England bishops, including both serving archbishops, have automatic seats in the Lords, and Canterbury and York receive life peerages on retirement. This, however, does not apply in Northern Ireland. When the Church of Ireland was disestablished by the Irish Church Act of 1869–71, the right to automatic seats in the Lords for Irish bishops was abolished. In one sense, therefore, it was a personal honour for Eames to have been offered a life peerage, and by implication an honour for his church – even though an important part of its membership owed their allegiance to a different state.

Because the offer was confidential, as it always is with things of this nature, Eames could not consult widely, but after thinking about it long and hard, he decided to accept the peerage. He recalls, 'It was made plain by London that this honour was in recognition of my personal work during the Troubles. I also felt that it could give me a further opportunity to bring a church perspective to Northern Ireland affairs at Westminster, and this opportunity had to be taken seriously.'

Eames characteristically seized the opportunity to make a contribution to the Lords, though because of the pressure of other duties he was unable to attend as often as he would have wished. He has, however, made a number of important speeches and although he does not address the House often, people listen to what he says.

He has also used his position to brief senior peers on Northern Ireland affairs, to inquire regularly about the rights and treatment of immigrants in Northern Ireland, to help lobby for financial aid to Northern Ireland's two universities – Queen's and Ulster – to support the cases of RUC and UDR widows, and other matters directly affecting Northern Ireland and its people.

Lord Dubs, who was a Labour Minister at Stormont for over two years from 1997, was responsible for Agriculture and the Environment and for Northern Ireland matters in the House of Lords. He says, 'I found Robin Eames' contributions very helpful. Because he spoke with authority, with experience and with principle, his words carried weight.'[1]

Clearly Eames likes being a member of the Lords, and appreciates the opportunity to meet other peers from a wide variety of backgrounds. One of his favourite haunts is the Lords Library where he finds space from his pressing diary engagements in order to read and to write sometimes copious letters in longhand. During his visits to the Lords he is known affectionately to the Library cleaners as the 'night watchman' because of the late and early morning hours he spends there.

On a broader scale he has been fascinated by the work of the House, and finds the debates to be generally thoughtful, well researched and informative. He says, 'Far from being a club for the retired, the House works long hours, and I am convinced that in any future constitutional reform, it is essential that the House of Commons does have a second chamber to scrutinise its work.'

He sits as a cross-bencher without any party affiliation, together with people like Lords Carey, Sheppard and Habgood. He would welcome the introduction of more peers representing denominations other than the Church of England and religions other than Christianity, and a reduction in the number of English bishops who are given automatic membership. He detects a tendency for English bishops to assume that the issues that concern the Church of England should automatically be representative of those facing people in the United Kingdom as a whole. He says, 'That is not necessarily so. My arrival in the Lords caused the English bishops quite a stir, but I made it plain that I was not one of them and that I would speak my mind freely. I believe that cross-benchers have a unique role in the Lords.'

When his peerage was first announced he found 'an amazing period of approval and congratulations from Northern Ireland church people' and 'a surprisingly small note of dissent from the Republic'. There may have been more dissent at that time than he realised, though attitudes have softened – partly because of his expressed wish not to use his title outside the Lords, and partly because some Irish issues simply fade away. Senior clergy in the South point out carefully that in the Church of Ireland Directory he is listed as 'Archbishop' and not as 'Lord' Eames.

The ambivalence of attitudes south of the border was summarised by Archbishop Neill of Dublin, who recalls the sense of pride that was shared by many in the Republic that Eames' role as church leader had been recognised by the Establishment. However, while Neill was pleased for him personally, he says, 'I was glad for him as I regarded it as a great personal honour, but I did wonder about its wisdom. Robin and I often talked about it. I was very supportive at first, and then I began to have some qualms, but overcame them. Robin rose above the negative opinions. You never hear anything mentioned of it now, and certainly it is never thrown in people's faces.'

Neill's predecessor Archbishop Walton Empey found much the same reaction. 'There was a feeling among some that he would always be seen as part of the British Establishment. Surprisingly, it came from some of those who appeared to be "Ascendancy" types. They thought it was the wrong move, but all this was overcome.'

Empey was also personally pleased for Eames, as was Bishop Samuel Poyntz, who had wide experience North and South of the border. Poyntz reflected that it might have been better if the peerage had been offered at the end of Eames' episcopate, but he also summarised the prevailing feelings at that time. He said, 'A number of Southerners would have felt that this was distancing Robin from the South, and the all-Ireland dimension. On the other hand a large number of people felt that he had borne the burden of the day, and that it was a just recognition for what he had achieved. I was also delighted for Christine who had been a wonderful Archbishop's wife and who had done so much as President of the Mothers' Union.'

Archbishop Empey's observation that all of this was a 'hiccup' at the time is an accurate summary of North–South perceptions within the long history of the Church of Ireland. A much more divisive issue, however, was the prolonged deadlock over Drumcree, which was one of the most serious challenges of Robin Eames' entire Primacy and one which pitchforked the Church of Ireland into a raging controversy which caused considerable pain and distress on both sides of the border. It was not for nothing that Eames referred to it often, and with considerable feeling both in public and in private, as his 'Calvary'.

15

Drumcree – the Passion
and the Pain

The Drumcree stand-off, which began in 1995 between Portadown Orangemen and the Roman Catholic residents of the Garvaghy Road, was one of the most difficult, dangerous and intractable problems of the entire Troubles in Northern Ireland. At the height of the confrontation it led to deaths, and to widespread rioting and considerable damage. It also led, on occasions, to a virtual paralysis of the Province, and, as further confrontation loomed each summer in early July, thousands of people deliberately took their holidays outside Northern Ireland – if they could – to escape from the atmosphere of danger and gloom.

The 'Drumcree factor' was blamed, to a greater or lesser degree, for adding to the difficulties of finding a peaceful solution to the Troubles, and also for making it much harder to attract tourists. In recent years the tensions have subsided markedly, though the stand-off has remained and affected most directly the Portadown area. At the time of writing, the problem remains unresolved.

There are hopes, however, that a peaceful solution can be reached sooner rather than later, but, as with much else in the tortuous history of Northern Ireland, the outcome is still unpredictable. The problem could quietly wither away, or it could explode once again into direct confrontation between some of those most closely involved – as it did in 2002 when the police were viciously attacked following the annual Orange service at Drumcree parish church. The fact remains that the wounds of Drumcree will take a very long time to heal, if ever.

For Robin Eames, Drumcree was a particularly heavy cross to bear. There was a supreme irony that this archbishop who had distinguished himself through his reconciling work within world Anglicanism and among the churches in Ireland seemed unable to achieve reconciliation in the heart of his own diocese.

There was also great pain for the Church of Ireland which nightly witnessed one of its churches in the television headlines amid vicious community upheavals, while the rest of the world looked on in a state of almost total incomprehension. Nearer home there was also the constant danger that the events at Drumcree would create deep and permanent divisions within the Church of Ireland itself.

Its members in the Irish Republic were aghast at what was happening and wanted the church to act decisively and to disassociate itself publicly from such sectarian mayhem by banning the Orange service in Drumcree church. Its members in the North, very many of whom were equally disturbed by what was happening, knew in their bones that there was no simple solution. Added to this was the human factor that many families in the Armagh diocese – men, women and children – had been deeply involved with the Orange Order for generations, and felt that this confrontation at Drumcree marked virtually the Orangemen's last stand.

In the middle of all this was Robin Eames, who knew intuitively, intellectually and politically the historical dimension of the events taking place all around him. He also knew the implications of putting a foot wrong, and he was aware that he would have to make decisions that his armchair observers, including his many critics, would never have to take. He recalls, 'Drumcree became a heavy cross to carry, because of the dilemmas and the unanswered questions, and the inevitable trouble year after year. As each July drew nearer, no matter what efforts had been made to try to solve it, you had this awful feeling of dread.' In addition, there was the constant pressure of continual criticism from outside, both founded and unfounded, and the sheer frustration of the failure to find a solution. He says, 'There was very, very strong hurt and pain. No single event in my time as Archbishop took more out of me than the Drumcree situation.'

The seeds of the Drumcree conflict go back many years, even centuries – depending on one's point of view. The issues

207

are complex, and the tortuous story would warrant a book in itself.[1] There is a risk in perhaps oversimplifying such a divisive issue in which all participants had their own clear and often opposing view of what was happening. However, in very broad terms, it was a quarrel about identity, a clash of cultures, a determination not to give ground to the other side, a total absence of trust, and a hardening of attitudes all round as the struggle increased in intensity year after year. In one sense it was a cameo of the divisions in Northern Ireland itself, though some observers felt that Drumcree was unique.

The dispute centred on two areas – the picturesque Parish Church of the Ascension where Orangemen from the Portadown district had attended a religious service each year since 1807. In later years it took on a special focus, which was the commemoration of the Battle of the Somme in 1916 where the 36th (Ulster) Division suffered enormous numbers of deaths and injuries. Traditionally the Orangemen completed the journey back to the centre of Portadown by marching along a country road which used to wind its way between green fields.

However, the geo-political map changed when members of the Roman Catholic minority in Portadown were rehoused in the Garvaghy Road area, along which the Orange march processed briefly. Though the first really major stand-off between the two sides occurred in 1995, the parade had been contentious for the previous twenty years, partly because the Orangemen had also been allowed by the security forces to proceed along Obins Street and through 'The Tunnel', a Nationalist area, against the wishes of the local Roman Catholics.

Partly in order to avoid this, the march was subsequently re-routed along the Garvaghy Road, but with the influx of more Roman Catholics to new local housing estates, this in turn became a flash-point area. For a number of years previously to 1995, residents' groups from Garvaghy had protested against the Orange march, but with time the protests became more substantial and more sharply focused.

In 1995 the whole issue came to a head when the security forces, in an attempt to prevent serious confrontation between the two sides, stopped the Orange march from proceeding along the Garvaghy Road, where a large number of Nationalists had gathered in protest. The Orangemen were taken by surprise by the ban but vowed to stay on Drumcree hill until their march was permitted to go ahead. Meanwhile, thousands of Orangemen from all over Northern Ireland made their way to Drumcree to add their support.

Thus the stand-off began, and continued during the early part of each July for nearly a decade, at the latest reckoning. Violence escalated in 1995 at Drumcree, and police retaliated by firing plastic bullets. Many roads across Northern Ireland were barricaded by Orange supporters, and the main road to the port of Larne was temporarily blocked. In effect a localised dispute in Portadown was deeply affecting life across the Province. After two days, the Orangemen were permitted to walk silently along the Garvaghy Road past placard-waving Nationalist protesters after an alleged compromise had been reached that the march would not be repeated – though this was later denied by Orange sources.

'Drumcree One', as it came to be called, created shock waves through Northern Ireland's political and community life, but, despite strenuous efforts to find a solution in the next twelve months, the stand-off occurred again in July 1996. There was even worse violence not only in the Drumcree area but in many parts of Northern Ireland, where for a short period several towns were cut off by Loyalist protesters. Hundreds of extra soldiers were again sent to Northern Ireland to assist the hard-pressed police. In four days alone there were 156 arrests, 100 incidents of intimidation, 90 civilian and 50 RUC recorded injuries and 758 attacks on police. More than 660 plastic bullets were fired.[2]

On the morning of 11 July 1996, the stand-off took a dramatic twist which was to have far-reaching consequences. The police, fearing that lives would be lost, decided on the controversial measure of allowing – many people would say 'forcing' – the parade down the Garvaghy Road against the wishes of the Nationalist residents. It transpired later that the police decision was taken because the army had warned that if the Loyalist protesters were to break through the security barriers beyond Drumcree, they would have to use live bullets to prevent them from reaching the Catholic housing estates on the Garvaghy Road. The potential loss of life would have been catastrophic.

To some it may have seemed the lesser evil to have allowed the parade to take place, but it proved to be a turning point for the worse. The Nationalists felt betrayed by the Government, with predictable rioting in Catholic areas across Northern Ireland. Attitudes on both sides hardened further, and a solution appeared even less possible, despite the enormous number of attempts to broker a solution in subsequent years.

The Drumcree crisis was not the only stand-off between members of the Loyal Orders and Nationalists, and there have been a number of flashpoints elsewhere each year, notably in North and South Belfast and also in Londonderry where, however, the locals seem to have been much more able to reach an accommodation.

Drumcree was typical, and yet atypical, of other disputes. It was seen by Orangemen as a last stand for 'Protestant' civil rights to march in their own land, even if that meant going through Nationalist areas where they had marched, as at Drumcree, for nearly two centuries. Equally it was seen by Nationalists as a test case for their ever-increasing self-assertion. They argued that Orangemen could not march as 'of right' in the Nationalist areas of Garvaghy, and by implication in other areas, and particularly if they were not prepared to talk to the residents face to face about it. And so it went on and on.

Meanwhile, Robin Eames became directly involved as Archbishop and Bishop of the Armagh diocese. It was 'his' church which was seen to be at the middle of the crisis. As he noted later, 'This particular situation could have arisen almost anywhere in Northern Ireland, but it came to a head at Drumcree, and therefore it became a "Church of Ireland" problem. However, a former Presbyterian Moderator remarked to me, "This could have arisen outside any Protestant church in the Province. It just happens to be one of yours, and our thoughts and prayers are with you." '

As the Drumcree stand-off developed, and the violence escalated, Eames had two major problems to consider – what could he do, if anything, to help lower the tension on the ground? Second, what could he do to hold the Church of Ireland together during the ongoing crisis, while ensuring that it spoke out courageously for its principles without allowing itself to be compromised either by its own lack of action, or by allowing itself to be dragged along by one side or other in the partisan arguments that raged in an atmosphere of violence and fear?

During the first stand-off in 1995, Eames first learned of the crisis from a news bulletin he saw while he was in an aircraft on his way to Australia to fulfil a series of lecture engagements. On his return he was taken aback to discover the full implications of the violence, which he condemned. He says, 'I did so without reservation, and came in for sustained Loyalist criticism for doing so.'

There was little he could do directly at that stage, apart from condemning the violence, but he tried in the ensuing twelve months to use his influence in his diocese and much further afield to try to calm the situation. He recalls, 'I also kept the House of Bishops fully informed, and received their unanimous support for my pastoral approach. They accepted that there was no easy answer.' Despite this, there was a widespread belief that the situation at Drumcree would not be repeated. Eames says, 'I knew differently in my heart, because of my knowledge of the depth of feelings in Portadown.'

Inevitably the 1996 stand-off was the result of a failure to find a solution in the preceding twelve months, and as it continued the situation worsened considerably. Eames went down to the hill of Drumcree, where the Orangemen and their supporters had taken up position. He recalls, 'Having issued a very loud and determined call for the protest to end, I went to see for myself what was happening. I was barracked and verbally abused by Loyalist supporters who felt that I had let them down totally, because of the stand I was taking. I was very disappointed by the attitude of those whom I thought would have been the first to understand why I had to condemn the violence.'

Meanwhile Unionist leaders were meeting the Prime Minister John Major in London to try to find a way out of the crisis, but without success. As the violence continued Eames became involved, 'almost as a result of desperation', in an attempt to bring together representatives of the Orange Order and the Garvaghy residents at a neutral place in the Portadown area, under the auspices of the church leaders. The chosen venue was the board room and other facilities of the Ulster Carpet Mills plant to the south of the Garvaghy Road, which the management had made available.

The meeting was a disaster, partly because of the mutual distrust between the representatives of the Orangemen and the

Nationalist residents. The church leaders present included, as well as Robin Eames and Cardinal Cahal Daly, who had already cut short a week of engagements in Austria, the Presbyterian Moderator the Right Reverend Harry Allen, and the Methodist President Dr Edmund Mawhinney. The previous day the Unionist leader David Trimble had met church leaders in Armagh, including Cardinal Daly who recalled later, 'We were being asked to bring the parties together to see if some agreement could be reached, and that's why I agreed to take part.'

The representative groups arrived separately at the factory around 8 a.m. and were taken to separate rooms. There was already a great deal of misunderstanding, with the residents' representatives believing that they were to meet with the Orange representatives face to face, which the Orangemen had made clear earlier they would not do. Much worse was to come, however. Within a comparatively short time the news had leaked out that the parade was going to be allowed to proceed down the Garvaghy Road, after all.

Brendan McKenna, the leader of the Garvaghy Road Residents' Coalition, was furious, and felt that he and his colleagues had been deliberately lured to the talks as a diversionary tactic while the security forces were making preparations to allow the march to proceed. The timing could not have been worse. Cardinal Daly felt badly let down, and Eames and the other church leaders were also taken aback.

Stephen Lynas, the Presbyterian Press Officer who was in the carpet factory recalls, 'I am unsure as to when we knew that the Orangemen were to march down the road. However, I remember that the church leaders were quite shocked, and fearful of the consequences. I recall Brendan McKenna leaving the building and hurling abuse at the church leaders, whom he considered were part of a plan to get him off the Garvaghy Road so that a march could be forced through.'

Eames said later, 'The first I knew that the parade was coming down was when word filtered through to the carpet factory. However to say, as some people have done, that the church leaders had conspired together to get the residents' leadership off the Garvaghy Road was a downright lie. We had attempted as church leaders to find a solution, and if we had not tried, we would have been guilty of even greater condemnation.'

The church leaders then retired to the Church of Ireland rectory at Seagoe, and Eames recalls an atmosphere of sadness and disappointment. He says, 'I remember Cardinal Daly sitting across the room from me, deep in thought and very, very silent, and then he got up and left. I feared that what had happened had put a certain strain on our friendship. Later on, I made a point of telling him categorically that I had not consorted with anyone in Government or the security forces, and that he had my word for it. I think that eased the situation, and it has not affected my relationship with him since then. I still feel as close to him as before all that took place.'

Cardinal Daly also recalls a sense of downheartedness after the failed talks in the carpet factory. 'No one was in a mood to talk. There was no joy in the atmosphere. We were tired because of loss of sleep the night before, and tense because of the efforts we had been making to the very last minute. I knew that the others might not have had the same perception as I had of what had taken place. I think Robin knew how I felt, and that the others did also. I suspected that they were embarrassed.'

Privately, Daly was angry at what had taken place. He recalls on the night before the march, the church leaders had spent long hours at the house of the Methodist President Dr Edmund Mawhinney in Belfast trying to refine the formula for bringing both sides together the next day. He says, 'There were many messages going back and forth, and it was conveyed to us that there was a deadline beyond which it would be too late to do anything.'

The Cardinal felt strongly that a decision had already been taken. He says, 'I am not pointing the finger of blame at anyone, but just recording the fact that I felt then, and I have felt since, that decisions had been taken already, and we were there to cover this up with some kind of veil of respectability and acceptability. I have no proof, that was only my instinct, and that determined what I had to say later about Drumcree '96.'

After meeting with the other church leaders in the local rectory after the failure of the talks the next day, Daly made his way to the Garvaghy Road where he received a hostile reception. This was daunting and difficult for him personally. He was an elderly man who had been up most of the previous night for the talks and had had only a few hours' sleep. He says, 'People banged on the car windows and shouted, "Get out, you traitor!"

I was excoriated by the Garvaghy people, and I never received so much "stick" in my life. They felt that I had let myself be used by "the Brits" – that was their term, not mine. They thought that I had done this knowingly, and I knew that I hadn't.'

The Cardinal strongly defended his position later in public, but he believed that he had been used. He says, 'I felt that we had been "used" in our good faith. I was sore about it, but time heals. It's over and done with.'

Stephen Lynas recalls, 'Some days later Cardinal Daly did an interview in which he heavily criticised the whole handling of the affair, both the Government and the RUC, and the forcing through of the parade. However, I don't remember him being in any way critical of his church-leader colleagues, endorsing the view that they had no prior knowledge of government intentions.'

Father Brian Lennon SJ, who had been working for a long time with the Catholic community in Portadown, acted as a facilitator with the Garvaghy Road residents and had been present in the carpet factory. He felt that the situation had been handled badly. He recalls, 'It was difficult beforehand to convince the residents that they were not being set up, and more difficult afterwards to convince them that this was not what actually happened.'

Eames says, 'If I was to live through it again, I would do it differently, and I would prepare the mechanics of it better, but in the same circumstances I would push for such a meeting. In the absence of anything else, it would be worth a try.' Eames was aware of the consequences of the failed meeting and the eventual march along Garvaghy Road. He recalls, 'The failure at the carpet factory ruptured my relationship with the Garvaghy Road residents, if such a "relationship" had indeed existed. I was angry at the continuing accusations of "connivance". I took those personally and I continue to deny most strongly that there was any form of collusion. After all that had happened, I felt totally gutted, and I asked myself, "Where do I turn to now as a basis for continuing dialogue?" '

That was a very difficult question indeed.

16

More Passion – More Pain

Although any room that Archbishop Eames had had to man-
oeuvre as a bridge-builder between the two communities had
disappeared following the acrimonious end to the carpet factory
talks in July 1996, he refused to give up his attempts to influence
the Orangemen. After the trauma of the first two years of the
stand-off, and particularly after 1996, it was clear that there
would be no easy breakthrough and both sides faced the long
haul – though, with hindsight, most people could hardly have
believed that the dispute would still be festering nearly a decade
later.

Eames realised that his personal dilemma was stark. He says,
'I had to decide between seeking an "easy" way out of ending
that particular Sunday service that had existed for generations,
or finding a means of keeping my diocese and my church
together by supporting efforts to find a consensus which would
bring about a lasting settlement.'

He decided that the so-called 'easy' solution could have led
to a split within his diocese and the Church of Ireland as a
whole. He says, 'After much prayer and dedication, I took the
hardest course of working endlessly to try to find an accommodation. I would probably have had a much easier life if at the
beginning I had bowed to the pressure to try to call a halt to
the service, to try to "discipline" the Rector and Select Vestry
of Drumcree parish church. I became convinced, however, that
I should not and could not walk away by taking the easier
course.'

He felt that if a solution could be found through reconciliation at Drumcree it would be a powerful symbol for Northern
Ireland as a whole, but he had no illusions about the task he

215

faced. Somehow he had to maintain his lines of communication with the members of Drumcree church, with the wider Church of Ireland which had a significant constituency in the Republic and a division of opinion on Drumcree within the North, and also with the Orange Order. He says, 'My relationship with the Orange Order was a mixture of condemnation of their actions, when I felt this was necessary, and also of attempts to get a solution. Often I tried to apply to the Drumcree situation the lessons I had learned internationally. Many a time I said to myself, "If I could transpose this situation into the terms of an international deadlock, what would I do?" '

At the same time, he had been building up a considerable network of international friends and acquaintances, but they found it difficult to understand what was happening at Drumcree. He says, 'They showed such incredulity at what was taking place outside a church in the years moving into the start of the twenty-first century. They just could not begin to grasp what was taking place.'

He did not have to go far from home to find many other people who felt the same, particularly in the Irish Republic, where Protestants and Roman Catholics alike viewed with distaste the nightly television bulletins of such naked sectarianism at Drumcree. They asked how on earth the Church of Ireland had become embroiled in such a bad situation and, more particularly, why Eames and his senior colleagues simply did not tell the Drumcree congregation to close their church to that particular march.

Archbishop Walton Empey summarises the feelings in the Republic during those days of high tension: 'Church of Ireland people were forever being pestered about Drumcree – people were asking them, "What sort of people are those Protestants up there?" They felt battered and betrayed and I believed that they needed someone to speak out for them. I hope I did it as rationally as I could. On the whole they were not blaming Robin. Some did, both Catholics and Protestants, but they did not understand the position he was in, and his comparative helplessness.'

The Rector of Drumcree the Reverend John Pickering felt that his duty was to keep the church open to all-comers. His Select Vestry, which had a strong Orange membership, felt the same. There was little likelihood that they could be persuaded to change their minds, much less to succumb to pressure from the Archbishop, or anyone else who was minded to close the church.

John Pickering, a mild-mannered yet determined man, had the sympathy of many other clergy in the Church of Ireland who did not envy him the position he was in – but not necessarily their backing for his views, which were very clear. He says, 'My position was quite simple. It was wrong to prevent anyone from worshipping God. I was ordained to bring people to hear the Word of God, and I would have been going against my own values if I had refused the Orangemen or any other group access to the church. The Archbishop knew all along what my views were, and it was a matter of my conscience as well.'[1]

Eames, however, was far from alone as he tried to solve his dilemma, and he had solid support from many members of the Church of Ireland, particularly in his own diocese. After the stand-off in 1998, a particularly bad year, the Armagh Diocesan Council at its meeting on 7 September commended Eames for his 'tireless efforts' to find a solution to the Drumcree problem and noted, 'with particular horror the fact that this year, despite the best efforts of the Orange Order, guns and other explosive weapons were used against the security forces, thereby posing a threat to life'.

Eames was particularly grateful for the strong support from his diocese. He says, 'Time and again my clergy urged me to maintain my joint approach of condemnation of violence and involvement in meetings and contacts geared to provide a peaceful solution. Without this support, I would have found the problem intolerable. It is not widely appreciated how much the people of the Armagh diocese have resented the criticism from afar, and how genuine has been their support for my efforts.'

Though many people were aware of Eames' acute dilemma – whether to try to withdraw permission for the church service on Drumcree Sunday, or face the long haul of patient negotiations – other voices were increasingly heard. They were asking whether it was better to aim to hold the church together, rather than to do what in their view was 'right' – that is, to withdraw permission for the service to be held because the Church of Ireland disapproved of what was happening in Drumcree, and to live with the consequences of that dramatic public act, come what may.

This debate lay – some would say still lies – at the heart of the Church of Ireland's reaction to the Drumcree crisis and the way it has handled the issue, not only through the actions of its Primate but the church as a whole. Drumcree was discussed at all levels but it was not until 1999 that the General Synod spent an entire afternoon in debating the issue.

This was partly due to the background work of a small group from the North, which included the Archdeacon of Down the Venerable Gregor McCamley, a Dubliner who had spent nearly twenty-five years of his ministry in Northern Ireland. He and Robin Eames were on good terms and had known each other since their college days. McCamley, in fact, had succeeded Eames as a curate in Bangor, Co. Down.

Archdeacon McCamley was respected throughout the Church of Ireland for his straightforward approach and his independence of mind. He, and the others in the small Northern group, thought that the Church of Ireland as a whole was not doing enough about Drumcree, and partly as a result of this a General Synod sub-committee on sectarianism was set up.

This, in turn, led to the full-scale debate at the General Synod in May 1999. This was preceded by a hard-hitting Presidential address from Eames who said that no issue in recent years had caused more heart-searching in the Church of Ireland than Drumcree. He said, 'Drumcree confronts us. Drumcree searches us. Drumcree tests us – and Drumcree can and does provide the Church of Ireland with a defining moment as we approach a new millennium.'

He said that the real question for the Orange Order to address was whether they wished to be regarded as members of a religious or a political movement, and added, 'In the light of events over the past four years at Drumcree, most outside observers would regard the Order as a political rather than a religious movement.'

In a particularly striking passage he said that what they had witnessed in the shadow of Drumcree church had been 'totally un-Christian, totally unacceptable in the vicinity of a church, and totally at variance with the teaching of the Church of Ireland'. He added, 'As I have frequently stated in the media, I see little of the Christ I believe in on the hill at Drumcree.'

However, there was also a very Eames-like passage which sought to provide a broadly balanced view. He said:

> I have always recognised that the vast majority of members of the Orange Order are decent, respectable and law-abiding men and women . . . There are also many who have told us of their moderation and disgust at the scenes on Drumcree hill. Their responsibility is immense. Have they the courage to speak out and to witness to their moderation? . . . Without a shadow of reservation I condemn in the name of the Synod and of the Church of Ireland the violence, intimidation, injury and deaths which have accompanied or been associated with the protest at Drumcree.

There were those within the Church of Ireland, however, who wanted more than words of condemnation. They wanted the kind of action that would demonstrate to the world the church's disapproval of what had been happening at Drumcree – in short, they were pressing for the closure of the church on Drumcree Sunday unless the Orangemen gave binding commitments in advance of their good behaviour.

Following an intense but dignified debate, the General Synod passed, by large majorities, three resolutions which indicated the church's strong moral stance on several issues. It resolved in effect that, first, only ecclesiastical flags should be flown from church towers or in church grounds (which by implication banned the Union flag and others with political implications); second, that while 'historic formularies' were an important part of the inheritance of the Church of Ireland, the Synod regretted that 'words written in another age and in a different context should be used in a manner hurtful to, or antagonistic towards, other Christians'; and, third, it called upon the Rector and Select Vestry of Drumcree to endorse three pledges sought by the Archbishop of Armagh from those attending the annual parade, and stipulated that the invitation should be withdrawn if the pledges were not adhered to.

Though the Synod had made clear their collective view, the resolutions were only a form of words that carried moral but not legal authority within the church. Only a Bill, if passed, would have become part of the law of the church. Archdeacon McCamley, among others, had had discussions with Eames several times prior to the Synod. He recalls, 'There were times when Robin seemed to be in favour of a Bill, and then he changed his mind, and was totally opposed to it.' This, McCamley believes, may have been for a couple of reasons – it might have been harder to win Synod's approval for a Bill, and if a Bill had gone through to empower the Archbishop to close the church for that one service, it might have been impossible to enforce it. He says, 'I believe that Robin felt that "no law" was better than a "bad" law – that is, a law that could not be enforced. For my part, I respected that point of view.'

However, the resolutions of the Synod were indeed only a form of words, though sincerely meant as a witness to the mood of the Church of Ireland in general over Drumcree. Almost immediately, dissenting voices were heard. The Rector of Drumcree, the Reverend John Pickering, had voted against all three resolutions, which was hardly surprising, given the situation in which he found himself.

Following the votes in the General Synod, Pickering made it clear that he would not be preventing anyone from attending a service in his church, 'and that is the view of the Vestry as well'. He also told journalists that the Union flag would continue to fly from Drumcree church.[2]

Another dissenting view was put forward by Norman Kelly from Ballymena who had resigned from the Orange Order some thirty years previously, over a different issue. In a letter to the *Church of Ireland Gazette*, he wrote: 'It seems to me . . . that in effect, the Church of Ireland is really nothing more than a holy club which exists for the benefit of "holier-than-thou" members . . . I will defend the right of all sinners – not only the Orangemen – to go to church. If we were all saints there would not be any need for either churches or clergymen.'

The practical test of the Synod's resolutions – indeed the church's 'resolution' – came at the subsequent Drumcree Sunday service several weeks later. The account of what happened, according to the *Church of Ireland Gazette* of 9 July 1999, makes fascinating reading:

> Despite the urgent pleadings of his Bishop, Archbishop Robin Eames, and an official letter from the Honorary Secretaries of the General Synod to withdraw the invitation to the

Orange Order to attend Morning Prayer, the Rector said his Church doors would remain open to all.

This letter requested that the invitation should be withdrawn because the Portadown District Lodges failed to confirm that they would adhere to the three pledges laid down by General Synod. These called on the Order to:

> *avoid any action before or after the service which diminished the sanctity of the worship:*
> *obey the law of the land before and after the service, and*
> *respect the integrity of the Church of Ireland by word and action and avoid the use of all church property or its environs in any civil protest following the service.*

However, the *Gazette* pointed out that the General Synod's resolutions were not legally binding, though passed by an overwhelming majority of clergy and laity, and that Mr Pickering and his Select Vestry were entitled to make their own decision. It then quoted the Church of Ireland Press Officer thus: 'We are not barring the doors of the Church to anyone, we are just asking the Orange Order to respect the law, not to bring the Church into disrepute and not to use the environs of the church for unlawful purposes.'

The *Gazette* then added, 'To the tremendous relief of all concerned, the Orangemen this year adhered to these requests.' Finally, the paper quoted Archbishop Eames who said, 'There has been dignity. There has been control. In the eyes of the world there has been a great deal to redeem the good name of the Orange Order. We wanted sanctity of worship, obedience to the law and protection of the church and its grounds. All three pledges have been kept at this stage.'

Overall the newspaper report seems to have summarised admirably a typically Irish solution to a typically Irish problem – the Church at large had asked for the Orange Order's pledges as to the Orangemen's good behaviour, the Orangemen had behaved accordingly on that Drumcree Sunday, the General Synod's earlier resolutions had been reached and faithfully recorded for posterity, the church had remained open, and the Union flag was still fluttering from the tower.

Archdeacon McCamley, who had proposed the Synod resolution on the flying of flags, reflects, 'It was passed by a considerable majority, but very few flags came down. That did not surprise me. I also accept that if we had tried to take action to stop the service on Drumcree Sunday we would not have succeeded, but at least we would have been seen to have been trying to do something.'

If the church had been closed, he believes, the situation might have gone even further. 'Drumcree might have seceded from the Church of Ireland, but things were so bad, and the image of the Church of Ireland was so poor worldwide, that I think this was a price that might have perhaps been worth paying.'

McCamley, by his own admission, has a tendency to confront things head on when he feels it is necessary to do so. He says, 'There are times when that is the right thing to do, and there are times when it is not the right thing to do, but we must always remember that it is not enough for justice to be done, it has to be seen to be done.'

Though he believes that Eames has been one of the 'giants' in the history of the Church of Ireland, he still feels that a firmer line should have been taken on Drumcree. He says, 'I have a great admiration for Robin, and diplomacy is one of his greatest gifts. However, in certain situations diplomacy can cease to be an asset and becomes a liability. There have been occasions when that has perhaps been the case.'

McCamley was satisfied, nevertheless, that his point of view, which represented that of others within the church, was properly heard. He says, 'I hope that I expressed that view in a reasonable and charitable way. It is too early for any of us to judge as to which approach was right. Only history will tell.'

Patsy McGarry, the respected Religious Affairs Correspondent of the *Irish Times* who covered the Drumcree crisis every year, also has clear views on the issues involved. He says, 'Archbishop Eames had the moral authority of the General Synod decisions, and he did nothing to assert that authority. It was flouted. Even when indications were given well in advance that it was going to be flouted, those flags still flew.'

Though McGarry has a high regard for Robin Eames' leadership of the church in many other spheres, he remains critical of his handling of Drumcree. He says, 'I like and respect the man a lot. We have clashed, and I have written and said very harsh things about him, but he has always come back to me.

There has been no personal animosity on my part, as I hope there has been none on his. However, I feel that he failed to give leadership on Drumcree which had the potential to be disastrous not only for the Church of Ireland but for the island as a whole. Robin has said that Drumcree was his "Calvary", and he is right.'

Eames was well aware of such criticisms, and regarded these as part of the price he had to pay for embarking on the course that he had chosen. He says, 'Everything is possible, in theory. In the earlier stages of the crisis it crossed my mind to try to close the church. It was not a constant thought, but it was there.' At one point he sought legal advice, which was typical of Eames the lawyer. 'I was told that by closing the church and preventing the service, I would be moving in to a particularly dangerous legal position.'

Eames was also aware of other realities. 'The Chief Constable had said to me, "Please do not stop the service. If you do that, Portadown will erupt, and we will be unable to contain the situation." Successive Secretaries of State said to me, "Our problems will only really begin if the service is stopped and the Orange Order marches to another location." '

Eames also considered very briefly the possibility of offering another parish church for the service, thus avoiding the Garvaghy Road dilemma. On reflection he felt this would have been unacceptable to the Orange Order, and he believed that, understandably, other clergy in his diocese did not want the problem passed on to them.

In his own mind Eames never considered closing the church as a serious option. He says, 'If I had closed the church – always supposing that it was possible to do so – the Orangemen would have come to Drumcree in their tens of thousands, and they would not have stopped coming to Drumcree. They would have held their service outside the church, or they would have gone into it. There would have been increased civil conflict and widespread rioting across Northern Ireland.'

He also had to consider the likely effect on the Church of Ireland itself. 'There would have been "rejoicing" from those who stood far from Drumcree and who did not really under-stand what was going on, but it would have split the church in the North. This is my raw nerve I am now talking about – if the church had been closed there would have been congratulations from "middle" Ulster, and the "middle" Church of Ireland, the people who never wanted to get their hands dirty; but you would also have had rectors put to the stake all across the North. If that had happened I don't think that I could have held the Church of Ireland together.'

Eames was also faced with another stark choice. 'If it had been decided to close the church and if the service had continued anyway, would that have been a better position where the Church of Ireland had mud on its face and was being seen as powerless to do anything in real terms; or was it better to do what I did, which was to condemn them, to tell them constantly that what they were doing was wrong, to seek another way, and to redouble my efforts to find a solution?'

His overriding decision was to seek consensus the slow, hard way. 'On balance the road I took was more likely to hold the Church of Ireland together better than if I had done the spontaneous "solve it for the moment thing" like closing the church, even if it had been possible. I might have solved something there, but it would have built up the problem a hundred-fold in other ways.'

In the years after the General Synod debate of 1999, which in one sense was the most intense period of the Church of Ireland's self-examination and heart-searching of its attitudes to Drumcree, the stand-off continued each July, without much real hope of a solution. However, Eames, who had kept in constant touch with the Orangemen, detected a change in attitude in early 2003. The year before there had been disgraceful scenes after the church service when a number of people violently attacked police at the barricade below the church. The Orange Order, despite its desire for a peaceful protest from 1999 onwards, had lost control of events on that day.

Eames strongly condemned the attacks on the police, but kept his lines open to the Orangemen. His aim was to convince them of the damage that had been done, to help them recognise that the impasse would not be broken unless they moved from their position of having no contact with the Garvaghy Road Residents' Coalition, and to bolster their confidence that they could indeed move forward and that public opinion would go with them.

In early 2003 Eames became aware of a new realism on the Orange side. 'I sensed that they were more open to guidance away from intransigence, and I believed that the Portadown Orangemen had a growing recognition that the Grand Lodge policy in Belfast of "no talks with residents' groups" was not going to help Portadown in particular.'

Behind the scenes within Portadown Orangeism, a gradual but significant change in emphasis was taking place, particularly after the vicious and dangerous stand-off in 1998. These were the voices which gave Eames something to work on. Richard Monteith, a Portadown solicitor who is also an Orangeman and a member of Drumcree parish church says, 'In earlier years it was harder for the Archbishop to do anything. Up to July 1999, all you were getting was tens of thousands of Orangemen who were perceived as being intent on forcing the parade down the Garvaghy Road. However, we decided to change. The Portadown Orangemen were prepared to adopt a different approach and to try to put their arguments over by persuasion, and by trying to show that they were worthy of being treated as a civilised organisation.'

Monteith says that the Orangemen were set upon this new course of action, irrespective of what the General Synod was doing, but it was essential for them to retain the Archbishop's support. He says, 'If we had lost that, we would have been friendless again, and if you could not get his support, it was almost as if you had lost in terms of the religious and church argument, and only a few hardline people would have been your friends. If you could convince him that there was merit in your case, you could always hope that you could convince others as well.

'Up to 1999, he was strongly articulating the position that "This can't go on!" but there has been movement since then in both directions – from the Orangemen towards something he can accept, and from him in return saying, "OK, you are now behaving in a way I can deal with." '

Denis Watson, one of the most senior Orange leaders and a moderate, felt that Robin Eames was always genuine in his attempts to solve the situation. 'I wasn't one of his flock, but I always had a very good relationship with him. Throughout all the difficulties, he stood shoulder to shoulder with us. Some of the Orangemen maybe did not recognise this as outwardly as they should have done, or would have liked to have seen it – probably because the Archbishop was in a difficult position with his own people, and had to keep them on board. He was under tremendous pressure all round.'

Watson underlines the importance of keeping in contact with the Archbishop. He says, 'I always felt that he was his own man, but I trusted him, and he was very open with me. I never believed that the Orange Order could be involved with seeing the Church of Ireland being pulled apart, but I also think that a number of Orangemen throughout the Province failed to realise the seriousness of the situation. I was adamant that the Archbishop had to be kept on side, and that if we ever reached a situation where we alienated him, we would be in great difficulty.'

When Eames saw the Orangemen's written proposals in the early summer of 2003 he was 'speechless'. He says, 'The most significant development was their recognition that there could only be future walks with the consent of the Garvaghy Road residents. The acceptance of the principle of consent, which I had spent months discussing with them, was clearly acknowledged in their proposals.'

Meanwhile Garvan O'Doherty, a Londonderry businessman who had helped to broker a solution to the controversial Derry parades, had agreed to sound out the Nationalist position at Garvaghy. In the event the talks broke down, partly because news of the Orange Order's proposals had leaked to the press and the Nationalists were annoyed because they had not been consulted.

Nevertheless, the 2003 Drumcree Sunday passed off peacefully. Eames says, 'I felt that although the Portadown Orangemen had not received enough credit for their actions, a historic corner had been turned. I knew that a hard road still lay ahead, but that we could not allow the advantages we had gained to slip away with us.'

Garvan O'Doherty had been impressed by Eames during the talks. 'He had shown courage and leadership not only over Drumcree but on other important issues. He had always been prepared to put forward a point of view which others might find unpalatable.'

He found Eames 'statesmanlike, with a reassuring style. Robin had confidence in his ability to deal with the Orange and they clearly listened to and respected him.' However, O'Doherty confirmed that the Garvaghy Road Residents' Coalition did not trust Eames because of the carpet factory incident. 'I don't know what had gone on there, but Nationalists felt that he had betrayed them. To some extent this was a handicap because it added a complication to closing a deal in 2003.

'On the other hand Eames' involvement with the Orange was important, because he was taking the broad view and he was putting himself on the line. We could not have gone so far without his help. The situation was moving from one of emotive reaction to pragmatism, and Robin played a crucial role in this respect, certainly on the Orange side.'

Brendan McKenna, chairman of the Garvaghy Road Residents' Coalition, confirms that they first became aware from media sources of the talks between Eames, the Orange Order and O'Doherty, and that there had been no direct contact with them. He says, 'No one spoke to us last year, no one forwarded us a copy of the Orange initiative until well after Drumcree. We had no part in it. What was being done was without any reference to the Nationalist community.'[3]

Time, literally, will tell whether or not Eames' overall stance over Drumcree since 1995 was right. His senior colleagues in the House of Bishops understood his problems, and hindsight helps everyone to view the tortured process within a wider perspective. Bishop Samuel Poyntz reflects, 'No matter what Robin did at Drumcree, he was going to be wrong. People now ask if by playing the "long game" did he get it right? It's hard to say "yea" or "nay" but from his point of view he probably did get it right. I don't think anyone could have done better, given the situation. Whether it should have been nipped in the bud sooner is another matter.'

Archbishop John Neill reflects, 'It's easy to be an armchair critic. In the early days we were very much polarised, and people felt that possibly the Archbishop had not been strong enough in the Drumcree situation, when it first exploded. Equally we were not as aware in the South of the complexity of the issues. Robin became stronger, and the Church of Ireland has moved on under his leadership to a much more critical stance over Drumcree.'

Father Brian Lennon believes that from the first stand-off in 1995, 'We were all in boxes. We all made mistakes. I don't know what else it was possible for Robin Eames to do. If you ask me, "Was he in an impossible situation, did he move too late?", I don't know the answer. It depended on what was going on in the wider picture. This is part of the "What if?" of history.'

Lennon, whose experience of working with the Catholic community in Portadown from the early 1980s gives him a particular insight into the problem, takes a longer view of Drumcree. He says, 'It's a pity that there was no dialogue between the Orange Order and Catholics living in the local area before 1995. The problem was there and it was not being addressed.

'All our churches were involved in pretty safe ecumenical efforts that were giving very limited witness to our call in the context of our divisions. I don't know what Robin Eames attempted at that time, but I would have liked much more involvement from the Protestant community. I believe that the Catholic community was willing to talk at that stage, and talks would have led to a more positive outcome.'

Cardinal Daly points out that Eames was ministering in one of the most difficult periods in Irish history. He says, 'Drumcree was an insoluble problem, and any efforts to resolve it were bound to be less than totally successful. However, his ministry has been so much more than Drumcree. It was his misfortune to be the leader of his church in that particular situation.'

The Cardinal feels that a church leader can only do so much. 'The only satisfaction is to feel that what you have said is right and true, and that you said it in total good faith. Therefore you have to leave the rest to God.'

The views of clergy in the Armagh diocese underline the depth of the dilemma Eames faced. Canon William Neely, the Rector of the border parish of Keady, knew the feelings on the ground. He believes that the Archbishop handled it as well as he possibly could and that he had to face so much criticism from people who did not begin to understand the problem. Neely says, 'If he had done what they wanted, which was to take the Orange Order by the ears and close the church, he would have done terrible damage to the Church of Ireland, not to mention the community. His decision to play the long game was gradually paying off. Some of the leaders of the Orange Order respect him now, whereas they would have greeted him with suspicion in the past.'

The Reverend John Pickering, the Rector of Drumcree, agrees with this view. He says, 'People felt that he should have been identifying more with them, in the way that the Cardinal did with his people. Around the time of the 1999 Synod there was negative reaction to the Archbishop, at Drumcree and in Northern Ireland. He may have been trying to bring people along for the good of the whole community, but if a person tries to bring everyone with him, he will please nobody. I think that Robin has recovered from that, and that people on the Protestant side have a greater regard for him.'

Pickering pays tribute to Eames' personal approach throughout the crises. 'He was my "Father-in-God", and we always kept in contact. He was a very good pastor. I don't see anything more he could have done, and he's been working away at it all the time. Like me, I think he would like to see it resolved before he retires.'

The Archbishop was always mindful of the human dimension behind the crises. He reflects, 'On the ground at Drumcree hill and on the Garvaghy Road, ordinary human beings found themselves prisoners of events. The world's spotlight would concentrate on violence, protests and barricades each July, but my mind often turned to what was happening to ordinary people who, for the remainder of the year, lived out ordinary lives away from cameras or media interviews.'

Among the Orangemen were people exposed to every conceivable pressure. 'At Drumcree they became, willingly or otherwise, participants in a cameo of Northern Ireland's problems. The vast majority saw nothing wrong in what they were doing. They may have had grave reservations about politicians or paramilitaries manipulating the situation – but to them it was a question of rights, freedom and traditions.'

On the other side were the Garvaghy Road residents. 'They found themselves caught up in a situation far from their experience of ordinary life. They had to deal with army barricades, and with being restricted to their homes if a parade was allowed. They were worried about their children, and encouraged to believe that a violent invasion of their area by Loyalists was always a possibility. They, too, were being shaped by events.'

Eames met Brendan McKenna, the spokesman for the Garvaghy Road Residents' Coalition, several times. He recalls, 'None of these were occasions of easy dialogue. He maintained that Cahal Daly and I had conspired in some way at the carpet mill to entice him off the street to allow a parade to take place. As I met Roman Catholic churchmen over the years and welcomed dialogue with them, I found their attitudes such a contrast. In other circumstances and at another time I always felt that he and I could have had a reasonable conversation, as I understood how easy it was for someone in his position to come under such intense pressure. He, too, was one of the human faces of the tragedy at Drumcree.'

Brendan McKenna retains his own clear opinions of Robin Eames and of the events at Drumcree. He says, 'Archbishop Eames may look on himself as an honest broker, but his actions since 1995 have been that of a partisan. He sees himself as having a very political role, as being the spokesperson for "unionism" with a small "u", and almost as an apologist for the Orange Order.'

McKenna claims that there is still a 'big question mark' about Eames' role in the 1996 talks in the carpet factory. He says, 'Those of us who were there are certainly convinced that the Archbishop knew that the march was going to be forced down the Garvaghy Road, and that all he was doing was almost creating a false sense of security among the community here, by ensuring that the leadership was somewhere else.'

Brendan McKenna regards Eames as 'your run-of-the-mill conservative church leader'. He says, 'Conservative forces link in with conservative forces. To someone from Robin Eames' perspective, the Orange Order is not the organisation as it is viewed in our community. There are various people in the Order who belong to various synods and that kind of thing. The Archbishop probably has a blinkered view of the Orange Order which, if anything, is itself a conservative organisation. I think that from early on Robin Eames saw himself as a representative of conservative unionists, with a small "u", and that coloured his dealings with us.'[4]

Notwithstanding the views of other people, from whatever quarter, Robin Eames himself believes that he made mistakes during the Drumcree crises. He says, 'I was not able to explain the depth of the problems to my fellow bishops in the Republic, or to explain to them what they could not have possibly understood. The Northern media was sympathetic to what I was facing and recognised what I could not do, but I did not succeed in convincing the Southern media of the difficulties.'

As time went on, Eames felt that there were so many obstacles and so many agendas being played out at Drumcree that he doubted if it could ever be solved. He reflects, 'As a churchman I discovered through the years that there were sinister angles to Drumcree which I would never be able to explain. I sometimes wondered if there were elements at a high level who felt that it would be of help to the overall situation vis-à-vis America, the Irish-American lobby and everyone else if it was proved that Drumcree was not necessarily solvable.

'It is totally foreign to me to say it, but if Drumcree had been solvable, we would have solved it. Somewhere along the line we would have found a solution before now. I don't know who to blame, but it seemed growingly incredible to me that given all the intellect, all the facilities of governments and all the world power that was focused on Northern Ireland, that no one could solve Drumcree.'

Robin Eames remains sensitive to the accusation that he allowed the situation to drift. He says, 'Too many people wrote off my action as "inaction". My so-called "inaction" was only reached after agonising, after prayer, thought and consulation. There was nothing I did through the entire situation that was simply letting something run. I may be judged right or wrong in the light of history, but I did what I thought was right. None of it was inaction – every single step was part of my engagement and my attempts to find a solution, which I have continued to do.'

He says, 'I still find it very hard to accept that people at a great distance from Drumcree were able to make critical comments through a total lack of appreciation of what others were going through, and the fact that we were taking decisions to try to defuse a situation that could have been a hundred times worse. Those who thought that there was a simplistic answer did not realise what the temperature was like in those days.'

Though Eames has been blessed with a robust constitution, the long Drumcree saga at one stage affected his health. During one period of stand-off he was hospitalised for tests because of stress, though he kept up communication with the outside world with the help of his office staff. His condemnation of the violence led to Loyalist threats, abuse and condemnation. The police warned him of a paramilitary threat to his life, and for a period they mounted a protection of his home.

He received critical letters from people on both sides of the argument. One Roman Catholic from outside the Drumcree area wrote, 'Let us not hear again about "the hours I have spent" and "the agonising I have gone through". When the responsibility of leadership which goes with your position was tested, you were found sadly wanting – or is there a latent Orange affiliation . . . and hatred of Catholicism occupying the Arch-episcopal See?'

On the other hand, a Protestant wrote to him from Belfast with the question, 'Who on earth do you think you are, laying down deadlines to people you obviously think are answerable to you, and if you think I am wrong in how you are seen by ordinary Protestants, just show your face at Drumcree Church on Sunday – but take at least half a dozen bodyguards.'

Eames says, 'Some of my closest colleagues and friends admit now that they did not know what I was going through. I greatly appreciate their acknowledgment of this, and I understand totally why they reacted in the way they did. They could not have felt otherwise, without having been there and having been involved with it.'

Despite all the setbacks on all sides, Eames believes that progress on Drumcree has been made, but at a personal cost to very many people – himself included. He says, 'The pressure and tension surrounding Drumcree was greater than I ever felt in any single episode of my life. All the suffering of the Troubles, and all the Drumcree situation – all of that will never leave me. I was born here, I have loved this place, I have been loved in this place, I will die in this place and I will take all the pain and the suffering of this place with me to my grave.'

17

Change and the Church
of Ireland

One of the keys to understanding Robin Eames is to realise the degree to which he is embedded in the Church of Ireland. He is an Anglican with a worldwide vision and mandate, he is a bridge-builder at home and abroad, he is a committed pastor, he is a family man, but also at the centre of his being is the Church of Ireland.

Eames' deep attachment to Anglicanism is all the more noteworthy because he was brought up in the Methodist tradition. Yet his consummation into Anglicanism seems to have been complete from the earliest stages of his journey as a would-be ordinand, then a priest, bishop and archbishop, and Primate. He has said to his close friends more than once, 'I live, sleep and breathe the Church of Ireland.'

Some people believe that he received the 'red-carpet' treatment from the start of his clerical career, not that he would have wanted it that way, nor would he think of his career in those terms. His ambition was to follow God's will, to become a member of the Church of Ireland clergy, and to follow wherever that path might lead him.

Early on he gained valuable experience as a curate in Bangor and later as a rector in Belfast. In Derry and Raphoe he learned about the complexities of a society locked in violence, and also a deepening understanding of a bishop's role. Bishop Edward Darling, who had known Eames since their days as curates, recalls a comment from a colleague: 'Robin left Down and Connor as a lad to go to Derry and Raphoe. Five years later he returned to us as a father-in-God.'

233

It seemed a matter of not 'if' but 'when' he would succeed to the Primacy. When the opportunity did occur in 1986, following the resignation of the ailing Archbishop John Armstrong, Eames was still only forty-eight. Bishop Samuel Poyntz believes that the House of Bishops gave Eames an almost impossible task. He says, 'A person can be so long in office that he gets tired, and the church gets tired of him. That has not happened with Robin, but it could have happened.'

Canon William Neely, who has known Eames well for forty-five years, says, 'Robin was never nakedly ambitious in that he pursued those in power, but he knew them and they knew him, and they respected him. If it had not been for that he would not have been Archbishop of Armagh. He is very cautious, but he never put a foot wrong. Robin always believed in his own destiny.'

Neely believes it would be wrong to be oversimplistic in this respect. 'Robin is a complex man, and his essential goodness, kindliness and wisdom have always been there. He was the right man in the right place at the right time, but he is a person who is very skilled at hiding himself.'

As Primate, Eames inherited a church that spanned two separate national jurisdictions and which was affected, to a greater or a lesser extent, by the terrible events taking place in Northern Ireland and – on occasions – in the Irish Republic.

The Northern church was fearful and felt besieged. Many of its members were murdered and whole families were bereaved by the Provisional IRA, while at the same time Protestants felt that the British Government was giving in to terrorism. In the Republic, Church of Ireland members were appalled by what was happening in the North, and much of it in the name of 'Protestantism'.

There was also a deeper irony. While Anglicans in the North felt themselves threatened, those in the Republic – after an earlier sense of uncertainty about their role in a relatively new state – were growing more confident about their place in society, and began to identify even more strongly with a new and prosperous Ireland.

Eames set about his dual, yet unified, role with characteristic determination and skill. He already knew the religious and political landscape in Dublin, but he systematically visited parishes across the South to sample life on the ground. By doing so, and also by his public speeches, acts and gestures, he dispelled any misgivings that he might be only a 'Northern' Primate, and that he was head of an all-Ireland church.

However, he had to work at it. Archbishop Neill believes that in the early days he was perceived by many in the South as a Northern bishop, but that he showed a willingness to identify with life in the South and emphasised that his Primacy was over all of Ireland. This was appreciated in the Republic. He has also been well regarded in the South generally. Neill says, 'He is respected in political circles in the Republic, and he is greatly admired by Catholics. They identify him with the voice of moderate Protestantism in the North. He has been there so long, and he has worked with three Roman Catholic Arch-bishops during his period of office.'

Archbishop Walton Empey believes that Robin Eames was well able to meet all the challenges. 'He has been totally and utterly at ease in the South compared to one of his predecessors, Archbishop Simms, who went from Dublin to Armagh. George Otto Simms was that holiest and most wonderful of men, for whom I had a high admiration, but it could never be said of him that he was at home in the North.'

While Robin Eames had an acknowledged 'Unionist' back-ground, Empey was a strong Irish Nationalist, but they worked well together. Empey recalls that the only time they had a 'spat' was in the aftermath of an important development in Dublin when the Irish President Mary McAleese, a Roman Catholic, partook of Holy Communion in the Protestant Christ Church Cathedral.

This led to strong criticism from the then Roman Catholic Archbishop of Dublin Dr Desmond Connell, and in face of the predictable public controversy, Walton Empey says he phoned Robin Eames with a view to letting others have their say. The next day, to his surprise, he read a press statement from Eames on the issue.

Empey recalls, 'I then wrote him a stinker of a letter, which I later greatly regretted! I was in a bad mood because I was getting it from everybody to "cut loose". However, I felt that to take apart the Vatican and the local Archbishop would have been to hurt our ecumenically minded Catholic friends and to put them into a defensive mode. Later on Robin pointed out that I had gone to see the Select Vestry at Drumcree without telling him. So it was tit-for-tat! It was only a minor spat.'

Although Eames won the respect and admiration of the vast
majority of Anglicans on both sides of the Irish border,
nevertheless the Southerners' loyalty to and concept of the
Church of Ireland was severely tested during the Drumcree
crisis.[1]

Overall his Primacy has been highly regarded by the entire
spectrum of the church episcopacy, ranging from the more
experienced to the most junior members of the House of
Bishops. The former Bishop of Derry James Mehaffey says,
'People would say generally that we have a good man in Armagh
who speaks for the Church of Ireland, and they listen to him.'
The relatively new Bishop of Cashel and Ossory, the Right
Reverend Peter Barratt, who himself experienced some of the
sharp end of the Troubles as Rector of St George's in Belfast,
says, 'The Primate has given a great sense of stability, continuity
and security. He knows the life of the church and its heartbeat
particularly well.'

In the North, Eames continued his pivotal role as a Protestant
church leader. As the Church of Ireland historian Alan Acheson
has noted, 'Eames was from the outset of his Primacy forthright
on public issues, fearless in avowing conviction, and (on matters
about which he felt strongly) at once passionate and plain-
spoken.'[2]

Eames, as Acheson also points out, had twin strategies from
the outset. He wanted to place the church on a better administrative and structural basis as well as addressing its spiritual
needs, and also dealing with major pastoral and theological
issues. Acheson notes: 'At the same time, the familiar historical
pattern of informal initiative reinforcing formal agenda was
again apparent in the Church, arresting decline, inspiring youth,
and enhancing her local effectiveness.'[3]

As with any organisation, the one constant factor that does
not change is change itself. While trying to address the major
needs of the church, Robin Eames as Primate was aware of the
changes that were constantly taking place within the institution
itself, at the same time as he and his senior colleagues were
trying to manage change. These developments affected the
entire life of the church, including its selection of candidates
for the ministry right through to the way in which the House of
Bishops acted as a collegiate body, as well as a need to
modernise the administration and governance of the church.

There was also the important external factors, not only of the continuing unrest in Northern Ireland but also of the increasing secularisation of society.

One of the most important developments since Robin Eames joined the ministry has been in the selection and training of ordinands. In the 1960s it was the prerogative of individual bishops to 'lay hands' on those they considered suitable for ordination. The church later developed a selection process involving an interview by a panel of those recommended by an individual bishop, who retained the right to make a final decision.

This was later replaced by a system whereby candidates are assessed by panels of experts in terms of psychological aptitude, spiritual preparedness, education and ability, and a sense of vocation. In the early days, students for the ministry attended Trinity College, Dublin and the Divinity Hostel at Mountjoy Square.

Today the Church of Ireland has its own Theological College in Dublin, but such education is expensive, and it costs some £63,000 to train a student over three years. Some people have argued that this is too much, that the college should be closed and that students should be trained elsewhere. Eames is opposed to this. 'If this happened, the Church of Ireland ethos would suffer. The ideal would be to maintain our own college, but to utilise more input from other traditions, including the Church of England. This would answer any allegations that we are "too parochial".'

Some people note pointedly that today's students miss the leavening effect enjoyed by those of Eames' generation who experienced the wider university ethos of Trinity College, Dublin, and that the broad 'churchmanship' of previous generations has virtually disappeared. There is also a strong Northern Ireland membership among today's students embracing a more evangelical outlook, thus reflecting the ethos of the Church at large, particularly in the North.

The lack of numbers in the ministry has meant that young clergy can expect much quicker promotion. Curates used to spend six to seven years in post before becoming a rector, but most are now promoted in roughly half that time. Eames says, 'Curates today have an expectation that would not have been possible or encouraged in the early days of my ministry.' He also believes that the vocation for ministry has been changing, and that clergy need to be much more involved in community affairs than in the past. He says, 'I have had to question the motives of some of those who have offered themselves for ordination training. I tell them that this is no cushy job if it is to be done well. Gone are the days of a comfortable, respectable and secure profession. Now they must ask questions of themselves and of their performance if their ministry is to be realistic and relevant.'

One of the problems facing Eames and all leaders has been the drop in church membership, due partly to a growing secularisation which some refer to as 'postmodernism'. Eames believes that in Northern Ireland the Church has lost a generation. He says, 'Many have dismissed the role of the church as an institution. Now it is the relevance of individual church leaders or laity which count much more than the institution.'

He believes that the spread of secularism has been slower than in England, but that it has taken root behind 'the smokescreen' of the Troubles. 'The Church of Ireland must not regard the secular society of the future as an enemy to be feared. It must listen carefully to it, and respond in new and imaginative ways.'

The comparative lack of clergy also poses other challenges. During his address to the Armagh Diocesan Synod in the autumn of 2003 Eames warned of the implications of a reduction in the numbers of clergy and of the need for new thinking. He says, 'It may sound too radical, but I can foresee that the majority of clergy will be part-time. Together with a permanent diaconate, a large number of part-time clergy, guided by full-time senior clergy from archdeacon to archbishop, could well become the pattern.'

The age profile of bishops has dropped considerably in recent years. When Eames was elected bishop at thirty-eight, he was by far the youngest of that era, when most were appointed well into their early sixties. Today the average age of the House of Bishops is just under fifty-three. Two are over sixty, six are in their fifties and four are in their forties.

There has also been a marked development of a more informal style among the bishops. This has been encouraged by Eames who remembers the strict formality of the Bench when he was appointed, though they were informal enough on one occasion to declare, 'Eames, part of your role is to make the tea!' He recalls how he was very much a listener in the presence of such Anglican 'heavyweights' as Archbishops Simms, Buchanan and McAdoo. The agenda was generally short and concentrated on policy, and much was left to individual bishops in their dioceses. 'In those days there was a strong feeling of authoritarianism in the House, and the proceedings were very formal. We addressed each other by the name of our dioceses, and there was an atmosphere of "us" and "them" when we met. Coming from a different generation, I found this daunting when I considered the developing attitudes in the dioceses.'

Eames systematically dispensed with the formality and encouraged a sense of collegiality. The House of Bishops meets regularly on a residential basis, and gets through an immense amount of business. Eames says, 'Years ago, there was a degree of aloofness about the authority of the House of Bishops. Today such aloofness is a luxury and is totally unacceptable.'

Many barriers have gone. 'The modern bishops work extremely hard, and are much more aware of the life of people "on the ground" than in previous generations. We have our differences of personality and of theological outlook, and these surface frequently, but the intellectual power and commitment of the current House of Bishops is impressive. I know how individual bishops have addressed their changing roles. Believe me, they no longer live or work on pedestals.'

The atmosphere has also changed throughout the church at all levels, and the meetings of important groups such as the Standing Committee, General Synod and the Representative Church Body remain businesslike, but with a sense of informality. Bishop Darling notes, 'Robin brought in a sense of levity to the proceedings. He could make a joke and the others would joke back. A person like Archbishop Simms was delightful but that was a period of formality, which is no longer there.'

There have also been significant changes in the administration of the church. The 'Priorities Committee', of which Eames was an early member, prioritised the work of the church for financial support and this has been an essential part of the church's life, dealing with many social and community issues as well as internal matters.

Though the Church of Ireland has considerable investments and benefits from large endowments, its financial outlay is considerable, and it is not as rich a church as some people suppose. Eames, though not a financier, keeps a close eye on such matters. He notes, 'Some years ago when the Church Commissioners of the Church of England found themselves in difficulties, the Church of Ireland investments actually showed a profit, due to the careful trusteeship of our advisers and investment managers.'

This is all part of Eames' ability to take a global view of church affairs, and also to take time to understand the details of church finances and administration. The relatively small size of the Church of Ireland compared to that of the Church of England or other Anglican provinces, makes it easier for Eames to stay in touch financially, but it is a useful quality in a leader who has so much else on his mind, locally, nationally and internationally.

Eames presides over the annual meeting of its ruling body, the General Synod, with a mixture of authority and familiarity, while pushing on with the business so that decisions are made. In doing so he displays an aptitude for hard work, as well as a discreet personal touch. 'It is taxing to preside over General Synod for most of the three days when it sits, and I do a great deal of preparatory work each year.'

He tries to remember the names of individual members, and to encourage first-time speakers at the rostrum. 'I also try to meet members at meal breaks and to welcome their attendance. The church has always been well served by its dedicated laity, and their support must never be taken for granted.'

It is important to underline that the Church of Ireland, like other churches on the island, has a cross-border membership, which is reflected at its annual meeting. As such, members of the General Synod include staunch Unionists from the North and committed Nationalists from the Republic, who may become involved in debates on controversial political and security issues affecting North and South. Eames handles these debates with deceptive ease, partly through his experience but also because of his sensitive political antennae.

His annual Presidential addresses have attracted widespread media attention, and over the years he has reflected accurately the 'gut feeling' of his church members on the important issues of the day, at a time of considerable change not only within the Church of Ireland but within Ireland itself. He has also been aware of the importance of General Synod meeting outside Dublin, including twice in Belfast and more recently in Armagh – oddly enough for the first time in its history.

Significantly, Eames retains a hard-headed view of the practical realities of maintaining the ecclesiastical headquarters in Armagh. He says, 'By tradition the Primate has been Archbishop of Armagh but it is far from Belfast and Dublin, and the Primate spends many hours in travel which is time-consuming and costly. Controversial it may be, but I could foresee a time when the Primate should live in Belfast, with an assistant Bishop in Armagh.'

Eames also believes that while the administrative centre of the church has been in Dublin, Northerners have shown an increasing awareness of this, but not a sufficient understanding of its implications. He argues that the distance and availability of the laity to play a part on central bodies has led to a dominance of the 'Dublin' work by Southerners. He says, 'I can foresee a great central administration in Belfast. Given greater and better means of communication, this should be possible, and in my opinion desirable.'

Administrative matters apart, one of the most important developments of Eames' Primacy was the decision by the Church of Ireland General Synod in May 1990 to admit women to the priesthood and episcopate. This was the first Anglican Church in the British Isles to do so, a fact which gave Eames no small sense of satisfaction. He says, 'I had long favoured this move, and I believe it was a decision whose time had come. I admired greatly the courage of our church to take this step, when our near neighbours had yet to do so.'

One of the major factors in this initiative was the length of time during which the Church of Ireland had been considering the matter. In 1970 the bishops had stated that there were no theological barriers to the ordination of women and while the debate continued for the next two decades, the church became used 'de facto' to women performing the duties of lay readers and deacons.

In 1976 the General Synod resolved to approve in principle the ordination of women 'subject to the enactment of any necessary legislation'. In 1979 the matter was debated again, and referred back to diocesan synods, prior to General Synod deciding in 1980 what the next step should be. However, during

241

that Synod a proposal to introduce a Bill for the Ordination of Women in 1981 failed to achieve the necessary two-thirds majority.

The issue did not go away, and in 1984 General Synod unanimously agreed to accept the ordination of women as deacons. During the debate Robin Eames, then Bishop of Down and Dromore, argued strongly in favour of Synod adopting the enabling legislative Bill. He said, 'If it is right that we should admit women to the order of deacon, then we should say "Yes" to the Bill, and not allow other considerations to cloud our judgment.'

The overwhelming acceptance of such a measure was regarded by many observers as a stepping-stone towards the ordination of women as priests at a later date, though opposition to this remained within some sections of the church. On 17 May 1990 the matter was finally considered at the General Synod. Eames recalls that the debate was measured, though the atmosphere was tense. He had to contemplate, however, the possibility of a split, but he felt that the Church of Ireland would not have to face the same degree of division as the Church of England on this issue.[4]

Eames recalls, 'The General Synod was its very best on this occasion – debating, praying and listening to each other. Unlike other provinces in the Anglican Communion, we had had a long period to reflect, before making a decision.' He felt that while there would possibly be a sizeable majority in favour, the church had to take seriously the reservations of those who were strongly opposed to the ordination of women. 'At all costs, we had to avoid a situation in which there would be any structural discrimination against a person's conscience-held views.'

During the debate, Eames emphasised that point. He told the Synod that his work with the Eames Commission on the ordination of women had given him an insight into the 'thoughts, feelings, considerations, aspirations, hopes and fears of our fellow members of the Anglican Communion far beyond our shores'. He said that while he regretted some of the things said within the Communion at large because they did no credit to the speakers or to the constituency they sought to represent, nevertheless their views had to be listened to carefully and prayerfully.

He said that the last thing he wanted to see in the Church of

Ireland on this issue was any sense of victory or defeat. He added, 'Whatever the decision, I will do all in my power to find ways through which the people of our church can continue to live together with difference, in compassion and understanding.' That philosophy also underlined his work on the Eames Commission on the ordination of women, and later on Anglican structures following the major controversy over the ordination of homosexual bishops.

In the event, the Church of Ireland did not split over the ordination of women. Eames says, 'I recall the future Archbishop of Dublin Dr John Neill, who originally opposed the development, speaking so honestly about his change of mind. Dean John Paterson of Christ Church, Dublin was the most notable opponent and, in fact, resigned as an Honorary Secretary of the Synod.'

Archbishop Neill, who was then Bishop of Tuam, reflected later, 'There are difficulties in being pioneers, and courage sometimes falters through pain, but the Church of Ireland is the first of the mother churches of Anglicanism to say to those women priests in America, in Africa and in Asia and Australasia: "God has called you, and we affirm you as priests of the one Holy Catholic Church." '

Eames underplays his own role in maintaining good relations with all sides during this sensitive period, but he saw as many dissidents as he could to assure them personally that their ministry would be as valued as much as ever, even though they felt unable in conscience to accept the ordination of women.

Bishop Darling says, 'Robin exercised a calming role. He diffused an awful lot of feeling, and addressed the worries and concerns that these people felt. An Archbishop of Canterbury could not have done this in England. The Church of Ireland is small enough to be personal and it is very much a family.'

Archbishop Neill confirms that under Eames' leadership there was no polarisation. 'I give him full credit for that. His role was holding the two sides together.' There were a small number of defections in the Church of Ireland, but the membership as a whole came to accept the new development, even though a rearguard action at the 1991 General Synod came to nothing. Neill notes, 'I was anxious that we would not do anything to undermine the decision that had already been taken. We came up with a form of words which John Paterson and I proposed to the General Synod, and that was the end of it.'

Several weeks after women's ordination was accepted in May 1990, the Bishop of Connor Dr Samuel Poyntz ordained Kathleen Young and Irene Templeton in St Anne's Cathedral, Belfast. In doing so, the Church of Ireland not only made history, but also took an important step into the future. Poyntz said later, 'Robin Eames has always shown wisdom to know the time and to be able to redeem it. This was well illustrated by the way in which he piloted through the ordination of women. He brought with him even those who were desperately opposed to it.'

The church historian Alan Acheson noted that the priesthood of women in both the stipendiary and auxiliary ministry commended itself in every diocese. 'The calibre of the women ordained, the character of their service, and their commitment above all to pastoral work, set new standards in ministry and stamped the seal of approval on the church's initiative.'[5]

Eames was acutely aware that in making the decision to admit women to the priesthood, the Church of Ireland, unlike some other churches, took care to draw no distinction between the priesthood and the episcopate. He says, 'I was strongly in favour of this, as I believed to do otherwise would be a false distinction doctrinally. It remains to be seen what will happen if and when a woman becomes a bishop in the Church of Ireland.'

Bishop Edward Darling notes, 'Robin had been conditioned by what was happening in the Church of Ireland, and I think that is how he dealt with the wider situation. There are still people who strongly oppose the ordination of women, but they are coming to accept that it is here and that it is going to stay.'

Another sensitive issue was the remarriage in church of divorced persons. This had been under consideration for some time, and although people had earlier been opposed to such a measure, the attitude of the clergy and laity was softening in the early 1990s – partly because of the increasing number of divorcees and partly because people were more compassionate and less judgmental about such matters. Edward Darling noted the change in attitudes. 'A lot of people had a sense of compassion and realised that you should not condemn a person if a marriage does not work.'

In 1996 General Synod approved regulations concerning

the marriage of divorced persons. Robin Eames as a pastor had long been aware of the heartache caused by marriage breakdown, but he was anxious that the Church would not simply be used by some people as a stamp of 'respectability' or 'convenience' for a subsequent remarriage.

He supported the legislation on re-marriage provided that, among other requirements, the new partnership intended to maintain a close link with the Church, that officiating clergy would have no problem of conscience in recommending the new wedding and that the parties were sincere in their wish to have a church blessing. He says, 'I do not see this situation as a contradiction of the Church's teaching on marriage, as some people do. I do feel, however, that it is an extension with clear guidelines of pastoral care and of the love and forgiveness of God.'

Though there were important developments in the Church of Ireland concerning faith, worship and doctrine, and on structural matters, Robin Eames continued to think deeply and prayerfully about what he termed 'the ethos' of the Church of Ireland in a rapidly changing and increasingly secular society.

He became increasingly aware of those within the church who were questioning the whole idea of episcopacy. He says, 'I do not doubt the vocation and earnestness of such clergy, but I sometimes ask myself if they would not have been happier in a non-episcopal setting. "Congregationalism" has become a real issue for the Church of Ireland, particularly in the North.'

While Eames remained long in favour of experimentation in worship – for example his introduction of a Sunday-night service at St Dorothea's for weekend caravanners returning home – he was anxious to retain as far as possible an essentially Anglican dimension to the worship. 'Response to the mood of the moment will always be an important ingredient, but it is vital that the Church of Ireland takes steps to be ahead of such influences.'

As a committed Anglican, he believes that the liturgy makes provision for almost every human experience. 'When I have encountered scant regard for an established liturgy, I wondered if the clergy concerned should have been ordained in another denomination. Perhaps the fault lay in a failure to understand fully the wealth of Anglican worship forms, or our failure to have taught those values in training.' He sometimes feared that too many of the clergy did not appreciate the rich heritage of the Church of Ireland worship and liturgy.

Given this background, liturgical reform in the Church of Ireland was important, and it was hoped that the new Prayer Book launched in 2004 would combine the riches of the past with the changes in recent years. Eames says, 'I pray that we may now settle after years of reform to allow our newest additions time to be used and to become part of a truly Anglican form of worship in Ireland. The secret will lie in educating our people in its use, but also in the loyalty of the clergy in knowing what true Anglican worship stands for.'

Hidden between the lines of Eames' expressed views about liturgy is a deep concern that the Church of Ireland may be moving away from a broad-church ethos to a more denominational attitude in the North, allied to a new-found sense of nationality in the South, and the kind of Anglicanism that is closer to and more easily identified with the Roman Catholicism of its neighbours. In the next few years it will be interesting to see whether the reaction to the controversial issue of the ordination of homosexual clergy will divide on North–South lines, and whether people in the Republic will be more tolerant.

Anglicanism at its best is both 'Reformed' and 'Catholic'. Eames says, 'There has also been the constant possibility of an all-Ireland institution reflecting the problems and the tensions of a divided island. I have been conscious of the dangers inherent in the two churches' syndrome, with the Church of Ireland in the North reflecting a different social, cultural and political outlook to its fellow members in the Republic. This has been a constant theme for all my work, but at times it has not been easy to keep the Church of Ireland together as a whole.'

One of Eames' main concerns, however, was the perception among some Northerners that the church was exhibiting a 'Romeward' trend because of its ecumenical activities, in which he himself had a high-profile role. He says, 'We have taken the initiative in many respects, and our theological position as being "Catholic" and "Reformed" has allowed us to identify with much of Roman Catholic practice.'

There have been difficulties, however, and not all from the

Church of Ireland opponents of ecumenism. Eames says, 'Several Edicts from the Vatican have caused genuine hurt among Church of Ireland people. To be told in the recent *Dominus Jesus* Edict that we were not a true church caused great consternation. In my many private contacts with Roman Catholic bishops I was surprised to find that they did not fully understand the degree of hurt we felt.'

It also gave ammunition to the critics in the Church of Ireland who said to Eames, 'There you are – even your friends in Rome don't accept you!' He underlines, however, that some of the strongest and best-informed critical comments on aspects of the Roman Church have come from Church of Ireland sources.

Overall, Eames has detected a sea change in attitudes. 'Earlier problems over inter-church marriages, for example, have largely disappeared. I am convinced that with growing secularisation our two churches will move closer on day-to-day matters. Theological and doctrinal differences will take longer to resolve.'

In personal terms, he long enjoyed the closest possible relationships with Roman Catholic bishops, clergy and people. 'Among them are some of my truest friends. In fact, during many private conversations with Roman Catholic bishops and others I have found greater examples of genuine Christian understanding and charity than would be found in many a Loyalist remark.'

Part of the significance of such comments from the head of the Church of Ireland is not just that Eames is saying the right things about fellow Christians, but that he has earned the right to say so, after many years of ploughing a difficult and sometimes lonely ecumenical furrow.

One development close to his heart was the Methodist–Church of Ireland Covenant which was completed in 2002 and signed in an evocative ceremony held at Chrome Hill near Belfast. It was here in 1787 that John Wesley himself had planted two entwined beech saplings in the hope of a growing under-standing between the two churches. Today they are sturdy and still entwined trees.

Work had been going on concerning an agreement for some time, and both Robin Eames and Harold Good, his friend from schooldays and the then Methodist President, spoke at the annual meeting of each other's church and were warmly received. Eames stressed that there would be no 'takeover' by the larger Church of Ireland and that the agreement was to work together as equal partners. Eames says, 'Both Harold and I talked to each other about the past, and my personal thoughts turned to my family's past and to my late father. I wonder what he would have thought of it all.'

Archbishop Neill, and other members of the Church of Ireland, noticed Eames' particular enthusiasm for the Covenant. 'I said to myself, "This is the two parts of Robin coming together." As you get older there is an awareness that if you have chosen a certain path that is different from the one with which you grew up, you want to reconcile the two.'

Bishop James Mehaffey, like many observers, voices the apprehensions of those who are aware that Eames must retire some day, but hopefully not yet. He says, 'He is a staunch Anglican with a deep love of the Church of Ireland. He has a broad view and does not come with a narrow agenda, theologically or ecclesiastically. He is a persuader and a respecter of different points of view. So long as he is in Armagh, the Church of Ireland is in a safe pair of hands.'

Some people claim that Eames' very strength as Primate is also part of his weakness, and that his perceived presidential style has made it more difficult for younger men to emerge. There is a general perception that he has become the 'face' of the Church of Ireland in a way that had not been quite so explicit previously. Perhaps this is because he has been in office for so long. The last time that this occurred was in the Primacy of Archbishop Gregg from 1939 to 1959, and since then the Primates have been a much shorter time in office.

To an extent, Eames has developed a presidential style not through choice, but because of the nature of modern society where leaders are expected to react swiftly with 'sound bites' for the media. Eames has done this well for several decades, but he is also aware of the need to stay in touch with his grass roots, which he has almost invariably managed to do.

He is willing to speak out on an important issue, rather than wait for weeks to gauge the reaction of a key church committee. He says, 'I am prepared to have the sleepless nights wrestling with something, rather than waiting for a longer-term reaction from the church, only to discover that the media have moved on.'

Within the Church of Ireland, there is wide praise for his

achievements or – to put it another way – there are few if any
substantive criticisms, or deeply held doubts and regrets about
his Primacy. It is generally agreed at all levels of the Church
that he has been one of the great all-Ireland Primates of the
past century, together with Archbishops Gregg and Simms.
Southerners in particular point to Gregg's leadership during
another period of extreme difficulty in Irish affairs, while others
single out the saintliness of Simms, though it is also acknowledged that he was out of his depth during the violent and
savage crisis in the North when he was Primate.

Even with hindsight, it is invidious to choose between Gregg
and Eames. They were different men facing different challenges
in difficult times, but both have been leaders of stature. Walton
Empey notes, 'History will be kind to Robin. He will be regarded
as one of the greatest Primates of the past century. From a
Southern perspective, however, Simms was loved and extremely
well known, and Gregg was admired not only for his astute
leadership at an extremely sensitive time, but also for his
wonderful scholarship. I think Robin will be up there with them.'

Bishop Samuel Poyntz believes that history produces leaders
of stature in every century. He says, 'In the twentieth century
the two Archbishops of Canterbury whose ministries enveloped
the whole nation were Randall Davidson and William Temple.
In twentieth-century Ireland they were John Allen Fitzgerald
Gregg and Robin Eames. Robin has been a father-in-God, just,
discerning and dignified, and with a mind that has been able
to judge timing to perfection, which is terribly important. He
has also been a very good communicator in the media age. All
these qualities have made him a quite remarkable Archbishop
and Primate for the twentieth century and beyond.'

Senator Martin Mansergh, an adviser to Irish Premiers and
himself a member of the Church of Ireland in the Republic,
believes that Eames has been a leader of considerable stature,
possessing a political astuteness that has been of great benefit
to the Church of Ireland in difficult times and also in making a
real contribution to the peace process. He says, 'Robin Eames
has been one of the most considerable figures to occupy the
Primacy in the twentieth century and beyond, and maybe
indeed the most considerable figure to do so.'

Such a judgment is not far off the mark.

18

Senior Primate

When Robin Eames pronounced the Blessing on Archbishop Rowan Williams at his Consecration in February 2003 he did so as Senior Primate on behalf of the world's 70 million members of the Anglican Communion. He was the longest-serving Primate, having been Archbishop of Armagh and Primate of All-Ireland since 1986. However, he earned the title not only because of his long service but also in a deeper sense because of his immense contribution to the Anglican Communion in which he had been a senior figure for many years.

He first joined the Anglican Consultative Council (ACC) in 1984 as a representative of the Church of Ireland, when he was Bishop of Down and Dromore. He attended the sixth ACC meeting in Nigeria from 17 to 27 July 1984 under the Presidency of Archbishop Robert Runcie, and he was accompanied by Barry Deane from Cork. Deane was the Honorary Secretary of the General Synod and the first layman of the Church of Ireland to attend such an ACC meeting.

It was here that Robin Eames first experienced in depth the global dimension of worldwide Anglicanism. At that meeting he played an active role in proposing a motion to the Council on mixed marriages in Ireland, and subsequently the ACC decided that the whole issue of inter-church marriages should be taken up directly with the Secretariat for Christian Unity in Rome.

There were, of course, many other dimensions to Eames' first experience of a major ACC gathering, at which he met many of the leading participants and forged friendships with a number of clerics within the Communion – including the then Reverend Winston Ndungane, who later became Archbishop of Cape Town as well as a close friend. To this day Robin Eames has kept a well-filled scrapbook on his visit to Nigeria in 1984, thus underlining his abiding love for travel as well as for new challenges.

Since then his work within the Anglican Communion has involved him in many different situations. He says, 'This has provided me with much satisfaction, deepened my experience of faith, made many friendships, and allowed me to be involved in work which has hopefully strengthened the life of the international church family.'

That work has ranged from membership of the ACC and its Standing Committee, to Chairman of the Anglican Communion Finance Committee (IAFC) with responsibility for the everyday life of the Communion as well as several Lambeth Conferences, membership of the Joint Primates-ACC Standing Committee as a representative of Europe, and, for almost twenty years, membership of the Primates' Meeting.

Eames has also been Chair of the Anglican Communion Staff and Appointments Review Group, and a member of the Personal Emergencies Fund, which allocates money for medical emergencies to Anglican priests and their families in the developing world. He has chaired the Archbishop of Canterbury's Commission on Communion and Women in the Episcopate, and the Anglican Theological and Doctrinal Commission, also known as *The Virginia Report*. Most recently he chaired the tactfully yet accurately named Lambeth Commission on Anglican Structures, following the controversy over homosexual clergy and the appointment and consecration of Dr Gene Robinson as Bishop of New Hampshire at the end of 2003.

Given his workload as Archbishop of Armagh and Primate of All-Ireland and the strains of ministering in a deeply divided society like Northern Ireland, it was long a source of wonder to many observers at home and overseas that Eames had also been able to play such a role within the Anglican Communion. He did so partly out of a sense of duty in responding to challenges that he encountered or was invited to consider, and partly because his robust constitution, his abilities and his self-discipline and time-management, as well as his appetite for long and sustained hard work, enabled him to undertake such a wide range of activities. In all of this he has had the steadfast support of Lady Eames, who is herself regarded with affection and respect all over the Anglican world.

Occasionally there have been quizzical eyebrows raised in Ireland as to where Eames may turn up next, but there has not been any suggestion that by travelling so much he has neglected his duties at home.

Although Eames' work has embedded him deeply within the structural and committee life of the Communion, he appreciates profoundly (and recalls in detail) the human dimensions to his many travels and encounters. He has visited Anglican churches literally around the globe, he has met the political leaders of many nations, he has witnessed human fear in the Gaza strip and Jerusalem, and starvation in the refugee camps of Uganda, he has met people suffering from AIDS/HIV in Africa, and he has encountered gangsters and drug barons in Brazil.

He says, 'I have seen at first hand the humanitarian work in the slums of the South African townships, in the civil war zone of Uganda, among the street children of Rio, among the rubbish dumps of Recife in Brazil where children search the stinking dumps for food accompanied by rats, and among war refugees in Lebanon.'

On one such visit Elizabeth Gibson-Harries, the Church of Ireland Press Officer who was with him, recalls that he was immensely moved by the suffering. She says, 'He was reduced to tears by the sight of human beings sifting through rubbish in order to help themselves stay alive. I remember him being deeply impressed by the fact that some of the little girls in a slum were wearing white socks. He saw that as their determination to maintain their human dignity in the midst of such terrible deprivation.'

She also tells the story of how he displayed his customary tact during a visit to a poor region in Latin America. She says, 'Robin is not always a good traveller in terms of "roughing it" and he is careful about what he eats, because he wants to be able to carry out his duties. One day, however, some people in a deprived area offered him food. It looked less than appetising, but he did not want to hurt their feelings or to offend them by refusing. He accepted the plate with thanks and later on slipped it over to me quietly, with the food uneaten. That was typically Robin's way of dealing tactfully with a delicate situation!'

As Eames continued to travel widely and to meet Anglicans

and others from many different backgrounds, he felt that in the light of some of their experiences, the situation in Northern Ireland took on a different perspective. When he heard the stories from Rwanda, Burundi, Argentina and other places during the years of dictatorships, he realised even more 'how comparatively fortunate we were in Northern Ireland'.

He heard the experiences of church leaders like Archbishop Desmond Tutu who have helped to overthrow repressive regimes, as in South Africa, of those church leaders whose clergy cannot be paid a living wage, of ministers who have to travel thousands of miles to celebrate Communion with their scattered parishioners, and of bishops whose families had been kidnapped or held for weeks in attempts to silence clerical criticism of injustices.

Ironically it was in his dealings with Archbishop Tutu at the 1988 Lambeth Conference that Eames' regional responsibilities in Ireland were directly challenged by the concern of the wider Anglican Communion concerning the repression and injustices of the apartheid regime in South Africa.

The Conference adopted a resolution indicating *inter alia* that it 'understands those who, after exhausting all other ways, choose the way of armed struggle as the only way to justice, whilst drawing attention to the dangers and injustices possible in such action.' The next day, however, Archbishop Eames made a powerful speech and pointed out that under no conditions should the Conference give the impression that the murder campaign in Northern Ireland – frequently referred to by those who supported it as an 'armed struggle' – was being afforded any succour by the resolution of the day before.

In the end the Conference accepted a resolution expressing 'solidarity with fellow-Anglicans and all the people of Northern Ireland in their suffering'. The Conference, 'in the circumstances of Northern Ireland', condemned all violence, and urged 'all political and community leaders to seize every opportunity to work together to bring about a just and lasting solution'.

Significantly, the seconder of the new resolution was Archbishop Tutu, who had backed the earlier resolution, and said that it would help those oppressed groups who had no recourse to democratic procedures. Earlier he had stated, 'Our people have used conventional means, and each time the response has been a violent response. We are not asking you to condone or condemn, but we are asking you to say to those of our people who have tried everything, "We understand." '

Eames recalls, 'Desmond Tutu came to that Lambeth Conference as the justified champion of South African resistance to apartheid, and we all admired him beyond words. I already had contact with him about the Christian response to violence and non-violent opposition. However, I tried to explain at length the fundamental difference between the two situations in Ireland and South Africa.'

In South Africa the 'armed struggle' was perceived to be opposing injustice. In Ireland the activities of the Provisional IRA were not seen by a large majority as part of an 'armed struggle', but as a means of inflicting violence on the people. Eames says, 'I am not sure that Desmond Tutu found the distinction easy to understand, but when he came to the Lambeth Conference I had to point out the difficulties for us in Ireland with the concept of an "armed struggle". To his credit he saw my point, and my amendment to his earlier proposal eventually won the support of the Conference. Much publicity was given to the debate, and in Ireland I received overwhelming support.'

Notwithstanding this difference of opinion, a firm friendship developed between Eames and Tutu. Eames recalls, 'We met on several occasions, apart from our communications by letter, and we shared many theories and thoughts. Desmond's ebullient character and deep spirituality, allied to his personal courage, made him the epitome of Anglican witness, and the award of a Nobel Prize to Desmond was welcomed by us all. When history is written, he will undoubtedly be the key figure of Anglican and Christian opposition to injustice and oppression.'

Archbishop Tutu recalls, 'I think Robin was for a blanket condemnation of the use of violence. I said that although we opposed violence, our situation in South Africa was quite different. People in Northern Ireland had the possibility of parliamentary action, but this was not an option available to us in South Africa at that time. I said that this made a significant difference, when people came to question the use of violence or not.' He adds, 'I cannot remember what exactly Robin and I said to each other at the Lambeth Conference of 1988, but we didn't end up throttling one another! We still talked to each other, and we agreed to disagree. Each of us had made his point.'[1]

This exchange at Lambeth in 1988 was a good example of some of the challenges Eames faced. Though he was a seasoned world traveller dealing with church business on a global basis, he did not always find it easy to collate this experience with what he faced back home in Ireland. It was generally perceived in world church circles that Irish Roman Catholicism was within the strongly conservative wing of Rome. Eames discovered that many international church leaders regarded what they saw as a 'religious war' in Ireland as a feudal expression of ancient religious hostility. When Eames talked overseas about the co-operation (which some observers in Ireland would describe as limited) between Protestants and Roman Catholics, he would be asked immediately that if there was progress, why did the Presbyterian Church in Ireland withdraw from the World Council of Churches?

There was a general belief in international church circles that Ireland was parochial, inward-looking, and counter to the prevailing world religious scene. Eames says, 'I had to spend a lot of effort to paint a positive picture of what was happening in Ireland, but the interlocking nature of Irish political and religious life did not make the task any easier.'

He feels that his experience underlined the importance of a local church being an integral part of a worldwide body such as the Anglican Communion. Only by such contacts could local parochialism be confronted by the realities of life further afield. This, however, was a two-way process. The Church of Ireland, though small in numbers compared to others in the Communion, retains its full autonomy, but Eames believes that Irish Anglicanism has vital things to say to the others. He says, 'The very diversity of the Irish scene has been a microcosm of the world diversity of the Communion, but our spirituality and our pastoral approach has opened many doors for me with my international colleagues. For example when I visit the United States I have always appreciated the Americans' warm affection for all things Irish.'

Eames has always tried to bring the structure of his own Church of Ireland more into line with international Anglicanism, and to open doors and windows to what is happening elsewhere. However, he feels that he has had limited success in broadening outlooks. He says, 'I have always tried to bring back to the Church of Ireland the impressions and lessons I was learning abroad. However, parochialism remains a very strong influence in Irish religious life. It will take a long time for grass-roots Irish Christianity to be as influenced by global progress as it is by the familiar paths of local intransigence.'

Nevertheless, he has always had a sense of pride in referring within the international context to the teaching and history of the Church of Ireland, and he has an impish sense of fun in reminding people that Armagh pre-dates Canterbury in early church history. He feels strongly that his international experience has given a dimension to his leadership in Ireland which he might not otherwise have had. 'I have been fortunate as an individual churchman to experience the winds of change and progress as well as the problems elsewhere in the Anglican Communion. In return, it is for others to judge what contribution I have made as an Irishman to the same Communion.'

It is significant that he refers to himself as an 'Irishman' within the international context. As Liz Gibson-Harries points out shrewdly, 'When Robin is abroad he is very definitely an "Irishman". Back home I am not sure he knows exactly what he is.' This was underlined by Eames' long heart-searching before accepting a life peerage, and also the somewhat mixed reception from part of his flock in the Irish Republic when he accepted the honour.

Significantly, however, the details of a person's nationality were on occasions much more than academic, as in the case of the Ulsterman Brian Keenan who was captured in Beirut in 1985 by fundamentalist Shi'ite militiamen and held captive in the suburbs there for more than four years. During this time he was shut off from all contact with the outside world and other people, apart from his captors and his fellow hostages, including John McCarthy.

The details of his capture and eventual release are related graphically and movingly by Brian Keenan in his book *An Evil Cradling*,[2] but perhaps less well known was the involvement of Robin Eames, with others, in trying to bring about his release from such harrowing captivity. Eames says, 'The capture of Brian Keenan and of all the others including Terry Waite and John McCarthy shocked the world. Brian's capture brought a new emphasis for me because he claimed membership of the Church of Ireland and his two sisters in Belfast contacted me to see if there was anything I could do to bring his case to the notice of the Anglican Communion and the British Government.'

Keenan held both a British and an Irish passport, and Eames – like other people who were trying to help – found himself in touch with the representatives of both Governments, with the danger of falling between two stools. A BBC Northern Ireland reporter Noreen Erskine brought Keenan's sisters, Mrs Brenda Gillhan and Mrs Elaine Spence, to meet Eames at Armagh. He listened to their story carefully and decided to contact the Archbishop of Canterbury Dr Robert Runcie, who was already deeply involved in the hostages' situation because of the incarceration of his special envoy Terry Waite.

Eames flew to London and talked to Runcie and his personal adviser John Little. He found the situation extremely complicated. The British Foreign Office was naturally very concerned about the fate of McCarthy and Waite, but diplomatic considerations in the Middle East hampered their efforts, and Syria was a key player. Eames immediately recognised the difficulties – Keenan's Irish citizenship brought Dublin into the picture, but the British saw his case primarily as a concern for Ireland.

Eames made several visits to the Department of Foreign Affairs in Dublin and found them equally perplexed, but anxious to separate the Keenan case from British involvement. He says, 'Lebanon was in a chaotic state, and there was great confusion as to who or what group had taken Brian Keenan. His sisters were greatly distressed and worried, and we were all very frustrated.'

Eames took two immediate initiatives. He went with the sisters to the Iranian Embassy in Dublin, and he also met the then Irish Premier Charles Haughey and senior government officials. The meeting in the Iranian Embassy was, according to Eames, 'quite an experience'. They were met by senior officials, who talked endlessly and showed great sympathy, but nothing concrete emerged. One official kept referring to the Koran, and there was an attempt by the Iranians to bargain with the Irish Government. They wanted more exchange visits for students and other concessions in return for their efforts to try to release Keenan. They intimated that they knew all about him, but would not specify any definite information.

Eames concluded privately that the Iranians wanted to keep out of the problem, but he promised to convey their suggestions to the Irish Government. He says, 'We concluded our meeting with promises to stay in touch, but I was not hopeful of their help. I told officials at the Irish Department of Foreign Affairs about the meeting and they were sympathetic, but again I could detect a general frustration with the whole situation.'

When Eames met Haughey and his colleagues he felt that they were powerless to influence Keenan's captors, and he formed the impression that the British were carrying the main burden. The rumours abounded, and no one knew whether the captives were alive or dead. Meanwhile, Brian's sisters were continuing to give media interviews in order to draw attention to his plight and to try to get as much help as possible.

The crisis dragged on to 1989. In the Spring of that year Robin Eames was due to attend a meeting of the Anglican Primates at Larnaca in Cyprus. He had been thinking continually about Keenan's situation and he believed that this would give him an opportunity to build a personal initiative on his behalf. Keenan's sisters also travelled to Larnaca, as did the BBC's Noreen Erskine.

In Larnaca, Eames met several priests from the Orthodox Church who had direct contact with Beirut. They met a number of times in a local monastery and in a hotel at Larnaca. Eames found them sympathetic but he felt that they knew more than they were telling him. 'On one occasion a tall American with a dark complexion was in the group. He said little, and although I was never introduced to him I found out later that he was Oliver North.'

Eames offered to travel to Beirut with any of the Orthodox priests who were willing to help move the situation forward by meeting people on the ground. There was a ferry service nightly between the ports, and priests made the journey frequently. It was agreed that one of the priests would accompany Eames on a secret mission to Beirut. On the day before they were due to go, Eames was asked to return to the monastery where he met a doctor who worked in Beirut. It soon became obvious that he knew a great deal about the hostage situation, and Eames formed the opinion that he had been asked for medical advice about at least one of the prisoners.

Eames recalls, 'There was an atmosphere of fear, and he was evasive about details. He said that he would soon have to return to Beirut, and he did not want his contact with me to become

258

known. Most importantly, however, he told me, "They are still alive", and that was the first indication that any of us had had about them. I found it tremendously encouraging.' Eames then talked with Archbishop Runcie who was also in Larnaca, and they compared notes.

They decided, however, that it would be too dangerous for Eames to travel to Beirut at that time. Runcie was extremely conscious that he had given similar advice to Waite before he had embarked upon his ill-fated mission, and the Archbishop did not want another captive on his hands. They also decided that Eames should tell as many Lebanese contacts as possible that he was in Larnaca and that he was most concerned about the welfare of Keenan.

At all stages, he kept Keenan's sisters fully informed of developments, and he introduced them to the contacts he had made. He says, 'Sometimes at night we could hear the sound of distant gunfire in Beirut, and this added greatly to the sisters' distress, but at least we felt we were making some progress.'

Eames later wrote movingly about walking with the sisters one evening along the beach at Larnaca and gazing in the direction of Beirut:

> Somewhere over there, always 'over there', lay that sad and strife-torn city, and somewhere among its ruins Brian Keenan was held hostage. His two sisters were silent. We had gone over in our conversation as we walked all we had found out, all we had heard and all we imagined we had heard, about him . . . He was almost four years missing and we had come to Cyprus because it seemed a good place to talk to people who might know.

There was no sound of gunfire from Beirut that evening.

> People told us they sometimes heard the sound of shells. But that evening it was as though there was nothing there beyond the horizon. It was Brenda who broke the silence. 'It's strange, isn't it. We've heard so much about what Beirut's like. Somebody said to me yesterday, "It's just like Belfast." ' [3]

During Eames' last evening in Larnaca he was introduced to someone who described himself as a Beirut 'businessman'. He told Eames that if a reward was offered and if the Irish Government would offer support for humanitarian and educational projects in the Lebanon, he could persuade people to release Keenan. Eames did not commit himself in any way but on his return to Dublin he briefed the Department of Foreign Affairs on what had happened at Larnaca.

Back in Ireland, Eames felt that the whole affair was becoming more and more complex. One of the real problems was to help keep alive the hopes of the Keenan sisters without being unrealistic about the fate of their brother. Eames says, 'I felt that while the Irish Government wanted to do all it could to gain Keenan's release, it did not have sufficient contacts in Beirut itself. The British Foreign Office had much more "clout", but I often wondered how really pro-active they were.'

Eames suggested to the Irish Government that they might make more progress on behalf of Keenan if they adopted a more independent approach on humanitarian grounds, divorced from any British effort, and he was told that this was to be Dublin's policy. He maintained his contacts with John Little, Runcie's adviser, and also the contacts he had made among the Orthodox priests in Beirut. He also met Terry Waite's brother who was campaigning on his behalf.

Then quite suddenly, just as dramatically as he had been kidnapped, Brian Keenan was released in August 1990, and later flown home to Dublin on the Irish Government's jet. As soon as he heard that Keenan was on his way, Eames issued a press release underlining his delight and that of 'thousands of people of all denominations in Northern Ireland and the Irish Republic'.

He added, 'I cannot speak too highly of the way in which the Keenan family have responded over the years to the strain and tension imposed on them.' Eames also paid tribute to the efforts of the Irish Government and also the church contacts in the Middle East and elsewhere who had given him such co-operation, and said, 'Our prayers must now be for the release of all hostages and an end to the nightmare of their families and friends.'

Back in Dublin, Brian Keenan met his sisters and also held a memorable press conference. Eames travelled to Dublin and met him for the first time. He found it a strange experience to talk face to face with a man who had been so high on his agenda for years.

Keenan was taken to a Dublin hospital to recuperate, and he asked Eames to meet him the next day. Eames noticed that he sat cross-legged on top of the bed because he could not lie under the bedclothes after sleeping so long on a bare floor in a cell in Beirut. Keenan knew something of the Archbishop's work on his behalf in Larnaca, and his sisters had told him some of the details. Eames found it a fascinating conversation, but the most important aspect turned to the fate of Terry Waite.

Eames says, 'Brian told me of seeing a man with "large feet" going past his cell in Beirut, and it seemed that they could only belong to Terry, who was a very tall man. He was convinced that Waite was still alive, and that was another breakthrough for all of us.' Eames told Archbishop Runcie and John Little what Keenan had said, but the Irish Primate felt a strong pastoral need to speak to Terry Waite's wife Frances.

It was decided that Brian should meet her face to face and that she should go to Belfast, where her family lived. The problem was trying to avoid the media who naturally had an intense interest in the whole hostage situation. The chosen destination for the secret meeting was the Business Centre at Aldergrove airport, far from the public view and away from the attention of the media who had no inkling of such an important rendezvous in those businesslike surroundings.

Eames was present at the meeting. He recalls, 'I will never forget it. Brian and Frances sat together and he told her the details of what had happened. It was the first time, I believe, that Frances had heard that Terry was still alive, and it was a very emotional occasion. When Terry was finally released, we met in London and all the pieces of the jigsaw started to fall into place. It transpired that the meeting at Aldergrove had given Frances the first full hope that her husband was still alive.'

Eames' one regret was that John Little, the Archbishop's adviser, had died suddenly, before he could see the outcome of all his work. Overall it had been an extraordinary time for everyone, including Eames who became involved in various cloak-and-dagger episodes at a time when he had more than enough to contend with in Northern Ireland.

Noreen Erskine, the BBC journalist who was closely involved with the Keenan story, sensed that Keenan's sisters had not been receiving much help from anywhere at the early stages of their campaign. She recalls, 'I felt that, apart from pushing journalistic buttons, here were two women who needed help, and publicity was one way of helping them.' She confirms that Robin Eames' support was appreciated, and says, 'The family believe that he made a significant contribution to getting Brian released.' Noreen Erskine also feels that the visit to Larnaca certainly helped. 'I am not sure that it was a turning point, but it was – to use one of Robin's phrases – "another piece of the jigsaw". It certainly gave Brian's sisters a considerable boost. When they came back they were a lot more reassured. In Larnaca people accepted that what Robin was doing was in good faith and even if they were not in a position themselves to do something, some of them knew people who might be.'

Eames sums up his role in only a few words: 'The whole experience introduced me to the complications of international politics, and what church sources could do to advise and to help to achieve, far ahead of established diplomatic activity.' Eames was always good with words, but when he wanted to, he could be masterly in his understatement. He had discovered yet again that being an archbishop in Ireland had its own responsibilities, challenges and rewards.

More than a decade later, in July 2001, Eames returned to the Middle East at the request of the Archbishop of Canterbury Dr George Carey who asked him to accompany him on a visit, together with Mrs Carey. Dr Carey was aware that the Anglicans in Israel and Palestine were disappointed that an American delegation had declined to visit them. The Americans were worried about the political situation, and felt that a visit might be too dangerous.

Carey recalls, 'Robin was *the* Primate I felt I could ask to go with me in that very delicate situation. He is the sort of person who is happy to "front" something, but who is also content to be "a number two". He doesn't always want to be in the hot seat. Robin has the capacity to be a disciple, the ability to go along with others, and at the same time an ability to energise a situation.'[4]

Archbishop Carey recalls that they had an 'amazing visit', where they met – among others – President Arafat and Prime Minister Sharon. He says, 'Out of that visit came the Alexandrian Declaration, and the process of trying to bring together the religious leaders of the Holy Land – Jewish, Muslim and Christian.'

Robin Eames also remembers the visit clearly. As he and Carey talked with Sharon, he felt some sympathy for Sharon's political dilemmas. He was aware that the Israeli Parliament was determined to safeguard the state, but on the other hand there was a growing recognition that dialogue somehow had to produce peace. Sharon said to him, 'After all that has happened in Northern Ireland *you* know how destructive terrorism can be.'

On the way to Gaza, Eames and his companions were held up for a long time at the frontier, even though they were on an official visit with the consent of the Israelis and the Palestinians. Eames noted that the Israeli troops were young conscripts who were officious and who made little attempt to speed things up. He says, 'If that was the attitude of the Israeli army to us, what must it have been like for the ordinary Palestinians?'

They met Arafat in his headquarters in Gaza city, surrounded by armed guards and much evidence of a place under seige. 'At that time there had been no political threat to Arafat's position, and he spoke in terms of "my people". His solution to the problem was dependent on an end to the building of houses on Palestinian land. I sensed a pessimism about the future. Again and again he stressed the humanitarian needs of his people.'

Eames feels that the visit helped to achieve a new awareness of the needs of the Christian communities in the Middle East and also a new awareness from Palestinians that the Anglican Communion was not only concerned, but also listening. He formed deep personal impressions of the sadness of the conflict. He says, 'I will long remember the image of the square at Bethlehem deserted except for an Israeli tank, as we prayed at the stable where Christ was born.'

On the journey back he had time to reflect on all that he had seen and heard. He concluded, 'There were memories of two peoples who were prisoners of their history. There were memories of fear brought about by violence. There were pictures of frightened communities. Again and again the image of my own native land reared its head. Change the colours, the climate and the labels and you had Northern Ireland again and again.'

19

Unity in Diversity?

During almost two decades of direct involvement within the Anglican Communion, Robin Eames has been conscious of its international role with other churches, and also of the change and challenges within the Communion itself. These have been made manifest in a long and complex search for an answer to the problem of living with an acceptable form of unity within considerable diversity.

Eames has become increasingly aware of the Anglican influence on the world scene, in terms of disciplined liturgical worship, and a spirituality leading to active social witness. He believes that its stance on ecumenical outreach provided new initiatives between world religions that would not have been possible without Anglican catholicity.

He says, 'Our official conversations with the Orthodox Church and with Rome have progressed far beyond other attempts at ecumenical understanding. Our Reformed character has produced real working agreements with Lutherans and Baptists. In all such ecumenism, we have adopted a truly inclusive approach, and what started off as "conversations" with one tradition have drawn in others.'

He feels that this is particularly true in regions where the Roman Catholics are strong. Anglicanism has been able to interpret for Roman Catholics the Reformed traditions in their own area, while the Reformed nature of Anglicanism itself has allowed approaches to many disciplines that found it difficult to interpret Roman Catholicism.

In his work outside Ireland – and this in itself is a significant point – he has been agreeably surprised at how quickly a genuine understanding had been fostered between churches through small initial steps, and how local ecumenical efforts had been encouraged by an Anglican knowledge of, and involvement in, other schemes elsewhere. He says, 'Without doubt, ecumenism has become a pillar of Anglicanism. It is certainly not without its frustrations, but frequent attention by Rome – both positive and negative – and to Anglicanism in general, indicates the serious way in which the Communion is regarded around the world.'

Within Anglicanism itself Eames has noticed significant changes. Throughout the years, the Communion has regarded certain structures as its foundation. These include the historic significance of the Archbishop and See of Canterbury, the Lambeth Conference, the Anglican Consultative Council and the Meeting of Primates. While the opinions of the Archbishop of Canterbury carry great moral authority and he is often perceived to be the 'official voice' of Anglicanism, this is true only up to a point. It is the Lambeth Conference that has the authority to speak for the Communion – though in practical terms this voice in the long periods between each Conference is that of the Archbishop.

Against this background, however, new developments have taken place. The numerical strength of the Communion has been most evident in the rapid growth of Anglicanism in Africa, and particularly south of the Sahara – to such an extent that some people argue that the centre of the Communion is now far from Canterbury and England. As well as this, differing attitudes to the nature of 'authority' have put pressure on relationships between the provinces and the centre, and between the provinces themselves, while external forces have questioned the ability of traditional Anglican structures to meet the demands of the centre.

In essence the Anglican Communion is a world family of churches that is characterised by its diversity in terms of nationality, culture, outlook, race and attitudes to church structures. Those differences are also, at the same time, its strengths and weaknesses. Eames comments, 'The strength lies in its amazing ability to maintain apparent unity of vision and purpose despite such differing outlooks. The weakness lies in its capacity, or lack of it, to produce coherent policies which command backing in each part or province.'

These strengths and weaknesses are visible at the highest

level in the Primates' Meetings, but it is noticeable in controversial issues such as women's ordination and homosexual clergy that the differing attitudes are clearly exposed to a wider public. A major part of Robin Eames' contribution to the Anglican Communion has been to grapple with these issues at the highest level, and to chair not just one but three major Commissions on varying aspects of the central challenge of finding unity amid diversity.

The issue of women's ordination had been around for quite some time before the Lambeth Conference in 1988. For example, the Church of Ireland had accepted as early as 1970 that there were no theological barriers to women's ordination, but it was to take another twenty years before this became a reality in Ireland. However, no woman has yet been ordained as a bishop in Ireland.

The focus on the ordination of women came to a head within the Anglican Communion when it appeared most likely that the Episcopal Church of the United States would proceed with the ordination of the Reverend Barbara Harris as a bishop in Massachusetts. The Americans were keen that the Communion should be aware of this possibility, and duly informed the Primates' Meeting. This led to immediate tensions, particularly among those who objected to such a development on theological grounds, and others – particularly in the developing world – who also had cultural difficulties in accepting a woman bishop.

This tension was reflected at the Lambeth Conference itself. Evangelicals and Catholic Anglicans found a strange commonality in their opposition, while the concept of male leadership in African and Asian cultures made the concept of women bishops unthinkable. Whole dioceses and provinces produced differences of approach.

The debate at the Conference was bitter and divisive. Outside the conference hall at the University of Kent in Canterbury banners were displayed, leaflets were distributed and calls rang out from opposing factions. Rome made it plain that any move to appoint a woman bishop would be a further obstacle to unity. The Orthodox Church issued dire warnings of what would happen if a woman was consecrated bishop.

In between there was a sizeable constituency that almost seemed to await the outcome before making a decision. Many people genuinely feared that the issue was so divisive that it could lead to the break-up of the Anglican Communion. (This in itself was a foretaste of the apprehension that surfaced some fifteen years later over the ordination of homosexual bishops.)

In the end the Lambeth Conference of 1988 produced a good old-fashioned Anglican compromise. Archbishop Runcie announced that there needed to be a consultation at the highest level by an international panel, and the temperature began to drop. Robin Eames was sitting beside a bishop from New Zealand when Runcie made his announcement and he said to Eames, 'God help the man who is asked to chair that one!' Within days, Runcie announced that Robin Eames was to chair the Commission on Communion and Women in the Episcopate. The New Zealand bishop wrote to Eames, 'I'm praying for you . . . !'

Runcie initially phoned Eames to ask him if he would consider chairing the Commission. The Archbishop of Canterbury had a high regard for Eames, and appreciated not only his legal background but his ability to deal with people. By that stage, in 1989, Eames was involved directly with women's ordination at home, and his suitability for the new challenge was not lost on his senior Irish colleagues.

Bishop Edward Darling points out, 'He was already being conditioned by what was happening in the Church of Ireland into thinking how to deal with the whole situation on a wider basis.' Bishop Samuel Poyntz says, 'Robert Runcie had a great ability to be able to spot people. That was one of his greatest gifts, and he made a good choice in appointing Robin to chair that Commission.'

Before Eames formally accepted, he had a long meeting with Runcie at Lambeth. They agreed that the real issues involved, apart from doctrinal differences, would be the effect on the relationships between the various provinces. Eames saw the problem in two ways: first, the need to resolve the theological issues where agreement was impossible and where there seemed no compromise on doctrinal grounds; and, second, the nature of relationships between provinces that could not reach agreement. Eames says, 'After much consideration and prayer I accepted the chairmanship on the grounds that the crisis had to be faced, and that I could be involved in nominating my team.'

The Commission needed an African voice that would command respect in the developing world, and Eames suggested Archbishop Joseph Adetiloye, the Primate of Nigeria, who was regarded as a strong and thoughtful African leader. In Australia, Archbishop Peter Carnley of Perth was emerging as a strong voice from a more liberal province, and he and Eames had worked together previously on constitutional issues concerning structures within the Anglican Communion. Carnley was eventually to become Primate of Australia, and at that time was highly regarded in the United States. Eames recalls, 'As the work of the Commission progressed, Peter's acute ability to discern theological issues made a great impression on us all. He was also excellent at making drafts.'

It was essential that an American voice should be included on the Commission. There was a long list of possibilities, but Eames was not interested in the leader of any faction within the Episopal Church of the United States. He wanted a moderate but knowledgeable input from someone who would command the respect of all the Americans. Eames and Runcie talked to the United States Primate Dr Edward Browning, and he suggested Bishop Mark Dyer of Bethlehem, Pennsylvania. He was a scholar, and a teacher and writer who had already made a name in the ecumenical field of Anglo-Orthodox relations. Eames says, 'Mark was a very gifted theologian and former Roman Catholic who was intimately aware of the US scene.'

Runcie suggested that the then Bishop of Wakefield, Dr David Hope – later to become Archbishop of York – should be on the Commission. He was among those who opposed women's ordination, and was a member of the Anglo-Catholic group. Eames says, 'David proved to be thoughtful and forthright, and he was imbued with a basic North of England common sense!'

Two theologians were added to the list – Dr James Reed, Director of the Toronto School of Theology, and Dr Mary Tanner from Church House in London, who was Theological Secretary of the Board of Mission and Unity of the Church of England. Eames recalls, 'Both were highly esteemed in their respective fields, and Mary in particular could bring an expert ecumenical approach to our work. She was a charming and gentle person who contributed a high percentage of the wording in the final report.'

Two co-secretaries were appointed: Dr Michael Nazir-Ali,

who was Co-ordinator of Studies for the Lambeth Conference of 1988 and later became a senior bishop in the Church of England; and Canon Christopher Hill, who was Runcie's Secretary for Ecumenical Affairs, and also later became a bishop. The Administrative Secretary was Deirdrie Hoban of the Anglican Consultative Council.

When the team was publicly announced on 12 September 1988, Eames was asked at the first press conference if the Commission was, in effect, supervising 'the end of the Anglican Communion'. He replied that its real task was to try to find ways in which it could continue to live and prosper as a community with its own differences. He says, 'Despite the controversy at the Lambeth Conference, the outcome had shown that we wanted to continue as a Communion. It was a time for honesty. I did not underestimate the difficulties, but I was reassured by messages of goodwill from right across the Communion.'

One message proved significant, in the light of future years. Archbishop Runcie received a communique from the Vatican, which warned of the problems raised for Roman Catholic–Anglican relationships posed by women's ordination. In particular, the Vatican viewed as devastating not just women's ordination, but the problems posed by the notion of a woman bishop.

Eames met with representatives of the Roman Catholic Commission on Unity from the Vatican, and having explained the remit for the Commission, he coined a phrase that was repeated by several sources in years to come: 'We must respect our differences, but in the end we must take each other as we are, rather than how we might like each other to be.'

Eames was acutely aware that while the Commission had to acknowledge conflicting theological views, its real task was to preserve the unity of Anglicanism. He says, 'Looking back now I see that challenge as one which was to re-emerge in the current controversies over sexuality.' In the meantime the role of the Eames' Commission, as it came to be known, was to examine the nature of communion as Anglicans saw it, and to suggest pastoral ways in which the Communion itself could face up to fundamental differences.

The Commission met initially in London from 23 to 25 November 1988, and in Long Island, New York from 13 to

269

18 March 1989. Presentations both written and oral were received from a wide spectrum of clerical and lay opinion within and outside the Anglican Communion. As well, formal and informal responses were received from provinces.

Just a few weeks before the scheduled meeting in New York, Barbara Harris was consecrated as the Suffragan Bishop of Massachusetts. Her consecration did not directly influence the ongoing deliberations of the Eames Commission as such, because the issues were already well known. However, it did underline the urgent need for clear guidelines to be set out, as far as possible, for the worldwide Anglican Communion on this vexed issue.

From the outset, the Commission acknowledged that it had been asked to examine a part, and only a part, of the issues that lay at the very heart of Anglican thought and experience. It took as its remit Resolution 1, which was accepted with an overwhelming majority by the Lambeth Conference in 1988, with 423 votes for, 28 against and 19 abstentions. The Commission also recognised, and Eames stressed publicly and privately, that it was not being asked to adjudicate between or within provinces on the ordination of women to the priesthood and episcopate. Rather, it was clear that its mandate was 'to discover how Anglicans can live in the highest possible degree of communion with differences of principle and practice on the ordination of women to the episcopate'.

The Commission lost no time in getting down to business, and it worked hard. Eames says, 'We toiled long hours, but I had to keep to a stringent timetable. The members of the Commission were very co-operative, and I had a high regard for the expertise they brought to their task, particularly in a theological sense.'

At the initial meeting there was a sense of caution, particularly as some members had previously expressed their opinions clearly on some of the issues involved. Eames felt that his responsibility was to build them into a team, and early on he decided to ask them to work in groups to deal with particular aspects of the business. He recalls, 'These methods worked well, and on those occasions when we reached an impasse in our debates, I would call a break, and in personal conversations with members we usually managed to create a consensus. Towards the end of our meetings, after some days, we were all exhausted, and I had to remember the pressures of international travel!'

One member who recalls vividly the hard work of the Commission, and the working methods of its chairman, is the outgoing Archbishop of York Dr David Hope. He says, 'Robin had a very genial style, allied to a certain formality. He always ensured that people's voices were heard, and this gave confidence to a group with very differing views. I had a sense that his own mind was working all the time on ways to find a path through it all.'[1] He believes that Eames was a good chairman. 'The discussion at times was very robust and strong, and Robin would do some straight talking when it was needed. He himself had questions to ask, and challenges to make to both sides. I never saw him frustrated or angry as chairman, or not in control.'

Dr Hope always felt that here was a strong person, who was in charge and that this arose out of his deep sense of God's purpose and his own spiritual depth. He comments, 'There are those who say that Robin Eames is a "wheeler-dealer". If you take only the surface of the person, or if you have only a passing acquaintance, that would be a wholly misguided view. Part of the reason why Robin wins the confidence of people is because he has a rooted spirituality. He is a very Godly man.'

The Archbishop of York also underlines a quality about Robin Eames that others have noted in different ways. He says, 'Sometimes there appears to be a blandness about some of Robin's statements, which is not blandness as such. It is partly his mind roving in a general kind of way. He is a master at the art of making something sound grand, but when you look at it, he has given nothing away. He knows exactly what he is doing when he is not particularly saying anything. That is what he intends! For example, it would have been fatal at the press conferences on the Eames Commission to have given away too much when the report had not been completed.'

Even though Hope was opposed to the ordination of women, and although it was clear where Robin stood, the chairman of the Commission did not let his own views intrude. Hope says, 'I was given a very fair hearing, and some parts of the final report went perhaps a bit further than Robin himself might have liked to have gone in addressing that constituency. However, he saw the reality and force of the arguments, and he saw it was right that they should be in.'

David Hope believes that the humanity of Robin Eames was, and is, clear in the exercise of his office. 'He is quite a "hefty" guy, and if that persona was exercised differently, it could be quite forbidding, even overpowering and quite authoritarian. However, being the person he is, the humanity comes out. When you sit with him around a commission table and when you have lunch with him afterwards, you don't see two different people.'

The Archbishop of York stresses that as chairman of the Commission, Eames did not indulge in any 'politicking'. He says, 'Robin did not take me aside and say, "We need to do this or that, let's do a deal." There was none of that. What was done was out in the open.'

David Hope provides an insight into the very heart of Eames as a chairman. He says, 'On the Commission he showed an ability to forge a sense of trust and belonging and of relationships. When those sorts of things begin to develop, that itself opens up to the work of the Holy Spirit, and people do tend to begin to work together and to try to find a resolution.'

During the meeting of the Commission at Long Island, presentations were made by a delegation of women with experience in the ordained ministry in the USA and Canada, including the newly consecrated Bishop Barbara Harris. Presentations were also made separately to the Commission by a group representing the Evangelical and Catholic Mission within the Episcopal Church, which was opposed to the ordination of women to the priesthood and episcopate.

Barbara Harris made an impressive entrance when she drew up outside the building with her companions in a stretch limousine. One observer noted that as the vehicle drew alongside the kerb a bystander was heard to ask under his breath, 'What have we here?' Clearly this was to be a meeting of differing clerical cultures.

Barbara Harris, by all accounts, argued her case well. Eames recalls, 'She was assured, confident and determined, and greeted members of the Commission as "old friends" even though none of us had met her before.' She faced the questioning fearlessly, and was convinced of the rightness of her episcopal ordination. Eames feels on reflection that she may have concentrated more on her arguments for women bishops than on addressing the issues of greater understanding among the Anglican provinces. He says, 'I would have thought of her as acutely politically conscious, but as with many members of ECUSA I have met over the years, not over-sensitive to the Anglican Communion's opinions. When she left the meeting in Long Island, I sensed a mixed reaction among the Commission's members. Most were impressed by her self-confidence, but some felt that she might not have realised the depth of feeling across the Communion on the issues involved.'

The Eames Commission prepared its final report for consideration at the Primates' Meeting in Larnaca in Cyprus in the Spring of 1989. It is worth noting, incidentally, that despite the important business of this meeting, which was considering the substantive report of the Eames Commission, its chairman made the time to make direct repesentations to local clergy and others in his attempt to help secure the release of Brian Keenan, the Ulsterman who was incarcerated in a Beirut prison cell. It was a good example of Eames' willingness to deal with a number of very tricky issues at the same time and also of his lawyer's ability to focus on the details of each situation without losing the wider perspective.

Naturally, a great deal of thought went into the presentation of the final report of the Eames Commission. The Archbishop of York Dr Hope recalls that there were 'fairly careful nuances'. He says, 'Robin was keen to ensure that the tone of what we were saying should be right. We knew that some of the key phrases and words were going to be heard by sharply divided constituencies which could be heard as repeating what they represented – but in a way which was conciliatory and not confrontational. That was very much Robin.'

The final report succeeded in setting out guidelines that attempted to embody the resolution accepted by the Lambeth Conference in 1988, both in the question of relationships between the provinces, and in terms of the respect and courtesy that the resolution required. It noted, among many other things, that 'both those who support and those who are opposed to the ordination of women are motivated by the common desire to preserve and remain faithful to the historic threefold ministry of bishops, priests and deacons'.

The Primates endorsed the guidelines at their Larnaca meeting, with the exception of one clause. They did not accept that the collegial participation of male bishops in the ordinations performed by a woman bishop was a 'practical or theologically appropriate way of achieving the recognition of those ordained by her'. The Primates believed that it would have the effect of questioning the validity of her own consecration and be demeaning to the woman concerned. The Primates, however, acknowledged that some Anglicans would feel unable to recognise the validity of ordinations presided over by a woman bishop. They also recognised that some provinces were not yet able to give such ordinations canonical recognition.

Overall, the Primates warmly recommended the report as a whole to the provinces for study and discussion and, with the exception of the recommendation on collegial ordination, they endorsed the guidelines as a means for furthering 'the highest possible degree of communion, in the spirit of the Lambeth Conference of 1988'.

The Commission had not produced, in fact could not produce, a perfect formula to please everyone, but almost against the odds it provided a working framework for the supporters and opponents of women's ministry and episcopacy to allow them to live with a certain amount of anomaly as well as clear diversity within the Communion.

As *The Times* of London noted on 7 July 2003, during the later controversy over the ordination of homosexual bishops, the handling of women's ordination by Archbishop Runcie (and by implication the Eames Commission) 'was maligned at the time as a fudge, but is now recognised as a remarkably successful example of ecclesiastical diplomacy'.

Despite the controversy at the 1988 Lambeth Conference and the considerable fears that it would split the Communion irrevocably, the Eames Commission had produced a *modus vivendi*, a largely workable solution to what had seemed an intractable problem. Considerable credit was due to the members of the Commission, and not least to Robin Eames, who had managed to square the circle.

By the time the Eames Commission had been completed, no fewer than five women had been consecrated bishops, more than one thousand had been ordained priests in the Church of England, and women had been admitted to the priesthood in Australia, New Zealand, Brazil, Burundi, Canada, Hong Kong, Ireland, Kenya, the Philippines, Scotland, South Africa, Uganda, the USA and West Africa. Without doubt it was a Commission whose time had come.

Robin Eames reflects, 'The Commission provided guidelines on how Anglicans might live together in the highest degree of communion possible while different views and practices concerning the ordination of women continued to be held within the Communion. The Commission saw this as a way of enabling an ongoing process of continued reception of the Anglican Communion within the world ecumenical fellowship. It also wanted to ensure graceful and charitable relationships, and to ensure pastoral care for one another.'

In essence, the Eames Commission opened the door to an examination of what true communion meant – theologically and practically – when world Anglicanism faced diverse reactions to women's ordination. Later on, two other major Commissions to be chaired by Eames would try to bring the process further. *The Virginia Report* would delve into what communion meant for the structures and thinking of Anglicanism, while the 2003 Commission on Anglican Structures was charged with taking the issue into ever new territory. As Eames says, 'We were asked to decide how the Anglican Communion can deal not only with divisions over sexuality issues, but how we can plan the way ahead, no matter what issues may arise to divide us in the unknown future.'

These were all matters for another day, but in the meantime Eames could feel justified in believing that his Commission and its members had helped to draw up a more than useful map in the Communion's continued search for unity within diversity. In doing so he had inadvertently attracted much notice within the worldwide Communion, and to his surprise – and not particularly to his liking – he found his name being mentioned publicly and privately as a possible successor to Dr Robert Runcie as the next Archbishop of Canterbury. It was, in one sense, a compliment that he was being talked about seriously in such circles, but it was something that he found personally unsettling as the speculation continued. He still had a major job to do in Ireland, and that remained the focus of his attention.

20

Canterbury Calling

The announcement of Archbishop Robert Runcie's impending retirement added impetus to the speculation about his successor, and Robin Eames from early on began to be talked about openly as a serious contender.

However, the then Provost of Southwark Cathedral Canon David Edwards was quoted in the *Daily Telegraph* as saying, 'No-one knows how the idea started. He is one hundred per cent Irish. The Church of Ireland is very small, and the Church of England is totally different.'

Nevertheless, Eames was given a high profile by a number of British national newspapers and religious publications which in the past had paid little attention to an Archbishop of Armagh. Eames' rise to prominence in the Anglican Communion had been mainly through his work with the Anglican Consultative Committee, and as Chairman of the Commission on Communion and Women in the Episcopate, following his appointment by Dr Runcie.

Eames and Runcie had respect and affection for one another, and it was known that Eames was Runcie's preferred candidate to succeed him. Archbishops of Canterbury, however, are not chosen by their predecessors, but rather by the tortuous procedure of the current Prime Minister choosing one of two names put forward by the Church Appointments Commission. It was felt in some church circles, however, that Eames would do well to be considered for the shortlist, never mind the final two.

Some of the media profiles of Eames during the long speculation about Runcie's likely successor make fascinating reading. Clifford Longley of *The Times* noted on 29 September

1988 that Eames was by then already 'a key figure in the convoluted and agonizing life of his native land. There he is becoming something like the one-eyed man in the kingdom of the blind, in the unique position of being respected and listened to by Margaret Thatcher and by Charles Haughey.'

Longley made an important point, however, which was shared by many people on both sides of the Irish Sea. He wrote, 'It would be sad to see him plucked from there merely to raise the tone of the otherwise unexciting line-up of possible successors to Dr Robert Runcie. Northern Ireland needs a good leader even more than the Church of England does.'

Mary Kenny wrote in the *Catholic Herald* of 15 September 1989, 'Whenever the name of Robin Eames is mentioned in the Anglican community, folks nod their head wisely and tap their noses knowingly: for he is the field favourite as the next Archbishop of Canterbury.' Ms Kenny interviewed him in Armagh and noted, 'He smiled a crinkly smile at me, and for some reason I instantly felt that I was in the presence of an ecclesiastical Terry Wogan.' She concluded, 'Should the Prime Minister indeed select Archbishop Robin Eames to lead the Church of England, she will find herself dealing with a clever man who is more adept at dealing with people than any churchman I have met.'

The passing of time did not diminish the speculation. On 19 May 1990 the *Daily Telegraph* ran a feature outlining what it claimed to be the main contenders, with Eames in the top six: the Archbishop of York Dr John Habgood, described as 'the cleverest'; the Bishop of Winchester Dr Colin James, the 'most likeable'; the Bishop of St Albans Dr John Taylor, with 'narrow vision'; the Bishop of Chelmsford Dr John Waine, with 'no enemies'; Archbishop Eames, 'for a while the bookmakers' favourite' but 'too Irish'; and the Bishop of Liverpool Dr David Sheppard, a 'popular success'. Another eight bishops were mentioned as possible contenders, but the name of Dr George Carey, the eventual successor to Runcie, was not included.

The list underlined the fun and the futility of such speculation, though the *Daily Telegraph* journalist who wrote the caption 'too Irish' under Eames' photograph made a telling, if unsubtle, point. At that stage in Anglicanism, before the elevation of the Archbishop of Wales Dr Rowan Williams to Canterbury in 2003, it was thought highly unlikely that a new leader of the Anglican Communion would be sought outside the Church of England.

Canon Colin Craston, who was at that time close to the selection process, observes, 'There never had been consideration of someone outside the Church of England. There was nothing in the constitution to preclude that, but people were simply not ready to consider such a step, though Robin Eames was very well regarded.' It was thought even more unlikely that a leader would come from the Church of Ireland which, as Canon David Edwards had made clear, was much smaller than, and totally different from, the Church of England.

Apart from such parochial considerations, however, there was no reason to suppose that Eames was not a leading contender. He had a good track record, he had made a significant contribution to the Church of Ireland and to the Anglican Communion, he had a lawyer's intellect, and he had gifts as a diplomat and bridge-builder. He was also a skilled communicator who would have made a national figure in the television age, and he was heart and soul an Anglican, and a part of the very fibre of the worldwide Church. As such, Eames was a credible possibility for Canterbury.

As the speculation continued, the Belfast-based Irish nationalist daily the *Irish News*, in its edition of 7 June 1990, turned the succession into the worldly language of horse racing. It declared:

> If the bookies are anything to go by, Dr Robin Eames can forget all about becoming the next Archbishop of Canterbury. William Hill has suspended betting on the succession stakes after a series of big bets were laid on the Bishop of St Albans.
>
> There has obviously been a considerable change in Dr Eames' fortunes over the past couple of months: when Dr Runcie announced that he was stepping down from Canterbury, Dr Eames was the early front-runner, being widely touted as his replacement. Now he is a dark horse, hovering on the edge of a pack of more fancied contenders.

The newspaper conceded that it did not know Eames' views on the matter, as he had chosen to decline all media interviews on the subject 'on the grounds that any such interview might cynically be interpreted as an attempt to pitch for the position'.

Their reporter was told by one of Eames' aides, 'I don't care if you are the Archangel Gabriel, you'll still not get to talk to him.'

The *Irish News* concluded, somewhat drily, that it was 'very difficult to gauge just how accurate are the succession rumours that are flying around Church of England cloisters and croquet lawns', but it also praised Eames for his role in Ireland, and offered him advice. It continued:

> One thing is, however, abundantly clear. Dr Eames is a man of vision and understanding, a man who loves Ireland and who loves and respects his fellow Christians in the Catholic Church . . . He has a lot to offer the people of Northern Ireland. He is committed to reconciliation and he is in the vanguard of the movement away from religious bigotry . . . he is in a unique position to assist ecumenism in Ireland. As head of the Church of Ireland which has both Catholic and low-church traditions, he is an important bridgehead between the non-conformists and the Catholics. His work is too important here for him to consider a move to Canterbury.

This underlined a widespread feeling that Northern Ireland could not afford to lose Eames, but no individual is indispensible. If Eames had gone to Canterbury there were many in the Church of Ireland who would have been delighted at the personal honour for their Primate, but would have been sorry to see him go. Others felt that a credible successor in Ireland might have been Bishop James Mehaffey from Derry and Raphoe, whose bridge-building in that troubled city (partly based on the earlier foundation laid by Eames himself) had been noticed by influential people both inside and outside the Church.

Eames made no public comment about the speculation over Canterbury. He was too canny to involve himself publicly in any speculation, and in human terms he found the pressure difficult to handle. He recalls, 'The announcement of Robert Runcie's retirement naturally provoked widespread speculation as to his successor. Like most people in the Church of Ireland I had a "touchline" interest in who would succeed him. It was therefore a complete shock when I found that my name was one of those being considered.'

The media attention increased, and Eames found it unsettling for his work in Ireland. 'I had to weigh up everything I said, even though it had nothing to do with Canterbury, but people were continually looking for a hint here or a nuance there. In both a public and a private sense, I found the ongoing speculation very difficult.'

Life continued at Armagh as usual, as far as possible, and Eames tried to reassure everyone that he or she should not take the media speculation seriously. 'However, friends in England told me that the speculation was indeed serious, and the media attention increased. I made it plain that my heart lay in Ireland and with the Church of Ireland which I loved. No non-Englishman had ever held the post, and I knew in my heart that there would be reluctance to give serious consideration to an Ulsterman. Robert Runcie went out of his way to try to assure me that he did not think I was right.'

The Crown Appointments Commission took soundings, and several fellow Primates told Eames that they wanted him to go to Canterbury. He and his wife Christine were invited to a reception in No. 10 Downing Street by the Prime Minister Margaret Thatcher, with whom he had developed a good working relationship on Northern Ireland. The reception, according to Eames, had been interesting but nothing more, and he later wondered to his wife what it had all been about.

Eames recalls, 'The pressure increased, and quite suddenly the Church of England became aware of the Church of Ireland. The meetings of the Crown Appointments Commission are guarded with secrecy, and it was only after George Carey's appointment that I discovered that much of the speculation had had a foundation. I was told that I had been on the shortlist.'

Eames was at a meeting in Cardiff with the Anglican Consultative Committee when Dr Carey's appointment was announced by Archbishop Runcie, who took him aside and told him the news beforehand.

Elizabeth Gibson-Harries, the Church of Ireland Press Officer, was with Eames at the Cardiff meeting, and she remembers clearly the announcement. 'There was a feeling that the name of the new archbishop was going to be announced, and many people including Robert Runcie were certain that it was to be Robin Eames. I believe that Robin had geared himself for any eventuality, but I think that when the announcement came it was still a shock.'

Eames says, 'I knew that my name would not have come out in that way if I had been the choice. I would have been sent for, by people elsewhere. I was honoured by having been regarded to have been "in the frame", and I was particularly honoured on behalf of the Church of Ireland which had never really been at that level.

'If I had been asked to take the post, a great deal of my time would have been spent with the Anglican Communion, because my heart lies there. My involvement in the international scene with the Anglican Communion still totally absorbs that part of me which might have responded to the job in Canterbury.'

However, when Runcie told him the news, his immediate reaction was one of relief that the speculation was over, and that although the issues were still difficult in Ireland, he would be remaining in Armagh. He says, 'I returned home from Cardiff and events were moving so quickly that I did not have time to think about Canterbury. The whole episode helped me to appreciate again how much I felt wed to Ireland.'

Even with hindsight, it is difficult to judge how big a disappointment or a relief this was to Eames. However, it could be argued that he ended up with the best of all worlds – he remained in his beloved Church of Ireland, he retained an important role within Northern Ireland, he still had a major international challenge through the Anglican Consultative Council, and he did not have to carry the awesome burden of Canterbury.

As Archbishop of Canterbury he would doubtless have done a good job, and his bridge-building skills would have been of benefit to the Church of England. However, with his Irish background he may have found it difficult to become absorbed into the culture of the English church, as opposed to worldwide Anglicanism. Though Eames can steel himself to take difficult decisions, his innate sensitivity might have left him vulnerable to the extreme pressures that are associated with Canterbury. He would not have shown it publicly, but he would have bled inside. As the very Welsh Archbishop of Canterbury Dr Rowan Williams noted wryly later on, 'Robin was admired by the English Establishment, but I think that he might have found some of the problems that the other Celts do.'[1]

There was also what Eames himself calls 'the Irish factor'. He says, 'It would have meant walking away from Ireland at a time when none of us could see the first gleam of light at the end of the tunnel. I had to ask myself, "Have you got a contribution still to make towards the creation of a new Ireland?", and I felt that I had. Overall I was terribly glad that, whether it was God or the Church or both, I had been told, "You are Irish and you have things to do over there." '

He believes that he would probably have taken the Canterbury position out of a sense of duty, but that 'it would have been a very, very lonely walk to that decision'. He says, 'There was a part of me through it all which prayed that I would not have to make that decision. Humanly speaking, I was relieved when the tension of the speculation ended, and relieved that in a sense the decision had been made for me. It was reassuring to have been allowed to stay with the familiar. We all need challenges, but God knows, Canterbury would have been a ferocious challenge. Having worked so closely with Robert Runcie, I knew a lot of the things that were involved in the job, and I also knew that I would have a mountain to climb culturally to understand and to be absorbed with English problems, because I had spent all my life in Northern Ireland.'

He had an excellent personal relationship with Robert Runcie, and they were in contact frequently. Eames recalls, 'He was wonderful company, and he had a great sense of humour, but he never used it in a hurtful way about anyone. His outward appearance of being an "English gentleman" in bearing and accent belied a sincere and caring man of deep devotion and faith. His "Englishness" and perceived "aloofness" hid a very genuine and compassionate man who was also quite lonely despite his sociability.'

Runcie shared many personal matters with Eames. 'He was frustrated on many occasions by Church of England problems, and while giving much time to worldwide Anglicanism, I know that he was often criticised in England for giving so much of his attention to the Communion. He had an acute awareness of the need for Anglican unity and of the problems faced by Anglicans. He was deeply interested in Northern Ireland, and he would phone me at home, often at night, after some tragedy had occurred.'

Dr Runcie came to Northern Ireland on a number of

occasions, including a visit in January 1988 to a world conference of young Anglican delegates in Belfast. Runcie took the opportunity to hold talks with Cardinal O'Fiaich, the Roman Catholic leader, and he told reporters that he detected a new 'atmosphere of hope' in the North, especially among the young people.

On international affairs, Eames found Runcie extremely supportive, especially during his work on the Commission on Communion and Women in the Episcopate. He says, 'Some people thought that Robert found it hard to make decisions. It is true that he welcomed consensus, but I witnessed him being very definite when it was needed. He was at his best when overseas, and when making contact with the local churches. His easy manner and warm greetings were greatly appreciated.'

Runcie had a close relationship with Archbishop Desmond Tutu. 'When Tutu was with us before returning to South Africa to face possible imprisonment, Runcie warned the Pretoria Government, "Touch Tutu, and you touch all of us." I found that very impressive. Robert was very loyal to his friends.'

Eames recalls that as one talked to Runcie, a solution to a problem often occurred simply because of the questions he posed. 'Though deeply spiritual, he was also worldly-wise. His wartime experience often influenced his attitude to events. He understood fully what violence did to a community.'

Eames met Runcie during his retirement when they both attended the House of Lords. 'Clearly he was ill, and his eyesight suffered. On one of the last occasions I saw him, I asked him how he was. His reply was characteristric. He said, "Robin, I am dying slowly, with my faith to keep me going." In my opinion, Robert Runcie did more than any other previous Archbishop of Canterbury to enhance the Anglican Communion. This, I believe, will remain his greatest attribute.'

If Eames himself had been appointed to Canterbury, it is a matter of conjecture whether or not the turmoil within Anglicanism would have become so pronounced. Perhaps even his consummate diplomatic skills could not have prevented the cracks from developing into such major divisions. However, looking back over the Canterbury speculation, Eames has no regrets that he was not appointed. He says, 'It would have been a challenge to have been in a position to influence the life of the Anglican Communion worldwide, but that is not to downgrade the work I was given to do in Ireland. Don't forget that the See of Armagh predates Canterbury, and that St Patrick came to these islands as a Christian missionary centuries before St Augustine.

'I believe that the right decision was taken when I was not asked to become Archbishop of Canterbury, because I feel that God was, and is, centrally involved in all of this. However we think in terms of what the Church of England wants, or the Anglican Communion wants, or a British Prime Minister wants, you have to believe – if you believe anything about Christianity – that in the ultimate analysis the only thing that matters is what God wants. And in that context I have been, and I remain, happy to let the matter rest.'

21

Virgin Territory

When it was announced that Dr George Carey was to succeed Dr Robert Runcie as Archbishop of Canterbury many people were taken by surprise. Carey's name had been mentioned by the evangelical lobby during the later stages of the process of selection, but he had not been regarded as a front runner. It was ironic that although Margaret Thatcher had chosen his name from the two supplied by the Church Appointments Commissioner, she had been replaced by John Major by the time Dr Carey took up office.

Robin Eames recalls, 'When Robert Runcie told me privately at the meeting of the Anglican Consultative Council in Cardiff about George Carey's appointment we were both surprised. He had not been mentioned prominently in the speculation about front runners, and none of us could claim to have known him well, before his appointment. His relatively short experience as a bishop posed questions about how he would deal with his new responsibilities, but George quickly won our confidence.'

One of Carey's first visits outside England was to Northern Ireland, where he presided at a meeting of Primates in the seaside resort of Newcastle, under the shadow of the Mourne Mountains. Also present was Archbishop Desmond Tutu. The assembled Primates listened to background briefings on Northern Ireland from Lord Molyneaux, leader of the Official Unionists, John Hume, leader of the nationalist Social Democratic and Labour Party, and also from this writer who was then a senior journalist with the *Belfast Telegraph*, and who remembers the occasion well. The briefings had been prepared and delivered as personal responses to a request from Robin

Eames, who had made the main arrangements for the Primates' meeting.

George Carey appeared fresh and enthusiastic about his new job, and willing to listen intently to briefings on the complexities of Northern Ireland where, at that stage, there was little hope of a breakthrough in the deadly cycle of political deadlock and violence. Robin Eames recalls, 'George was warm and friendly, and he impressed Northern Ireland people by his sympathy for our difficulties. His wife Eileen accompanied him, and she was to play a key role in his future work and leadership. This was to be very much a joint ministry with Eileen, and I felt at times that the magnitude of the Church of England problems and the Anglican Communion's problems wearied them both.'

Eames feels that Carey was basically a teacher who had spent much of his life in academic circles, and that it was soon obvious that his teaching ministry would be important to his future leadership. He was clearly an evangelical in the English sense, and they talked long and often about the Irish situation.

Eames recalls, 'He said to me on more than one occasion that as an evangelical he felt that he could talk to fundamentalists in Northern Ireland if that would be useful. There was political criticism in Northern Ireland of some of his comments, which worried him. He was most supportive of my work in Ireland, and he gave me full encouragement in my contact with paramilitaries.' (As has been noted earlier, he helped to facilitate directly a meeting between the Prime Minister John Major and Robin Eames, which had a constructive outcome resulting in the first Loyalist paramilitary ceasefire in Northern Ireland.)

A great deal changed in the Church of England during Carey's term of office. Eames says, 'During the speculation about Robert Runcie's successor I was deeply conscious of those in positions of influence who could not consider an "outsider" being appointed. It is to George Carey's credit that he did much to remove the parochialism of the Church of England.'

Eames and Carey developed a good working relationship, and Carey appointed Eames to chair media briefings and conferences at all meetings of the Primates. They would talk in depth before each briefing, and agree on priorities. Eames says, 'I came to know how his mind worked on divisive issues, particularly abroad, and I did my best to guide him in what he said.' Carey, however, was his own man, and did not always accept advice. Eames says, 'On occasions he created ripples at home by what he said abroad.'

Archbishop Carey, for his part, appreciated the skills that Eames had to offer, and his capacity for hard work. He says, 'His name was very much around, at the time of my appointment. Frankly, I don't know why they ignored him because he would have been an absolutely splendid Archbishop of Canterbury, and I would have been honoured to have been one of his bishops. In my time as Archbishop, he was the most outstanding Primate in the Anglican Communion.'[1]

There was no real surprise when Carey asked Eames to chair the Inter-Anglican Theological and Doctrinal Commission which was a response to the call of the Lambeth Conference in 1988 to consider in depth the meaning and nature of communion. Eames did not see himself as a theologian, but he had shown outstanding qualities as a chairman of the Commission on Communion and Women in the Episcopate.

George Carey says that he had noted Robin Eames' training as a lawyer and his ability to analyse and sift information. He also appreciated Eames' 'Irish' jocularity and his ability to defuse a difficult situation. 'He did so with a joke, or a gentle smile or a way of expressing something which took the sting out of a very dangerous situation. During my time as Archbishop of Canterbury, if I wanted anyone to do a difficult job I would turn to Robin Eames. He had that judicious, mature and wise way of being able to assess a situation and suggest possible means of dealing with it.'

There was another reason why Carey chose him to chair the new Commission. 'Robin was also a good theologian, though he himself would dispute that. He was a difficult person to pin down theologically. You couldn't say he was evangelical, or Catholic or liberal. In a sense he was all of those things.' Eames, he believed, had a liberal background, but he also had a strong understanding of evangelicals and how they would think. 'He had a commitment to the Scriptures, and he was a person whom people could respect and trust. That capacity of being able to be trusted by all sides made him ideal for a senior job in the Communion.'

Eames accepted the chairmanship of the Inter-Anglican Theological and Doctrinal Commission. As a tribute to the Bishop and Diocese of Virginia and the staff of the Virginia

Theological Seminary in the United States, who hosted the main meetings, the final document was called *The Virginia Report*. The sixteen members of the Commission represented theologians and leaders from most of the Provinces in the Communion. While the work continued over the years from 1994 to 96, the full Commission met at the Virginia Theological Seminary twice to finalise the report.

Eames set the tone of the final document in his Introduction. He wrote:

> At the heart and centre of the Anglican pilgrimage lies the concept of communion. From it we derive so much of our belief and practice. It is not itself a static concept. It has become with our pilgrimage a living and developing reality. Yet that fact alone demands understanding which cannot be tied to any one period in our history or to any single cultural approach.

Eames reflected later on, when he was asked to chair yet another Commission (this time arising out of the controversy over homosexual bishops), 'The words of my Introduction to *The Virginia Report* reflected and influenced my whole approach to the Anglican Communion, and in the light of my later responsibilities, it helped to point a way forward. I believe in communion for worldwide Anglicanism. The issue for *The Virginia Report*, as it continues to be, was how this moving concept can be translated into a practical and agreed reality.'

Though the essence of *The Virginia Report* centred on theological and doctrinal issues, Eames believes that there were several broad conclusions affecting Anglicanism worldwide. *The Virginia Report* underlined among other things that to understand communion, Anglicans must also understand the real nature of the trinitarian faith. He says, 'It was hoped that the Report would open up the possibility of creative change which would strengthen the ministry and mission of the whole people of God. The Church is the icon of the future towards which God is directing the history of the world. The Anglican Communion must recognise its place in that progression.'

The Virginia Report underlined that the mutuality and interdependence of each member and each part of the Church was essential for the fulfilment of its mission. It also indicated that while an important function of communion was for each part to remain attentive to one another, particularly when conflict arises, it was necessary also to remember its central beliefs and its reference to shared concepts. Eames says, 'The relationship of Scripture, tradition and reason for the Communion means that the mind of God has constantly to be discerned afresh, not just in every age but in every context. The life of belonging together, with its characteristic ethos within the Communion, is supported by a web of structures which hold together and guide a common life of belonging. Hence we have autonomous provinces, episcopal oversight and leadership and synodical government.'

It was also important to emphasise that a central authority should have a subsidiary function, performing only those tasks which cannot be performed at a more immediate or local level. *The Virginia Report* concluded that serious issues needed and deserved a Communion-wide mind if a life of interdependence was to be preserved. It was therefore necessary at times for the universal Church to say to the local church that a local practice was wrong and would lead to disputes, as happened over the issue of homosexual bishops.

In effect *The Virginia Report* took the Anglican Communion's understanding of 'koinonia and communion' to a new level, and it related the theology of communion to the actual instruments of unity. It also raised, possibly for the fist time, serious questions about the role of the Archbishop of Canterbury. The Report considered, for example, 'Does the Archbishop of Canterbury have sufficient back-up? Does the Primate of the Anglican Communion always need to be the Archbishop of Canterbury? Does the Archbishop always have to be an Englishman? Does the Primate of the Anglican Communion need to reside in England?'

Robin Eames comments, 'Without realising it then, by building on the concepts of the Eames Commission we envisaged the current problems which later faced the Communion. In *The Virginia Report* we questioned seriously the inter-relationships of Anglican unity.'

In its time, the report of the first Eames Commission had introduced the concept of 'reception', and *The Virginia Report* centred on collegiality, communion and subsidiarity. Eames says, 'Personally I found my thinking on communion was

289

developed greatly by my work with Virginia. In a sense both "Eames" and "Virginia" provided the preface for my further work on the Commission on Anglican Structures.'

The Virginia Report had been produced and published in an atmosphere of calm theological detachment, compared to the controversy surrounding women in the ministry. Although the Eames Commission had produced a way forward on this issue involving gender, and also theology, the whole question of homosexual clergy was bound to erupt with a vengeance, sooner or later. Within the Anglican Communion, George Carey had to grapple with division perhaps even more so than his predecessor Robert Runcie, who had more than enough with which to contend – including women and the episcopate and the incarceration of his special envoy Terry Waite in Beirut.

Eames reflects that in George Carey's time, the situation was changing rapidly, and that he was very conscious of the problems faced by the African bishops over the developments in the United States and Canada concerning homosexual clergy. 'Carey, I believe, had little patience with what he considered was the complexity of contradictory attitudes among the United States bishops. While supportive of the United States Primate Frank Griswold, he often spoke firmly about the influence of the religion-politics of the United States clergy on the Anglican Communion. However, he also took major steps to source financial aid for the Communion through the establishment of Communion funds, based on American generosity.'

The bitter division over homosexuality surfaced at the 1998 Lambeth Conference, when Carey asked Eames to chair a day-long debate. Eames recalls, 'In some parts of the United States and Canada, same-sex unions were being blessed and indeed encouraged, and this was bitterly opposed, chiefly by Primates from Africa, the Caribbean and the Far East. Alignments were emerging and we were seeing another definite threat to the unity of Anglicanism.'

The debate was robust, and one observer – Canon Michael Burrows, later Dean of Cork – wrote, in the *Church of Ireland Gazette* of 14 August 1998, about 'a long, hot plenary session on sexuality'. The Archbishop of Canterbury in a pastoral letter issued soon afterwards noted that prior to the Conference, no province had asked for homosexuality to figure as a major item on the agenda, but that nonetheless the issue was hotly debated.

He added diplomatically, 'We found that our diversity of theology and culture, often a source of blessing, was becoming a "differing" that could so easily have resulted in bitter confrontation.' In other words, tensions were high, and Eames had to handle a difficult debate. He recalls, 'It was an experience I will never forget. I prepared myself at great length because the real problems I faced were on procedure and the decision-making process. Each province had its own way of making decisions, but there was a complete divergence of methodology.'

Eames devoted several days to preparing for the debate, and he was inundated with advice and lobbying. He says, 'On the day, the tensions were obvious, and I decided to be as open and honest with the Conference as I could. In my opening statement I talked about divergent methods, and pointed out that the only way to proceed was to permit a clear expression of views couched in terms which would not further divide us.'

The background tensions and passions were described some years later by Archbishop Carey. He recalls meeting a delegation of African bishops who were very worried. He said, 'They told me that they were in a cleft stick. They said that if they went home and indicated that they agreed with the sexual statement, they would be vilified. Yet in conscience they could not agree with the wild statements coming out of West Africa.'

They asked Carey if a compromise could be reached. 'They needed to say very clearly that they believed practising homosexuality was wrong, so I made a suggestion with which they agreed. That won the day, and Robin helped to push it through, but it was very tense indeed. During that debate Robin was a superb chairman. He showed his judicious qualities and his ability to defuse difficult situations, to a consummate degree.'[2]

The Lambeth Conference passed the resolution on sexuality by 526 votes to 70, with 45 abstentions. It endorsed traditional teaching on marriage, and expressed a commitment 'to listen to the experience of homosexual people'. It rejected homosexual practice as 'incompatible with Scripture', but called on all its people 'to minister pastorally and sensitively to all, irrespective of sexual orientation' and 'to condemn irrational fear of homosexuals, violence within marriage and any trivialisation and commercialisation of sex'.

The resolution also stated, in a clause that became critically significant in the light of later developments, that the Lambeth

Conference 'cannot advise the legitimising or blessing of same-sex unions, nor the ordination of those involved in same-gender unions'.

Predictably, opinions varied about the outcome of the debate. Canon Michael Burrows in the *Church of Ireland Gazette* noted that the resolution was 'a pretty strong conservative endorsement of traditional teaching, and people will argue as to whether it is expressed in loving or judgmental tones'. He also noted that the agreed resolution was much less forceful than certain alternative texts proposed by African provinces whose bishops wanted homosexuality condemned as a 'sin'. He added, however, 'although it provides a form of words with which a majority of Anglicans may manage to live, it is likely, as several bishops admitted, to cause considerable pain in the Gay Christian community.'[3]

Burrows wisely noted also that the resolution 'like many Anglican texts demands close reading'. Archbishop Carey in his pastoral letter concluded that:

> For the majority of us involved in that debate, the friendships that had been established, coupled with a desire to listen to each other, enabled us to transcend our differences. Nevertheless, I recognise that for some parts of the church, there was considerable pain to be endured, both in the debate itself and its outcome, and so the listening must go on, not only to Scripture but also to one another.

Carey also outlined in his pastoral letter the many other issues with which the Conference had dealt – including international debt, civil strife, the impact of technology, the needs of the poor, and many other important issues. In the same way, his successor Dr Rowan Williams would plead later on for a wider perspective on the challenges facing the Church, as well as issues of sexuality.

Important though these subjects were, and continued to be, the issue of sexuality so hotly debated at Lambeth in 1998 refused to go away, even though it seemed at the time that the outcome of the debate, handled so deftly by Eames, would provide a breathing space for the Church as a whole.

Eames reflects, 'I said at the end of the debate that we should regard a vote as an indication rather than as a final word, as experience had taught me that Anglicanism had moved again and again.' The basis for his approach at that controversial debate was his view that the Lambeth Conference could only produce moral leadership, rather than a legislative decision. He says, 'I knew that views were so strong that individual provinces would continue to "do their own thing" at home. I chaired the debate, with frequent calls for a pause and prayer, and the tone was enouraging. However, looking back now I recall little of the individual contributions, as I was concentrating hard to advise on procedure.'

As a chairman, a churchman and a lawyer he had indeed been encouraged at the way in which the debate had evolved, and the response to the procedural method he had adopted. However, he was not over-optimistic that this would be the end of the matter. He says, 'Despite any personal satisfaction I felt at the time at the way the debate had gone, I knew in my heart that the problem was only beginning.'

This recollection of his immediate instincts at that time may have benefited to a certain extent from hindsight, but not for the first time his hunch proved to be right. The problem indeed was going to get much worse.

22

Sex and Sanctity

The appointment of Dr Rowan Williams as Archbishop of Canterbury came as no great surprise, in contrast to that of his predecessor Dr George Carey. Despite the best efforts of the Crown Appointments Commission, Rowan Williams' name appeared in the media early on as an almost certain appointment to Canterbury.

So it proved, but in the run-up to the announcement of the appointment, the speculation continued. During this period Rowan Williams, at that time Archbishop of Wales, came to Northern Ireland for a church engagement, and he met his old friend and colleague Robin Eames.

Eames recalls how they had shared primatial leadership in the 'Celtic Fringe', which enabled a particular bond of friendship to grow between the Archbishops of Ireland, Scotland and Wales. Eames could empathise with Williams, from his own experience in the Canterbury stakes, as the widespread speculation focused on the evangelicals' views of Williams as a 'liberal'. Eames says, 'I knew that if Rowan were asked to take the post, he would accept it, but I was a little surprised to find that he was hurting so much. I mused to myself that if he was appointed, the future would be interesting for Church–State relations in England, let alone within Anglicanism at large.'

Eames advised Williams, 'Don't say too much before your Enthronement that could haunt you later.' He was convinced that Rowan Williams' intellect and spirituality, his academic achievement and his ability as a speaker and communicator would give his leadership in Canterbury a particular distinction in writing and teaching. He feared, however, that the structure of Williams' role at Lambeth might prove a heavy burden and perhaps dull the gifts that had marked him out for the position. 'As someone said to me at the time, "I don't doubt Rowan's great gifts, but will the pressures of administration suffocate his ability to give spiritual leadership?" '

Over the years Eames had come to see what those pressures had been on Robert Runcie and George Carey. 'I prayed that Rowan would put his own stamp on Lambeth. My hope was that he would be given space to develop his knowledge of the worldwide Communion while never losing opportunities to bring his scholarship and teaching to Anglicans around the world. My fear remained that in time he would become submerged in the practicalities of the job, to the extent that his great gifts would be diminished. If that were to happen it would be a tragedy.'

Rowan Williams was duly appointed, and enthroned in Canterbury Cathedral on 27 February 2003. It was a memorable occasion in the presence of the main representatives of the Church of England, the Anglican Communion and worldwide Christendom. Despite the previously expressed reservations of those who disapproved of his 'liberal' views on sexuality and other matters, there was a widespread feeling that something of significance was taking place within the Church at large.

During the Enthronement ceremony, Robin Eames pronounced the Blessing on the new Archbishop, on behalf of the Communion, but this was more than a ritual honour which fell to the then senior Primate. It meant a great deal personally to both men, as Williams confirmed later on.[1] He said, 'The prayer was very special to us both, not least because of the last meeting I had attended with the Celtic Primates as Archbishop of Wales. They held a little ceremony one morning at Eucharist to send me on my way. Robin prayed on that occasion, and I remembered that at Canterbury. I have a real respect and veneration for Robin, and it was a very personal moment when he pronounced the Blessing at my Enthronement. It reminded me of that more private moment at Llandudno when the Celtic Archbishops said, "Good-bye".'

As colleagues they enjoyed many lighter moments. Williams tells the story about one meeting of the Standing Committee of Primates on finance. He had celebrated the Eucharist earlier that morning, and Eames, who was chairing the later meeting, thanked him for leading the service. Then Eames told him, with a grave face, that he had some bad news about the finances of the Anglican Communion. There had been a reassessment, and it was discovered that the Welsh Church was some £2 million behind in its contributions.

Rowan Williams says, 'My face was a picture but Robin said helpfully that they had had a whip-round to help make a contribution on behalf of Wales, and he then produced a large leek and gave it to me!' It was no coincidence that the meeting was taking place on St David's Day.

Rowan Williams made a good impression at the Primates' Meeting in Brazil from 19 to 27 May 2003, where he presided for the first time as Archbishop of Canterbury. There were many examples of his teaching skills as he led Bible study, and his gift for communication was clearly apparent to all.

However, it was during this meeting that the issue of homosexuality among the clergy surfaced again, partly because it had never gone away – despite the careful wording of the relevant resolution that had been passed with a huge majority vote at the Lambeth Conference in 1998. Since that time George Carey had somehow managed to keep the lid on it, but the pent-up pressure added to the vehemence of the argument on both sides when the debate erupted right at the start of Rowan Williams' Primacy.

The Primates Meeting in Brazil had emphasised the desire for unity, and underlined the Lambeth resolution of 1998, but this approach was undermined by events in the United States where it became clear that the Episcopal Church was determined to proceed with the appointment and consecration of Dr Gene Robinson, a practising homosexual, as Bishop of New Hampshire.

Eames recalls, 'Rowan Williams could not have had a more difficult "baptism of fire". While rumours circulated at Brazil, few people realised the impact that events in New Hampshire were to have, so soon. It was quite a challenge to the communiqué from Brazil when New Hampshire pressed ahead with its intentions, and from my contacts with a number of fellow Primates during that period, there was a great deal of unease – and also annoyance – that despite what had taken place in Brazil, this was happening.'

Some people felt that the Archbishop of Canterbury should stand by the Brazil communiqué and await reactions. Others argued that he should be seen to act quickly. He chose the latter course by inviting all the Primates to a special meeting at Lambeth Palace on 15–16 October 2003. It was significant that in his invitation he mentioned New Hampshire and also New Westminster in Canada, which had been involved in same-sex blessings. No one could doubt, therefore, the connection between the Lambeth meeting and events in the United States and Canada. The Archbishop's action was seen as 'decisive' but many viewed the meeting with foreboding and, as in the controversy that arose over the issue of women and the episcopate more than two decades previously, there were fears about a deep schism within the Anglican Communion.

Meanwhile back in England, the Archbishop of Canterbury's problems were being compounded by the announcement on 20 May from the Diocese of Southwark of the appointment of Canon Jeffrey John as the Suffragan Bishop of Reading. Canon John was a celibate homosexual, but the prospect of his appointment and planned consecration on 9 October raised the ire of the strong evangelical and conservative wing of the Church of England. Many would have agreed with the Bishop of Liverpool, the Right Reverend James Jones, who told the BBC that Canon John's appointment was 'premature', and that it had come 'at a critical time in the life of the Church before a point of consensus has been reached'.

Rowan Williams was caught in a cleft stick. If he condoned the appointment he would have the approval of many liberals, but would face intense opposition from the evangelicals, and vice versa. In the end, Jeffrey John was asked to attend a meeting with the Archbishop at Lambeth Palace, and following this it was decided not to proceed with his appointment. Predictably, however, Williams was criticised by the liberals and still regarded with suspicion by the evangelicals, who felt that his natural instinct was one of tolerance towards homosexual clergy including Jeffrey John, who was seen by some people as the innocent victim of current circumstances. (He was appointed Dean of St Albans in 2004.)

The Dean of Southwark, the Very Reverend Dr Colin Slee, issued a strong statement on 6 July 2003, just after Jeffrey John announced his withdrawal from the Reading appointment. He claimed that Canon John had become the victim of 'appalling prejudice and abuse which has its main proponents within the

Church of England and about whom the Church at large should be deeply penitent'. He added, 'The Church has to address the manner in which this relatively small group has sought to undermine the authority of the Archbishop and thereby the Church as a whole.'

The episode was a bruising reminder that an Archbishop of Canterbury, while trying to wrestle with problems on a world basis, was also required to deal with great difficulties in his own backyard, in the same way that Eames, the Anglican reconciler on the world stage, had had to deal with immense challenges when facing the very different but also very divisive problem of the Drumcree stand-off in his own Diocese of Armagh.

Back on the wider stage, however, the pressure continued to build on the issue of homosexuality and the clergy, and in the run-up to the Lambeth special meeting Robin Eames issued a special and carefully argued statement titled 'What Price Unity?' in which he examined some of the questions facing Anglicanism at large. This statement was issued primarily to his own Church of Ireland, but it was distributed and widely read throughout the Communion.

Eames declared that he was in no doubt that the decision of ECUSA to endorse the appointment of Canon Gene Robinson had provoked a crisis for the Communion, and that this had once more brought into question the whole issue of unity and relationships, and also the divisions between the provinces on sexuality issues.

Once again, they were facing the old question, 'How can Anglicans live together with differing opinions and differing cultures, but maintain some semblance of active communion?' Eames, despite the problems, remained positive. He wrote, 'I believe that Anglicanism will survive this current controversy. The question is: in what form?'

He pointed out that the Communion had lived through generations without basic regulations, rules or legal structures. He was aware that the election of Canon Robinson undoubtedly challenged Resolution 1:10 of the 1998 Lambeth Conference and he further noted, 'It is clearly in breach of the views of the majority of bishops in 1998. It is clearly contrary to the view of a large number of Anglicans.'

Eames, like others, was also well aware of calls for ECUSA to be expelled from the Communion, but as a lawyer he asked, 'Expulsion from what? . . . To put it plainly, if no constitutional or legal rules exist for what constitutes membership of the Anglican Communion, there are no rules for the expulsion of a member Church.' In asking such a pointed and timely question he underlined in effect that 'laws apart, opinions apart and sensitivities apart . . . diversity of culture, practice and life-styles have been and will most likely continue to be the experience of a world family such as the Anglican Communion'. Once again the question had to be faced: 'How do we live with and how do we understand difference?' It was clear that the special meeting at Lambeth would not – and could not – produce any 'quick fix'. The search for a path to unity within diversity would continue to be a gruelling one.

The Primates made their way to the emergency meeting at Lambeth with mixed feelings. There were some who questioned whether or not it was an overreaction by Canterbury and wondered if it would solve anything. Eames recalls the kind of questions in many minds: 'Would we stay together for two whole days? Would what we issue at the end be anything more than a fudge? Did this really mark the parting of the ways? Would the US Primate Archbishop Frank Griswold have anything new to tell his fellow Primates?'

Eames recalled the sense of unease much earlier when the Communion had to face the issue of women and the episcopate, but this current argument over homosexuality was different, and it seemed more dramatic and divisive. Many of the Primates had already given their views to the media before setting off for London, and few believed that the US Church would refuse to proceed with the election and consecration of Canon Robinson.

The Primates were staying in a hotel near Lambeth. Unavoidably members of various pressure groups appeared in the hotel lobby, but most of the Primates were keeping their thoughts to themselves – though it was rumoured that a group of conservatives had already held a preliminary meeting elsewhere in London.

The Primates were driven across to Lambeth for their first meeting, and used a back entrance to avoid protesters at the main gate. Each Primate was met individually by the Archbishop of Canterbury, and later they all met around a large conference table, in the absence of any personal staff.

The meeting began with an open forum to discuss the reaction within individual provinces. The tone was measured, but it was clear that few had changed their minds about the likely outcome. A majority made it obvious that they could not, and would not, condone the election of a practising homosexual as a bishop, or the blessing of any same-sex unions, as had been taking place in New Westminster, Canada.

Everyone was courteous, and although people held firmly to their points of view, two elements appeared to emerge from the divisions – it was clear that no one wanted the end of the Anglican Communion as such, and no one doubted the central importance of Scripture in the whole issue.

Eames, as at all previous Primates' Meetings in Carey's time, was deputed to deal with the media. During the first afternoon, he told the numerous correspondents encamped at Lambeth that the Primates were searching for a consensus, but that as time wore on, this seemed to be more difficult to achieve.

The Primates had agreed that Eames would brief the media during the second session. He recalls, 'As I walked across the square at Lambeth to meet more than a hundred members of the media, I was struck by their feeling of expectancy, and by the level of interest in our deliberations. Rarely had church affairs commanded so much attention.' Eames explained to reporters that it was too early to predict an outcome, that the debate was under way, that no Primate had left the meeting, and that while a final communiqué would be issued, there was a general acceptance among the Primates that they wanted to preserve the Anglican Communion.

This was quintessentially Eames, who was dubbed by the media as 'the divine optimist'. One correspondent noted, tongue in cheek, that when Robin Eames tells the media that there has been a blunt but constructive discussion at a meeting, there must have been one hell of a row going on behind closed doors.

Archbishop Rowan Williams and Canon James Rosenthal, the Anglican Communion's Director of Communications, both recognised and appreciated Robin Eames' skills with the media. Williams says, 'Robin commands trust. He will not shuffle or evade, but if he has nothing to say very much, he will say it with authority. Sometimes you have to have someone in that position, who can say no more than "We've had a very interesting day

300

and that's all I am going to tell you." However, what Robin does not say is also important. Everything is carefully weighed. He doesn't waste words, and that's where the authority comes from.'

James Rosenthal says, 'I have always insisted at the highest level for Robin to be the spokesperson because he can rise to the moment. The content of what anyone says is reflected in how they say it. Robin can say simple things well, and that is a true gift. He is the only Archbishop I know who can respond on his feet without getting into a terrible mess, but there are times when I have rolled my eyes and asked myself, "Where did he get that from?" '

Rosenthal points to one of Eames' particular skills as a communicator: 'He is able to lead a journalist or a fellow archbishop at least into a thinking mode which says, "We have not got where you want us to be, but here's the road we are on." He can engage them without making them feel that something is bland, and he can satisfy them – which is a very big thing to be able to do. I have never had a journalist complain about anything Robin has said or the way in which he has handled them. That's a huge plus.'

The outgoing Archbishop of York Dr David Hope is another senior churchman who appreciates Eames' communication skills. He notes, 'People will sometimes say that there's a bit of Irish blarney about Robin, that he can "sweet talk" his way out of things. You sometimes hear him speak and you ask yourself, "What has he said?" – not a lot really. There are elements there, but very often he has been in these situations where it has not been possible to say too much, but he has all these press people around. They are all listening to him and he has said nothing – how does he do it?'

Dr Hope partly answers his own question by another observation. 'Robin is a robust person, and a person of charm in the right sense of that word, and that is not a pretence. It's part of who he is. He's a very human person, and often it's the human dimension that inspires confidence. He is tenacious for reconciliation because that is at the very heart of the gospel, and that is in the very heart of God, and it springs from his own deep well of spirituality.'

Eames, and the others, needed all the 'tenacity for reconciliation' they could muster, as the emergency meeting at

Lambeth continued. The discussions in the plenary session moved from the purely descriptive and individual provincial reactions to a reflection on what was being said. In private conversations over meals, any evidence of a possible consensus was seized upon, but such evidence was limited.

The meeting reached a catharsis on the second day. People were saying, 'This is the moment of truth,' and, 'We can move no further.' Deadlock loomed. There was a gulf between opinions, there was little evidence of movement, there was regret, pain and genuine apprehension. At that point the urgency of learning to live with difference became more and more of a reality.

In the atmosphere of a shared Eucharist in the crypt of Lambeth Palace there was further opportunity to reflect on what they had in common, and not just what was dividing them. The opposing views remained, but crucially the tone had begun to change. There was also the stern reality that they would have to emerge sooner or later and to tell the world, through the media, what they had decided. Eventually a statement was agreed, and four senior clergy – Archbishops Williams, Eames, Griswold, and Gomez of the West Indies – went across to Church House, Westminster to meet the assembled media.

Predictably, Williams explained the communiqué, Griswold justified the actions of ECUSA, and Gomez spoke clearly of his opposition and those who agreed with him. Despite the measured words of the official statement, the mood within the Communion was sombre, and many Primates were alone with their thoughts. It was obvious that there would be no medium-term compromise of the kind that had taken place after the debate at the Lambeth Conference in 1998. It was also clear from the press conference, and what had preceded it, that the divisions were indeed deep.

The announcement by the Archbishop of Canterbury of a new Commission to report further on the matter, and the plea for a period of reflection, were seen as genuine attempts to find a breathing space for all concerned. It was equally clear, however, that even then the Americans were determined to go ahead with the ordination of Canon Robinson as a bishop in two weeks time, and they announced their intention just hours after the emergency meeting at Lambeth had ended.

Rowan Williams was already warning of a 'huge crisis' looming within the Communion. Eames said that the decision to go ahead with Robinson's ordination 'as a whole flies in the face of those pleas from the Lambeth meeting for a period of reflection. I am not disappointed at the results of the Lambeth meeting but at the reaction of our American colleagues.'[2] The divisions were pronounced – the Anglican Communion as a whole was not prepared to approve of the ordination of Canon Robinson, and the Americans were not prepared to back down. The battle lines were being drawn in public as well as in private even before the role and the membership of the new Commission was announced.

Eames reflected later on the emergency meeting at Lambeth, and its aftermath. 'As in 1988, we did not disintegrate. As then we produced a carefully drafted statement which contained a mixture of reassurance and warning. We had been renewed. We had been honest with each other and we had understood more about each other. We recognised the differences and understood more about why we differed. But those differences were clear and determined.'

In a few weeks Canon Robinson would be consecrated as a bishop, and in twelve months or so a Commission would present its findings on the structures and differences in the Anglican Communion. What would be the future shape of that Communion, and who would relate to whom in the meantime? Eames recalled, 'God alone knew, but for the moment the challenge of "unity in diversity" had spelt out its own message. We did not want to destroy the Anglican Communion – but we disagreed on what to do next.'

While preparations continued for the consecration of Canon Robinson in New Hampshire, the shape of the new Commission and the identity of its chairman was being determined at Lambeth and elsewhere. The obvious candidate for chairman was Eames – given his experience as chairman of the two previous Commissions – but would he be willing to serve?

Rowan Williams had known for some time that the whole subject of homosexuality and the clergy was going to become a controversial issue within his Primacy. He says, however, 'I didn't realise quite so much, and quite so soon.' He had no doubt about whom he should ask to chair the new Commission, and he was very aware of the possible results of setting it up.

'The whole point was about dealing with diversity and about the fact that the American church does not see why its decisions have anything to do with the church in Africa, whereas the African church assumes without question that what the Americans do affects them, and commits them almost, so they feel that they have been pushed into a false position by a decision taken elsewhere.'

Williams' 'best-case scenario' at that stage was a report from the new Commission within twelve months which would clarify how certain provinces could distance themselves from others in a way that did not totally break relationships. He hoped that the report would provide some guidance on what it would mean to be a Communion 'that could call itself a Communion, but where a number of bilateral relationships were broken or changed'.

His 'worst-case scenario' would be a situation where the provinces wanted to detach themselves from each other and from Canterbury in a way that did not allow the Archbishop to act as some kind of overseer or honest broker. 'That would be very difficult, but then we would have ceased to be a Communion and the Communion might have to reinvent itself. What I didn't really want to see in the future was the church of the North and South dividing, because we need each other.' That, he believed, was absolutely central to the work of the Commission and its chairman.

Eames seemed to be most people's first choice as chairman, and his qualities were appreciated by many, including Rowan Williams, who first met him at the 1988 Lambeth Conference. 'From the start I formed the impression that Robin was someone in whose hands you could safely place very difficult subjects. He had an extraordinary gift of summing up the heart of an argument, and he carried huge moral weight. He also had an immensely genial presence.'

Eames, he believed, was definitely not an 'English' archbishop. 'This was partly his ability not to come to issues with the boxes in working order. In a way he was not compartmentalised. He looked very hard and very deeply for ways around a problem, with a kind of lateral thinking. Maybe that was his Celtic dimension.'

Williams felt that Eames was the obvious person to chair the Commission. 'He had previous experience of chairing

Commissions on impossible subjects, and the report on women and the episcopate was and still is a classic point of reference.' There was also the consideration that he was Primate of the Church of Ireland. 'That was a small factor, but it was there. He represented enough of the feeling of the Mother Church, the heartland of Anglicanism, but he was not "English" and therefore there was not a kind of colonial echo to what he said.'

In sheer practical terms he had a good track record of chairing important committees. Williams says, 'In every meeting of the Primates Robin is one of the people who can most clearly help to articulate a consensus. He is often active in drafting an agreed statement, and refining it so that everyone can go along with it. He also has a solid reputation as a chairman. In all sorts of ways people look on him as a person of absolutely dependable judgment.'

Apart from his long experience within the Anglican Communion, and his chairmanship of two previous Commissions, Eames had the right background in church politics and was classified neither as an evangelical nor as a liberal. Williams says, 'He was somebody who was not identified with an agenda, and therefore people trusted him to a very remarkable degree. This is partly why I asked him to take on the appallingly difficult job of chairing the Commission. Frankly we all asked a great deal of him, but I knew that he had a selfless devotion to the Church and I felt that I could only but ask him if he would take on the chairmanship of the Commission. To be honest, I felt a sense of relief when he said, "Yes!" '

23

Troubleshooter

The new Commission on Anglican Structures was announced on 28 October 2003 by the Archbishop of Canterbury, who named its Chairman, Archbishop Eames, and its sixteen other members, representing a wide range of views within the Anglican Communion. Dr Williams said that the Commission's main task would be to offer advice on finding a way through the situation that currently threatened to divide the Communion.

The Primates, he said, were clear that the Communion could be approaching a crucial and critical point in its life. 'The responses of provinces to developing events will determine the future life of our Communion in a profound way, and we need to take time for careful prayer, reflection and consideration to discern God's will for the whole Communion.'

A press release issued on behalf of the Anglican Communion noted that the Commission would 'take particular account' of the decision to authorise a service for use in connection with same-sex unions in the Diocese of New Westminster, Canada, and the expected Consecration of Canon Gene Robinson as Bishop Coadjutor of New Hampshire on 2 November, only a few days away.

Robin Eames, as Chairman, said that he was conscious of the importance and delicacy of the work that the Communion would have to undertake, and stressed that they had not been charged with finding answers to the questions of sexuality 'but with assisting the Communion to respond to recent developments in our churches in North America in a way which is fully faithful to Christ's call for the Unity of his Church'.

The mandate for the Commission was carefully worded by

Rowan Williams himself. It was wide-ranging yet precise. The statement from Lambeth pointed out that the Archbishop of Canterbury had requested the Commission:

(i) To examine and report to him by 30 September 2004 . . . on the legal and theological implications flowing from the decisions of the Episcopal Church (USA) to appoint a priest in a committed same sex relationship as one of its bishops, and of the Diocese of New Westminster to authorise services for use in connection with same sex unions, and specifically on the canonical understandings of communion, impaired and broken communion, and the ways in which provinces of the Anglican Communion may relate to one another in situations where the ecclesiastical authorities of one province feel unable to maintain the fullness of communion with another part of the Anglican Communion.

(ii) Within their report, to include practical recommendations (including reflection on emerging patterns of provision of Episcopal oversight for those Anglicans within a particular jurisdiction, where full communion within a Province is under threat) for maintaining the highest degree of communion that may be possible in the circumstances resulting from these decisions, both within and between, the churches of the Anglican Communion.

(iii) Thereafter, as soon as practicable, and with particular reference to the issues raised in Section IV of the Report of the Lambeth Conference 1998, to make recommendations to the Primates and the Anglican Consultative Council, as to the exceptional circumstances and conditions under which, and the means by which, it would be appropriate for the Archbishop of Canterbury to exercise an extraordinary ministry of episcope (pastoral oversight), support and reconciliation with regard to the internal affairs of a Province other than his own for the sake of maintaining communion with the said Province and between the said Province and the rest of the Anglican Communion.

The Commission was also charged with taking due account of the work already undertaken on issues of communion by the Lambeth Conferences of 1988 and 1998, as well as the views expressed by the Primates in their communiqués and pastoral letters arising from their meetings since 2000.

This, then, was the formidable brief facing Robin Eames and his Commission colleagues who had been drawn from all branches of the Communion. They included well-known conservatives such as Archbishop Gomez of the West Indies, Archbishop Iduwo-Fearon from Nigeria and Archbishop Malango from Central Africa, as well as a leading evangelical, Bishop Wright of Durham, and the liberal Bishop Paterson from New Zealand, who was also Chairman of the Anglican Consultative Council.

Reflecting later on the challenge facing the Commission, Robin Eames referred to the wide degree of early misunderstanding by the outside world of the purpose of its work. 'Its role was not to discuss sexuality except insofar as this subject had provoked the crisis. Its purpose was to find guidelines which would allow provinces to live together in the highest degree of communion, while facing disagreement. It also had to take on board the previous examinations of the meaning of communion, as set out by the earlier Eames Commission and *The Virginia Report*, and to apply that thinking to the current crisis.'

It was also important to realise that if the new Commission was successful, its recommendations should be applicable to any further divisive issues that might arise. He said that Anglicanism needed to look much further. Another important task, he felt, was to study the role of the Archbishop of Canterbury. 'I felt, and I put this to Rowan Williams direct, that while I would be updating him at every opportunity, the Commission must maintain, and be seen to maintain, its independence. It could not simply be seen as the Archbishop of Canterbury's "voice".'

Three days after the official launch of the Commission on Anglican Structures, Canon Gene Robinson was consecrated as Bishop Coadjutor of New Hampshire. It immediately provoked strong reaction around worldwide Anglicanism, and further afield. The conservative American church publication *The Christian Challenge* called it 'The Consecration that Shook the Anglican World'.

It described the Consecration of Gene Robinson as 'a shot heard around the 77-million member Anglican Communion, one that has left the global fellowship shuddering, and in some places, shattered'.

The magazine stated that the consecration had

defied two Lambeth Conference resolutions, and the admoni-
tions of two Archbishops of Canterbury and the majority of
Primates. Just two weeks earlier, in fact, all the Primates
attending an emergency meeting in London had warned
that the gay cleric's consecration would cause such a breakdown in fellowship as to imperil the global church, with
majority support remaining only for the faithful remnant of
ECUSA now seeking a new dispensation in the Communion.

The report also pointed out: 'As thousands of Episcopalians
celebrated Robinson's consecration, for Orthodox Episcopalians it was a day of wrenching grief.'[1]

The language of the article may have been regarded by
liberals as over-dramatic, but the headlines in the British press
two days after Robinson's consecration showed that the secular
world was in no doubt about the seriousness of the developments. The *Daily Telegraph* ran as the front page headlines,
'Day the Church split; Leaders of 50 m. Anglicans reject gay
bishop; Williams fights to keep control'. *The Times* of London
had the headline, 'World's Churches Cut Links Over Gay
Bishop'.

In a joint statement the Primates of the Global South,
involving most of Africa, Asia and the West Indies, said they
were appalled by Bishop Robinson's consecration and would
not recognise his ministry. They claimed that a state of
'impaired communion' now existed both within the American
church and between America and most provinces of the
Communion.

In a separate statement the Anglican Church in Kenya said it
would sever ties with the church in America. Bishop Thomas
Kogo was quoted in *The Times* of 4 November 2003 as saying,
'As a Church, we are not going to support homosexuality in the
Church, primarily because it is a sin.'

Even though such reactions were predictable, it looked to
outsiders – perhaps also to church insiders – that a schism was
inevitable. However, *The Times* advocated caution, and stated
in its leading article of 4 November 2003, 'Dr Williams must
hope that, his warnings of schism having been ignored, the
Church will stop short of making its divisions permanent.'

The newspaper advised that the Archbishop 'must use time, his considerable influence and institutional mechanisms to effect a cautious reconciliation. This should be a private healing; the anger is still too raw for retractions or a reaching across battle lines. But he may, with tact, forestall an irrevocable breach. The Church stands on the edge of a precipice – it would not recover from the fall.' It was wise advice directed to Lambeth, but the man most directly charged with finding a path through the ecclesiastical minefield, and trying to lead his colleagues in the right direction, was Robin Eames.

There was a residual feeling among many liberals and conservatives that the Americans had forced the pace over the issue of homosexuality, and that there was a kind of American ecclesiastical colonialism that had taken scant notice of the cultures and feelings of many other parts of the Anglican Communion. The *Church of Ireland Gazette* concluded in its leader of 14 November 2003 that ECUSA had 'followed its own mind and convictions and went its own way' in proceeding with the consecration of Bishop Robinson. In doing so it had left Archbishop Eames and his new Commission to 'pick up the pieces'.

Before the first formal meeting of the Commission in Windsor, England, during the second week of February 2004, Eames had his own period for reflection – apart from his endlessly busy schedule dealing with his responsibilities in the Church of Ireland and the Anglican Communion. He had made plain his personal views on homosexuality and had told his Armagh diocese, just prior to Robinson's consecration, that the ordination of a practising homosexual to a clerical post in the Church of Ireland would be in conflict with accepted practice.

He told his Synod, 'Holy Matrimony involving a man and a woman blessed by God is the norm recognised, proclaimed and supported by the church. The ordination of anyone to the diaconate, priesthood or episcopate in the Church of Ireland who is known to be in an active homosexual relationship would be in conflict with the mind and accepted practice of this church.'

Eames reflected privately that there was a legitimate distinction between a celibate person with homosexual orientation and one who was in a practising relationship. 'Some of the finest pastoral clergy I have known would also have been of a homosexual orientation, but celibate. I respect them for this standpoint, but to the best of my knowledge I have never ordained a candidate who was in a homosexual relationship, although some would undoubtedly have had that orientation.'

Eames had long believed that it was a gospel imperative that the Church must reach out to everyone, irrespective of lifestyle. However, he could not see how a bishop who is supposed to be the focal point of unity to his or her people could be capable of fulfilling this role if he or she was a practising homosexual. He said, nevertheless, 'I realised that this was a very private and personal opinion, and I did not intend to allow it in any way to influence my work on the Commission.'

As he prepared himself to start work on chairing the Commission, Eames wondered privately whether Anglicans in the United States as a whole had realised the consequences of the New Hampshire developments for the wider Anglican Communion. 'I wondered, in fact, if many of the Anglicans in the pews across America had a consciousness of the Anglican Communion itself?'

He worried also about the effect on worldwide ecumenism if the Anglican Communion did split. 'Rome already opposed the ordination of women, and the Pope had expressed his opposition to Robinson's appointment. If we broke up, would any other world faith take the Anglican Communion seriously?'

He worried too about the church's sense of priorities. 'In my preparatory work for the Commission I reflected upon the challenges for an international church like ours, including HIV/AIDS, hunger, injustice, famine, refugees and other issues which seemed to be far more pressing. More than once I asked myself, "Have we lost a sense of balance?" '

Many observers inside and outside the Church pointed to two main camps within Anglicanism – the conservative/evangelicals and the liberals. Eames believed, however, that there was a third important group. 'There was a large middle ground which was bewildered and perplexed by it all, and they were also asking us questions about the Anglican Communion's priorities.'

He had long emphasised that communion did not mean conformity. 'Diversity was a clear characteristic of Anglican Communion. While we accepted this, it seemed to become of secondary importance once differences of opinion surfaced. Some of the strongest advocates of provincial autonomy were also the strongest critics of what other provinces did. This seemed to me a sort of ecclesiastical hypocrisy. I felt that we could not have it both ways.'

Eames was also worried about what he described as 'degrees of anti-American feeling' which, he believed, had nothing to do with the Anglican Communion. He said, 'I had heard phrases such as "America is the new imperialism . . . with her money she expects the rest of the world to follow". I feared that these emotions would present the Commission with added difficulties.'

While Eames reflected privately, there were few people within the Anglican Communion who felt that he and the other members of the Commission would have an easy task. This mood was summarised by Canon James Rosenthal, the Director of Communications for the Anglican Communion. He said, 'It was more than a question of church order; we were talking about the future. Robert Runcie used to say that Anglicanism was "provisional", and that it was always going to be something else, part of a bigger Church.'

The reality, Rosenthal felt, was that something had to give. 'You could no longer compartmentalise anyone in the Anglican Church, nothing fitted into patterns any more. Yet Robin Eames had to try to pull it together in some way. I didn't think there was anyone else who could have done it, but we could not live in "cloud-cuckoo land" about what the end result might be. My sense was that we might be surprised or disappointed, but I prayed that we be realistic and that we did not continue to pretend that something was there, which might not be there.'

This sense of caution about the outcome was echoed by two senior church figures. Former Archbishop (now Lord) Carey had associated himself publicly, in a letter to *The Times* on 6 November 2003, with the views of the Primates of the Global South in their reaction to the consecration of Bishop Robinson. However, he cautioned 'all those most deeply affected not to drift away from each other, but to strengthen the bonds of affection that remain at the heart of Anglicanism'.

Privately he was pessimistic about the Commission's chances of finding a lasting solution. He said, 'I didn't think it was going to come up with anything new. I didn't have any great hopes for it, apart from the fact that Robin Eames was chairing it, and therefore it had the capacity to find a way forward, and to bring people together. In other words, all it could hope to achieve was to give us some breathing space, to find a way in which we can live together.'

Carey thought it significant that Rowan Williams had asked Eames to be chairman. 'Robin has that great proven ability to hold disparate groups together and to find a way through. If I had still been in office I would have chosen him to chair the new Commission, very definitely.'

Dr David Hope also felt that Eames was the right person to chair the Commission, but he had no illusions about the enormity of the task. He said, 'If anybody could make it happen, Robin Eames could, but it was a very tough assignment. There was a deep chasm of views and it was not going to be easy to build bridges.'

Bishop James Jones of Liverpool, who had got to know Eames when he conducted a clergy retreat for the Archbishop of Armagh in the beautiful isolation of Donegal, also came to appreciate his qualities, and what he might realistically achieve through the Commission. He said, 'His leadership skills would be tested in the Commission itself and that is also where he would have his authority proved. I didn't think that the Commission would come up with a solution, but I hoped that it would provide a basis for the church to move forward. I didn't think that that was too much for Robin and the Commission to deliver, and I believed that he had the authority to do so.'

Eames, however, continued to harbour no illusions, in private or in public, about the challenges of the Commission. Privately he was aware of the consequences of failure, both personally and with regard to the future of the Church, but he felt that he had no option but to try. He held preliminary meetings with groupings in the American church prior to setting off for the first formal meeting at Windsor on 10 February 2004. He told the *Belfast Telegraph*, 'I already sense that there will need to be a great deal of understanding across the Anglican Communion if we are to provide proposals which will last. I have always been an optimist, but I am also a realist, and I recognise that there are immense difficulties ahead.'

It is also worth reflecting at that stage that despite the success of the earlier Commissions that Eames had chaired, the practical results had been limited enough – though nearly all of these had been outside his direct control. By February 2004, almost a decade after the first women priests had been ordained within the Church of England, there were no women in the English episcopate. Anthony Howard, the columnist, noted in *The Times* of 10 February – the same day that the third Eames Commission began its work – that, in the decade since the original thirty women priests were ordained at Bristol Cathedral on 12 March 1994, progress had been painfully slow.

Howard wrote:

There are still episcopal areas – and even the occasional diocese – where no woman wearing a dog collar is encouraged to show her face. Worse than that, in some ways, are the isolated pockets of resistance – individual parishes where, under the C of E's current rules, a resolution can be passed denying the right of a woman priest to celebrate Holy Communion, or even to give absolution at matins and evensong.

Against that, it should be pointed out that by mid-February 2004, women deans had been appointed to the great cathedrals of Leicester and Salisbury. But there was a long way to go, even if Anthony Howard believed that 'Slowly but remorselessly the C of E is being brought to realise that it cannot hope to hold the line against women bishops for much longer.'

Ironically, only four days after Howard's article was published, *The Times* of 14 February 2004 – Valentine's Day – quoted Canon Malcolm Widdecombe, a Bristol vicar, thus: 'The Lord wants male leadership in his Church. It's not about the capability of women to do the job, I'm sure some do it far better than some men, but it's the "allowability" of women to be priests that I question.'

Nearer home, Eames was aware that although the Church of Ireland had agreed as long ago as 1990 to accept women to the episcopate, there was little prospect of a woman bishop in Ireland within the foreseeable future. Judging by past practice, it was clear that whatever the new Commission would recommend on Anglican structures, following the controversy over clerical homosexuality, the results would take a long time to work themselves out.

Prior to the meeting in Windsor, Eames travelled to Virginia in the USA to attend the diocesan synod and to meet ECUSA representatives on both sides of the argument. He had known of the sharp divisions in the USA, but he found it very sobering to listen to them face to face. He says, 'I saw and heard the two dimensions – the depth of division and the pain and uncertainty on both sides. I was amazed at the welcome I received. Without exception they were most anxious to have someone "in authority" to listen to them.' Eames found it an invaluable preparation for the Windsor meeting. 'No one doubted that I had come with my new responsibilities to be fair and to listen, but it was a very disturbing experience.'

When the Commission assembled at Windsor in February 2004, it could not have failed to notice a carefully timed statement from the Primates of the Global South underlining that, in their view, the action of ECUSA in persisting with the appointment and consecration of Bishop Robinson had created a situation of 'grave concern' for the Anglican Communion, and that such actions were a 'direct repudiation of the clear teachings of the Holy Scriptures'. This underlined clearly that the work of the Commission would come under the severest scrutiny from people on both sides of the divisions.

It was noticeable that the new Commission's public statement following its first formal meeting underlined pointedly that its members had been 'saddened that tensions within the Communion, exacerbated by the use of strident language, have continued to rise in recent months'. Significantly, the Commission bluntly requested 'all members of the Anglican Communion to refrain from any precipitate action, or legal proceedings, which would further harm the bonds of communion in the period while it completes its work. Mission and ministry, including prayer for unity, remain the priorities.'

The Commission set out its work plan for the succeeding months, and organised small working groups to study and reflect on five key topics – issues of process in the Communion, the nature and purposes of communion, the obligations of communion, authority, and the rule of the instruments of unity in preserving fellowship. The Commission announced that its next meeting would be held in the USA in June. Apart from the statement quoted above, there were no other public utterances, and neither the Chairman nor any other Commission member spoke directly to the media – though the main papers were available on the Internet.

Despite the Commission's public expression of sadness over the strident language that was being used in the public debate within the Anglican Communion, Eames was somewhat encouraged by the tone of the first meeting. There was a desire to act with integrity, to avoid coming up with a 'fudge', to avoid 'demonising' any opposing points of view, and to avoid seeking unity for unity's sake. Significantly, there was a strong desire that the Anglican Communion should continue.

However, as they began their work, Eames had several conflicting emotions. The situation confronting the Commission was much different from that of the 1980s, when the ordination of women was foremost. He recalls, 'Feelings this time were much more international, chiefly due to the depth of feeling on a cultural rather than on a purely theological basis.'

Technology had advanced so rapidly that instantaneous reaction to events from across the Anglican world had allowed people to take up set positions long before localised discussions had taken place. Eames recalls, 'This led to confrontation over long distances. There was also the overlap of international politics and church affairs. The anti-American feeling in many parts of the world led to initial suspicion, particularly in parts of the Far East, of anything American. Added to this was the emergence of degrees of independence in Provinces of Africa, India and the Far East, whose new confidence stemmed from a widespread belief that the centre of Anglicanism was no longer in historical Canterbury, or indeed the West, but south of the Sahara.'

There was also the fundamental question of the authority of Scripture. For years, Anglicanism had lived with a gradual growth in the recognition that Scripture was open to several interpretations. The more evangelical wing of Anglicanism had become prone to the fundamentalist outlook in which Scripture was absolute, whereas reason and tradition had become more and more important to the West. Eames says, 'I was convinced that had the crisis over sexuality not become the touchstone for serious differences, something else would have arisen to do likewise. Looking back to the Eames Commission period, I was somewhat surprised that though the interpretation of Scripture

316

over the role of women was important to the debate, it occupied less prominence – relatively speaking – than in the new crisis.'

At Windsor, Eames became even more aware of the powerful forces on the fringe of the crisis, which were to play an ever-increasing role. He says, 'These forces were closely linked to financial power. It was no secret that certain individuals and groupings, particularly in the USA, were prepared to finance those who held influence in certain parts of the Anglican Communion, but would require support. This was a powerful lobby, and I was uneasy as to the precise role such influences were playing.'

Meanwhile, the language being used to expound positions was becoming more vehement. Eames reflects, 'I greatly regretted this, and it was to make the work of the Commission more difficult. It was no coincidence that, in our press release issued after the Windsor meeting, we drew attention to this development and publicly deplored it.'

Tensions were high throughout the United States and Africa. Eames says, 'I was alarmed to find the degree of manipulation of individuals that was taking place. In one instance an African leader for whom I have the highest regard told me that while maintaining a position of integrity over the sexuality issue, he felt that he had allowed himself to become a prisoner of those with other agendas. I was devastated by this, but it helped to bring home to me, as Chair of the Commission, the very human side that was facing us.'

From the outset at Windsor, Eames warned the members of the Commission of the danger of having too high expectations of what might be achieved, and underlined that no matter what the Commission would recommend, there would inevitably be more pain and casualties. Eames was aware that Archbishop Malango was about to preside over a meeting of his bishops in Africa, and as Chairman of the Commission he sent fraternal greetings to them.

Eames indicated his awareness of the desire of some provinces to break their links with ECUSA, but asked the African bishops to allow the Commission time to complete its work, because any decision to break links would make the agenda more complex. Having bought time, the Commission could look foward to its next meeting in a few months at Kanuga in North Carolina.

Here they met face to face with the various representatives of the differing groups within ECUSA. There was close questioning and also clear explanations. Eames again found the expectations of the Commission's work overpowering. He recalls, 'To be honest, at times I felt that the USA which had exercised its secular world power in invading Iraq and had come to be viewed by some as "the new imperialism" was yet to be really conscious of the needs of a world church communion.' He wondered at the oversimple beliefs expressed, and that there seemed to be no real difficulties in inviting extra-diocesan episcopal oversight where parishes had lost faith in their own bishop. He recalls wryly, 'As I listened, questioned and led the discussion, the complications of Drumcree seemed light years away.'

By the time they met at Kanuga in June 2004, Eames had a very acute sense that whatever they proposed in their report, the Anglican Communion was very different from that which had looked forward to his report on women's ordination in the 1980s. He also faced the added difficulty that so many of the media continued to view him and his colleagues as a Commission on sexuality alone.

He felt that the traditional instruments of unity within Anglicanism were under strain, simply because so much had depended previously on unwritten practices and agreements. Only when a major crisis arose did they stand back and ask fundamental questions about how they related to one another. He reflects, 'I felt that the integrity of honestly held positions on all sides became debased by the way in which the power blocks were making use of different scriptural interpretations for their own reasons.' High among those agendas was the question of who or what should actually control the Anglican Communion. Eames says, 'The Archbishop of Canterbury was facing definite challenges within and from beyond the Church of England, not alone to his own stated position on sexuality, but to the historic significance of Canterbury as the centre of the Anglican Communion. In my conversations with him, I was acutely conscious of how well aware he was of this.'

The next meeting of the Commission took place back in Windsor, interrupted only by the sounds of the changing of the guard at nearby Windsor Castle. Eames had urged the Commission not to be overconscious of the need to write a report, but to engage in deep analysis of the problems. Again he urged them to think of what was actually possible. The final report would most likely reflect upon the development of the concept of communion and relationships, based on the reality that basic agreement on procedure was essential if the Anglican Communion was to enjoy something more than 'bonds of affection'. He recalls, 'I was quite certain that one of the significant criteria by which our final report would be judged would be whether or not we produced guidelines that would be helpful for generations to come, whenever or wherever any crisis arose. The issues we faced had a long-term significance far beyond the sexuality issue. I kept stressing to the Commission that no matter what good ideas emerged in our work on structures they would be seen merely in academic terms unless there could be agreement at the level of each individual province.'

At one point, Eames suggested to Rowan Williams that it would be of paramount importance for the Primates to be given an opportunity to 'own' the final report, even if it meant delaying its eventual publication. He pondered also as to how the Anglican Consultative Council, with its lay representation, could also figure in the process of reception.

Throughout his work as Chairman of the Commission on Anglican Structures, as before in his work with the other Commissions, Robin Eames displayed the touch of a good chairman with a legal mind and with long experience of Anglican affairs. Most important of all he was ever conscious of the long-term effect of the report and its impact upon the Anglican Communion.

He summed up, 'It seemed obvious to me, even as we began our work, that one of the first tests of all that we had been attempting to solve would come when the Archbishop of Canterbury would issue his invitation to the new worldwide Lambeth Conference. What would be the response of the others if Bishop Gene Robinson were to be invited? What would be the response to the location of South Africa as a venue? Not alone would the authority of our Commission be tested by such issues – so, too, would be the authority of the Archbishop of Canterbury.'

Whatever the outcome of the potentially divisive Commission report, and the reaction of the Church at large, it was clear that the chairmanship of the Commission would most likely be Robin Eames' final significant contribution to the Anglican Communion, as the prospect of his retirement loomed in the not-too-distant future. By any standards he had given remarkable service to his own Church of Ireland and to the wider Anglican community, and his impending departure – at whatever time of his choosing – was not being relished by his senior colleagues in Ireland or the wider Communion.

Dr David Hope once described Eames as a 'troubleshooter'. He said affectionately, however, 'Robin came to have an "iconic" status. People would say, "Robin Eames, he's the troubleshooter of the Anglican Church. If you have a problem, bring in someone like Eames!" '[2]

However, there was much more to him than that, as Dr Hope stressed. He said, 'When Robin chooses to go, he will definitely be missed. The Church of Ireland will have lost a very substantial and notable Archbishop of Armagh, and the Anglican Communion will lose a very distinguished, mature and experienced Primate. There is no doubt about it.'

The Archbishop of Canterbury Dr Rowan Williams said simply, 'I don't at all look forward to Robin's retirement, though he will still be there as a friend. I have great affection for him, as someone I can confide in and talk to, and whom I can trust without reservation.'

Rowan Williams believes that there is no one quite like him within the Anglican Communion. 'Robin does have an utterly distinctive role within the Anglican Consultative Council and the Primates' Meetings, in the fellowship of people who have those kinds of responsibilities. The fact that he comes out of a situation of deep conflict in Northern Ireland, where he has earned his stripes, is all part of his authority. Without doubt Robin Eames is a world figure within Anglicanism and he has been one of the outstanding Archbishops of his era. His absence will be felt as a real wound.'

24

Nobody's Fool

Robin Eames is every inch an archbishop in his bearing, style, manner of speech and presence. Yet there is also the man behind the clerical collar. That is not to say that there are two different people, or that he puts on a public face which is totally different from that of the private person.

Yet there is the reassuring human dimension that this archbishop, who is totally competent in chairing a major Anglican Commission or handling a tricky press conference or 'live' broadcast, might have difficulty in putting up a shelf that won't fall down. Like many other intelligent and street-wise people he is not 'good with his hands', and yet he is a capable sailor, he held at one time a pilot's licence to fly light aircraft, and he is a painter – in his limited spare time.

Many people will instantly recognise Archbishop Eames in his clerical attire, but when he walks into a room in 'civvies' there is sometimes a need for a quick visual double take as one begins to realise that the man in the sweater and slacks is the same Robin Eames one sees on television or in a pulpit. This is something that appeals to his impish sense of humour, like the occasion when two people in a supermarket collided with each other's trolley while they pointed out to one another that the man at the end of the aisle was indeed Archbishop Robin Eames.

A sailing colleague tells the story about the occasion when Eames was competing strongly in a yacht race at Strangford Lough, and his craft came far too close to another vessel. One of the crew of the other yacht yelled out at this burly man in racing gear, 'Shove off, you stupid bastard, you're far too close!' – whereupon the rival skipper barked to his crew member,

'Watch your language! That bloke you're yelling at is the Archbishop of Armagh!' It's a story that still affords Eames much amusement.

Despite the storms and swirling currents of public office, Robin Eames' home port and haven are his wife Christine and close-knit family. They have two sons, who are both medical doctors, and five grandchildren. Their elder son Niall, a consultant surgeon, is married to Rosemary, and they have three children – Christopher, Sarah and Nicola. Their younger son Michael, a senior registrar in surgery, is married to Elizabeth, and they have two children – Joanna and Patrick.

Niall Eames says, 'Dad is a very good father and grandfather. He travels all over the world, but he constantly stays in touch with the family, and he always brings back a present for the children. My Mum and Dad are as close as it is possible for any couple to be. They talk to each other non-stop, and they seem to have an almost telepathic relationship. My Mum is a huge force in his life.'

That closeness between Robin and Christine Eames has been noted by many people throughout the Anglican Communion, and not least by the Archbishop of Canterbury Dr Rowan Williams, who knows them well as a couple. He says, 'I have a high regard for Robin, and Christine is another person of huge integrity and authority. Sometimes in a marriage you see one stronger and one weaker partner, but sometimes you also see in a marriage two strong people supporting each other in their strength. That's how I see Robin and Christine. They are strong and independent individuals, but they complement each other wonderfully.'

Lady Eames is a law graduate of Queen's University, an accomplished public speaker, and a former President of the worldwide Mothers' Union, a post she held for six years. Robin Eames says, 'I am very proud of Christine and of what she has achieved. Even today my senior colleagues from Africa and other continents send greetings to "Mamma Christine". They still speak of their love for her, and of their gratitude for all her encouragement. The work could not have been more demanding, physically or spiritually.'

Their close bond as a couple has been important to both of them. Robin says, 'My home has always been vital to me, and at the centre of this has been the love and support of Christine.

Her highest possible standards of devotional life, her humour and her care for people have been a rock to all my work, and her discernment and judgment of people and events have always provided me with a wealth of support.'

Lady Eames says, 'I've always tried to be supportive of Robin, and I have never been asked to do anything I did not want to do. I've never thought of it as a "job", but rather as a response and an opportunity. I have been totally privileged to be able to identify with the life of the Church, and to do whatever that requires.'

Robin Eames' family paints an affectionate picture of the Archbishop when he is off duty – though in a sense he is never 'off duty'. His elder son Niall says, 'I cannot recall a harsh word or act from my Dad. He was always there to support us in good or bad times. There were occasions, of course, when he was cross. I remember learning to drive his car round the See House in Derry and going through a bush in the process. When he saw the extent of the scratches in daylight he was not best pleased, understandably, but I have never seen him blow his top at anything. When he is cross you know it, and that is more impressive than with someone who habitually "loses it".'

Eames, however, has been known to blow his top on the rugby field. He himself tells the story of a Saturday afternoon encounter playing against an opponent, when they actually came to blows. 'I ended up with a cut lip and he with a black eye. We were both warned by the referee as to our future conduct. This was in my time as a curate in Bangor, and on the next day I was the guest preacher in a different parish. When the offering was brought up to the altar, one of the collectors was sporting a black eye, and he spotted my lip. We looked knowingly at each other, but I think this secret has been kept until now!'

Though Robin Eames has been extremely busy all his life, he has always made time to be with his family. Christine says, 'Robin works very hard, but he doesn't manufacture difficulties when there aren't any. He is straightforward. His great strength is his faith, but he doesn't burden those of us who are close to him with his strong sense of duty. When he relaxes, he really does relax. Robin is great company. He reads and takes in a lot, and he retains it. He's also a very positive sort of person.'

One of the family's most enjoyable experiences has been sailing. Niall says, 'Dad is a good seaman. He understands and loves the sea, and he engendered in Michael and me a great love for it.' He believes, however, that they were more competitive than their father. Niall says, 'Dad was competitive too, but without being ruthless. He was a benign dictator on the boat. He would let Michael and me do all the hard work while he contentedly ran the show!'

In times of difficulty or danger, Robin Eames' inner strength came through. His son Michael says, 'If anything was going wrong on the boat, or with the weather, Dad was always the person everyone looked to. He had a calming influence, and he could instil confidence. Dad always made his presence felt.' His brother Niall agrees. 'I have been in situations on the boat when I have been frightened, but Dad always said, "We'll be all right. Don't worry." It was something he said not just to give leadership or reassurance. He had this sense of a deep inner confidence. There is no superficial faith in him at all. He doesn't wear his archbishop's badge on his sleeve, and he keeps his faith very close to him, but he practises what he preaches, very much so.'

At the same time Niall paints the endearing picture of a man whose forte is not DIY. 'Dad's strength is not in mechanical things. If his car breaks down he would not be the best person to dive under the bonnet – but he knows how to get a mechanic to come and fix it. When he is sailing he is at one with the sea and the wind, and because of his faith there is nothing that will frighten him. However, the thought of him screwing one of the winches onto the deck – now that *would* be scary!'

Paradoxically, Robin Eames used to hold a pilot's licence to fly an aircraft, a skill that requires a good knowledge of things mechanical. Typically, he learned to fly in order to overcome a fear of flying. He still hugely enjoys air travel, and until the introduction of stricter regulations concerning aircraft security, he usually wangled an invitation to visit the cockpit during a flight. Even today he will embark on a long air journey, armed with relevant maps and a working knowledge of the prevailing weather. One of his former associates notes, 'Robin could sometimes be a pain in the butt on a long flight – he went on and on about cloud formations and that sort of thing!' This sophisticated archbishop retains a small boy's innocent enthusiasm for boats, planes and trains – which is probably why he has remained such an inveterate traveller.

His capacity for travel and for work is legendary. His son Michael observes, 'Dad is never off call. He works incredibly hard, and he can't just drop everything and go on holiday. He has to have things sorted out before he can do that. I don't know where he gets his energy from.' Robin Eames admits to being 'a man in a hurry'. He says, 'The death of my father taught me the fragility of life. I am the sort of person who says every morning, "I am still here," but I have been very conscious in my work of how suddenly a life can end, and with it ends the possibility of what a person might still have achieved.' Yet despite being aware of the passage of time and of the importance of getting things done, Robin Eames is also noted for his infinite patience – such are the paradoxes of the man.

When he does have time, he likes to relax by painting or reading. He has been a constant 'doodler' and caricaturist during long church meetings – when he is not using another acquired skill of lip-reading. He learned to lip-read as a curate because one of his parishioners was deaf and dumb, and Eames still retains enough lip-reading skill to make him aware of what is going on at a conference. He says, 'I can always spot a sudden sub-committee meeting which is taking place in the body of the hall and although I don't always know what they are saying, I can lip-read enough to get the gist of what their questions might be. This is particularly useful on the international stage.'

He is a more than useful amateur painter, a skill that was first developed during a programme with Ulster Television when local celebrities were taught the basics by a professional artist. Some time later when Eames was at a conference in Hong Kong he was stopped by a local in the street who said enthusiastically, 'You painter!' The UTV programme had been sold to a Hong Kong television station, and the man had seen it. Eames recalls, 'We talked for quite a while in broken English about my painting, thousands of miles from home.' He continues to paint when he can, and the annual Archbishop's Christmas card is more often than not a picture of an Armagh diocesan landscape.

His favourite writers include T. S. Eliot and the Irish poet Seamus Heaney. He says, 'Both of them teach me something about the art of communication. They both write about the co-relation between success and failure, hope and despair. Life to me is balanced between those two parameters, and when I talk about the spiritual life I counsel people not to be disappointed if one day they can almost touch the hem of Christ's garment, and the next day they feel that maybe there is no God. That's why Christ taught by giving examples – he knew that life was not going to be a red carpet for everybody and that the road might lead to Calvary.'

The theme of challenge, suffering and pain has been intertwined with his entire clerical career, not only in the Troubles – the deaths, the bereavements, the sustained rage over Drumcree – but also in his mission to keep together the Church of Ireland and in his work as a mediator within the Anglican Communion during a period of heart-searching and of potentially great divisiveness. As ever, there have been the two dimensions to Eames – the sensitive inner man, and also the archbishop who has the right word for every occasion, even in the worst of circumstances.

His son Michael describes the occasion when he accompanied his father to the aftermath of a bomb blast in Armagh. He recalls, 'He was terribly moved by what happened, but he also had to find the right words not only for those directly involved but also for the world at large. Time and again he would witness devastation, and within minutes someone would put a microphone under his nose, and yet he was able to find the right words. I don't know how he was able to get himself together to do that.'

While Robin Eames has always been a man of deep caring and infinite patience, sometimes to the point where some of his strongest critics accused him of following events rather than of shaping them, he is nobody's fool. His legal brain and his political astuteness, allied to a 'street-wise' pragmatism, mean that he has survived in situations that would have swamped lesser figures. He has long remembered the advice of the late Bishop Arthur Butler, a former military chaplain: 'The secret of real leadership is never to go so far ahead of your troops that when you look over your shoulder, nobody's there.'

Eames reflects, 'When there have been major difficulties or differences of opinion I have tried to take people with me as far as I can, and certainly to the point where I can say to them, "Trust me – I am going to take the next step. Will you follow me?" I have judged my work by that standard, and while at times this seems to have been successful, I cannot say that I have succeeded all the time.'

Different people have different views on Robin Eames, depending on their own agendas, but there is general agreement that one of his greatest achievements has been to hold together the Church of Ireland during a period when it could easily have been torn apart. He has his own worries about the way the church is shaping, and the differing cultures between North and South which create a certain natural tension between people of different state loyalties and aspirations. Eames is also perplexed at the growing 'evangelicalism' of the Northern church and a move away from traditional 'broad-church' Anglicanism, but that is a phenomenon facing all the established churches.

There are also those who wonder whether or not Eames has stayed too long at the top, thus stifling growth among the younger clergy. That view has to be measured against the fact that, despite his presidential style, Eames has been keen to present a collective voice and to delegate where possible. He is also keenly aware of the danger of staying too long in the job, but his views about retiring are tempered by the need to ensure that a successor will have as much experience as possible before taking on the considerable responsibilities of Primate. Barring any unforeseen disasters, Eames' major achievement in Ireland will be to hand over to his successor a church that remains in relatively good shape.

On the vexed subject of Drumcree, Eames' supporters and critics are unlikely to change their minds. His supporters feel that, again barring a huge flare-up, Eames' tactic of playing the long game will prove to be right. His critics will continue to argue, however, that he should have moved earlier and more decisively, and that he should have given a stronger lead by closing the Drumcree church and showing the world that the Church of Ireland visibly disapproved of what had been taking place there. If he had done that, he would have made a strong moral point, but he might well have lost control of his church and at the same time lost any influence he had with the Portadown Orangemen.

Ironically, the Church of Ireland may end up by having the best of both worlds – it made its voice indubitably clear at the

1999 General Synod, and yet the long game of its Primate may in the end bring about a peaceful conclusion. As others have pointed out, only history will show who was right – if ever there is a simple 'right or wrong' answer to such a complex problem.

One of the keys to the later development of Drumcree was that the Orangemen at last began to consider changing their tactics away from mob violence and confrontation around the same time that the General Synod had called for demonstrably peaceful protests. If that had not happened Eames might have lost the plot, and he might have been crushed between the rock of his church and the hard place of Drumcree – but he was astute enough to retain the confidence of the Orangemen and help to lead them to a point where dialogue offered more hope of a solution than confrontation.

On the other hand he failed in his attempts to win or to keep the trust of the Garvaghy Road residents, because of the fallout from the unsuccessful carpet mill talks in Portadown in July 1996. He discovered the hard way that a reconciler cannot build a reliable bridge unless its supporting structures are rooted in the ground on both sides of the chasm.

In the broader field of peacemaking in Northern Ireland, Eames made a valuable contribution, not only in talking to prime ministers and other leading policy-makers, but also in engaging in dialogue with paramilitaries and their political representatives. He also talked directly to Loyalist paramilitary commanders, and also to Sinn Fein politicians.

In his early days in Derry he secretly met a Republican paramilitary, during the same period in which he was also burying the victims of Provisional IRA violence. He was taking a high risk, because if the news had leaked out he would have been very severely criticised in general, and most probably roundly denounced by his own people in particular. However, he believed throughout the Troubles that risks had to be taken if the community was to be edged towards peace.

In doing so he displayed an inner courage and toughness beneath his measured and calm exterior. Lady Eames reflects, 'There is a steel in Robin, and he has had to have that inner toughness to come through what he experienced. There were matters to be resolved and they were not going to be won by sitting around and uttering platitudes. I suspect that he is a tough man to fight when he comes out of his corner. I could never see him "bawling" people out, because he is naturally a courteous person, but I don't think that he would let them kick him twice. He's a reconciler, but he is also resilient.'

At the height of the Troubles there were many angry people in Northern Ireland who made a point of phoning the Archbishop at home. His wife says, 'I have listened while some have shouted pretty awful things to him down the phone. Some of those people concerned me, because they were deeply hurt and felt let down by all kinds of situations. Perhaps it was a good thing that in a small society like ours, people felt that they had accessibility to Robin, but there were some nights when I could not begin to make an evening meal before 10 p.m. because of the phone calls. What else could we do? We learned to develop another layer of skin and to get on with it. That's what life demanded of us, and it wasn't easy, but we lived through it.'

There were many other good moments of privilege and of opportunity, and the mutual support within a strong marriage and a closely knit family. 'Of course Robin has been shaped and changed by the events he has lived through, and he has grown and developed as a human being, but he is essentially the same person I married. He is also the same person at home as he is in public. He doesn't have a public face and then a private face. He's essentially "Robin", wherever he is. I think he's even nicer at home, and I would put kindness very high on his list of good qualities. It's really hard for me to sum him up in a few sentences, but I'd happily marry him again tomorrow!'

Outside his home and his native land, Robin Eames' work for the Anglican Communion has been very significant. The Report from the Commission on Communion and Women in the Episcopate, which he chaired, became a blueprint for practical yet principled compromise on a vexatious issue. His chairmanship of the Commission that produced *The Virginia Report* was also astute and productive, and the Report itself provided a deeper understanding of the nature of communion within the church.

His third major commitment, the chairmanship of the Commission on Anglican Structures, has been arguably the most difficult undertaking, with no guarantee of eventual success – given the nature of the problem, and the passions and hurts surrounding it. Whatever happens, there has been no better equipped or more experienced Primate in the entire

Communion to try to chart a peaceful way forward for Anglicanism in the twenty-first century.

In all of these varied activities, it is clear that Robin Eames has been nobody's 'man', and certainly nobody's fool. In the most subtle yet determined of ways he has remained his own man, but the search to find and to understand the inner man has been possibly the most elusive path of all – for himself and for his biographer, to whom he has talked openly and at times intimately about the private person behind the headlines. He is in some ways a simple man, and yet he is also complex.

One public clue to this apparent paradox lies in his media statements. Some of these say little, because there is little to say. Others seem to say little, but the real meaning lies between the lines or has been left out. Yet others, particularly of late, have been meaty indeed.

A former Presbyterian Moderator, the Very Reverend Dr John Dunlop says, 'Robin had to be a moderate voice when it would have been easy to provide a tribal leadership which would have tipped this society into civil war. He was one of those people who held Northern Ireland back from total anarchy, and he did that well.'

Dunlop, underlines the problems facing every church leader. He says, 'I know as a preacher that it is possible to put so many conditional clauses in a sentence in order to make the message accessible to those who don't necessarily like you or agree with you. However, to keep those people on board and to move them forward you might end up by not saying decisively what you needed to say. In a classic sense that is where the prophetic word sits uneasily with the pastoral word.'

This is a general argument which Eames accepts, but he makes the point: 'My definition of a prophet is the person who makes the greatest progress without having lost touch with the grass roots. If I had lost the pastoral touch I could not have been a prophet or commentator on bigger events. During the Troubles I did not have time other than to try to give leadership in "instant theology", but things have changed. Now it is possible to spend more time thinking about things, and framing a judgment. One of the greatest compliments I have been given was when someone said to me, "In the heat of the battle, you managed to hold the line." '

It all depends, of course, on where one believes that 'the

line' should be held, and the point might well be made of all church leaders. There is no doubt, however, that in recent years Robin Eames has become more outspoken and assured, and more confident of the way he wants to go. His Presidential Address to the General Synod in 2003 in Dublin was rightly described as 'statesmanlike', and was one of the best speeches by any Irish church leader in recent years.

In his address, he challenged the Ulster Unionists to find a new self-confidence, and to move away from their 'siege mentality'. He urged the Roman Catholics in Northern Ireland to accept that they were no longer 'second-class citizens', and to recognise that there was general goodwill towards them in much of the Protestant community which, like them, had made mistakes in the past.

He also endorsed a new and significant Church of Ireland report on sectarianism, *The Hard Gospel*, as 'one of the most significant documents in the long history of the Church of Ireland'. As well, he challenged the growth of materialism in society, and he called for direct government taxation to provide 'a permanent contribution . . . for the poor of the world'.

In the press conference afterwards, he was even more frank, a point noted by seasoned journalists, who had heard him speak many times before. Patsy McGarry of the *Irish Times* says, 'It seemed that the lawyer was pushed back and the leader took over. He showed that he could be inspirational, although I don't think that this has been a feature of his period as Primate. He has not been as prophetic, possibly, as he could be.'

However, McGarry also makes the point:

Robin is a complex figure, and there is a complex regard for him, not unlike my own. I would be critical of his handling of Drumcree, but I would admire him for a lot of other things, particularly on the international stage. It was a compliment to the Church of Ireland and to him personally that he was in the running for Canterbury, and was very close to it, some say. Many people in the United Kingdom would have preferred him to George Carey.

Archbishop Rowan Williams has also noted an even stronger emphasis of late in a number of Eames' public statements. He says, 'For years Robin has had to make difficult judgments on when and how to say certain things, when there may have been factors that made it unconstructive to speak out. I think he has made a judgment of various areas and he has decided that now is the time to say more. I respect his judgment of the situation.'

Eames' continued reassessment of a wide range of crucial issues is partly that of the street-wise lawyer who wants to keep abreast and often ahead of developments, but also part of the inner man who frequently agonises over saying something that would increase the burden on others, particularly his clergy, in sensitive situations.

He reflects on the responsibility of having to make so many public statements, often at times of political and community crisis. 'There is a loneliness in decision-making, because you are scrutinised in everything you do or say. My real worry is before I put pen to paper. How will what I say affect someone else's life? Will it help to ease the pressure on my clergy, or will it make the pressure worse? I have been very careful in terms of what I have said in public. It's not self-protection, and it's not the "bland" thing – it is trying to work out what effect my words might have. I am a sensitive person, and I am easily hurt, but my faith is not to hit back. It's to state the truth as I see it. Nevertheless, I am always my own severest critic.'

The former British Prime Minister John Major, who worked closely with Robin Eames on Northern Ireland affairs, rejects any notion that the Archbishop was 'bland'. He says, 'It's a devil of a job being Archbishop of Armagh, or Archbishop of Canterbury for that matter, because you have to hold the ring against sharply competing views, without cutting yourself off from people on either side. So people accuse you of being "bland". You are not. You are extremely skilful to be able to do it. People sometimes mistake politeness for blandness, and they sometimes mistake people who don't react sharply or hysterically as people who don't care or don't know. That is a bad misreading of character. It's weak men who strike attitudes. Strong men don't. They want results.'

Robin Eames never felt totally alone, but he experienced loneliness in his job. In fact the concept of 'loneliness' is a regular part of his vocabulary. Despite his abundant social skills, and his affability and lively sense of humour, he needs to create his own space and his own sense of privacy. He says, 'I mix a great deal with people and I hugely enjoy doing that, yet I know that some might look upon me as solitary, and I don't have a close circle of intimate friends. My family and my church are the rocks of my life. I have discovered that I am more sensitive than I had realised, and I can be easily hurt, but I steel myself not to show it, particularly when I have to make decisions that don't come easily.'

He has not cultivated a circle of intimate friends, partly because he does not want to confuse friendship with judgment or his duty to make difficult decisions. He says, 'I have friends who are really close to others, but I have not allowed that to happen to me. I am extremely conscious of the fact that a person to whom I have become very close might well be the same person to whom I might have to say "No" as Archbishop – and I don't want to put them in the position of saying, "Oh, I thought you were closer to me than that." '

He confides a great deal in his wife Christine. 'She knows and has known about virtually everything I have been involved in. There are things that she knows, but there are others about which she would never ask me because she knows that there are some things I can never talk about. If someone comes to me with an enormous burden I say to them, "I might not be able to solve your dilemma but at least I can promise you total confidentiality." '

It is this inner sanctum of Robin Eames' life that holds the key to the man, that part of him which is known only to himself and to God. His son Niall observes, 'There is a relationship between him and God which is between them, something which we are not party to, nor necessarily can be.' He believes that his father surrounds himself at times with caveats of complexity, but that at heart he is a simple man. 'He is not good at bluffing. I have never seen him try to lie or deceive, it's just not in him.'

Perhaps one of Robin Eames' problems, unfairly for him, is that some people believe that he is just too good to be true. They say, 'All that charm, all that ability, all that way with words, all that religious background – there has to be a catch somewhere!' Niall Eames notes the point, but does not accept it. He says, 'Good friends of mine who have been introduced to him through our friendship have also become close to him. You can see them saying to themselves, "This man is not in any way a 'goody-goody' on the surface, and then deep down there is something quite different. He is what it says on the label."

There's his faith in God and his family, and that's it. What you see is what you get. There's nothing hidden, strange or startling about him. He is a good man, a very good man.'

During his career, Robin Eames has received many public honours, including his life peerage and honorary doctorates from Cambridge, Lancaster, Aberdeen and Exeter Universities, as well as Trinity College, Dublin, the University of Ulster and his *alma mater* the Queen's University of Belfast. Yet he wears his honours with a refreshing informality, and his irrepressible sense of humour offsets his natural gravitas.

As Archbishop Desmond Tutu points out, 'Robin's humour is part of his attractiveness. He is very Irish in his capacity to be able to "take the mickey" out of himself. He has very consider-able dignity, yet he is also someone who does not stand on ceremony the way you would quite expect. He is fun.'[1]

Archbishop Rowan Williams believes that Robin Eames is, in one sense, every inch an archbishop, and yet in another sense he comes across as a very 'unchurchy' person. He says, 'He is not narrowly religious in the sense of being a "professional" churchman. He would not describe himself as a theologian first and foremost, and yet he is solid in that sense. He has a strong, adult faith that does not need discussing very much or airing in public. It's just there. At the same time, however, he is subtle, but that is not in opposition to a real and a basic simplicity.'

Bishop James Jones of Liverpool makes the general point that those who hold public office may not survive internally unless they know who they are. He says, 'So much is projected onto you that is false. If you did not know who you were, that would get to you, and undermine your very being. So there needs to be an internal security to detach the office from the person. Robin Eames is a man who has many different roles, and I don't think that he could cope with all of that if there wasn't his internal security. If you are on a journey of knowing who you are, then you can cope.'

The fact remains that Robin Eames the man and Robin Eames the archbishop and pastor are indivisible. For some three decades he has signed his name 'Robert Derry', or 'Robert Down' or 'Robert Armagh', but rarely 'Robin Eames', except, as he notes with characteristic humour, when he signs his cheque book! Robin Eames does have a bedrock of internal security of the kind to which James Jones refers, and he is confident about his internal 'journey'. Jones further makes the point: 'He's a pastor, but he's also a bit of a bruiser. Robin Eames has had a few knocks in his time, and he knows what it's like. He is someone who understands the rough and tumble of public life.'

Yet in a long episcopal career where he has been buffeted by many violent storms in Ireland and within the Anglican Communion there is a human vulnerability as well as a deep inner strength in this archbishop who has had to be a man for all seasons. On a much deeper level he admits, 'If you ask me, "Who is the 'real' Robin Eames?", I could hardly tell you sometimes. The job and I are one. It's absolutely total.'

Perhaps this explains part of Robin Eames' continued commitment, as evidenced in his willingness to drive to 'Ballygobackward' for Evensong because he has been invited and therefore doesn't want to let people down, or – at the other extreme – his willingness to take on yet another challenging Anglican commission at the age of sixty-six. Indeed, the latter is more understandable because, as Niall Eames points out, his father thrives on challenges. He says, 'No matter what profession he had chosen, he would have needed to have been sorting out the big issues, in order to drive him along. When he has the big issues to sort out, he can work whatever hours are necessary.'

Robin Eames' endless commitment, however, is more than the ethic of hard work. At the heart of the man is his unyielding, undying sense of duty, and at the heart of that sense of duty is his loyalty to the memory and example of his earthly father, as well as his duty to his Heavenly Father. As the former Church of Ireland Press Officer Elizabeth Gibson-Harries astutely pointed out, 'This is metaphorically but clearly stamped on his forehead.'

The relationship between Robin Eames and his late father is complex, but alive and real. He says, 'He installed in me a sense of discipline and duty, and I have never forgotten that. I don't know why, but there is hardly a day passes that I don't think of him. I had always believed in the communion of saints, and as an Anglican I still believe it implicitly. The influence of my father became even more significant after he died, and there have been many times in my ministry when I would have loved to have had him there for me to talk to. I hope that he would have approved of all that I've tried to do.'

Above all, there is his Heavenly Father. Robin Eames' daily routine rarely varies, apart from when he is travelling. He is at his desk first thing in the morning, with his diary open to say his prayers. He reflects, 'Since becoming a bishop I have prayed each morning for my diocesan clergy by name. As Primate I pray every day for all the bishops, knowing as I do the problems they face. I have a silent prayer before any interview or appointment. At the end of the day, I seek forgiveness for my failures.'

He believes implicitly that the love of God does not end at the grave. 'There must be a greater purpose to life than only the experience of living in this world. There will be some sort of judgment undoubtedly, but my only personal comfort is that this justice will not depend on the vagaries of human judgment. It will be an experience of divine justice far above anything we know on earth.'

Whatever form this judgment takes, he believes that he will have to answer for the way in which he used the gifts and opportunities that God gave him. He says, 'The prime question we will all face is not "Were you successful?" The real question will be "Were you faithful with what I gave you to do?" '

The answer to that in human terms must be very largely in the affirmative, though not totally so. In the Divine judgment, however, the answer to that question must lie between the Most Reverend Dr Robert Henry Alexander Eames – Peer of the Realm, Archbishop of Armagh and Primate of All Ireland and Metropolitan – and his God.

Notes

2: Between Two Worlds

1. B. Walker and A. McCreary, *Degrees of Excellence: The Story of Queen's Belfast 1845–1995* (The Queen's Institute of Irish Studies, 1995).
2. ibid., p. 108.

4: The North-West Frontier

1. The role of Archbishop Eames and of the Church and clergy during bereavement is discussed at greater length in Chapter 10.

5: Walking the Tightrope

1. In an interview with the author in Derry in 2002.

6: More Trouble and Strife

1. Some years later he was appointed Dean of Belfast.
2. Reprinted in *The Listener*, 11 September 1980.

7: The Road to Armagh

1. *Irish Times*, 8 February 1986.

8: The Footsteps of St Patrick

1. Alf McCreary, *St Patrick's City: The Story of Armagh* (Blackstaff Press, 2001), pp. 219–20.
2. David McKittrick, Seamus Kelters, Brian Feeney and Chris Thornton, *Lost Lives* (London and Edinburgh: Mainstream Publishing, 1999).
3. The Drumcree issue will be discussed at length in later chapters.

9: Across the Divide

1. A concise outline of this important topic is an essay, 'Ecumenism', by Ian M. Ellis in *A Tapestry of Beliefs*, ed. Norman Richardson (Blackstaff Press, 1998), pp. 263–73.
2. In an interview with the author, published in *Omnibus*, Summer 1994, pp. 9–13.
3. ibid.

10: The Valley of Death

1. John Donne, 'Meditation XVII'.
2. Gordon Wilson, with Alf McCreary, *Marie: A Story from Enniskillen* (Collins Marshall Pickering, 1990), p. 34.
3. ibid.

11: Cross-Border Politics

1. Tom King, later Lord King of Bridgwater, was talking to the author in the House of Lords in November 2003.

12: The Road to Downing Street

1. In an interview with the author in the House of Lords, 18 December 2003.
2. ibid.
3. In an interview with the author in London, 22 January 2004.
4. In an interview with the author in the House of Lords, 18 December 2003.
5. In an interview with the author in Dublin, 22 October 2003.
6. In an interview with the author in the House of Lords, 18 December 2003.

13: Paramilitaries, Politicians and Paisleyism

1. In an interview with the author at the Cardinal's home in Belfast, 20 December 2002.

14: Unfinished Business

1. In an interview with the author in the House of Lords, 22 January 2004.

15: Drumcree – the Passion and the Pain

1. A comprehensive account is contained in Chris Ryder and Vincent Kearney, *Drumcree: The Orange Order's Last Stand* (Methuen, 2001). A good summary of events from 1995 to 1998 is contained in Sydney Elliott and W. D. Flackes, *Northern Ireland: A Political Directory 1968–1999* (Blackstaff Press, 1980, fully revised and updated 1999), pp. 239–40.
2. Elliott and Flackes *Northen Ireland*, p. 239.

16: More Passion – More Pain

1. In an interview with the author, 14 May 2003.
2. *Church of Ireland Gazette*, 28 May 1999.
3. In conversation with the author at the Drumcree Centre, Portadown, 15 March 2004.
4. ibid.

17: Change and the Church of Ireland

1. As discussed in an earlier chapter.
2. Alan Acheson, *A History of the Church of Ireland 1691–2001* (Columba Press, 1997, 2002), p. 244.
3. ibid., p. 245.
4. The role of the Eames Commission on Communion and Women in the Episcopate will be discussed in later chapters.
5. Acheson, *History*, p. 246.

18: Senior Primate

1. In a conversation with the author at King's College, London on 4 March 2004.
2. Brian Keenan, *An Evil Cradling* (hardback: Hutchinson, 1992; paperback: Vintage, 1993).
3. R. Eames, *Chains to be Broken* (London: Weidenfeld and Nicholson, 1992), p. 1.
4. In an interview with the author at the dedication of a new Benedictine monastery in Rostrevor, Northern Ireland, 18 January 2004.

19: Unity in Diversity?

1. In an interview with the author at the Archbishop of York's Palace in Bishopthorpe, 21 January 2004.

20: Canterbury Calling

1. In an interview with the author at Lambeth Palace, 17 December 2003.

21: Virgin Territory

1. In an interview with the author, 18 January 2004.
2. ibid.
3. *Church of Ireland Gazette*, 14 August 1998.

22: Sex and Sanctity

1. In an interview with the author at Lambeth Palace, 17 December 2003.
2. Quoted in the *Belfast Telegraph*, 17 October 2003.

23: Troubleshooter

1. *The Christian Challenge*, October–November 2003, pp. 20–1.
2. In conversation with the author at the Archbishop of York's Palace in Bishopthorpe, 21 January 2004.

24: Nobody's Fool

1. In an interview with the author at King's College, London, 4 March 2004.

Index

80, 83–5, 90–1, 94, 125, 153–7;
Downing Street Declaration *see*
Downing Street Declaration (15
December 1993); Good Friday
Agreement (10 April 1998) 125–6,
158, 160, 176, 194–205; role of
Church in post-Troubles 127; *see
also* cross-border relations
Peacocke, Bishop Cuthbert 47, 55
peerage, conferred on Eames 202–5,
256, 334
people-management, Eames' skill in 110
Personal Emergencies Fund 251
Philbin, Bishop William 74, 114
Pickering, Revd John (of Drumcree
parish church) 215, 216–17, 219,
220, 221, 228–9
plastic bullets, use of during
Drumcree stand-off 209
police: attacks on 42, 196, 206,
208–9, 224; funerals of 43, 59,
129, 130–1, 132, 133–4, 189
politics: alienation, sense of ordinary
people from 39–40, 71, 174,
185–6; changing order following
Good Friday Agreement (1998)
125–6; criticism of Church
involvement in 86; of cross-border
relations, overview of 144–57;
Eames' flirtation with possible
career in 22–3, 31; Eames'
meetings and work with
politicians and prime ministers 3,
90–1, 94, 122–3, 144, 153, 163,
170, 171–2, 184, 200, 286, 328;
gulf between politicians and
Church 78; political divisions
mirrored at Queen's University
21–2; political process *see* peace
process; political skills of Eames
326–7 *see also* political gifts, of
Eames; role of Eames during
Lebanon hostage crisis 256–62; *see
also* Anglo-Irish Agreement
(November 1985); Downing Street
Declaration (15 December 1993);
Good Friday Agreement (10 April
1998); Major, John, MP; Thatcher,
Margaret, MP
Portadown: Drumcree stand-off
14–15, 105–6, 206–32, 235–6, 298;
and Lurgan, first pastorate of
William Eames 7
post-Troubles scenario, challenge to
Church 126

Poyntz, Bishop Dr Samuel 88, 89,
154, 204–5, 227, 234, 244, 249,
267
prayer, integral to Eames' Primacy
336
prayers, requested by Tony Blair at
start of meetings with Robin
Eames 200
Presbyterian clergy, and views of 123,
124, 125, 185, 190, 212, 255, 330;
see also ecumenical relationships;
Magee, Revd Roy; Paisley, Revd
Ian
presidential style of Eames 248, 327
Priestland, Gerald 86
Primates of the Global South 309,
312, 315
Primates' Meetings 251, 258, 265,
266, 273–4, 296–7, 320
'Priorities Committee' 239
prophetic voice, of Eames 192, 330,
331
protection rackets 185
Protestantism: impact of grievances
and fears on cross-border
relations 147–56; impact of
hunger strikes on relations with
Roman Catholicism 81–3;
international perception of Irish
Protestantism 255; North-South
divisions within Church of Ireland
234–5; perception of Eames as
spokesman of 123–4; Protestant
fears in relation to peace process
55–6, 64, 83–4, 154–5, 164–6,
168–74, 178–93, 234; *see also*
bridge-building, between Catholic
and Protestant communities;
Church of Ireland; Drumcree
stand-off; ecumenical
relationships; Loyalism; Orange
Order; Unionism
Provisional IRA: Armagh, attacks in
103–4; ceasefire 159–60, 178–9,
182, 183, 189, 190, 192; Claudy
bombing (July 1972) 69–70, 127;
Co. Tyrone bombing 161;
condemnations of 116–17, 145,
170–1, 188–9, 254; in context of
cross-border relations 145, 148,
149, 153, 234; Derry, attacks in
39, 51–2, 55–6, 59, 65; emergence
of 38–9, 43; Enniskillen
Remembrance Day bombing
136–43, 170, 198; hunger strikes